Ross Alexander, signed photograph.

ROSS ALEXANDER:
The Life and Death
of a Contract Player

John Franceschina

BearManor
Media

Orlando, Florida

Published in the USA by
BearManor Media
1317 Edgewater Dr. #110
Orlando, FL 32804
www.BearManorMedia.com

Softcover Edition
ISBN: 978-1-62933-584-1

Printed in the United States of America

Table of Contents

Prologue: 2 January 2020   ix

Act One: Brooklyn to Broadway

1.   Early Days   1
2.   Boston Stock   13
3.   Louisville Stock   41
4.   *The Ladder*   53
5.   John Golden's Broadway (1)   71
6.   The University Players Guild   87
7.   John Golden's Broadway (2)   93
8.   *The Wiser Sex*   109
9.   Summer Stock   121
10. Back on Broadway   133
11. *Social Register*   157
12. John Golden's Broadway (3)   165

Act Two: Hollywood

13. *Flirtation Walk, Gentlemen Are Born,* and *Maybe It's Love*   179
14. *A Midsummer Night's Dream*   207
15. *Going Highbrow* and *We're in the Money*   233
16. *Shipmates Forever* and *Captain Blood*   253
17. *Boulder Dam* and *Brides Are Like That*   279

Act Three: The Aftermath

18. *I Married a Doctor, Hot Money,* and *China Clipper*   307
19. *Here Comes Carter* and *Ready, Willing and Able*   339

Epilogue: 2 January 1937   367
Bibliography   387
Index   397

For Ray DeMattis and Sue Lawless,
who know such things are true

Prologue: 2 January 2020

A good actor ought to be able to make
the telephone directory sound convincing.

—Ross Alexander

"Allow me to be frank at the commencement: you will not like me. . . . You will not like me now and you will like me a good deal less as we go on. Oh, yes, I shall *do* things you will like . . . , but Do Not WARM TO ME, it will not serve. . . . What I require is not your affection but your attention. I must not be ignored or you will find me as troublesome a package of humanity as ever pissed into the Thames." Thus begins the prologue (with marked ellipses) of Stephen Jeffreys's 1994 play *The Libertine*, spoken by John Wilmot, Second Earl of Rochester as a prelude to the (not always factual, but thoroughly entertaining) dramatization of his life and career.

I am always reminded of those words whenever I commence the task of reducing a person's life to words and still images declaiming probabilities and possibilities based on discourse that is objective (or discernably factual) and subjective (personal interviews, opinions, and innuendoes). Rare is the instance of a biographical study (or any book or artifact, for that matter) that pleases everyone, for an audience tends to approach fiction and nonfiction (in art, on film, and in the theatre) with subjective expectations that emphasize particular aspects or probabilities of the narrative. Such has been the relationship between audiences and artifacts from the beginning of recorded history and often described as a "taste" for a particular style, or subject, or structure, and authorship (of a book, fine art, music, theatre, or film) has ever been held accountable to the public. As David Garrick proclaimed in prologue to the opening of Theatre Royal, Drury Lane in 1747:

> Hard is his lot, that here by fortune placed,
> Must watch the wild vicissitudes of taste;
> With every meteor of caprice must play,
> And chase the new-blown bubbles of the day.
> Ah! let not censure term our fate our choice,
> The stage but echoes back the public voice.
> The drama's laws the drama's patrons give,
> For we that live to please, must please to live.

Two prologues, nearly 250 years apart, both spoken by actors trading on an anticipated relationship between author and audience. The 18th-century classical iteration (entitled *Ode to Drury Lane Theatre, on dedicating a Building and erecting a Statue, to Shakespeare* and written, by the way, by Samuel Johnson of *Dictionary* fame) admitted to changing tastes and fads and cajoled the audience to embrace the difficulty the theatre experiences in keeping up with contemporary trends. The 20th-century prologue, trading on an audience's expectation to empathize with, or even like a principal character in a play, berated the spectators and immediately tried to frustrate their anticipated responses. The author's use of reverse psychology was quite effective in piquing the audience's interest in the character, just as Garrick's audience was enraptured by his rational and methodical ability to negotiate their "wild vicissitudes of taste."

Flash forward to 2019 when fans of the cable television megahit *The Game of Thrones*, disappointed with the final season, took to media outlets to demand that it be rewritten and reshot—at the expense of the producers, of course, who also went to the media to defend their original choices. The spectators' passionate response to the season demonstrated an investment that enabled them to believe that they were worthy and necessary co-authors of the artifact. As Herbert Blau wrote in his seminal book *The Audience*:

> The privilege of the spectator was like a natural phenomenon. When somebody in authority said the audience wouldn't accept this or that, we might have incipient doubt about the nature of authority or would be stubbornly willing to run the risk, but there was very little disagreement about the audience as an arbiter or about some perceptible unity in its judgment and taste. . . .Where performance and commerce meet there is still a perceptible unity, an audience that echoes its edification through all the changes of fashion—theory of value and acting method inscribed with the price of the ticket, along with standards of credibility. The entertainment industry—from recurrently desperate Broadway to the astral optimism of Spielberg and Lucas to bigtime sports . . . more than knows its audience, give or take a few errors in the market surveys and Nielsen ratings. (1990, 4)

I am going on about the audience because of its importance to this study of Ross Alexander. During the period of this inquiry, 1907–1937, fans and fan magazines flourished and certain types of behavior were concretized on stage and film to appease and (sometimes) broaden audience tastes. From 1925 to 1936, Ross Alexander was a living artifact, created by the roles he performed, moulded by stage and film directors and producers, and fetishized by an appreciative, if not always adoring, public. His story is the story of theatre and film actors as it was in the twenties and thirties, and as it is today: how performers must accommodate their private lives to their public audience, without whom their careers would disappear. The period included, and was shaped by Prohibition, the Great Depression, and the enforcement of a Motion Picture Production Code and was characterized by the free-wheeling spirit of the 1920s followed by the more conservatively conventional atmosphere of the 1930s.

It was during the writing and rewriting of an off-Broadway-bound musical (which during previews appeared to please the performers more than the audience) that I first encountered Ross Alexander in a Dick Powell-Ruby Keeler military musical film entitled *Flirtation Walk* (1934). His electric personality enlivened every scene in which he appeared—often even stealing scenes from Dick Powell. Impressed by his performance, I went to the American Film Institute's catalogue of feature films and the Internet Movie Database to explore Alexander's resume before turning to reference works and articles searching for biographical information. What I discovered was both reductive and surprising. I learned that even though he had a short film career (1934–1937), newspaper and magazine articles called Ross one of Warner Brothers' fastest rising stars, an opinion shared evidently by most (though not all) critics and gossip columnists. Turner Classic Movies' online biography "Starring Ross Alexander" reported that in 1936, Ross was considered "an up-and-coming leading man at Warners, ranking fifth among all the studio's stars in fan-mail volume." However, in Larry Langman's *Encyclopedia of American Film Comedy*, Alexander was listed as a stage actor during his teen years prior to performing supporting roles in Warner Brothers musicals and comedies "until his career faltered and he began to get parts only in low-budget features. His death was reported as a suicide" (1987, 9). David K. Frasier's *Suicide in the Entertainment Industry* reiterated that Alexander's career had faltered in 1936 and suggested that "the studio no longer considered him star material" (2002, 9) adding that, at 18, Ross made his Broadway debut in *Enter Madame* with Blanche Yurka. Although many sources repeat this credit, Ross actually debuted in Boston with Blanche Yurka, not on Broadway. While Frasier spends the majority of his entry for Ross Alexander about the suicide of Alexander's second wife, Aleta Freile (Freel), in December 1935, and Alexander's suicide by gunshot in January 1937, he continued, citing the authority of Lawrence J. Quirk's Bette Davis biography *Fasten Your Seatbelts*, "the bisexual Alexander was seduced by older actors and kept by a series of wealthy men when not working" (2002, 9). Alexander's bisexuality was reaffirmed by William J. Mann in his groundbreaking book, *Behind the Screen: How Gays and Lesbians Shaped Hollywood, 1910–1969*, where he placed Ross among a group of gay actors who went to Hollywood and achieved "varying degrees of fame: Nils Asher, Gavin Gordon, David Manners, Douglass Montgomery, Richard Cromwell, Louis Mason, David Rollins, Ross Alexander, Alexander Kirkland, Tom Douglas, John Darrow, and, of course, Charles Laughton" (2001, 110).

Mann made no further comment about Alexander's sexuality, but, citing the authority of Jerry Asher, a gay publicity agent and confidante to Bette Davis, Quirk added that "Opportunistic and self-despising, Ross hated his homosexual side, and later went on a wild overcompensation swing by romancing several prominent actresses" that included a "wild crush (which Jerry Asher called an obsession) on [Bette] Davis" (1990, 135). Psychologist Alan Downs agreed with Quirk's prognosis and suggested in his book *The Velvet Rage* that "While denying our sexuality, we may have become hypersexual with women, needing to always have the most beautiful, sexy woman we could find on our arm. We denied our attraction to men and attempted to convince ourselves and everyone else that we were really straight—or at a minimum bisexual" (2012, 44). Down's argument was also supported in Ray Stricklyn's autobiography, *Angels and Demons*, when he wrote: "I told [Paul] how unhappy I was being homosexual. Just saying the word nauseated me. . . . I told myself, I would be a *man*. I would be *straight*, so help me God! . . . In my sincere efforts to be 'straight' I had only succeeded in making myself more miserable, not being able to satisfy the woman or myself. . . . It was following these abortive attempts at a heterosexual lifestyle that I came to realize that you can't be something different from what you are" (1999, 86, 126).

In addition to citing Alexander's obsession with Bette Davis, Quirk reported that after sinking into a deep depression, Ross picked up a "male hobo on the highway, and had sex with him," following which the man threatened blackmail, forcing a team of Warner Brothers lawyers "to hush the matter up" (1990, 137). Because Quirk played fast and free with dates and generalizations, his and Asher's claims about a Bette Davis affair and the hobo incident have been challenged by Laura Wagner in her series, *Overlooked in Hollywood*: "Ross Alexander, 'His Eyes Suggest Tragedy'" (2016/17, 53). Wagner argues that "Because Asher died in 1967, there is no way of knowing if these claims are true, in fact, there's no way of knowing if Asher even made these claims. This, however, has not stopped other 'historians' from presenting them as fact and even embellishing them with the usual lies so popular in the celebrity fantasy bios of today" (2016/17, 53). Wagner does, however, follow the trend of other historians with the mistaken notion that, although he was born in Brooklyn, Alexander grew up in Rochester, New York. According to census documents and city directories, Ross was a teenager who attended Erasmus Hall High School in Brooklyn prior to moving to West High School in Rochester in the early 1920s.

John R Allen, Jr's online article "Ross Alexander: Fleeting Star" delivers an excellent chronology of Alexander's career, the most complete and detailed summary available of the actor's career and serves as an invaluable starting place for students and biographers with a general interest in theatre and film in the 1920s and 1930s and a specific emphasis on Ross Alexander. Allen is especially helpful in providing the chronological order in which Alexander appeared on stage and film.

Other important sources of information about Ross Alexander exist in *Movie Mirror* articles, including "Ross Alexander the Great," by Katharine Hartley (October 1936); "Why Ross Alexander Married Again," by George Madden (February 1937); and "The Real Reason why Ross Alexander Killed Himself," by Caroline Somers Hoyt (April 1937). Because these articles involve interviews with Alexander, they are especially illustrative of the actor's personality and private life. "Bachelor Father" (in *Screen and Radio Weekly*) by Clarke Wales offers a fine portrait of "Maternity Acres," Alexander's farm-like estate in the San Fernando Valley and other reports of the actor's proclivities and idiosyncrasies can also be found in the memoirs of John Golden (*Stage-Struck: John Golden*, 1930); Norris Houghton (*But not forgotten: The Adventure of the University Players*, 1951) Henry Fonda (*Fonda: My Life as told to*

Howard Teichmann, 1981); and in the inter-office memos and production reports at Warner Brothers collected by Rudy Behlmer (*Inside Warner Bros. [1935–1951]: The battles, the brainstorms, and the bickering—from the files of Hollywood's greatest studio*, 1985). Gossip accounts of Alexander's comings and goings are also available throughout a variety of industry magazines including *Motion Picture, Photoplay, Film Daily, The Hollywood Reporter*, and *Variety*.

The suicides of Ross Alexander and his second wife were captured in newspapers and magazines throughout the United States and found particular mention in Kenneth Anger's *Hollywood Babylon* (1975), in which Alexander's suicide is erroneously cited as caused by sleeping pills, and Michelle Morgan's *The Mammoth Book of Hollywood Scandals: Scandalous Lives, Scandalous Deaths, and Everything in Between.*(2013), in which an entire chapter is devoted to the events.

In the following pages I have cobbled together a history of Ross Alexander from the sources already mentioned, from newspaper accounts, documents recovered from Ancestry.com, playscripts, shooting scripts, publicity photographs (of which there are many), and videos of Alexander's films. As a contract player, Ross had little control over his film roles or the many duties for which he was responsible beyond simply performing before a camera. He was required for publicity shoots, personal appearances (and tours) to advertise a coming film, radio spots, and whatever fan-related event or interview that Warner Brothers arranged. What first may have been exciting could quickly become a drudge for an actor who always had to look fresh and friendly and vibrant for the public. Often Ross appeared defiant and aggressive in an interview, a "Mr. Hyde" kind of mood that invariable dissolved into the warmth and kindness of a Dr. Jekyll. Accepting his position as a member of a film factory, he knew that he had to present to the public the image of him that they had in their imaginations. But, in reality, like John Wilmot, Second Earl of Rochester, Ross was looking not for affection but their attention.

In her interview with Ross, Caroline Somers Hoyt noted:

As we parted, he said something which, I've thought since, explains why

Ross was what he was—spoiled, arrogant, cynical—and why he couldn't be anything else.

He said, "Why are you taking the pains to talk to me like this? No woman has ever done that before. They've only wanted kisses." And there were tears in his eyes as he said it.

"They've only wanted kisses," when the thing that Ross Alexander needed most from the women who loved him, never having had it at all, was "cold turkey" talked by someone who could forget his charm and be concerned with his soul. He needed someone who could, for a change, dish it out and make him take it.

But he never found anyone like that. (1937, 102)

To present the life of Ross Alexander in a way that both suits and challenges the imaginations of a readership, I have sought the attention of many whose cooperation has been invaluable in the development of this biography: Mary K. Huelsbeck, Assistant Director, Wisconsin Center for Film and Theater Research; Alexandra M. Griffiths, Interlibrary and Document Services, The New York Public Library; Tom Lisanti, Manager, Permissions and Reproductive Services, The New York Public Library; Mary Haegert, Public Services, Houghton Library, Harvard University; and David Boynton, whose many helpful suggestions assisted in the preparation of this manuscript.

The book is full of anecdotes, vintage photographs of Alexander's theatre work, publicity shots from his various films, a few newspaper images, and a great many quotations from the plays and films in which Ross appeared. I crave your indulgence if my choice of illustrations is not exactly to your taste, or if I seem to spend too much time describing a play, or film director. Theater and film practices of the twenties and thirties form an important part of Alexander's character and provide a vibrant background to his career. So, with these provisos in mind, let's begin with the "Answer Man" in the February 1935 issue of *Photoplay Magazine*: "Ross was born [Alexander Ross Smith, Jr.] in Brooklyn, New York, July 27, 1907. He is six feet, one-and-a-half inches tall; weighs 160 pounds and has brown hair and blue eyes." I should also note here that Ross is left-handed, a knuckle-cracker, a member of the Hollywood Erin Club (along with Pat O'Brien and James Cagney among others), and still sleeps in a night shirt. He enjoys watching prize fights and ice hockey and likes model ships but doesn't delight in building them. For his studio biography, he roguishly added: "He has no suppressed desires, no economies that he practices, no favorite extravagances, no hobbies, and only one or two aversions.... Neither politics nor religion have an interest for him. He isn't superstitious" (*Modern Screen* 31 March 1936, 88).

ACT ONE
Brooklyn to Broadway

1. Early Days

In the 1970s, Sue Lawless, my friend and collaborator on a number of musical and dramatic projects in and around New York City, bought a brownstone on Union Street in Carroll Gardens, Brooklyn, not many blocks from 95 Second Street where our story began some hundred years earlier. At the Second Street address, a thirty-four-year-old bricklayer named Albertson Smith and his wife, Margaret Augusta Smith became the proud parents of their third son on 31 August 1879. The newly christened Alexander Ross Smith was welcomed by his older siblings, Chester (8) and Walton (6) with more curiosity than empathy, but with somewhat less surprise than the brothers exhibited five years later when they were introduced to Harriet, their infant sister. By the turn of the century the Smiths had moved up a block to 329 Carroll Street; Albertson had become a building inspector, and his two oldest sons continued the family bricklaying business. Alexander was rather less inclined to manual labor and applied himself instead to the business of salesmanship, in the pursuit of which he met and married Maude Adelle Cohen on 30 January 1901. Maude was the fifth child—and first daughter—born on 11 December 1877 to William Henry Cohen, a packer of canned goods, and Catherine Woodruff Cohen. Maude's grandfather, Morris Cohen, a Polish Jew, emigrated to the United States in the early nineteenth century, prior to the birth of his son William in 1838.

Not long after the nuptials of Alexander and Maude Smith, the couple moved to 780 St. Johns Place in the Crown Heights neighborhood of Brooklyn. Originally called Crow Hill, Crown Heights was a desirable residential area in Brooklyn marked by elegant mansions and limestone row houses along tree-lined streets. After the completion of the Eastern Parkway, the world's first six-lane highway, in 1868, the splendor of the grand boulevard made the northern part of the neighborhood especially fashionable. By the turn of the century, attractive brick and brownstone row houses were built, and the predominantly Jewish neighborhood became home to young professionals (Manbeck 1998, 78–80).

In 1905, Alexander became the Brooklyn representative of the American Hide and Leather Company, an Ohio Foreign Corporation. Two years later Alexander Ross Smith, Jr., was born on 27 July 1907. Little is known of Alexander's youth: he made his theatrical debut at the age of four playing the part of a nestling in his kindergarten production of a pageant entitled *A Nest of Birds*. Around the same time, Ross enjoyed the companionship of a boy named Phil Regan who lived in the neighborhood and who shared Alexander's interest in playacting. The two went around impersonating cowboys and Indians and the variety of character types they encountered in and around Crown Heights during the second decade of the twentieth century. It didn't occur to either boy at the time that they both would become contract players at Warner Brothers in the 1930s and even work together on a film (*We're in the Money*) in 1935!

Following kindergarten, Alexander was enrolled in the Brooklyn Dramatic Model School where he studied acting and dancing and music as well as rudimentary academic classes that he did not enjoy. He did, however, enjoy spinning a top in and out of the classroom and, in spite of (or perhaps, because of) his teacher's reprimands, Alexander earned the rank of champion top spinner of the New York Public Schools. When he was seven years old, he kissed a girl in his class named Helen Stebbins, much to the amusement of the girl's mother, although the event was met with recriminations in the Smith household. Alexander's parents were firm and not overly strict but they drew the line at their son's youthful manifestations of affection. Irrespective of his parents' leniency, Alexander recalled his childhood as difficult in a *Movie Mirror* interview with George Madden: "We weren't very well off. There were lots of things the other kids possessed that I couldn't have; and while that doesn't matter now—and I'm glad for the hard knocks that put me on my own early in life—those things are tough on kids. And so I kept myself happy by forgetting the things I didn't have and thinking only of those things I would have when I became a rich and famous actor; for I had my mind set on an acting career as far back as I can remember" (February 1937; 56, 78). Alexander's commitment to acting, however, did not liberate him from youthful tantrums when his artistic choices were challenged. At the Model School, a patient dramatic coach became one of many victims of Alexander's childish outbursts when he disagreed with her direction. As Alexander described it:

She was coaching our class play and I was in it. She was a good sort; worked hard with us. Used to help me with my part after school. Always seemed pleased when we kids took an interest in things. One day we disagreed over the way I was to say some lines. I've always been crazy about acting but I guess I've always, too, wanted my own way about it.

Patiently, she tried to tell me she thought her way was best. I wouldn't listen. I got mad. Tore up the script and threw it at her. Said I wouldn't be in the play and stalked out. As I looked back at her from the doorway, I saw that she was crying. I was sorry about that, terribly sorry. I went to her home that night and apologized. And I tried to give her what was, then, my most cherished possession, a green ever-sharp pencil but she wouldn't take it. . . . She forgave me. I went on in the play and she was as nice as ever. But I've never forgotten what I did, because it was so unnecessary. I think about it every once in a while, even now, and wish I hadn't made her cry. (Hoyt 1937, 100)

In 1936, Alexander also spoke of a longing for the quiet of rural living and farming lifestyle in an interview with Rosalind Shaffer published in the *Chicago Tribune*. Claiming that he inherited such taste from his great-grandfather who had earned the record of being the most professional liar in New York State, Ross continued: "Last year a guy won the championship as the year's greatest liar with one of Great-Grandfather Kingston's stories. . . . My favorite was the time he came in out of a bitter New York blizzard and said to great-grandmother as he threw several little lumps of ice on the table, 'Get out the frying pan, mother, and thaw out those things. I said something out in the yard, and I want to see what it was'—meaning his words froze when he spoke them" (26 July 1936, 70). Eleven-year-old Alexander's love for the outdoors and the land led him to join Troop 22 of the Boy Scouts before it had been officially chartered in May 1920. The Scouts taught the young Alexander survival skills as well as veterinary techniques that helped him throughout his private life. Given contemporary accounts about Alexander's later homosexual pursuits, his interest in boys might well have begun during a camping trip with the Scouts.

On midnight of 17 January 1920 the National Prohibition Act came into effect. The bill, perhaps better known as the Volstead Act or "Prohibition" was designed to define and enforce the provisions of the Eighteenth Amendment to the Constitution that prohibited the production, sale, and transport of intoxicating liquors. Of course, whatever is prohibited becomes immediately desirable and challenges to the Volstead Act surfaced almost as soon as the Act became law with speakeasies and other places of business finding surreptitious methods of circumventing it. In the same year, the Alexander Smith Family moved to 1241 Union Street, about five blocks south of their St. Johns Place address, and Alexander began high school at the highly revered Erasmus Hall located across town at 899-925 Flatbush Avenue.

Founded in 1786 as a private institution, Erasmus Hall Academy became a public high school in 1896. In the early 1920s, enrollment at the high school began to burgeon, with the school term beginning on 1 February 1922 boasting the highest enrollment in the history of the school: 5,390 students in a building with space enough for only 3,100! Given the overcrowding between 1920 and 1922, Erasmus Hall allowed Alexander a recklessness that seemed incorrigible. In addition to his aversion for academic subjects, Alexander's objections to Erasmus Hall boiled down to one simple fact: the school did not have a dedicated theatre department. Instead, elocution was taught in the Departments of English and Speech and musical and variety shows were presented to raise money for athletics at the school. Before he left Erasmus Hall, Alexander had participated in several of these productions, including the most successful fundraiser to date: the 1921 school production of Gilbert and Sullivan's *The Mikado*. Such experiences, however, were too few to satisfy the rambunctious lad and school administrators were relieved when Alexander announced that he was leaving the school because his father had moved on from the American Hide and Leather Company and created his own company, Lang and Smith, in collaboration with a Rochester, New York, firm that would obviously require the family to move to upstate New York. Alexander's parents were well aware of their son's difficulties at Erasmus Hall and the move was well timed to save the family the embarrassment of Alexander's actually being expelled from so noble an institution.

Erasmus Hall, from a contemporary postcard.

It is unfortunate that Alexander was hotheaded and, like many teenagers, unyielding in his belief of his own righteousness because Erasmus Hall was then and continued to be an important training ground for professional actors, writers, artists and musicians. Famous names that emerged from the Hall included actors, Mae West, Norma Talmadge, Clara Bow, Mary Anderson, Susan Hayward, Barbara Stanwyck, Barbra Streisand, Jane Cowl, Eli Wallach, Jeff Chandler, Moe Howard; writers, Arthur Laurents, Mickey Spillane, Betty Comden; artists, Joseph Barbera, Elaine de Kooning; musicians, Laine Kazan, Gilbert Price, Marky Ramone, Beverly Sills, Oscar Brand, Artie Butler, Neil Diamond; the list of notables goes on and on, and even includes a champion chess player by the name of Bobby Fischer!

Rochester may have presented both challenges and opportunities for the elder Smith running the Lang and Smith factory at 115 Mill Street, but for Smith Jr., school presented only challenges. On 16 January 1922, a headline in the *Rochester Democrat and Chronicle* announced: "Will Bar from High Schools for Varying Periods Pupils Who Fall Behind in Studies," and the article that followed revealed that the Board of Education has taken a stand that "High school pupils must do their work well or forfeit the privilege of high school attendance." The Smith family had found a new home on 378 Troup Street across the Genesee River in West Rochester, not far from West High School on Genesee Street.

West High School, from a contemporary postcard.

In addition to a traditional academic curriculum, West High had a newspaper (the "Occident'), glee clubs, soccer and basketball teams, and a dramatics department that should have inspired and fulfilled Alexander's theatrical desires. But instead of taking advantage of what West High had to offer, the six-foot tall teenager continued to get into trouble: "I don't remember what the final straw was that broke the principal's patience," he told Katharine Hartley, "but there had been a lot of things. Hookey, broken windows, spit balls, beebee shot, mutiny rebellions, glue in the furnace which closed the whole school for one day, because of the stink—I was really quite ingenious. You see I didn't like school" (October 1936, 63).

The faculty at West High School during Alexander's reign of terror.

Alexander's expulsion from West High was a relief to all involved. Teachers could return to their classrooms without fear; students who went to school to learn could do so without interruption; and young Smith was free to pursue private acting training. This he found with the elocutionist and theatre director Hugh William Towne (born 22 March 1890) who had recently moved from Cambridge, Massachusetts where he was connected with the Boston Little Theater, to Rochester where he became the director of dramatics at the University of Rochester and produced plays privately at the Towne Studio of Dramatic Art located at 186 East Avenue. Private study required a private income so, retracing the footsteps of actors immemorial, Alexander needed to find the proverbial "day job." The first place he looked was at the MacFarlane Outfitting Company, a clothing store young Smith had been frequenting for about a year, and which was about to commence the "biggest sale in history." Denied employment by the company manager, Mr. Bellows, Alexander hurried down to the suit department and in two hours he succeeded in selling four overcoats and seven suits, the sales of which he entered into the stock book along with his initials A.R.S. When Bellows reviewed the books at the end of the day, he was so impressed that he (albeit begrudgingly) hired young Smith.

Working in a high-end clothing story was a mixed blessing for a teenager who had a weakness for clothes. In fact, since employees could charge their purchases against their salary, every payday, Alexander ended up owing the company money. After weeks of working in the red, Alexander requested a transfer to the boys' clothing department where he proudly "turned out some pretty smart boys!" In an interview with Katharine Hartley, he explained:

Of course [the boys'] families never recognized them when they got home. I was crazy about color in those days, colored shirts, socks, etc. (shades of Broadway), and Rochester hadn't quite accepted it yet. But eventually the mothers coming back for exchanges got the best of me. I argued one woman into a faint one day, and Mr. Bellows sent for me. "Smith," he said, "I don't think you're happy here." The school principal had started his dismissal speech the same way. I saw what was coming. But I staved it off for a while. "It's that department," I said. "You know, I think I could do much better as a window trimmer!" And so he gave me a chance at it. You see, I was still so in debt I had to stay on for a while longer. (*Movie Mirror*, October 1936, 113)

Alexander caused a great stir as a window trimmer by placing only a single hat in MacFarlane's largest (half a block long) window, but his celebrity was cut short the moment he threw a hat stand at the envious head window trimmer. A subsequent nine-to-five job as an office boy at a manufacturing firm was also short lived because Alexander kept an erratic work schedule, sometimes coming in three hours late because he wanted to spend the morning eating breakfast. His capricious handling of work schedules will plague him throughout his acting career making it clear that the only timetable Alexander would follow was his own.

He had more success—because he was his own boss—as a restauranteur. Starting with a capital of only $35, he rented a room on percentage across the street from the Eastman School of Music, furnished it with second-hand tables and chairs, and created a bohemian atmosphere by means of a crate filled with old candles. He named the restaurant "Le Coq D'Or," and served as cook, waiter, and cashier. He didn't make a profit, but in the four months he was in business, he always broke even:

You see I couldn't make any money because I had to cook with electricity and I didn't have adequate refrigeration so I had to buy in small quantities at retail. One thing I really am proud of, though—the Thursday Evening Open Forums I instigated. You see the restaurant was right across the street from the Eastman School of Music, and because of that I had contact with quite a few important people. He doesn't remember it, but [Rouben] Mamoulian talked there one night, and so did Vladimir Rosing of the Rochester Opera, and [Norman A.] O'Brien, one of the prominent politicians in the town. Who knows, if the Eastman school hadn't closed for the summer, and my restaurant along with it, I might have become one of the literati! (*Movie Mirror*, October 1936, 114)

Following the summer closure of Le Coq D'Or, Alexander traveled to East Jaffrey, New Hampshire where he spent the summer with Hugh Towne at the Pine Knoll Inn. The pair gave recitals of poetry, dramatic readings, and songs with Alexander providing accompaniment at the piano. The thirty-five-year-old Towne and eighteen-year-old Alexander Ross Smith (spelled "Smythe" in the hotel registry) had formed a strong bond during acting classes in Rochester and were inseparable throughout the summer. Whispers that the pair were engaged in an unnamed "special relationship" noised about the town

9

like the sound of mosquitos sawing through the thick summer night, even though Townes was a favorite son of East Jaffrey and a previously married man with a fifteen-year-old stepdaughter. When Towne died suddenly in 1931, his obituary made no mention of a wife and daughter but reported that he was survived only by a brother and sister. There is a record of his marriage to a thirty-two-year-old widow, Grace W. Merchant, on 25 December 1913 but I have located no account of a divorce. Census and City Records indicate that Towne's wife and daughter did not accompany him to Rochester in the early 1920s so a divorce or separation would have had to occur before then.

Earl Carroll Theater Building, 755 Seventh Avenue in Manhattan.

Returning to Rochester in September, Alexander finally convinced his family to give him the money ($500.00) to return to New York City for a six-week crash course in theatre at the Packard Theatre Institute, beginning in mid-October at the Earl Carroll Theater Building, 755 Seventh Avenue in Manhattan. He took up residence in a boarding house with the single bathroom at the end of a hall (and he swears this is true) with trained seals floating in the bathtub! The building was a sort of hostel for vaudevillians and unemployed actors, the kind of place familiarized by backstage musical films, where jugglers rehearsed in the lobby to the gasping tones of an aspiring Juliet, preparing for her "big" audition; trained dogs scuttled up and down the stairs while the next Luisa Tetrazzini chirruped the "Mad Scene" from *Lucia*, accompanied by an inattentive pianist bludgeoning an out-of-tune piano; and a fledgling magician tried to disappear a disobliging rabbit in a hat. Ballerinas, chorines, exotic dancers, female impersonators, working girls and guys, all provided Ross with an education that was more profound and realistic than the acting training he received from the Packard Institute, though studying English and Psychology under the esteemed Professor Hahn, Alexander progressed quickly and earned his Actors' Equity Card upon graduation.

The quality of education Alexander received at the Theatre Institute was unimportant. What was significant was the fact that the Institute was attached to the Packard Theatrical Exchange, an agency that arranged for actors to work in theatre companies. A close association existed between the Theatrical Exchange and the Henry Jewett Players, then appearing at the Repertory Theatre on Huntington Avenue in Boston, where the celebrated actress (and diva extraordinary) Blanche Yurka had committed to guest star with the company in Ibsen's *The Wild Duck*, followed by Gilda Varesi and Dolly Byrne's comedy *Enter Madame*. The Jewett Company was filled with talented and experienced actors; what it lacked was a plausible juvenile to act the role of Yurka's son in the comedy.

All a-flutter, Madame Yurka materialized in the Packard offices like the Queen of the Night in *The Magic Flute* and demanded a juvenile, any juvenile that could act passably, take direction, and not upstage her (not necessarily in that order). As luck would have it, Alexander had just graduated and looked right for the part. He so often told the story of his first meeting with Yurka, that in one (dubious) version of the tale, he was the only one in his graduating class, and so picked by default; in other (more verifiable) versions, he was chosen out of several young men in the graduation class. As he told the story:

Blanche Yurka took me up to Jewett, so there was no difficulty in getting

11

a hearing. But the Packard Agency in Boston had told me to get $75 a week if I got the job. I had that figure firmly in mind when I went into Jewett's office.

Jewett, a typical old-school actor, adjusted his monocle and looked me up and down. Then he said: "Well, laddie, what experience have you had?"

I lied like a trooper, and then Jewett said: "What is your salary?"

When I said $75 he looked me up and down again and said: "And what, laddie, do I get for $75 a week?"

"Youth and a fair amount of intelligence," I said.

"For that, laddie, I will pay $30."

I gulped and said: "Make it $35 or I won't stay." I went to work for $35 a week. (*Oakland Tribune*, 23 August 1936, 85)

2. Boston Stock

Famous for being actress Julia Marlowe's leading man, venerable Australian actor-director Henry Jewett (1861–1930) settled in Boston not long after 1900. By 1910 he had established a theatre company, The Henry Jewett Players, to produce Shakespearean plays, first at the Boston Opera House and later (beginning 10 November 1925) at the Repertory Theatre located at 264 Huntington Avenue, close to the Museum of Fine Arts and Symphony Hall. Jewett would be uncomfortable with the title of this chapter because he viewed the concept of a "stock company" as an inferior kind of theatre troupe. In 1921, Frank Chouteau Brown explained that Jewett "considers the term 'Stock Company' beneath the just merits and present ambitions of his organization, and insists that it be dignified by the name 'Repertory,' instead. There is justification for this to the extent that no member regularly plays 'leading' parts, but all are moved around in the cast from week to week, from important to minor roles. But the company is nevertheless not run on the European Repertory system by means of which several plays are put on within the week, but instead, follows the usual American fashion of playing each play for a week or more at a time" (*Theatre Magazine* vol. 34, 1921).

The Repertory Theatre of Boston. Detail from a 1927 commemorative plate
designed by Joshua Wedgewood.

For Alexander Ross Smith the concept of a "Stock Company" seemed
more like "Shock Company" for no sooner had he been hired as Blanche
Yurka's son, John, in *Enter Madame*, and accepted into Actors' Equity
as "Ross Alexander," than he was moved, on 7 December 1925, into the
company's lodgings—called the "Nursery" after English Restoration actor
George Jolly's school of acting—and called for rehearsal at 10:00 A.M. on 8
December the afternoon following Blanche Yurka's triumphant debut at the
Repertory as Gina Ekdal in Ibsen's *The Wild Duck*. The "one-a-week" stock
system was designed to rehearse a play during the daytime while another
play was performed in the evenings and on matinees. Usually each play was
given thirty hours of rehearsal so it benefitted the actors if they were familiar
with the script prior to the whirlwind rehearsal schedule. Because Blanche
Yurka had been approached to play the lead in *Enter Madame* prior to its
Broadway run she knew the play intimately; Ross had been handed the script
only days before rehearsals began and his professional theatrical debut would
be a baptism of fire. After a week of table readings, blocking rehearsals, and
what seemed like an eternity of criticisms from Henry Jewett the director,

at 8:10 P.M. on 14 December 1925, after a full day of dress rehearsals, Ross Alexander made his professional theatrical debut before an elite and critical Boston audience.

Set in Boston, *Enter Madame* unveils the story of a great opera star, Madame Lisa Della Robbia (Blanche Yurka) whose husband, Gerald Fitzgerald (Arthur Behrens) has tired of trekking as a nonentity behind his peripatetic wife and her entourage, Bice (Agnes Scott), her maid; her personal physician (Horace Pollock); Miss Smith (Carolyn Ferriday), her secretary; and Archimede (John Thorn), her chef. Gerald decides that he wants a divorce so that he can marry Flora Preston (Lenore Chippendale), a widow who lives in his apartment building. Not untypical of comedies of this ilk, Madame Lisa manages to reawaken the romantic spark that drew Gerald to her originally, and in spite of the fact that they are now divorced, they spend the night together and, to avoid the scandal of being caught having sex out of marriage—Boston was especially Puritanical about such things—the couple decide to elope to Buenos Aires, where Madame has accepted a singing engagement. Rounding out the cast are Tamamoto (William Kershaw), Gerald's manservant, Madame's son, John Fitzgerald (Ross Alexander) and his fiancée Aline Chalmers (Peg Entwistle),

A fledgling electrical engineer, described by his father as a "manly, likeable chap, though heaven knows we were never very congenial" (I, 10), John is the normative character in the play, the rational voice of Bostonian scruples and devotion to mother. On his entrance (with his fiancée), he surprises his father who is kissing the widow Flora and exclaims "What again!" a rebuke not taken kindly by his father who continues to be scolded by his son throughout the play. While John is openly contemptuous of his father, he exhibits only affection for his mother as in the only extended scene between him and his fiancée:

John. Disgusting! Never mind, Aline. I know you'll love mother. She's wonderful!

Aline. She must be John—because she is your mother.

John. Do you know sometimes I wonder how I can love you both so much. You are so different.

Aline. Perhaps that's why. With such a famous mother I don't see how you can be interested in me. I'll never be famous. Will that matter?

John. Why no. Don't ever change. Always be just you.

Aline. My poor little engagement! I thought it was such big news last night. No one said a word about it except to mention the fact that it's all rot!

John. (*Coming to her*) Mother won't make fun of it. You wait. I don't know what to do. I don't dare go down for fear of disgracing her with my long legs. . . I hope mother won't mind too much that I'm a man. (1, 32–33)

At the end of Act One, the dutiful son pledges his life to protect his mother. Although the lines on the page are often mawkish, Alexander's youthful enthusiasm and poignant line readings rendered John's dialogue natural and effective. John's rational approach to life is especially displayed in his Act Two scene with his mother:

Lisa. Now you are my son and yet you do not understand me, nor I you. You stand up there, and there's blood of mine running very busy in and out of all the little veins; there should be thoughts like me darting about the brain I gave to you—why are there not?

John. I grew up away from you. I confess, it's hard for me to understand you.

Lisa. Yet you love me?

John. Yes, mother, very much.

Lisa. You love Aline?

John. Yes, mother, very much.

Lisa. You say the two alike, there is not one speck of difference in the tone. You don't feel just alike?

John. You can't go about feeling and shouting about it, you know. It isn't done.

Lisa. (*With a flash of understanding.*) Ah! (*Then thoughtfully.*) What would you do if Aline should say to you: Go away, go away. I don't want to see your face again.

16

John. I'd go.

Lisa. To stay?

John. Of course.

Lisa. Could you live without her?

John. Yes, if I must.

Lisa. Monstrous! (77–79)

For the first two acts of *Enter Madame*, John might have been interpreted as something of a prig had it not been for Ross Alexander's natural charm. Critics often speak of an actor throwing himself or herself, or their self, into a role, becoming one with the character to help an audience believe in the probability of what is happening onstage. Alexander had not yet perfected that technique but his imposing stage presence and innate (if still somewhat naïve) theatrical instincts enabled him to hold stage with theatre veterans Blanche Yurka and Arthur Behrens.

In Act Three, when John discovers that his recently divorced father and mother have spent the night together, his innate prudishness collides with emotional outbursts that demonstrate that he is, after all, Madame's son. Embarrassed that his fiancée has been witness to his parents' indiscretion, and desperately trying to forestall the scandal that is certain to occur after Flora discovered Gerald and Madame's dalliance, John takes charge of the situation in an emotionally charged, farce-paced scene:

Lisa. (*Phone rings.*) Oh John, tell [the reporters] you are coming down to them!

John. I will if you promise to do just as I say. (*Gerald motions her to say yes. Phone rings.*)

Lisa. We'll do anything you want.

John. (*At phone.*) Stop this noise. I am coming down to you. Yes, this is Mr. Fitzgerald. I am coming. (*Rings off. Turns to parents.*) Now you'll do as I say. I've stood enough from you. You're an awful responsibility.

Gerald. (*Loudly.*) All right. Keep your voice down. Don't shout!

John. (*Furiously.*) Will you answer me one question?

Gerald. Certainly

John. Did I ask to be born? Did I ask to be born? Answer me that.

Gerald. (*In a fit of laughter falls into the armchair, then recuperating:*) Why, we gave you the gift of life.

John. Oh, that's no good. That won't work nowadays. You tell me if it's right to treat me like this, when I never asked to be born. I didn't choose you to be my parents, God knows, but I've got to put up with you and you've got to put up with me. You can't go on living as if I weren't here. You've got to think of me, and of my future, and of the dignity of the family— (*Goes threateningly to Gerald.*) The dignity of the family, do you hear?

Lisa. Yes, yes, Johnnie you are right. Now if you will go down and get those wicked reporter's away—I promise that we will do anything you want, anything at all.

Gerald. There now.

John. First, I want to see father leave this house.

Lisa. But he can't, at the door there are men.

John. Well, he can go by the back door.

Lisa. (*Soothingly.*) All right, Gerald, go by the back door, go by the back door. . . . There—there . . . he is gone—Now you go down and save the family honor! The family honor, it rests with you!

John. All right, I will— (*Goes. You hear his voice outside.*) Here I am gentlemen—I can explain everything to you. (3, 167–171)

Although Ross Alexander spent a great deal of time onstage and served an important function in the comedy, his debut went unnoticed by the critics. *The Boston Globe* (15 December 1925) summarily noted that other than Blanche Yurka, "[t]he rest of the cast has little to do," and except for Arthur Behrens and Lenore Chippendale, "the others seem to think the play is farce." Although this criticism has much to do with the direction of the play, it does, perhaps, suggest that Alexander's performance was as broad as that of the farcically-written characters of Madame's entourage.

At 10:00 A.M. on the day following the opening of *Enter Madame*, Alexander began rehearsals for the dramatic fairytale *Snow White and the Seven Dwarfs* written by Winthrop Ames under the pseudonym of Jessie Braham White. Peg Entwistle, who had played Alexander's fiancée in *Enter Madame* was cast as Snow White and Ross was given the relatively thankless role of the handsome but monosyllabic Prince Florimond of Calydon. Prior to his entrance in the play we learn that, as an infant, the prince had met his cousin, Princess Snow White, when their royal fathers visited one another and even shared a baby carriage with her; but even though he sent Snow a valentine every year, he had no idea what she looked like grown up. When he enters in scene one, Florimond meets a young woman whose "hair was black as ebony; her skin whiter than snow; her lips were redder than a drop of blood" (1, 27); he dances (and sings) a duet with her, and immediately falls in love with her. When told that his father intends him to marry his cousin, he refuses until he realizes that the woman he had met and fallen in love with just moments earlier is, in fact, Snow White! Jealous of her step-daughter's beauty and charisma, Queen Brangomar (Lenore Chippendale) forces the prince to wait for a year before he can marry the princess. Disappointed, but not disgruntled, the prince exits the stage and reappears to claim his bride a year (and five scenes) later, only to be told that Snow White is dead. Overcome by grief, Florimond "sinks sobbing on the steps of the throne" (6, 82), but his sadness is quickly abated by the entrance of the very-much-alive princess whom he marries and, as per the stage directions: "With stately grace the Prince leads Snow White to the throne and reverently sets the crown on her head. Then he kneels before her, and all the Courtiers follow his example, and all the trumpets in the palace blare. Rising and unsheathing his sword, the Prince cries: Love and homage to our little Queen" (6, 88)!

All in all, Florimond spoke only 28 lines and sang only 5 lines of lyrics in the fairytale. As written the role of the prince was neither witty nor especially clever. It simply required the actor to be charming and handsome—qualities that Ross Alexander had in ample supply. Though he might have preferred one of the more challenging (and less laconic) male roles in the production, given the hectic rehearsal schedule and heavy performance load at the Repertory Theatre, Ross certainly appreciated a role that he could execute with little effort. While *Enter Madame* continued in the evenings for a second week, beginning Monday 21 December, *Snow White* opened on Monday afternoon and played matinees on 23 and 25 December, and at 10:30 (A.M.) on 26 December (followed by a matinee and evening performance of *Enter Madame*).

During the busy Christmas week, the repertory company found time to rehearse Mary Kennedy and Ruth Hawthorne's comedy *Mrs. Partridge Presents* starring (and also directed by) Blanche Yurka making the most of her stay in Boston. Set in the Washington Square apartment of the fashionable modiste Mrs. Masie Partridge (Yurka), the comedy portrayed the efforts of Mrs. Partridge to render her son and daughter "independent" by forcing them into careers and life choices that she wished she had made in her own life. Ross was cast as Masie's son Philip, another dutiful son who wants to be a civil engineer (recalling John's ambition to be an electrical engineer in *Enter Madame*) but who forces himself to be an artist to please his mother. Ross was again paired with Peg Entwistle who played his sister unsubtly named Delight. Since Mrs. Partridge missed her opportunity to be on the stage, she determined that Delight was destined to be an actress and spared no effort in making that dream a reality. Delight, however, took little interest in an acting career—she knew she was untalented and eventually managed to trade a Broadway debut for marriage to the millionaire farmer she loves.

Although Philip Partridge often was given fine comic dialogue and glib banter (foreshadowing the kind of material that would bring Ross acclaim in films), most of his stage time is spent in deference to his mother, either by setting up his drawing board in an obvious location (the living room) where he can be seen to be working on a sketch, or by trying to get her permission to do the thing he thinks he wants to do. When his friend Charlie Ludlow (John Thorn) invites him to go to Spain to work with him on the construction of a bridge, the following scene ensues between Philip, Charlie, and their friend Sydney:

20

Philip. Gee, that's swell! I knew you'd get it. I'd love to.

Charlie. You'd have charge of paying off the men. Sort of timekeeper. Check them up in the morning! Check them off in the evening! There is scarcely any salary attached to it, and you would have to pay your own way over.

Philip. That sounds great. Gee, I hope Maisie will let me go.

Charlie. My God, you haven't got a wife!

Sydney. His mother.

Charlie. Oh, your mother. She may not like it, but after all you have to live your own life.

Philip. You see, it's—well, my father is dead.

Charlie, So is mine.

Philip. Then you know how I feel. I can't disappoint her. She wants me to be an artist, and if I don't work at it, she'll find out I hate it. . . .

Sydney. No offence, old man, but you ought to get out and decide for yourself. You don't owe everything to a parent and don't let them kid you that you do. (2, 58)

It is telling that Philip is willing to pay to escape his mother's domination. Later in Act Two, he explains the situation to Stephen Applegate (Dallas Anderson), his mother's lawyer:

Philip. Steve, I don't dislike painting, but I hate Art Schools. I hate artists, for that matter. I want to see the world.

Stephen. You and Delight have been all over Europe.

Philip. With Maisie! Between the spring and summer openings. Do you honestly think that is what I want? I don't want to be rushed like that. Masie hurries me so. It's the same thing about my life. All I ask is to be left alone. I may turn out to be anything if I can only get a chance. (2, 71):

In Act Three, with ticket in hand for the boat about to leave for Spain, Philip finally forces himself to confront his mother about the trip:

Philip. Gee, didn't I tell you? You see, Ludlow's an engineer.

Masie. An engineer?

Philip. I'm going to help him build the bridge. I've come to the conclusion that a man should work out of doors. That's the way to live.

Maisie. You don't mean you'd like to be an—what about your painting?

Philip. I'm taking the old sketch book. (*Taking it from his pocket.*) See, right beside my ticket. I can do that on the side, anyway.

Maisie. Oh, perhaps you can. I had a notion that one should give one's whole life to it.

Philip. Well, the way I look at it is this, Maisie. I want to work, not just sit on the side and daub paint on a blank canvas.

Maisie. I see. It seems like that to you. Why daub paint on a canvas at all?

Philip. I don't know. I guess because it was always expected of me. We always do what's expected of us, don't we?

Maisie. Only till something wakes us up! Philip, wake up! And tell your mother the truth. Do you want to be an artist? If you could do only one thing in the world, only one thing, as long as you lived—would it be painting?

Philip. (*Considers.*) No. I think—no.

Maisie. Then do only one thing for me. Don't be an artist on the side. Philip, I couldn't bear a child of mine to be an artist on the side. Give me that sketch book. (*She takes it and tosses it on the sofa.*) Now, my son, go and be a good engineer. (3, 87)

Mrs. Partridge Presents opened on 28 December before a large and appreciative high-class audience. Although Ross Alexander was not singled out in *The Boston Globe* review (29 December 1925), the appraisal was generally complimentary noting that "There are three admirable feminine comedy characters who are on the stage the greater portion of the time, as well as a number of well-acted male roles, and by far the greater portion of the speeches throughout the play prove to be signals for hearty general laughter." The notables in the cast were all women: Blanche Yurka, Peg Entwistle, Carlotta Irwin, a new member of the company who played the effervescent family friend Katherine Everett, and Agnes Scott as Ellen the maid. The review concluded that "Each of the other members of the cast was thoroughly satisfactory."

Two days after the opening of *Mrs. Partridge Presents*, on the afternoon of Wednesday 30 December, Ross was among the 300 attendees that included Henry Jewett and his wife Frances, Blanche Yurka, members of the repertory company, and invited guests from Boston society, at the season's opening meeting of the Repertory Theatre Club of Boston, the governing board of Jewett's theatre company. The Jewetts enumerated the difficulties of establishing a repertory theatre in Boston, and Yurka extolled the repertory system in a dramatic and impassioned address designed to inspire financial contributions from Boston's wealthy theatrephiles: "One must play a variety of characters to enrich the content of the color of one's character. To play comedy one should have back of it the warmth and pathos of a great romance. That is the way great acting must be developed. . . . To do that we must have a laboratory theatre, performance, and the public. You have your theatre. E.H. Southern, Cyril Maude and Louis Mann visited here yesterday and declared that it is a perfect place, with permanent equipment for a great national theatre. I personally feel that if any set of circumstances should prevent this theatre from reaching the ultimate pinnacle of achievement it would be the worst tragedy that could happen to the artistic life of America." (*The Boston Globe*, 31 December 1925).

Prior to the speeches was a program of songs and recitation by members of the repertory company: Yurka performed Czechoslovakian folk songs in costume; Dallas Anderson gave a reading from J.M. Barrie's play, *What Every Woman Knows*; John Thorn sang "Dear Old Pal of Mine"; Agnes Scott sang "Caro Mio Ben"; Horace Pollock recited Robert W. Service's "The Cremation of Sam McGee," a popular program piece; and Ross Alexander rounded out the entertainment portion of the afternoon singing "I Must Down to the Seas Again," John Ireland's setting of the famous John Masefield poem. The afternoon culminated with a reception and a receiving line that included the entire repertory acting company. Never one to believe in (or tolerate) ceremony, Alexander considered the afternoon "dog-and-pony-show" a completely misspent effort: if the powers that be wish to raise money, he thought, let them do it on their own time. To paraphrase a remark attributed to Queen Victoria, Ross was not amused!

After a week of performing in *Mrs. Partridge Presents* in the evenings and *Snow White* on matinees, Ross found himself in rehearsal for Shakespeare's *Much Ado about Nothing* during the day and free in the evenings when Ibsen's *The Wild Duck* returned, marking the final week of Blanche Yurka's residency at the Repertory. Although Ross was cast in the small role of Conrade, one of Don John's villainous flunkies, and appeared in only four scenes in the play (in one of which he had no lines), he felt ill-equipped to play the role. For many actors, particularly those without extensive training in the classics, Shakespeare's elevated language inspired a fear not unlike what one might experience when going to the dentist; and with only thirty hours to mount a five-act play, director Henry Jewett (who was also playing the demanding role of Benedick) had little time to assuage his actors' fears.

The table reading on the first day of rehearsal provided Ross with a sense (but not much more than a sense) of what the play was about: a double love plot involving a serious couple: Hero (Peg Entwistle) and Claudio (Charles Meredith), and an ironic couple: Beatrice (Eva Walsh Hall) and Benedick. The wicked Don John (William Kershaw) and his minions, Borachio (Charles Stillwell) and Conrade, sow discord between Hero and Claudio by making her appear unfaithful. Claudio calls off their wedding, Hero goes into hiding and is subsequently reported dead. Through the ministrations of a blundering Master Constable Dogberry (John Thorn) and his men, the conspiracy is unmasked and wedding bells chime for both couples.

Conrade first appears onstage in Act One, scene three, where he serves as confidant to Don John, leading him to reveal his animosity toward his brother, Don Pedro (Dallas Anderson) by means of an organic expository dialogue. Conrade has only one speech longer than a single line, but one that provides significant information: "Yea, but you must not make the full show of this till you may do it without controlment. You have of late stood out against your brother, and he hath ta'en you newly into his grace, where it is impossible you should take true root but by the fair weather that you make yourself. It is needful that you frame the season for your own harvest" (1.3.18–24).

24

Ross found the line difficult to memorize and impossible to paraphrase since he had no idea what he was saying.

Conrade's second appearance occurs in Act Three, scene three, where he acts as a comic foil to his fellow-flunky Borachio, forcing him to overexplain the success of the scheme to convince Claudio of Hero's infidelity. Once again, Conrade has only one speech longer than a single sentence, a witty turn of phrase that again escaped Ross's understanding: "All this I see, and I see that the fashion wears out more apparel than the man. But art not thou thyself giddy with the fashion too, that thou hast shifted out of thy tale into telling me of the fashion" (3.3.139–142). Lying in wait, Dogberry and his watchmen overhear Borachio's detailed confession of villainy and summarily arrest the pair.

Borachio and Conrade are put on trial in Act Four, scene three, where they do little but state their names and plead not guilty to the charges in spite of overwhelming evidence against them. When told that they are to be bound and brought before Hero's father Leonato (William Mason), the Governor of Messina where the play is set, Conrade calls Dogberry an ass—an epithet that sends the Master Constable into a fourteen-line tirade at the end of scene. In Act Five, scene one, when the defendants appear before Leonato, Dogberry issues a formal complaint against Conrade for calling him an ass. Since Conrade has no lines in the scene, we can only imagine his standing sheepishly, a fettered object of scorn. Given the difficulties Ross experienced with the few lines he was taxed to speak in the production, he threw himself into the mute scene in Act Five and created a more fully rounded Conrade without dialogue than he had in any of his spoken scenes. *Much Ado About Nothing* opened at the Repertory on 11 January 1926 to mostly positive reviews. *The Boston Globe* (12 January 1926), for example, praised Jewett, Hall, Entwistle, Anderson, and Thorn in their roles of Benedick, Beatrice, Hero, Don Pedro, and Dogberry, but found Mason only a competent Leonato, and Kershaw too much of the "slinking type of villain." The company as a whole was found to be deserving of "much credit for the performance," even though "more careful enunciation" was needed.

Speaking of the experience to Clarke Wales ten years after the fact (*Oakland Tribune* 23 August 1936), Alexander explained:

> I was 17 years old, playing in *Much Ado About Nothing* with the Jewett Stock Company. I was the villain with a long grey beard. [Note that in January 1926, Ross would have been 18, on his way to becoming 19.]
>
> Everything might have gone all right if a girl in the company [Ethelyne Hoizman] who was supposed to sing a romantic song ["Sigh No More, Ladies"] hadn't frozen up with stage fright at the last minute. Jewett adjusted his monocle and looked at me. "Laddie," he said, "can you sing the song?" I said I could. "Very well, then, you will sing it tonight."
>
> Well, I sang the song and played the villain and rushed out to get the papers the next morning. I supposed I expected to be hailed as a combination of Booth and Caruso. But one notice said: "In Mr. Jewett's company are two groups of players, those who seem to know something about Shakespeare and those who apparently have no idea of what they are doing. In the first group are Mr. Jewett, et al, et al, et al; in the second group is Ross Alexander."

Much Ado About Nothing remained at the Repertory for two weeks during which Ross continued to struggle to make sense of Shakespeare in the evenings and on matinees. In rehearsal was *Captain Brassbound's Conversion*, an early comedy by George Bernard Shaw. Ross Alexander was given the role of (Kid) Redbrook, son of the Reverend Dean Redbrook and one of Brassbound's pirates who first appears in Act Two sprawling on the cement floor of a room in a Moorish Castle in Morocco, overcome by the midday heat. Shaw's description of the character continues: "One of them, lying with his head against the second saddle seat, wears what was once a fashionable white English yachting suit. He is evidently a pleasantly worthless English

26

gentleman gone to the bad, but retaining sufficient self-respect to shave carefully and brush his hair, which is wearing thin, and does not seem to have been luxuriant even in its best days. The silence is broken only by the snores of the young gentleman, whose mouth has fallen open, until a few distant shots half waken him. He shuts his mouth convulsively, and opens his eyes sleepily" (Shaw 1, 627). What Redbrook sees is an English adventuress, Lady Cicely Wayneflete (Agnes Scott) ministering to a wounded man (George Stillwell), and her much older brother-in-law, Sir Howard Hallam (Horace Pollock) complaining about his treatment at the hands of Captain Brassbound (John Thorn), who he discovers is his vengeful nephew who blames him for his mother's death and loss of his inheritance.

In the name of justice, Brassbound had arranged to turn over Sir Howard to Islamist Sheik Sidi el Assif (James H. Bell) but Lady Cecily charms the captain into buying him back, even though the only price Sheik Sidi would accept in return is the woman. The transaction becomes moot when the overlord Cadi Muley Othman el Kintafi (William Mason) appears brandishing a letter from Captain Hamlin Kearney (Charles Meredith), the very handsome commander of an American warship, ordering the Cadi to release Sir Howard and Lady Cecily. To which end, the Cadi arrests Brassbound and his men and removes them to the jail in the Moroccan seaport city of Mogador. At the home of a Scottish missionary (William Kershaw) Brassbound and his men are brought before Commander Kearney who presides over a court of inquiry into Brassbound's behavior. Lady Cecily manages to charm the commander into dropping any charges against the captain, who subsequently reveals his affection for her and proposes marriage. Lady Cecily is about to accept when gunfire from the Thanksgiving, Brassbound's ship, calls him back to sea and the lady celebrates her lucky escape from marriage.

Beginning 25 January 1926, Ross Alexander played the role of Redbrook on evenings and matinees for two weeks. Although the role was not particularly noteworthy, it did clearly express the bigotry of the British establishment at the turn of the century. When Brassbound accuses his crew of mutiny because of their reticence at turning over Sir Harold to the sheik, Redbrook explains: "Not at all, governor. Don't talk Tommy rot with Brother Sidi only five-minutes gallop off. Can't turn over an Englishman to a nigger to have his throat cut" (Shaw 1, 650). Even if his portrayal of Redbrook did little to earn Alexander kudos from the Boston critics, it did, at least, prepare him for an eminently noticeable role ten years later: Jeremy Pitt in the critically acclaimed Warner Brothers film *Captain Blood* (1935)

The theme of British prejudice continued in the next Repertory Theatre offering, John Galsworthy's *Loyalties*, a play about anti-Semitism. A young nouveau riche Jew Ferdinand De Levis (John Davidson) accuses retired British war-hero Captain Ronald Darcy, D.S.O. (Charles Quartermaine) of stealing £1000 and takes him to court instead of settling the matter quietly. Darcy's friends rally around him and strive diligently to prove his innocence, and even when it is proven that he is actually guilty of the crime, his lawyer Jacob Twisden (Horace Pollock) and his wife Mabel (Peg Entwistle) struggle to help him avoid scandal. Cast as Twisden's much younger partner Edward Graviter, Ross Alexander is given another innocuous character that enters only in the last act of the play and has little to do with the action, but assists in extending the "loyalties" trope to the legal profession:

Graviter. What's to be done about Dancy?

Twisden. Can you understand a gentleman—?

Graviter. I don't know, sir. The war loosened "form" all over the place. I saw plenty of that myself. And some men have no moral sense. From the first I've had doubts.

Twisden. We can't go on with the case.

Graviter. Phew! . . . (*A moment's silence.*) Gosh! It's an awful thing for his wife.

Twisden. Yes.

Graviter. (*Touching the envelope [of incriminating evidence].*) Chance brought this here, sir. That man won't talk—he's too scared.

Twisden. Gilman.

28

Graviter. Too respectable. If De Levis got those notes back, and the rest of the money anonymously?

Twisden: But the case, Graviter; the case.

Graviter. I don't believe this alters what I've been thinking.

Twisden. Thought is one thing—knowledge another. There's duty to our profession. Ours is the first calling. On the good faith of solicitors a very great deal hangs. . . .

Graviter. By Jove, I don't like losing this case. I don't like the admission we backed such a wrong 'un.

Twisden. Impossible to go on. Apart from ourselves, there's Sir Frederic [trial counsel]. We must disclose this to him—can't let him go on in the dark. Complete confidence between solicitor and counsel is the essence of professional honor! (3.1.249–250)

Loyalties began a two-week run on 8 February 1926 and was met with popular and critical approval. After complimenting the principal players, *The Boston Globe* (9 February 1926) concluded: "Approval was pretty well spread over the rest of the cast. Each player got a big share of the laughs, gripping silences and the applause. The play is crowded with incident, suspense never wavers, and altogether it is a fine piece of workmanship."

Loyalties was followed on 22 February 1926 by what *The Boston Globe* called the "most ambitious [production] yet attempted by the Repertory players" (23 February 1926), Shaw's sprawling *Caesar and Cleopatra* in its full five acts without "disfiguring cuts." Ross was given the most colorful role of his Boston tenure, that of Apollodorus, a Sicilian purveyor of beautiful things, described by Shaw as "a dashing young man of about 24, handsome and debonair, dressed with deliberate aestheticism in the most delicate purples and dove greys, with ornaments of bronze, oxidized silver, and stones of jade and agate. His sword, designed as carefully as a medieval cross, has a blued blade, showing through an openwork scabbard of purple leather and filigree" (Shaw 3, 412).

Entering in Act Three with carpets to furnish Cleopatra's (Mary Servoss) apartments in the royal palace Apollodorus is immediately censorious of the Roman sentinel (Frank Thomas) standing guard: "I am Apollodorus the Sicilian. Why, man, what are you dreaming of? Since I came through the lines behind the theatre there, I have brought my caravan past three sentinels, all so busy staring at the lighthouse that not one of them challenged me. Is this Roman discipline" (3, 412–413). When asked for the password to enter the palace, Apollodorus executes the following exchange:

> **Sentinel**. So you are a carpet merchant?
>
> **Apollodorus**. (*Hurt*) My friend: I am a patrician.
>
> **Sentinel**. A Patrician! A patrician keeping a shop instead of following arms!
>
> **Apollodorus**. I do not keep a shop. Mine is a temple of the arts. I am a worshipper of beauty. My calling is to choose beautiful things for beautiful queens. My motto is Art for Art's sake.
>
> **Sentinel**. That is not the password.
>
> **Apollodorus**. It is a universal password.
>
> **Sentinel**. I know nothing about universal passwords. Either give me the password of the day or get back to your shop. (Shaw 3, 413)

When Cleopatra enters rather than concern herself with Apollodorus's carpets, she demands to be given a boat by which she can escape to Caesar (Charles Quartermaine) from her incarceration in the royal palace. After her maid, Ftatateeta (Agnes Scott), chastises her saying that she "cannot go on the water except in the royal barge," Apollodorus wins Cleopatra's respect by replying: "Royalty, Ftatateeta, lies not in the barge but in the Queen. (*To Cleopatra*) The touch of your majesty's foot on the gunwale of the meanest boat in the harbor will make it royal" (Shaw 3.413).

Of course, the Roman sentinel continues to hinder Apollodorus from helping Cleopatra into his boat and a sword fight ensues between them, ending only when a Centurion (George Stillwell) enters with reinforcements:

> **Centurion**. (*to Apollodorus*) As for you, Apollodorus, you may thank the gods that you are not nailed to the palace door with a pilum for your meddling.

30

Apollodorus. (*urbanely*) My military friend, I was not born to be slain by so ugly a weapon. When I fall, it will be (*holding up his sword*) by this white queen of arms, the only weapon fit for an artist. And now that you are convinced that we do not want to go beyond the lines, let me finish killing your sentinel and depart with the Queen.

Centurion. (*as the sentinel makes an angry demonstration*) Peace there, Cleopatra: I must abide by my orders, and not by the subtleties of this Sicilian. . . . (*sulkily*) I do my duty. That is enough for me.

Apollodorus. Majesty: when a stupid man is doing something he is ashamed of, he always declares that it is his duty. (Shaw 3, 417–418)

As the scene progresses, Cleopatra rolls herself into one of Apollodorus's carpets and manages to be transported in Apollodorus's boat as a gift to Caesar who, in the meantime, tosses into the sea a bag of incriminating letters from Pompey and his Egyptian associates. Moments later, Apollodorus's arrival is met with displeasure by Caesar, his aide Rudio (Louis Leon Hall), and his secretary Britannus (Ralph Roberts):

Caesar. (*Taking him into his confidence in his most winning manner*) Apollodorus: this is no time for playing with presents. Pray you, go back to the Queen, and tell her that if all goes well, I shall return to the palace this evening.

Apollodorus. Caesar: I cannot return. As I approached the lighthouse, some fool threw a great leathern bag into the sea. It broke the nose of my boat; and I had hardly time to get myself and my charge to the shore before the poor little cockleshell sank.

Caesar. I am sorry Apollodorus. The fool shall be rebuked. Well, well: what have you brought me? The Queen will be hurt if I do not look at it. . . .

Apollodorus. Caesar: it is a Persian carpet—a beauty! And in it are—so I am told—pigeons' eggs and crystal goblets and fragile precious things. . . .

Rufio. Swing it up by the crane, then. We will send the eggs to the cook, drink our wine from the goblets; and the carpet will make a bed for Caesar.

Apollodorus. The crane! Caesar, I have sworn to tender this bale of carpets as I tender my own life.

31

Caesar. (*cheerfully*) Then let them swing you up at the same time; and if the chain breaks, you and the pigeons' eggs will perish together. (*He goes to the chain and looks up along it, examining it curiously.*)

Apollodorus. (*to Britannus*) Is Caesar serious?

Britannus. His manner is frivolous because he is an Italian; but he means what he says. (Shaw 3, 427–428)

After Cleopatra is raised by the crane and presented to Caesar, she soon realizes that her presence is unwarranted and unwanted:

Caesar. (*Gravely*) Cleopatra: when that trumpet sounds, we must take every man his life in his hand, and throw it in the face of Death. And of my soldiers who have trusted me there is not one whose hand I shall not hold more sacred than your head. (*Cleopatra is overwhelmed. Her eyes fill with tears.*) Apollodorus: you must take her back to the palace.

Apollodorus. Am I a dolphin, Caesar, to cross the seas with young ladies on my back? My boat is sunk: all yours are either at the barricade or have returned to the city. I will hail one if I can: that is all I can do. (*He goes back to the causeway.*)

Cleopatra. (*struggling with her tears*) It does not matter. I will not go back. Nobody cares for me. . . .

Caesar. (*still more gravely*) My poor child: your life matters little here to anyone but yourself. (Shaw 3, 430–431)

As the Egyptian army draws closer to the Roman forces, Apollodorus demonstrates that the only escape lies in swimming to a ship a quarter of a mile away:

Apollodorus. Defend yourselves until I send you a boat from that galley.

Rufio. Have you wings, perhaps?

Apollodorus. Water wings, soldier. Behold! (*He runs up the steps between Caesar and Britannus to the coping of the parapet; springs into the air; and plunges head foremost into the sea.*) (Shaw 3, 432)

Wildly excited, like a schoolboy, Caesar follows him into the water and, offering to carry Cleopatra on his back, orders Rufio to pitch her into the sea.

Because Caesar enjoys the company of Apollodorus, his presence is tolerated through the rest of the play. He joins Caesar in battle proclaiming his readiness "for Art—the Art of War" (3, 460), yet after the battle, he expresses little solidarity the soldiers: "I could not stand any more of the roaring of the soldiers! After half an hour of the enthusiasm of an army, one feels the need of a little sea air" (Shaw 3.463). Before he returns to Rome, Caesar bequeaths the art of Egypt to the care of Apollodorus saying, "Remember, Rome loves art and will encourage it ungrudgingly," to which Apollodorus replies, "I understand, Caesar. Rome will produce no art itself; but it will buy up and take away whatever the other nations produce." Stung by Apollodorus's cynical response, Caesar exclaims, "What! Rome produce no art! Is peace not an art? Is war not an art? Is government not an art? Is civilization not an art? All these we give you in exchange for a few ornaments. You will have the best of the bargain. (Shaw 3, 466).

Ross Alexander had a plum role in Apollodorus and his efforts did not go unnoticed by the critic of *The Boston Globe* who concluded that "Mr. Alexander [was] a pleasing disciple of 'art for art's sake'" (23 February 1926). The same reviewer also noted the ubiquitous presence of the prompter feeding Caesar his lines during the opening performance. One of the drawbacks of the repertory system lies in the difficulty for actors to remember their lines, rendering them often imperfect studies on opening night. Ross Alexander did not particularly like doing repertory for that very reason. He felt that the play finally begins to gel in the second week of a two-week run and complained that by the time the actor feels comfortable in a role, the run is over! There is much to be said for his point of view.

On Thursday 4 March, only days before *Caesar and Cleopatra* completed its run, Ross was a featured entertainer in an after-the-theatre dance and midnight revel, entitled *The Silver Forest,* given in Repertory Hall, a rehearsal and meeting space adjacent to the theatre. Dancing began at 11:00 after the conclusion of the play and a tableau, *Cleopatra's Night*, presented by all the members of the Repertory Company followed at midnight. Supper was also served at 1:00 A.M. Stars from all the plays and musicals in Boston were invited guests, and the entertainment and dance music were broadcast on the radio channel WBZ.

During the final week of *Caesar and Cleopatra* Ross understudied the role of Randall Utterwood in Shaw's *Heartbreak House* which opened for a week's run on 8 March, and during that run, he rehearsed the role of Fred Minick in *Minick*, George S. Kaufman and Edna Ferber's popular comedy. Fred, who is trying to establish himself in the mail-order business, and his wife Nettie (Mary Servoss), who is trying to establish herself in a Chicago women's club, both decide that Fred's recently widowed father would be better off living with them in their five-room flat rather than in some home for the elderly. Set in his ways, Father Minick (Frank Thomas) disrupts the household, compromises Fred's business and embarrasses Nettie in the middle of an important women's club meeting, all of which leads to a blowup between Fred and Nettie who storms out of their living room with an ultimatum: "Either your father goes out of this house or I do, Fred Minick—and I don't care which it is" (2, 93). Following the tense scene between husband and wife, Father Minick makes an unwelcome entrance with the attitude of a father "who is going to remonstrate with his little boy" (2, 94):

Minick. Now, Fred! I want you to listen me.

Fred. (*A gesture of a man who has all he can stand and will hear no more.*) Father!

Minick. I don't know what Nettie had to say to you, but I want you to tell me about this nonsense [the mail-order business] of yours.

Fred. Father, for God's sake! Will you—

Minick. All right! But I'm going to take hold of things just the same. I remember when you were nine years old—

Fred. But I'm not nine years old any longer. You don't seem to realize that!

34

Minick. I realize you got no right to jump into a thing like this without coming to me about it—

Fred. Father, for God's sake! You're an old man. What do you know about modern business? If you'd only stay out of my affairs— (*Exits and slams the outer door.*)

Minick. (*Stands for a moment, dazed.*) An old man—that's what he said—an old man. (2, 94)

When he learns of a vacancy at an old folks' home, Father Minick decides to leave but, out of a deep-seeded feeling of filial responsibility, Fred and Nettie talk him into remaining. Proving perhaps that the older man really does know better than the younger, Father Minick steals away to the home leaving his son and daughter-in-law to get on with their lives.

Minick began a two-week run on 15 March 1926 and was enthusiastically received by audiences and critics. *The Boston Globe* (16 March 1926), for example, found Frank Thomas "convincing" as the elder Minick, dubbed Ross Alexander "a capital young son trying to make his mark in business," and called the supporting cast first rate. As soon as *Minick* was in production Ross began rehearsal for the next offering at the Repertory, W. Somerset Maugham's 1921 play *The Circle*, in which he was cast as the pithy and loquacious Edward {"Teddie") Luton, a planter in the Federated Malay States. Edward is in love with Elizabeth Champion-Cheney (Peg Entwistle), the wife of Arnold Champion-Cheney, M.P. (William Kershaw) whose mother Lady Catherine ("Kitty") Champion-Cheney (Ruth Taylor) eloped with a married man, Lord Porteous (Horace Pollock), ruining his political career. Elizabeth, who is in a loveless marriage, finds Lady Catherine a romantic figure but, in fact, what had been a romantic elopement on her part has proven to be an exercise in tolerance rather than affection. Added to these characters who are enjoying a day at Aston-Adey, Arnold Champion-Cheney's country house in Dorset, England, is Arnold's father, Clive Champion-Cheney (Charles Quartermaine) who advises his son that the best way to keep a wife is to give her her freedom, counsel that proves useful when Arnold discovers his wife's affection for Edward Luton. Because Arnold offers to let Elizabeth divorce him, she becomes unwilling to leave him saying, "How can I accept such a sacrifice? I should never forgive myself if I profited by his generosity. . . . Let's say goodbye to one another, Teddie. It's the only thing to do. And have pity on me. I'm giving up all my hope of happiness" (3, 169, 171). Her behavior evokes Luton's commentary about England in Act One: "England seems to me full of people doing things they don't want to because other people expect it of them" (1, 104). In rebuttal, Luton looks into Elizabeth's eyes and the following scene occurs in the presence of Lady Kitty and Lord Porteous:

Teddie. But I wasn't offering you happiness. I don't think my sort of love tends to happiness. I'm jealous. I'm not a very easy man to get on with. I'm often out of temper and irritable. I should be fed to the teeth with you sometimes, and so would you be with me. I daresay we'd fight like cat and dog, and sometimes we'd hate each other. Often you'd be wretched and bored stiff and lonely, and often you'd be frightfully homesick, and then you'd regret all you'd lost. Stupid women would be rude to you because we'd run away together. And some of them would cut you. I don't offer you peace and quietness. I offer you unrest and anxiety. I don't offer you happiness. I offer you love.

Elizabeth. (*Stretching out her arms.*) You hateful creature, I absolutely adore you. (*He throws his arms round her and kisses her passionately on the lips.*) . . .

Teddie. Let's make a bolt for it now.

Elizabeth. Shall we?

Teddie. This minute.

Porteous. You're damned fools, both of you, damned fools! If you like you can have my car.

Teddie. That's awfully kind of you. As a matter of fact, I got it out of the garage. It's just along the drive. . . .

Porteous. Do you mean to say you were going to steal my car? . . .

Teddie. Hang it all, I couldn't carry Elizabeth all the way to London. She's so damned plump.

Elizabeth. You dirty dog!

Porteous. (*Sputtering*.) Well, well, well! . . . (*Helplessly*.) I like him, Kitty, it's no good pretending I don't. I like him.

Teddie. The moon's shining, Elizabeth. We'll drive all through the night. . . . We'll drive through the dawn and through the sunrise. (*Teddie stretches out his hand and [Elizabeth] takes it. Hand in hand they go out into the night*.) (3, 171–173)

The Circle began a two-week run on 29 March 1926. Ross Alexander was singled out by *The Boston Globe* as "a perfect correspondent," (in its usage meaning "paramour" or "the other man" in a case of adultery) and the reviewer found "the acting throughout was completely worthy of the play" (30 March 1926).

During the run of *The Circle*, *The Wild Duck* was put back in rehearsal in preparation for a two-week run beginning on Tuesday afternoon 13 April. Ruth Taylor replaced Blanche Yurka as Gina Ekdal and Charles Quartermain replaced Arthur Behrens as Werle, but Peg Entwistle (Hevig), Horace Pollock (Old Ekdal), William Kershaw (Gregers Werle), and Dallas Anderson (Hialmar Ekdal) reprised their roles from the two earlier productions of the play at the Repertory. Ross Alexander was cast as Molvik, a student of Theology and downstairs neighbor of the Ekdal family. He enters in Act Three, dressed all in black, with his roommate Relling (Louis Leon Hall), a doctor. The men seat themselves at table with the Ekdal family to whom Relling reveals the daemonic side of Molvik's personality:

Relling. Molvik was frightfully screwed yesterday, Mrs. Ekdal.

Gina. Really? Yesterday again?

Relling. Didn't you hear him when I brought him home last night?

Gina. No, I can't say I did.

Relling. That was a good thing, for Molvik was disgusting last night.

Gina. Is that true, Molvik?

Molvik. Let us draw a veil over last night's proceedings. That sort of thing is totally foreign to my better self.

Relling. (*to Gregers*.) It comes over him like a sort of possession, and then I have to go out on the loose with him. Mr. Molvik is daemonic, you see. . . . And, daemonic natures are not made to walk straight through the world; they must meander a little now and then. (3, 48)

Another side of Molvik's personality is in evidence when dinner is being served:

Relling. And a slice of bacon for Molvik.

Molvik. Ugh; not bacon!

(*A knock at the garret door.*)

Hialmar. Open the door, Hedvig; father wants to come out.

(*Hedvig goes over and opens the door a little way. Ekdal enters with a fresh rabbit-skin, she closes the door after him.*)

Ekdal. Good morning, gentlemen! Good sport today. Shot a big one.

Hialmar. And you've gone and skinned it without waiting for me—

Ekdal. Salted it, too. It's good tender meat, is rabbit; it's sweet; it tastes like sugar. Good appetite to you, gentlemen!

Molvik. (*Rising.*) Excuse me—; I can't—; I must get downstairs immediately—

Relling. Drink some soda water, man!

Molvik. (*Hurrying away.*) Ugh—ugh! (*Goes out by the passage door.*) (3, 49)

Molvik disappears until the final scene of the play when it is discovered that Hedvig has shot herself. As everyone onstage responds the Hedvig's death in a way that suits their characters, Molvik quotes from the Gospel of Matthew 9: 24, "The child is not dead, but sleepeth." In the Gospel, however, the girl is brought back to life physically, not metaphorically. Molvik continues mumbling with Genesis 3:19, "Blessed be the Lord; to earth thou shall return; to earth thou shall return—," to which Relling replies, "Hold your tongue, you fool; you're drunk" (5, 86–87).

On Monday 12 April, the day before the opening of *The Wild Duck*, Ross Alexander appeared on Samuel Wren's 7:00 P.M. radio show "Theatrical Gossip," broadcast on station WBZ. This would be the first of many radio broadcasts in which Ross participated during his career. Three days later, on Thursday afternoon, Ross was joined by Hugh Towne in the performance of ballads and classical songs at a literary and musical entertainment sponsored by the Repertory Theatre Club. The program also included Henry Jewett who gave a dramatic performance of "Shamus O'Brien" and Charles Quartermaine who recited from a variety of plays.

On 26 April, James M. Barrie's *The Little Minister* opened at the Repertory with Ross Alexander in the small, but dramatically important supporting role of Sergeant Davidson, a character who appears only in the first and last act of the play. Lady Barbara "Babbie" Rintoul (Peg Entwistle), daughter of the lord of the manor (Charles Quartermaine) disguises herself as a gypsy and runs through the forest warning the villagers that her father has sent soldiers to arrest them for protesting his treatment of the weavers. Gavin Dishart (Dallas Anderson), the young minister of the town protects Babbie from being arrested by allowing Sergeant Davidson to believe that she is his wife. Neither Gavin nor Babbie realize that, according to Scottish law, if a couple claim that they are married in front of witnesses, the marriage is legal. Eleven days later, when Gavin is forced to accept the legality of his counterfeit relationship, it is Sergeant Davidson who reveals that it is not the gypsy who is Gavin's wife, but Lady Barbara—a fact that his soldiers confirm.

Sergeant Davidson was Ross Alexander's last credited role of the Repertory season. *The Little Minister* closed on 8 May and was followed by week-long productions of Ferenc Molnár's ironic fairy tale, *The Swan*, and Karel Čapek's forward-looking science-fiction drama, *R.U.R.* Ross was not a cast member of either play; instead he served as understudy to Dallas Anderson in the role of Dr. Nicholas Agi, a twenty-four-year-old tutor who falls in love with Princess Alexandra in *The Swan*; and understudy to Charles Knowlton as Primus, a Robot, in *R.U.R.* After five months of a grueling repertory season, often performing two different plays while rehearsing a third in a dozen-performance week, Ross rather enjoyed his role as understudy. He had to prepare the roles and learn the staging—he even had to be in the theatre during performances in case the principal actor became ill—but he no longer felt the pressure of performing a role on the fly, a feeling he often had in his earliest weeks at the Repertory.

After *R.U.R.* Closed on 22 May 1926, Ross spent a few days with Hugh Towne in East Jaffrey, New Hampshire. Ross had been invited to audition for a new Broadway play and sought Towne's advice in preparing for it. Just as it is impossible to verify the exact nature of the relationship between Ross Alexander and Hugh Towne, it is equally difficult to determine the exact course of theatre study that passed between them. It does not seem likely that Ross was coached in Shakespearean diction since, throughout his career, he considered it a foreign language, but Towne was first and foremost an elocutionist and certain behaviors that permeated Alexander's stage and film careers suggest that he was an apt disciple of the craft delineated in prominent elocution texts of the period. In *Advanced Elocution* (1910), Rachel Walter Hinkle Shoemaker emphasized the importance of an "expressive countenance" of the speaker (260), a guideline reinforced by Grenville Kleiser in his *Talks on Talking* (1917): "Let your standing position be manly, erect, easy, forceful, and impressive" and "your gesture should be graceful, appropriate, free, forceful, and natural" (86). Kleiser goes on to declare that one's voice should be "musical and well-modulated" (58); and "it is difficult to overestimate the power of words . . . with ten thousand words at his command [one] should be able to express himself with greater precision and effectiveness" (62). Evidently Ross embraced the power of words since, throughout his career, he was determined to learn a new word every day. It is not known whether his "hot-potato-voice" delivery, which often drew censure from contemptuous critics, was the result of Towne's training or in spite of it, but Ross's physical bearing and organic gesticulation, not to mention the fluency with which he managed personal interviews, clearly allude to his elocutionary training.

3. Louisville Stock

On Tuesday 25 May 1926, three days after the close of Boston's Repertory Theatre season, the (New York) *Daily News* reported that "A play entitled *The Ladder*, written by J. Frank Davis, has been purchased by Brock Pemberton, who will place it in rehearsal shortly for an out-of-town tryout next month, and for fall showing on Broadway. Davis is a fiction writer living in San Antonio, Texas, and used to be a newspaperman himself in Boston." Perhaps best known as the creator of Broadway's Antoinette Perry ("Tony") Awards, Pemberton had been a newspaper theatre critic and press agent before launching his career as an independent producer-director with the Broadway production of *Enter Madame* in 1920. Well-acquainted with the work of Blanche Yurka and Henry Jewett, Pemberton was in attendance at the premiere of *Enter Madame* at the Repertory Theatre in December 1925. While the production fulfilled his high expectations, Pemberton was especially impressed with the work of Ross Alexander, whom he kept in mind when casting future productions. It was thus not surprising that, at the end of May, Pemberton invited Ross to audition for the juvenal role in *The Ladder* and cast him on the spot.

Rehearsals for *The Ladder* began on 31 May in New York City and two weeks later the play began a tryout run in New Haven, Connecticut, followed by a week in Stamford. On 27 June 1926, *The New York Times* offered a positive critique of the tryouts:

41

Enthusiastic reports, especially from Stamford, precede the New York premiere of *The Ladder* in the Fall. Brock Pemberton is the producer and J. Frank Davis is the author. An account of the play in *The Stamford Advocate* reads as follows:

"In these four lines by Josiah Gilbert Holland,

'Heaven is not reached at a single bound

But we build the ladder by which we rise

From the lowly earth to the vaulted skies

And we mount to its summit round by round.'

programmed with *The Ladder*, is expressed the entire meaning of the piece. 'Life is a ghastly riddle,' Mr. Davis tells us, 'and there is no answer.' That we gain our happiness from the lessons learned in our other lives is the theory of the story. And so, when Wilma Newell, the luxury-loving daughter of a New York business man, finds herself in a dilemma as to making a choice between one or the other of two suitors, one of whom offers her love while the other pedestals his riches, she is taken back—yes, way back—by Prince Rama Singh, an Arabian seer, who causes her to look into her past and her ancestors and to learn their mistakes so that she may build her life accordingly. Mr. Pemberton delves into four interesting periods—1300 A.D., 1679 A.D., 1844 A.D., and, of course, the present time."

After the two-week tryout in Connecticut, Pemberton decided that *The Ladder* needed substantial rewrites prior to opening in New York City and released the cast for the remainder of the summer. Ross returned to New York and was immediately hired as the principal juvenal for the Wright Players, the stock company performing at the Strand Theatre in Louisville, Kentucky.

During the first days of July Ross Alexander moved to the housing provided by the stock company and spent the Fourth of July celebration becoming acquainted with his fellow-actors enjoying the comradery and fireworks display. The following day the company began rehearsals for Monckton Hoffe's sentimental melodrama, *The Faithful Heart*, scheduled to open a week's run on 12 July. Ross was cast as Gilbert Oughterson, the well-spoken, wealthy, upper-class brother of Diana (Susan Freeman) to whom Lieutenant Colonel Waverly Ango (Robert Warwick) is engaged. Unannounced, a young lady, Blacky II (Helen Flint), presents herself to Ango, claiming to be his daughter—the offspring from a dalliance with a woman named Blacky (Helen Flint) twenty years before, while he was in the merchant marine. Ultimately, Ango decides that his fatherly affection and sense of duty trump his marriage to a socialite, so he becomes captain of a tramp steamer bound for the Cape of Good Hope and takes his daughter with him.

The Strand Theatre, circa 1950.

Oughterson's chief function in the play is to encourage Ango to make the most of upper mobility in order to support his sister in the manner to which she is accustomed:

Oughterson. You turn up your nose at a staff appointment without giving the matter sufficient thought. I say, accept that appointment. *Accept* that appointment, and within two years my uncle, or someone or other, will see that you obtain a position that will be not only lucrative but attractive in *every* way. . . . In the meantime, my grandmother would undoubtedly regard it as a duty to make a certain marriage settlement—that I am sure of. . . . A settlement that would enable you to provide for Diana in a proper manner. (1, 26)

Ross certainly had the stature and demeanor for the role and, given his training in elocution, he was easily able to convey the lucidity of the posh English gentleman.

The Faithful Heart was followed on 19 July by Vincent Lawrence's critically acclaimed comedy, *Two Fellows and a Girl*, in which Ross portrayed Johnson, the butler. In the play, Lee Ellery (Helen Flint) flips a coin to decide which of her two suitors she will marry. She chooses Jack Moorland (Fred Sullivan) and the loser, Jim Dale (Irving Mitchell) departs, only to reappear several years later as a very rich man. Lee rekindles her interest in Jim—a behavior that arouses Jack's jealousy—but the arrival of flapper Doris Wadsworth (Susan Freeman) makes it clear that Jim's interest in anyone but her is purely Platonic. As the butler, Ross portrayed another proper gentleman's gentleman not unlike Oughterson, though, without an English accent.

The day before *Two Fellows and a Girl* opened the *Chicago Tribune* (18 July 1926) ran an article called "Pink Powder Puffs," that aggressively complained about the recent fad of men wearing makeup:

> It is time for a matriarchy if the male of the species allows such things to persist. Better a rule by masculine women than by effeminate men. . . . Is this degeneration into effeminacy a cognate reaction with pacifism to the virilities and realities of the war? . . . How does one reconcile masculine cosmetics, sheiks, floppy pants, and slave bracelets with a disregard for law and an aptitude for crime more in keeping with the frontier of half a century ago than a twentieth-century metropolis?

Do women like the type of "man" who pats pink powder on his face in a public washroom and arranges his coiffure in a public elevator? . . . It is a strange social phenomenon and one that is running its course not only here in America but in Europe as well. Chicago may have its powder puffs; London has its dancing men and Paris its gigolos. . . . Hollywood is the national school of masculinity. Rudy [Valentino], the beautiful gardener's boy, is the prototype of the American male.

Hell's bells. Oh, sugar.

Ross Alexander was ever vigilant not to appear effeminate on stage and off, and the *Tribune* article identifying the zeitgeist of the period suggests a reason why.

Beginning 26 July, Ross portrayed the minor role of Joe Wells in Samuel Shipman and Max Marcin's popular melodrama, *The Woman in Room Thirteen*, an over-the-top melodrama about a vengeful ex-husband, blackmail, lust, and murder. About to leave on an extended business trip, Paul Ramsey (Irving Mitchell) hires a private detective, John Bruce (Fred Sullivan), to protect his wife Laura (Helen Flint) from his lecherous boss. Since the private dick is, in fact, Laura's vengeful ex-husband, he manages to persuade Paul that his wife is carrying on an affair with the boss in room 13 of a New York apartment hotel. In Act Two, in a room directly beneath room 13, Joe Wells appears as one of John's operatives who had placed a hidden microphone in the room above so that Paul might hear the goings on allegedly between his boss and his wife. Since Paul refuses to hear the actual conversation, John instructs Joe and a female operative (listening on headphones) to repeat the lusty conversation, imitating the tone and inflections of the upstairs voices. Infuriated by their performance, Paul rushes upstairs to catch the couple *in flagrante* and seconds later a shot is heard. Of course, Paul is arrested for the murder of his boss and put on trial, during which his wife, who was never actually in the upstairs room, confesses that she was in order to vindicate her husband's outburst according to some accepted "unwritten law." The lie convinces the jury to vote

"Not guilty!" and, as the curtain falls, Paul learns that it was really not his wife who was the woman in room thirteen.

For a change of pace, *No More Blondes*, Otto Harbach's risqué, crude, and often vulgar farce, opened for a week's run on 2 August. Never having been performed in Louisville and a twenty-nine-performance flop on Broadway, the play depicts the plight of automobile salesman James Howells (Irving Mitchell) from Cohoes, New York, who brings his fiancée, Millicent (Susan Freeman) to New York City to get married. Immediately after the wedding ceremony Howells takes a blonde business associate to lunch while the unhappy wife cools her heels at the Martha Washington Hotel. Not knowing where his wife is, and having nowhere to stay in the big city, Howells finds himself house sitting on Riverside Drive. While he is asleep, the blonde woman of the house, Mrs. Eve Powell (Helen Flint) returns unexpectedly and the following morning Howells finds himself in the company of the woman wearing a negligee. Eve's wild-Western brother, Battling Hogan (Ross Alexander) suddenly appears and mistakes Howells for her husband, slapping him on the chest and back with such force that the man nearly collapses. Mr. Powell (Fred Sullivan) and Mrs. Howells arrive to find their spouses accused of infidelity by Tanner (Don Costello), a blackmailing butler. Ultimately the Powells and the Howells work through the spicy coincidences in the play and James and Millicent return to Cohoes, wishing they had never come to the big city.

Still waiting for a principal role in the Wright Players season, Ross was a delight as the broadly comic wild-Western brother, earning every laugh and guffaw he received. His next role was the romantic Henry Marchant in Rachel Barton Butler's *Mamma's Affair*, the prize-winning play from George P. Baker's English 47 class at Harvard and Radcliffe. Henry is engaged to Eve Orrin (Eleanor Martin), caregiver for her valetudinarian mother to whom she is obsessively devoted. Henry's histrionic (and often hysterical) mother is the dearest friend of Eve's mother and also a significant enabler of Mrs. Orrin's hypochondria. Both mothers see the marriage of their children as a continuation of their old and deep friendship. While Henry appears to be entirely invested in the engagement, his fiancée is less so:

Henry. (*Taking Eve's hand—sits left of her.*) You look a great deal paler today. Are you quite well?

Eve. (*Nervously.*) Oh yes, Henry, quite. Only—the past few weeks everything seems to make me—cross.

Henry. I have noticed—you've been somewhat irritable.

Eve. Oh, have I shown it—with Mamma?

Henry. (*Impatiently.*) Oh, can't you forget your mother for one moment—we have few enough of them alone.

Eve. (*Timidly.*) Henry—if you can—get along without holding my hand—

Henry. (*Rise, stiffly withdrawing.*) Pardon me. I did not know I was forcing my caresses upon you!

Eve. (*Rise, following him, eager to explain.*) Dear, please don't misunderstand. It's only that I'm always nervous when there's a new doctor coming for Mamma....

Henry. (*Sulkily.*) You worry foolishly over your mother.

Eve. Oh—perhaps I do! But she's all I have, Henry!

Henry. (*Tartly.*) Haven't you me?

Eve. Yes, dear—but you're not my mother, you know.

Henry. I'm beginning to believe you love your mother more than you love me!

Eve. Oh—Henry—dear! ... You promised you'd never again—

Henry. I know I did! (*With a sudden burst.*) I tell you I can't help it! When I kiss you after twenty-four hours of what might as well be complete separation—your eyes are on her door and your ears are listening for her. When I talk to you about our marriage vows you are wondering if she needs another pillow!

Eve. Henry—she loves me!

Henry. So do I!

Eve. With her it is more than just love! I have never slept a night away from her. Sometimes she comes and watches me, when she thinks I am asleep—she wants me *every moment*.

Henry. You hardly need to tell me that. I'm wondering what she will do while we are on our wedding trip!

Eve. I don't know. It worries me to think!

Henry. (*With suppressed wrath and sarcasm.*) Perhaps we'd better plan to have her with us.

Eve. (*Rises—naively.*) Oh, Henry, could we? (1, 21–23)

Coming to attend to Mrs. Orrin, Doctor Brent Jansen (Irving Mitchell) sees that Eve is suffering from a nervous breakdown and orders her to take a complete rest, away from her fiancé and their mothers. During the rest cure Eve falls in love with Brent Jansen and agrees to postpone the wedding on doctor's orders, a decision that does not sit well with Henry who rants: "Have you gone mad? There's nothing the matter with you now. This quack of a Doctor is preying on you, and bleeding you for every cent he can make out of you. Well, I'm a man! He can't befuddle me! I do not consent to any postponement of our marriage" (2, 73). Bravado, charm, understanding, simple desire—none of these works for Henry in his attempt to win Eve's love and he exits the play in a rage, warning her, "Remember! I'm not going to endure any more nonsense! You're going to marry me tomorrow" and scolding the doctor, "Understand, please, that only the presence of my mother and the presence of my future wife prevents me from thrashing you for a cad and a scoundrel" (3, 97).

Ross appreciated the opportunities that Henry Marchant provided: a ubiquitous stage presence; a wide emotional range; clever, perceptive dialogue; and a chance to figuratively chew scenery in bold, emotional outbursts. I once saw an actor actually chew a piece of scenery during a production of Molière's *Tartuffe* at the Geva Theatre in Rochester, during the late 1970s. The device was quite effective. Ross, of course, does not go that far with his histrionics, but at the end of the play he might well have taken a bite out of some canvas backdrop had the script allowed.

Publicity photograph of Ross Alexander in *Whispering Wires*,
from *The Courier-Journal*, 15 August 1926.

Kate L. McLauren's dramatization of Henry Leverage's *Saturday Evening Post* story, "Whispering Wires," followed on 16 August. Hated Millionaire businessman Montgomery Stockbridge (Truman Quevli) opposes the marriage of his daughter Doris (Eleanor Martin) to Barry McGill (Irving Mitchell), a retired military Captain and son of one of Stockbridge's former partners. Having received a recent death threat, Stockbridge hires Triggy Drew (Fred Sullivan), a private detective, to hunt down the culprit and keep him safe. After compiling a list of suspects, including former business associates Morphy and Vogel, Drew stations plainclothesmen throughout the millionaire's house, including the tall, good-looking Delaney (Ross Alexander) who stands, carrying a gun, right outside the library where the millionaire is positioned. Suddenly the phone rings, Stockbridge answers it and immediately collapses, exclaiming with his dying breath, "Ah! Sing" (1, 63). The remainder of the play is spent discovering the who, why, and how of Stockbridge's murder and preventing a similar fate to fall on Doris, the victim's daughter. Suspicion is accordingly concentrated on McGill, but he is eventually exonerated and the real perpetrator is brought to justice.

Delaney is Drew's righthand man, carrying out his orders, on and off stage. He is a source of information useful to the solution of the mystery: "Morphy's sleeping sweet behind the bars" (1, 51); "Flood's with the cop a block down the avenue. O'Toole came and I shot him off to see what Vogel's up to. Harper is right across the street—you could see him from the window there. Peters is doing the cellar and then the upper floors . . . We've got you covered at every angle, Mr. Stockbridge" (1, 59); "Drew, I got Sing Sing, talked to the warden. Morphy and two other men killed a guard and escaped" (2, 90); "Office just 'phoned, Chief, the police nabbed Morphy in a house up on Fifty-Second Street" (3, 124). The efficient plainclothesman, however, is not without humanity: "Say, I'll be glad to get off this case. Nobody's stuck a gun at my head—not even in a dream! I ain't been asleep—ain't even laid down—I been on my feet doing my bit since we got here last night. I haven't even washed my face. . . . Say, Chief, if you don't want me right now, they're passing out tea and sandwiches in the dining-room. I think I'll go and get mine" (2, 76–77).

The final offering of the Wright Players' season was Roi Cooper Megrue and Walter Hackett's "Farcical fact in three acts" called *It Pays to Advertise*, in which soap-magnate Cyrus Martin (Fred Sullivan) and his secretary Mary Grayson (Eleanor Martin) connive to force Martin's son Rodney (Irving Mitchell) to earn a living. Rodney decides to go into the soap business to compete with his father and enters into a financial partnership with Comtesse de Beaurien (Ann Constant), a con artist pretending to be a French aristocrat desirous to acquire the rights to sell his father's soap in France. A theatrical press agent, Ambrose Peale (Ross Alexander), convinces Rodney that advertising is the key to success with a speech that anticipates the sharp, fast-talking dialogue that would typify many of Alexander's film characters:

Peale. Oh, you're one of those guys who don't believe in advertising, are you? Now, don't get me talking advertising. That's where I live, where I have my town house and country estate, my yacht and motors. That's my home. Maybe you think love is important? Piffle. Advertising, my boy, the power of suggestion, the psychology of print; say a thing often enough and hard enough and the other chap'll not only believe you, he'll think it's his own idea, and he'll fight for it. Some old gink, a professor of psychology, showed forty Vassar girls the other day two samples of satin, one blue, one pink, same grade, same value, same artistic worth. One he described as a delicate warm old rose, the other a faded blue. He asked them to choose their favorite. Thirty-nine out of the forty picked the old rose. Why? Because they were told it was warm and delicate; no faded blue for theirs! What did it? The power of suggestion—advertising! . . . You heard me tell that girl of yours a few minutes ago that "The Belle of Broadway" was the biggest hit in town. Ask her to go to the theater. Give her her choice and I'll bet you four dollars to a fried egg she picks "The Belle of Broadway." Advertising! . . . Ninety-seven percent of the public believe what they're told, and what they're told is what the other chap's been told—and the fellow who told him read it somewhere. When you see a thing in print about something you don't really know anything about, you come pretty near believing it. . . . Can you tell the difference between a vintage wine and last year's champagne? Sure you can: it costs more. Son, the world is full of bunk. Ninety-seven percent of the people are sheep, and you can get 'em all by advertising. (1, 27–30)

After spending all of his money on advertising, Rodney is unable to manufacture the product that has been so successfully advertised; but since demand is great for his "13 Soap" at a dollar a bar ($15.00 in 2020 dollars), Cyrus Martin buys out his son's company and becomes a convert to the power of advertising, Rodney and Mary get married, and Peale foils Beaurien's plot to "trim" Rodney's father for $15,000 on the bogus French rights to his soap:

Peale. Where's the contract? Come on—gimme—gimme—

Countess. You mean you've been on all the time?

Peale. Sure.

Countess. And you let me sit there and emote all over the place.

Peale. Gimme—gimme—

Countess. Oh, I suppose I've got to. Oh, I'm sick of soap anyhow. Thirteen may be a lucky hunch for you boys, but it has been a hoodoo for me.

Peale. And now, my little hearts of lettuce, this concludes your portion of the evening's entertainment.

Countess. But at that, don't give me away, will you?

Peale. I like you, you've got brains. Most chickens are just chickens.

Countess. You are eighteen-karat, kid. (3, 103)

On the morning of 23 August, Ross Alexander, Susan Freeman, Irving Mitchell, and Eleanor Martin appeared at Chandlers's Boot Shop to celebrate the opening of the new Louisville store and to introduce the latest autumn fashions in shoes, all advertised at just $6:00 a pair! The personal appearances of the actors also served as publicity for *It Pays to Advertise* which opened that evening and also demonstrated the popularity that Ross enjoyed with the locals. As *The Courier-Journal* (22 August 1926) noted, "Mr. Alexander in the brief time that he has been in Louisville, has been a great hit."

The Wright Players season closed on Saturday 28 August and, after having appeared in 63 performances of seven different plays in as many weeks, Ross rushed back to New York City to resume rehearsals for *The Ladder* in preparation for his Broadway debut.

4. *The Ladder*

Broadway has ever been a place where dreams and myths abound, where theatrical productions can achieve legendary status by being superlative examples of dramatic art, or critical and financial disasters. Ross Alexander's first show on Broadway, *The Ladder*, was legendary for being "that milestone in the history of theatrical ineptitude" (*The New Yorker*, 26 November 1949), the longest-running, most-expensive flop of its generation, playing 789 performances on Broadway, and losing $1,255,384.11 ($17,625,593 in 2019 dollars).

The accepted myth surrounding the genesis of *The Ladder* begins with Brockton-Massachusetts-born, multi-millionaire philanthropist Edgar B. Davis who made his fortune consecutively in shoes, rubber, and oil; and Brockton-born newspaperman J[ames] Frank Davis who tripped on the ice and seriously injured his spine at the North Pole where he had been sent to interview Admiral Robert E. Perry. Both men (and all newspaper reports emphasize that, in spite of their identical surnames, they were not related) attended Brockton public schools and, because seating was alphabetical, they sat in the same row, one behind the other, and became friends. After going off on separate careers, the pair became reacquainted in San Antonio, Texas, where J. Frank had settled because of his health. Riley Froh reports that during numerous hands of bridge, the subject of reincarnation was introduced: "J. Frank pointed out to Edgar B. the statement that Jesus made about John the Baptist in Matthew 11:14: 'And if ye are willing to receive it, this is Elijah that is to come.' Edgar, who was a Biblical scholar, was also steeped in Emerson's essays and quite familiar with the theme of 'Compensation.' Along with Emerson, he believed that sometime, somewhere, there was eventual happiness for everyone" (1984, 63). After hearing about J. Frank's physical misfortunes and difficulties finding work as an author, Edgar commissioned him to write a play that espoused the philosophies they had been discussing and paid him the equivalent of a year's salary for his efforts. Moreover, he pledged to produce the finished play on Broadway. This was a fortuitous coincidence for J. Frank because in his correspondence with Nellie Revell, a press agent who suffered from a similar spinal injury, he had promised to write a play and get it produced (*Variety*, 27 October 1926).

Advertisement for *The Ladder* in Detroit, from the *Detroit Free Press*, 19 September 1926.

During the three weeks of rehearsal in New York City, *The Ladder*, which had been considerably revised since the summer tryout, continued to be pushed and pulled by director Brock Pemberton, author J. Frank Davis, actor Edgar Stehli, and ghost-writer Edward Knoblock, the monocle-wearing British author of *Kismet*. Rehearsals were particularly difficult for Davis who, because of his spinal injury, could only sit upright for limited periods of time. After three weeks' rehearsal in New York, the company left on another series of out-of-town tryouts scheduled for Cleveland and Detroit where the critical reaction was lukewarm:

Detroit saw *The Ladder* Monday night, and the critic of the *News*, though greatly impressed with its "pictorial grandeur and engaging cast of solid reputation," found it "a not altogether articulate dramatization." He adds, however, that "J. Frank Davis, the author, was inspired by an ambitious idea." The theme, according to this review, concerns the theory of reincarnation as presented first through "flappers and their boyfriends, dice and jazz in a modern New York setting," and later through feudal England of the 14th, 16th and 17th centuries, each representing a new phase in the incarnations of the heroine. The reviewer had the warmest praise for the cast . . . . *The Ladder* has been scheduled for a September opening in New York, but the difficulty of finding a theater adapted to its elaborate presentation will delay its entrance until the week of October 4. (*Dayton Daily News*, 25 September 1926)

The authors and director continued to tinker with the extravaganza during the month between the tryout and the actual Broadway opening at the Mansfield Theatre. After nine weeks of rehearsal and two dress rehearsals on 21 October, *The Ladder* finally opened on Broadway on 22 October and was greeted by critical notices that were tepid at best. In *The New York Times* (23 October 1926), J. Brooks Atkinson concluded that "Surrounded by agreeable scenery, and attired in the toggery of the respective periods, the actors gave a letter-perfect performance. They did not miss a petal of the verbal efflorescences strewn lavishly through the dialogue. . . . 'Declamation roared whilst Passion slept.'" About the author, Atkinson suggested that "However earnest the author may be in his philosophy, he obviously is unaccustomed to writing for the stage. According to rumor, Edward Knoblock took a hand in preparing the script for the stage. His hand was not conspicuous last evening." In the *Daily News* (23 October 1926) Burns Mantle concurred: "It is a play of considerable variety of scene but not much variety of thought or expression. The episodes vary dramatically only in externals. Speech and language are changed to some advantage, but the adventures are basically similar, and there is no definite or reasoned progress for any character." Mantle did, however, find much to compliment among the cast with Ross receiving his first Broadway review: "Short parts are well played by Irene Purcell and Ross Alexander." *The Brooklyn Daily Eagle* (23 October 1926) was especially irate: "By far the most burdensome and most politely boring of the season's new plays was unveiled last evening at the Mansfield and disclosed, among other things, that the age of honest and adulterated hokum has not yet departed. J Frank Davis, an unknown—and perhaps justly so—playwright ... in earnest conjunction with Brock Pemberton, foisted upon this innocent metropolis a saccharine drama so devoid of substance that its ultimate crumbling was heralded with the curtain descending on the first scene."

Pemberton, who took on the project out of friendship with Edgar B. Davis argued that it was, in fact the money man who stood in the way of the play's success: "Knoblock did a workmanlike job of doctoring it. The play wasn't a bad one at all. That is, it was really not a bad spectacle. . . . Damn it, it was Davis himself who stood in the way of possibly putting the thing over. Every change that was made had to be O.K.'d by him—it had to fit his theme. I was in show business and that wasn't show business" (*The New Yorker*, 26 November 1949). In the same article Pemberton even suggested that the critics were enraged by the first night audience made up of Davis's Brockton friends whose expenses he paid to attend the premiere: "There were two hundred ladies, all wearing enormous orchids, with their husbands tagging along behind. These people applauded, laughed, and generally carried on until it's a wonder the critics didn't choke on their gorges."

Bolstered by the occasional kind notice in the press, Ross, however, remained positive. When he had returned to New York from Louisville he went back to the boarding house with the single bathroom at the end of a hall, but the trained seals had left to tour the vaudeville circuit! For Ross, the prospect of earning the Broadway minimum of $150 weekly ($2105 in 2019 dollars) and appearing in New York City in a show produced and directed by the highly revered Brock Pemberton—and paid for by a multimillionaire who was adamant about keeping the project alive—all far outweighed the deficiencies of the script that went before the opening night audience.

The basic outline of *The Ladder* provided in newspaper reviews and subsequent magazine articles told the story of a composer, Margaret Newell (Antoinette Perry) who must choose to marry either Stephen Pennock (Hugh Buckler), a wealthy financier without heart, or Roger Crane (Vernon Steele), a poor but honest believer in reincarnation who is offered a job in Buenos Aires. Stephen's money and position can advance Margaret's musical career but Roger can offer her love. Alone in Stephen's sumptuous home adorned with several medieval tapestries, Margaret falls asleep at the grand piano and dreams of her various incarnations: first, at an English castle in 1300, as Lady Margaret Percy, accused by Stephen, Earl of Orleton (Hugh Buckler) of murdering her husband and betrayed by her lover Sir Roger Clifford (Vernon Steele); next, at a house on Pall Mall, London, in 1670, as actress Margaret Sanderson, mistress of Stephen, Earl of Arlington (Hugh Buckler) who has rented her services to King Charles II, over her objections and those of her lover Captain Roger Harcourt (Vernon Steele), who is murdered for supporting her; and finally, at the Covill home in New York City in 1844, as Margaret Wright, an invalid niece of Roger Covill (yes, Vernon Steele again) whose brother Stephen (Hugh Buckler), a financier without a heart, is running for Governor of the state of New York. After deciding that "we have to go through hell to get to heaven," Margaret awakens in the present at the piano in Stephen's home and accepts Roger's proposal—a denouement that was easily anticipated in the first scene of the play.

None of the synopses made mention of Ross Alexander and Irene Purcell whom, you will remember, Burns Mantle cited in his review. Their "small parts" were actually significant to the development of the plot and structure of *The Ladder*. In the first scene, Purcell plays Betty Pennock, Stephen Pennock's daughter, whom Margaret is nurturing following the death of Betty's mother. She is described as "a pretty girl of 18 with all the typically aggressive assurance of the modern New York young woman. She wears a pretty dinner frock. She is smoking a cigarette" (1, 9). Ross enters as Betty's boyfriend, William ("Billy") Patterson, described as "a young fellow of 22 . . . wearing a motoring coat. Over his arm he has Betty's coat and brings her hat as well" (1, 11). Alexander's first scene on a New York City stage involved the following exchange between him, Betty, and Steven Pennock:

Billy. Betty, have you gone to sleep? (*Seeing Margaret.*) Oh, Miss Newell—I beg your pardon—Good evening, Mr. Pennock.

Stephen. How do you do! —I hear you're taking my daughter out.

Billy. She's taking me out, sir. It's *your* car.

Stephen. Good lord! Do you belong to the same famous school of quibblers as Betty? You two must have a bully cock-fight, picking each other's feathers.

Billy. I let her do most of the picking, sir. (*Billy helps Betty into her coat and gives her her hat.*)

Stephen. You're older than I thought.

Billy. I'm playing a long game.

Stephen. Don't make it too long. Try putting your feet down every now and then or you'll find you won't have a leg to stand on.

Billy. I know when to put on the breaks.

Betty. Listen to the babe!

Stephen. Seriously. I want you to promise me to look after Betty properly.

Billy. I promise to love, honor and obey her—till death do us part.

Betty. Gosh! Why look at the gloomy side of things? There's always divorce! (1:1, 11–12)

Ross Alexander and Irene Purcell in modern dress. Posed publicity shot. White Studio (New York, NY) Museum of the City of New York. 68.80.477 © The New York Public Library.

Following their exit in scene one, Ross and Irene rushed to their dressing rooms to change into authentic-looking medieval English costumes, complete with wigs, smock, lacings, petticoats, doublet, stockings, hood, cape, and cote-hardie. No sooner had they dressed when they heard their cue to enter as Master William Ashley, attendant on Lord Orleton (Hugh Buckler) and Mistress Betty, Lady Margaret's (Antoinette Perry) attendant, on a stage that depicted the Great Hall of Orleton Castle:

(*William Ashley, a youth of 19, comes running down the stairway. At the same moment Mistress Betty comes from the lower door right. They meet breathless.*)

William. Good morrow, sweet mistress Betty!

Betty. Good morrow, Master William!

William. (*Coming close.*) One little kiss? I have not seen you all the morning.

Betty. I'm in no mood this day for kissing.

William. So stern? What have I done?

Betty. You? Nothing! Nothing. Heard you no noise at dawn up in the great tower?

William. Not a sound! —Yet stood I guard upon the battlements.

Betty. For the love of Jesu then, swear to lock in your heart what I shall betray to you!

William. What is't? You look pale! Speak!

Betty. This self-same sunrise, my Lady's drunken Lord—Hush! (*She points to the arch.*) Sir Roger! —Move there! And let me whisper in your ear. (*She draws him down into the corner right, where she whispers to William who shows signs of consternation at her confidences. Sir Roger Clifford has entered down the stairs and through the archway. He is reading a manuscript book bound in parchment He looks up and sees the couple whispering.*)

Roger. (*Pleasantly.*) Ha! Whispering again of love? Is spring then everywhere?

William. (*Pertly.*) We cannot all love musty parchments! (1:2, 1–2)

When it is discovered that Margaret's husband is dead, to divert suspicion from Margaret, her lover Roger accuses Betty of bewitching William into murdering the man: "Then to her lover did I hear her say: 'Strike! Strike Sir Walter dead! —He has wronged me vilely. If you deny me this, never again I'll bed with you'" (1:2, 17). Although William vehemently denies the accusation, the Earl of Orleton calls for torture to reveal the truth: "Call me the hangman! Have the thumbscrews brought! Prepare the rack" (1:2, 18)! Before his rather excessive commands could be carried out, Margaret admits her involvement in the death of her husband to save William and Betty from further distress: "I struck my lord and master! I—with these two hands.

Struck him and slashed him with my riding whip. And left him staggering—but not dead—not dead" (1:2, 18)! However, when she calls upon Sir Roger to support her testimony, he betrays her, claiming never having loved her at all, and Margaret is led to the dungeon as the curtain falls on Act One.

During intermission Ross transforms himself into Lord William Sedley, an English aristocratic gentleman during the reign of Charles II, by adding a moustache, frilled breeches, a lacey cravat, a feathered hat, square-toed-high-heeled shoes, a cloak, and multi-colored ribbons all over his body. He enters midway in Act Two at Margaret Sanderson's house as messenger to her from the King. Before he can deliver his charge, Margaret witnesses Sedley's behavior towards Mistress Betty Holden (Irene Purcell) and determines that he is in love:

Margaret. You have the fever badly.

Lord William. I'll die of it—if she cure me not with her eyes.

Margaret. Will her glances not quicken it?

Lord William. Sooner die of a surfeit than of starvation.

Margaret. Best not die at all and use your good fortune.

Lord William. True Enough! I *will*, I promise you. (2, 17)

Following a brief philosophical repartee, Lord William remembers his instructions from the King and presents Margaret with a diamond ring:

Margaret. This ring—for me?

Lord William. His Majesty's appreciation of your performance this afternoon.

Margaret. The King is most gracious.

Lord William. He begs but one thing in return That you will wear that ring tonight at the Masquerade.

Margaret. I shall wear it always. (*She slips the ring on her finger.*)

Lord William. You'll be masked, of course, like all the world. Find yourself by the portal of the Banqueting Hall on the stroke of midnight. I shall be there. Show your ring thus. (*He holds his hand to his breast.*) And I'll lead you straight to where the King awaits you. . . .

Margaret. (*Realizing the purpose of the ring*.) I understand. So that's the kernel of your errand? A pretty profession for a man of your breed—is it not? . . .

Lord William. And with that, I must go back to the palace. Other duties call me. Mayhap less difficult, but also less—shall we say—interesting. I shall expect you at midnight. Your servant, Madame. (*He bows and goes off by the double door right. Margaret stands a moment looking after him, then at the ring. After a moment's reflection, she draws it off, goes to the dressing table, deposits it there.*) (2, 18–19)

Almost immediately Margaret discovers that the dalliance with the King was promoted by her vindictive lover, the Earl of Arlington, so to punish him, she sends Betty Holden off to the masquerade in her place, giving her the King's ring, her mask, and masquerade costume. When the clock chimes midnight it is Betty with whom Sedley will rendezvous, not Margaret who is visited at her home by Captain Roger Harcourt, a former lover whom she believed dead. Arlington bursts in on them and, calling Margaret a whore, he challenges Harcourt to a duel during which he fatally stabs Harcourt in the heart. Curtain!

In Act Three, set in New York City in 1844, Ross plays William Covill, the headstrong and impulsive twenty-one-year-old son of Stephen Covill, a successful businessman and candidate seeking election as Governor of New York. William is intent on marrying an actress, Betty Lee (Irene Purcell) against the wishes of his father, an ancient theatrical plot, perhaps, but one that permitted Ross (figuratively) to chew a fair amount of scenery:

Stephen. That's got nothing to do with me—his tying up with a common harlot!

William. (*Rushes in from the parlor.*) You're a liar! —Say that to my face.

(*Betty and Roger [William's uncle] have followed William who tries to rush at his father. Roger restrains him.*)

Roger. Willie!

Stephen. (*Coldly.*) So they *are* here—my son and this dirty little strumpet!

William. You dare! I'm going to marry Betty.

Stephen. If you do you shan't have a cent of my money.

William. I don't care. I can make a living. (3, 25–26)

To avoid what he considers a scandal—the marriage of his son to an actress!—Stephen offers to pay Betty to go away, providing William with ample opportunities to emote excessively:

Stephen. (*To Betty.*) What's your price?

Betty. Price?

Stephen. Well it's pretty damn obvious you're out for blackmail.

William. Don't you use that word! You shan't say that—by God! (*Moves as though to strike his father. Betty between them holds him back.*)

Stephen. (*Ignoring him, and completing the sentence to Betty.*) Go on! Name the figure! . . . How much? (*Takes out pocket checkbook.*) How much for my boy? I promise I won't stop payment on the check. (*Sits to write check.*) . . .

Betty. (*Wetting her lips.*) Five thousand dollars.

William. What? You mean—

Stephen. Two thousand and not a cent more.

Betty. All right. For God's sake give it to me and get this over. (*Stephen writes the check.*)

William. Betty! You're not going to take it!

Betty. (*To Stephen—in a hard voice.*) Come on! Give it to me! (*Stephen hands her the check.*)

William. She's taken it! She's taken it! (*To Betty.*) Betty! You're all the things that father said you were.

Stephen. Of course, she is. Now you see perhaps who really cares for you.

William. Care for me? You? Damn you. I don't want ever to see you again. Neither you—nor *her* as long as I live! You each are as rotten as the other! (*William exits hurriedly into the hall.*) (3, 27–29)

It will come as no surprise that Betty tears up the check and admits to giving William up for his own good; in no time at all, he would realize that an actress would make an unsuitable bride among his class of people. The relationship between Margaret and the young people comes full circle: in the first scene of the play, Margaret feels out of her depth in dealing with Betty and her aggressively modern views; however in Act Three Margaret is able to counsel the actress Betty, another social misfit and advise her to see the danger in her marriage plans. The many critics who argued that Margaret did not change dramatically through the play were the ones who completely ignored the importance of William and Betty in the dramatic structure. Ross threw himself into his roles to great effect; after the show each night ladies and attractive young men gathered at the stage door to meet him. In fact, moneyman Edgar Davis considered Ross the perfect juvenile saying that the whole venture was worthwhile if only for the pleasure of seeing him perform. Moreover, as proof that Davis's remark was not only hollow praise, when Ross asked him for a raise later in the run, Davis doubled his salary!

Ross Alexander and Irene Purcell in antebellum costumes. Posed publicity shot. White Studio (New York, NY) Museum of the City of New York. 68.80.491 © The New York Public Library.

The romantic subplot between William and Betty finally resolves in marriage in the Epilogue when the party to which Betty planned to take Billy turns out to be located in a wedding chapel! Margaret decides to marry Roger—no surprise there—after coming to the realization that love and understanding provide the greatest happiness.

Although a legitimate (if unsuccessful) Broadway production, *The Ladder* was not unlike the stock productions in the estimation of Ross Alexander: performances on the evenings and matinees, and rehearsals during the day. On 26 October, *Variety* reported that *The Ladder* "will undergo revision and recasting" and, as a result, not a week went by without changes to the script—J. Frank Davis remained for three weeks after the opening to tinker with the book; $6,000 richer, Edward Knoblock returned to England to distance himself from the project: "Never did I work harder. And I made money too. But the work, when I look back on it now, fills me with shame. It was either hack work or utterly uninspired" (Knoblock 1939, 344); and Edgar Davis paid highly for advice from neophyte writers, including a "Miss O'Conner" and a "Miss Curtis," and seasoned professionals including Eugene O'Neill who was offered a small fortune to rewrite the play, but he didn't even respond to the invitation! Calling Davis "a credulous and seemingly demented Texan, who poured thousands of dollars into a play called *The Ladder*," a newcomer named Moss Hart considered applying for the job and asking Davis to subsidize him until he found his place in the theatre (Hart 1989, 157). Murdock Pemberton, Brock's brother, initially hired as press agent for *The Ladder*, wrote eighteen versions of the script and saw four of them actually produced. It was fortunate for Ross that Murdock found him exceptional in his roles because in each of the revisions, he embellished and enlarged Alexander's part so that he "had most of the show and ran away with it" (Pemberton 1939, 156).

Along with rehearsals came luncheons at the Ritz for the cast and crew. Murdock Pemberton recalled that they were "happy days for the cast, stage hands and electricians when the luncheons would come around. Davis always insisted that everyone come, there was no caste distinction in our company. The luncheons were rich and long, and often, as when Davis came back

65

from abroad, they would be marked by little tokens: silk shawls, beaded handbags for the women, pipes, lighters, sweaters from Scotland for the men" (Pemberton 1939, 83).

After a month at the Mansfield Theatre, playing to less than half houses, *The Ladder* moved to the new Waldorf Theatre, opening there on 22 November 1926. Ross enjoyed the change of scenery and the ability to hang out with the young men and women in the ensembles of the various musicals that were playing all around him, including *Sunny, Deep River, Naughty Riquette, Countess Maritza, The Ramblers, Katja, The Wild Rose, Oh, Kay!* and *The Desert Song.* Alexander also began to associate with the casts of the homosexually-inclined plays, *The Captive* and *The Virgin Man,* as well as the prized classics, *Abie's Irish Rose, Broadway, An American Tragedy,* and *The Emperor Jones.*

Because *The Ladder* had been playing to poor houses at the Waldorf, Brock Pemberton advertised free seats for the two performances on Christmas which proved to be a Christmas present to both the audience and the cast, who enjoyed performing for a full house. After the holidays, however, *The Ladder* returned to playing to poor business, which, since the opening in October had never earned enough to pay the expenses. Brock Pemberton continued to press Edgar Davis to close the show, but Davis would not hear of it. Unwilling to bear the reputation that he was taking advantage of his Broadway "angel," Pemberton withdrew from the project on 15 March 1927 and issued an explanation in *The New York Times* (16 March 1927):

I produced *The Ladder* on the insistence of Edgar B. Davis, a personal friend of many years' standing and not an "angel" I unearthed, as the idea for the play as well as the money to promote it was his. He retained full control and I merely acted in the capacity of his agent. Mr. Davis is desirous of continuing the play and of trying exploitation methods new to show business.

He produced the play for the most idealistic reason, and as he has already expended a fortune on it, I asked to be allowed to withdraw, a request that was granted amicably. Thus my withdrawal gives him a free hand to market his play and negates the rather unsavory rumor that I have been taking an "angel" on a long, flat-tired buggy ride along Broadway.

Davis acquired Pemberton's interest in *The Ladder* through the United Actors, Inc., a corporation he established to carry on with the play. On 4 April, Davis announced that the price of a ticket would be refunded to any audience member who was dissatisfied with the production and, later in the month, he offered a five-hundred-dollar prize each week for the best two-hundred-word essay written about the play. Unfortunately, because New York State law did not require entrants to actually see the play, the contest, which ended on 20 June, awarded $8,000 in prizes but did nothing to improve attendance.

As summer approached, and anticipating a move from the Waldorf to the Cort Theatre, Davis called the cast together and asked them how they would like to proceed. Ross and the rest of the company saw the closing notice approaching. They huddled together and agreed to take a salary cut in order to keep *The Ladder* running throughout the summer. When they delivered their decision to Davis, he rejected it saying that he had no intention of lowering their salaries: he was simply wondering if they would mind not giving two performances on Saturday until September. Needless to say, Ross and company were delighted to get a five-day week and two days off during the summer heat without a change in salary.

The Ladder stumbled on through the summer months to audiences of no more than ten or thirty people but still the cast pushed on through September with more rehearsals of revisions penned by J. Frank Davis, Murdock Pemberton, and Edgar Stehli, under the direction of actress Margaret Anglin. The company took a hiatus of a week beginning 29 September in order to perfect what the newspapers called the "fifth version" of the play scheduled to reopen at the Cort Theatre on 6 October 1927. It was business as usual for Ross until celebrated designer Robert Edmond Jones was commissioned to recreate the sets and costumes for the production. Jones took an immediate interest in Ross who duly returned his attention. What transpired between them during Jones's tenure with *The Ladder* is now the object of vivid imagination, but for Ross, the experience of being on Broadway was Dickensian: It was the best of times. It was the worst of times. Ross enjoyed the attention he received on and off stage and the sensation of feeling desired even though, in reality, he felt completely undesirable and unworthy of attention, often describing himself as looking like "the west end of a horse going east," punctuated by "And don't think I'm kidding when I say that" (Hartley 1936, 114).

The new version of *The Ladder* did little to improve box office receipts, but it did present an amusing situation that disclosed the absurdity of the show's run. According to Murdock Pemberton, the vice president of United Actors, Inc.:

It was during the Anglin regime that one of the minor amusements occurred. Miss Anglin's husband, Howard Hull, had been in the habit of aiding and abetting her labors with sandwiches and snacks during the long rehearsals. But Mr. Hull didn't follow our schedule carefully and one afternoon he walked down the aisle of the Cort Theatre, leading a terrier and holding aloft a sandwich. He didn't see his wife but he saw a few people on the stage and a few in the seats. Approaching the footlights, he cupped his hands and shouted: "Here's your lunch, Babs. I'm going out with the dog." The few bewildered patrons didn't know whether this was a part of the show or not and the cast took some minutes to recover. You see, *The Ladder* had moved over from rehearsals to performances. (Pemberton 1939, 83)

The story was a favorite of Alexander's who enjoyed bragging about his misfortunes on Broadway, and the joke was not unappreciated by producer Edgar B. Davis who moved the show to the Lyric Theatre on Halloween 1927 and, when receipts dropped to $15.00 a day, he began offering free attendance on Thanksgiving to continue indefinitely until the play reached "its ultimate goal." *The New Yorker* (26 November 1949) reported that when the free ticket policy was initially announced, "a mob of three thousand stormed the Lyric Theatre for tickets, police reserves were called, and Agnes Brauneskey, of 635 Lafayette Avenue, Brooklyn, was badly cut when she was pushed through a glass door" (44). In addition, as soon as free tickets became available, speculators gobbled up large blocks of tickets and proceeded to sell them at a premium to harried last-minute purchasers and unsuspecting out-of-towners. Still offering free tickets, *The Ladder* moved to the Belmont Theatre on 12 December 1927 and remained there through the spring of 1928. By the time members of The Morning Call Dramatic Club saw the play in early February, Margaret had been rewritten from an ambitious composer in search of a career to a self-willed and spoiled young artist who, after breaking her engagement because of the seeming infidelity of her fiancé (as in the plot of *No More Blondes* by Otto Harbach), fails in her attempt to support herself through her art; and facing eviction from her studio-apartment, she attempts suicide, the gas fumes sending her dreaming about earlier lives. In her first dream, she is a liar and thief in 1850 New York City; in her second vision she is an unfaithful mistress during the English Restoration; in the third, set in the fourteenth century, having murdered her uncle for his gold, she is subsequently abandoned by her lover and murdered by her cousin. She is ultimately revived and gathers sufficient strength to approach the footlights and directly address the audience, imploring them to believe that "right will triumph, and as they must have seen from her different lives, that tolerance and faith are the truer guide" (*Chicago Tribune* 22 July 1928).

The newspaper accounts of that performance determined that the most entertaining and beloved actors were Ross Alexander, still in the ever-ballooning role of William, and Edward J. McNamara, a former New Jersey policeman, in the role of Giuseppe, an Italian tenor and artist's model. McNamara had been involved with *The Ladder* since the beginning, playing the small singing role of Wat of Hampshire. Murdock Pemberton saw a lot of untapped potential in his performance, and in every one of the eighteen versions he produced, along with Alexander's role, he enlarged McNamara's part.

Moving back to the Cort Theatre in April, *The Ladder* continued to stagger along free of charge until 11 July when, this time charging $3.00 top, another version opened to an audience numbering seventy-five, including the ushers. On 25 July 1928, *Variety* announced that during the previous week the total gross for the show was only $300, an insignificant amount considering that *The Ladder* needed to take in $10,000 weekly to break even.

5. John Golden's Broadway (1)

In all, Ross Alexander spent twenty months with *The Ladder*: two in rehearsals and out-of-town tryouts, and the rest in performances (and rehearsals) at five different theatres on Broadway. In March 1928, however, two occurrences persuaded Ross to withdraw from the endlessly revised and poorly attended show: a wedding and an introduction to Broadway producer-writer-director John Golden.

The wedding was Alexander's first, registered under his given name Alexander R. Smith, to the actress Helen Burroughs on 19 March. Six years older than Ross, Helen Burroughs was born and raised in Boxborough, Massachusetts, the daughter of George and Mary Burroughs. She attended James Madison University where she was a member of the prestigious Lanier Literary Society and, after graduation in 1923, she moved to New York to become an actress in vaudeville. Little is known about when and under what circumstances Helen met Ross, or the length and nature of their courtship. In an article by Caroline Somers Hoyt in *Movie Mirror* (April 1937) Helen is portrayed as "more poised and sophisticated than Ross. He was only eighteen when they were married. But she loved him devotedly—and let him break her heart" (101). Of course, the article pays scarce attention to dates, since by March 1928, Ross was well on his way to becoming twenty-one—though it should be mentioned that in virtually all of his press, Ross is depicted two or more years younger than his actual age. The couple lived together at 34 Bethune Street in Manhattan, a block away from the Hudson River and, although in interviews Ross claimed that they had a "swell little girl," the census records between 1928 and 1930 do not indicate a child living at that address, and I have not found any birth certificates in New York naming Ross and Helen as parents. In any event, Ross relished being loved by a cultured and reasonably affluent woman as much as he enjoyed the attentions of older, talented men, although the way in which he balanced romantic and sexual attractions often led to disastrous results—but not always. Enter John Lionel Golden.

John Golden in Miami, Florida.

Born in New York City on 27 June 1874, actor, songwriter, playwright, director, and producer John Lionel Golden began his theatrical career as the butler in the New York City production of Henry Guy Carleton's *Ye Earlie Trouble* at Proctor's Twenty-third-Street playhouse in 1892. Not being an especially accomplished actor, Golden soon realized that he could earn a better living as a lyricist and composer for Broadway, especially when his melodies created on a dusty violin were embellished into a full piano-vocal arrangement by Max Dreyfus the president of the renowned musical publishing houses of T.B. Harms and Chappell. Early hits included (the now forgotten) "Willie Off the Yacht," "Yvette," and "Pretty Kitty," but a whopping success came in 1916 with "Poor Butterfly," lyrics by Golden, music by Raymond Hubbell. With a steady income from the royalties of "Poor Butterfly," Golden began mounting shows on Broadway, gaining the reputation as a producer of clean, wholesome entertainment that included the long-running *Lightnin'* (1918–1921), *The First Year* (1920–1922), and *Seventh Heaven* (1922–1924). Golden first encountered Ross Alexander at a performance of *The Ladder*, a play he judged to be completely unworthy of Alexander's talent, for which he predicted a fine future.

An avuncular relationship developed between Ross and "Uncle" John that exceeded the boundaries of a professional friendship. Were it not for respected film historians such as Lawrence J. Quirk revealing that, in his early stage career, Ross had been "seduced by several older actors and two prominent stage directors" (1990,135), one might not infer that Alexander's relationship with Golden was anything other than professional. Quirk's statement, however, taken up as fact by other writers without question, compels us to investigate more profoundly into Alexander's mentorship with a man thirty-three years older, especially as it reflects his relationship with Hugh Towne, a man seventeen years older. Both Towne and Golden were theatre professionals who saw potential in Ross and encouraged him to pursue his dream. Ross may well have approached both relationships opportunistically but, in both cases, Ross became infatuated—perhaps, even in love—with his mentor. He spent an idyllic summer alone with Towne and, as we shall see in future pages, his correspondence with Golden is filled with romantic expressions, headed by the word "Unk," for uncle, the accepted code name of the sugar daddy in both hetero and homosexual relationships. On his part, Golden was more reserved in his expression of friendship, but his allowing Ross to live in his theatre—whenever the actor couldn't afford an apartment—displayed a trust and bond that exceeded Golden's relationship with other actors and collaborators. More on this will follow as we chronicle the mutually satisfying careers of Ross Alexander and John Golden.

Golden finally persuaded Ross to leave *The Ladder* by promising him a role in Philip Dunning's dramatic comedy *Night Hostess*, scheduled to begin rehearsals in June 1928 in preparation for an out-of-town tryout mid-July. Ross was cast as Rags Conway, "a breezy youth of about 23 years" who "affects the loud clothes of a vaudevillian" (Dunning 1928, iii). He makes an entrance midway through Act One "*carrying a suitcase with umbrella stuck through straps and grip. Also music case and light overcoat. A Variety stuck in his suit coat pocket; a cane hangs from his breast pocket*" (1, 34). Rags's first bit of dialogue with inside doorman Tish (Porter Hall) conveys the wit and sensibility of his character:

Rags. What, no more guarded doors to pass? Am I all the way in now?

Tish. Yea—all the way.

Rags. Ain't you goin' to take my finger print or nothing?

Tish. Not right now—no. (*Rags puts down his bags.*)

Rags. Before I got by the lookouts I had to show 'em everything but my birthmark.

Tish. Say—is this all you brought?

Rags. I left the Zeppelin outside. (*Looks around the place.*) So this is the "Little Casino?"

Tish. Yeah.

Rags. Say, this is some swell hash-hut, ain't it?

Tish. Huh?

Rags. I say, this looks like a hot spot. (1, 34)

Marguerite Churchill ("Buddy") and Ross Alexander ("Rags) in *Night Hostess.*

Rags accepted the offer from Ben Fischer (Maurice Freedman) principal owner of the Little Casino, to leave the vaudeville circuit (forty weeks of sharing the bill with trained monkeys and acrobats) and go undercover as a bartender at the club in an attempt to discover who in the business has been skimming off the top. Rags's fiancée, vocalist "Buddy" Miles (Marguerite Churchill), also works at the establishment, though her interest in Rags has waned in favor of "improving herself" through a relationship with Chris Miller (Averell Harris), Fischer's racketeer partner, who is currently cooling his affair with Julia Barnes (Gail DeHart), the ex-wife of policeman Tom Hays (Charles Laite). When Julia threatens to reveal Miller's crooked dealings at the casino if he leaves her, Miller strangles her and disposes of her body in a trunk. Rags and Tom manage to take possession of the trunk, which Miller had scheduled to be sent to Chicago, and accuse him of murder. All of Miller's fraudulent activities are laid bare, but in the scuffle over the possession of a gun, the villain manages to escape, only to back into an open elevator shaft and tumble down five stories to his death. Realizing that she had been foolish to trust Miller, Buddy concludes that "I'm only a poor sap of a kid—I want somebody who'll be on the level with me, Rags. This is such a wicked town" (3, 164). In answer, Rags and Tish end the play with the following brief dialogue:

Rags. Well, we shouldn't complain about the town—after all, we only paid the Indians a bottle of whiskey for it.

Tish. Sure, what the hell can you expect? (3, 164)

Night Hostess opened under the direction of Winchell B. Smith at Mamaroneck, New York, on Thursday 19 July 1928, followed by a production in Hempstead on Friday 20 July, and a performance at the Great Neck Playhouse on Saturday 21 July. On Monday 23 July, the play began a week's run in Atlantic City to near-rave reviews, earning $9,800, the season's record for drama in that city. Plans were underway to bring the production to Elmira, New York, early in August but instead, Golden opted to continue preparing the show for a two-week engagement at Minneapolis/St. Paul beginning on 26 August prior to a 12 September opening at the Martin Beck Theatre in New York City.

In his autobiography John Golden wrote that "At the try-out, a youngster named Ross Alexander played the leading role and he showed great charm and acting ability" (1930, 197). Shortly before *Night Hostess* left for the Minnesota tryout, however, *Variety* (22 August 1928) reported that Ross had been struck by a hit-and-run driver and taken to the Polyclinic Hospital, 341–351 W. 50th Street, with a broken jaw. *The Brooklyn Daily Eagle* (5 October 1930) suggested that Ross Alexander was "a sort of discovery of Mr. Golden's and during the two weeks that the production played out of town prior to its New York opening, critics hailed Ross as a 'find.' Then, as these things happen, with his big chance just twenty-four hours away, a speeding taxi careened crazily down a side street—and Ross Alexander lay in a hospital bed, a coin's toss between life and death."

New York Polyclinic Hospital, from a contemporary postcard.

In the Winter 2016/17 issue of *Films of the Golden Age*, Laura Wagner added that "A *Daily Star* reporter claimed that Alexander was badly disfigured and that 'many expected that he would be unable to continue his career,' but a plastic surgeon performed what was called a 'modern miracle.' It was later revealed that he had lost almost all his teeth and fractured his jaw in the accident" (52).

Night Hostess opened in Minneapolis/St. Paul with Norman Foster in the role previously played by Ross Alexander, and Ruth Lyons in the Marguerite Churchill role. The change of performers did little to help the show. The *Variety* (5 September 1928) review noted that "The main love affair between the small-time vaudevillian and the hostess heroine rouses little interest, due to the weakness of the characterizations and the ineffective handling. . . . Even the efforts of the club's proprietor to rid himself of the manager and other thieving employees creates more suspense than the main love affair." In addition, the box office receipts amounted to only about $6,700, much less than anticipated because night club and crook melodramas had little interest for the audiences in Minneapolis/St. Paul.

Ross was lying unconscious in his hospital bed on 12 September when *Night Hostess* opened on Broadway and on the days that followed when Norman Foster received the critical plaudits that John Golden had meant for Ross Alexander. St. John Ervine, writing in the *New York Morning World* (14 September 1928) was especially effusive in his praise:

I now abase myself before Mr. Norman Foster, whose acting of Rags Conway was the jolliest and most attractive performance of its kind that I have seen for many months. What luck for me in my first week in New York to see so fine a play so well produced and so splendidly acted. The whole of this company must go to London. I warn Mr. Foster, however, that if he goes, he will probably not be allowed to come back to New York.

Advertisement from *The Boston Globe*, 7 November 1928.

Ross was still recuperating on 10 November 1928 when *The Ladder* finally closed in New York and moved to Boston for a two-week engagement at the Boston Opera House beginning on 12 November. What the predominantly Back-Bay audience saw would not have been unfamiliar to Ross: the jealous fiancée plot, the suicide business, and the gas-induced journey to previous lives remained from previous iterations. What may have been new to him was the prologue set during World War I, just before the Armistice, when David Newell lies dying in a dugout. He reveals to his friend Roger Crane that he had had an affair with a French girl named Letitia whom he intended to marry after the war, and who is pregnant with his child. He begs Roger to take care of them and to swear never to tell David's family about the affair. Roger swears and David dies. Albeit sober, the first night audience reportedly laughed at the comedy, applauded vigorously at the ends of acts, and recalled the company for several curtain calls at the end. Although the critics were divided regarding the merits of the production, the general consensus dubbed the show "a flop." Still, *The Ladder* grossed $3,000 the first week and $5,500 the second, signs of approval that encouraged Edgar B. Davis to begin making plans to produce the show in his hometown, Brockton, Massachusetts before Christmas, and to take *The Ladder* on the road again, after the first of the year.

Ross was released from the hospital just as *The Ladder* was completing its run at the Boston Opera House. The bills from his extended hospital stay, including fees for reconstructive surgery and other specialized costs all but ruined him and his wife financially. Nearly all the money he earned from *The Ladder* was spent on doctor bills, even after insurance claims were settled. He needed work but he was not sufficiently recuperated to hazard a stock company or even eight performances a week on Broadway. Coming to his rescue, "Uncle" John Golden arranged for Ross to produce a radio series of five-minute "movie chats" that aired at 6:15 P.M. on Channel WCAU, Camden, New Jersey, throughout the month of December, and in January 1929, Golden cast the recovered actor in his production of Rachel Crothers play, *Let Us Be Gay*, scheduled to open under Crothers's direction at Broadway's Little Theatre on 19 February 1929.

In the role of Bruce Keen, Ross Alexander portrays a young man whose fiancée, Dierdre Lessing (Rita Vale) has a roving eye. Described as "young, tall, and good looking in a fresh straightforward way" (1, 35), Bruce confronts Dierdre about her interest in Bob Brown (Warren William) in their first extended scene together at her grandmother Mrs. Boucicault's (Charlotte Granville) Westchester estate:

Bruce. Awfully nice for some tennis now. Want to play?

Dierdre. Um—no—I don't believe I do—thanks.

Bruce. Why not?

Dierdre. Well—I seem to have done enough. I think I'll call it a day.

Bruce. It's been a pretty dumb day for me. I haven't seen anything of you at all.

Dierdre. Well—don't you think it's rather a good idea not to be together *every* minute?

Bruce. No I don't. Every minute I'm not with you is just so much time wasted....

Dierdre. You know you get bored with me, *once* in a while.

Bruce. Listen. If I was ever bored with you for a second—I wouldn't want to marry you.

Dierdre. (*Trying to evade his seriousness.*) Now, darling—

Bruce. (*Getting stronger as he goes on.*) And that's just exactly the way you felt about *me* till exactly three days ago when this Brown guy hove in sight. I'm jealous as a pup and pretty much scared and I think you're making a congenital idiot of yourself. (1, 56–57)

Concerned about her granddaughter's interest in Bob Brown, the cigar-smoking Mrs. Boucicault invites Kitty Brown (Francine Larrimore) for the weekend to break up the affair, unaware that Bob and Kitty are a divorced man and wife. Even though Dierdre suspects her grandmother's plot and accuses Kitty of seducing Bob, she continues to be infatuated with him, a feeling that Bruce is convinced she will learn to overcome. The emotional final scene between Bruce and Dierdre is illustrative of the culturally enforced double standard governing male and female behavior:

Bruce. If you threw yourself away on that man you'd want to kill yourself afterwards. . . . I want to see you through this. Believe me there's nothing in it but what you'll be terribly sorry for—and ashamed of afterwards. . . .

Dierdre. (*Softening and putting a hand over his.*) Listen, Bruce—I like you better than anybody in the world. Maybe we are the best bet for each other. But I'm not crazy about you the way I am about Bob.

Bruce. Take it from me—liking is better than craziness.

Dierdre. (*Drawing her hand away.*) Now, don't talk to me like Santa Claus. I want to know what I'm doing because I know—*myself*. Not because somebody's telling me what I ought to do.

Bruce. If you'd use your bean and tell yourself the truth you'd know what to do.

Dierdre. I *am* using my bean. That's just it. I'm not swallowing any old stuff.

Bruce. Now get this. There's no new slant on this old stuff at all. Either a girl's decent or she isn't. There's no half way business about it—and when a fellow gets down to brass tacks, he wants the girl he's going to marry—the one who is going to be the mother of his kids—to be the straightest, finest, cleanest thing in the world.

Dierdre. Pearls you learned at mother's knee. And if a girl wants the darling boy she marries to be the same thing—where the hell is she going to find him?

Bruce. It's not the same thing at all for you and me.

Dierdre. It is! . . . exactly the same thing. . . . Why shouldn't I have Bob for a while and marry you, too?

Bruce. (*Rising and walking away.*) *Because you can't.* You simply can't. That's all there is to it.

Dierdre. Do you mean to tell me if I'd *had* an affair with Bob—and it helped me to know I wanted to marry you—you wouldn't marry me?

Bruce. Oh, Dierdre, I love you. I want to help you. There isn't anything I wouldn't do for you. Can't you see you're— (3, 143–146)

The couple's lightning-charged discussion is cut short by the entrance of Boucicault, Kitty, and Bob who reveals that, even though he and Kitty have been divorced, he still considers her his wife. Bruce exits before the revelation explodes Dierdre's infatuation and does not bear witness to her humiliation.

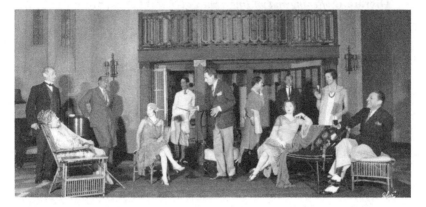

Let Us Be Gay theatre still. White Studio (New York, NY). Museum of the City of New York 48.210.1347©New York Public Library.

Detail of Ross Alexander.

The opening night critics were divided about Alexander's performance. The *Variety* (27 February 1929) review found Ross to be completely miscast in a role "calling for a personality of greater maturity," while *The Brooklyn Daily Eagle* (22 February 1929) wrote, "A young actor named Ross Alexander gives a clean-cut, manly, unadorned performance as the boy whose fiancée wants to ditch him." Neither the *Daily News* (22 February 1929) nor *The New York Times* (22 February 1929) mention Ross by name but both found the cast uniformly well-chosen and directed.

Unaccustomed to appearing on Broadway in a critically lauded play—Alexander's personal experience taught him that only critically panned productions run for years—Ross bet Francine Larrimore a week's salary that *Let Us Be Gay* would never reach 250 performances. By early September, the show had reached that goal and Ross acted a week without pay—a small price to pay for success, he thought. During the summer, his photograph had begun to appear in the newspaper publicity for the play and, bolstered by the attention and the regular paycheck, Alexander felt that he had finally "arrived." That is not to say that everything in his life was roses. His accident and subsequent convalescence took a toll on his marriage, with both parties beginning to wonder why they entered into a union in the first place. Feeling smothered at home, Ross took to spending most of his time at the theatre and at theatre parties, living the Broadway highlife while his wife continued to struggle as an all-but-anonymous actress in third tier vaudeville houses. She viewed Ross as self-centered and distant; he saw her as controlling and needy. Both found a way to coexist in their Bethune Street home; neither was prepared for the Wall Street Crash that began on "Black Thursday," 24 October 1929.

On Wednesday 6 November 1929, *Variety* published an article disclosing the effect of the stock market crash on the theatre industry under the banner headline: "Broadway Takes the Slap": "Broadway, kicked, heeled, punched and gouged by Wall Street, came within an inch of its night-life last week, shattering all records for gloom in the country through the Great Break. As a business center—with joy on sale—no other locale or community suffered a greater depression. Main stem had no buyers. The bottom dropped out of hilarity. . . . Utterly washed out, with gags and songs and dancing, worthless commodities, the Street famed for its mirth and jollity, became the locale of misery. . . . Viewed generally, the situation as it concerns Broadway made history, catapulting the Street into the dankest despair it has ever experienced." *The Film Daily* (18 November 1929), however, reported that the chaos on Wall Street has not injured the movie business throughout the country: "Popular-priced showings of pictures haven't been hurt anywhere by the market. All over the country business at the box office is fine." Whether or not Ross Alexander had considered acting in films prior to the Stock Market Crash, the durability of motion pictures even in the worst of times began to feed his strong survival instincts. He would not have to wait long for an opportunity to become a contract player in the film industry, though success would not necessarily come with every opportunity.

A victim of the Depression, *Let Us Be Gay* closed in December 1929 after spending 43 weeks (353 performances) on Broadway and immediately went of tour playing the Broad Street Theatre in Newark, New Jersey, during Christmas week, followed by a run at Werba's Jamaica Theater in Queens, opening 6 January 1930, and three months at the Studebaker Theater in Chicago, beginning on 27 January where the presence of Francine Larrimore and generally superlative reviews kept the weekly box office receipts hovering around $15,000 for the run. Ross loved everything about being in Chicago: the bohemian atmosphere he discovered at Bughouse Square; the gay-friendly Dill Pickle Club, where he could rub shoulders with artists, jazz musicians, and gangsters; the theatres, where he could enjoy drag shows and sexually-charged entertainments; and the cabarets and speakeasies, where he could sit at the piano and improvise away the early hours of the morning. The possibilities open to Alexander in Chicago were not all that dissimilar to those that were available in New York City, but being away from home seemed to allow Ross the freedom to expand his horizons, to explore experiences that he would never allow himself in Manhattan. He also especially enjoyed his accommodations at the Lorraine Hotel, Wabash Avenue at Van Buren Street, an easy block away from the theatre. A private room away from a suffocating marriage reminded him of how much he valued his freedom.

In March, while *Let Us Be Gay* was still in Chicago, John Golden returned to New York from his seasonal holiday in Florida and announced his plans for a summer tryout production of Hugh Stange's play *After Tomorrow*, with Ross Alexander in a principal role. Golden had spent the winter months golfing in Miami and Palm Beach, a practice that he felt accounted for much of his success as a producer: "I have found this method of going off and letting somebody else do the real work so effective that I am tempted to make it Rule I in the search for hits. When Rachel Crothers brought me her play, *Let Us Be Gay*, my thoughts were occupied almost entirely with the problem of whether it were better to go to Miami and play golf or to Havana—and play golf. Miss Crothers . . . solved my problem neatly by suggesting I give her *carte blanche* and the able assistance of Dixie French, my business manager, and go South or any other place that looked good to me. This I did, and when I returned, I found *Let Us Be Gay* playing to capacity audiences at my Little Theatre of hits" (Golden 1930, 187–188).

On Monday 28 April, Ross took part in the midnight broadcast of the National Vaudeville Artists, commencing at 11:30 P.M. over radio station WBZ-WBZA. Appearing with Ross were prominent stars of stage and screen, including Fred Stone, Ethel Barrymore, Eddie Foy, Jr., Thomas Mitchell, Pat Rooney, and Charlotte Granville, in addition to several jazz bands that contributed to the evening's festivities. Ross liked being in the company of famous actors, and the enjoyment was mutual. Stars found little to dislike in Ross. He was tall, talented, handsome, and charismatic, with a Puck-like sense of humor, and a sensuality that commanded the interest of men and women alike. Moreover, he was left-handed, something of an oddity in a right-handed universe, but a trait that supported his anti-establishment, left-leaning principles, which he could turn on or off like a faucet depending on his audience.

For *Let Us Be Gay*, 12 May 1930 marked the beginning of a limited engagement at the Broad Theatre, 4813 N. Broad Street, in Philadelphia. The show closed after two weeks of good business on 24 May, fifteen months after its New York opening. Ross suddenly found himself out of work, though not really, since he had committed to the summer tryout of *After Tomorrow* some months earlier; but since rehearsals would not begin until July, he needed somewhere to go and something to do. He did not relish the idea of returning to his Bethune Street apartment where the wife he abandoned kept threatening a costly divorce, so he scoured the trade papers for summer stock employment—anything to keep him away from New York City. Suddenly something caught his eye.

6. The University Players Guild

What captured Ross Alexander's attention was the notice of a summer theatre in Falmouth, Massachusetts, about to begin its third season on 30 June 1930. The company, called the University Players Guild, had been formed in 1928 by two enterprising (and well-to-do) college students—Charles Crane Leatherbee from Harvard and Bretaigne Windust from Princetown—who had met during Christmas vacation and discovered their shared theatrical ideals. Believing that theatre professionals who went to New York right out of high school had advanced more quickly in their careers than those coming from four-year colleges, Leatherbee and Windust wanted to give themselves and those like them a leg up, so to speak, in show business. Simply put, they created a summer theatre venture staffed only by college students to prove that theatre professionals could emerge as easily from universities—even those without designated theatre programs—as from a traditional theatre apprenticeship whereby actors and technicians learn their craft in professional venues by performing roles and services that start small and grow as they become more practiced.

The pair decided to set up their theatre in Falmouth, first at the Elizabeth Theatre, a movie house, where they performed on Monday and Tuesday evenings, and next at Silver Beach, in a conveniently located abandoned power-and-light-company plant that provided the space for "an auditorium, stage and lobby facilities, and also space for a café and dance floor on the end overlooking the water" (Houghton 1951, 77–78). The original housing for the company had been a cottage in Quisset, Massachusetts, for the women, and *Brae Burn*, a yacht Charlie's father had converted from a World War I submarine chaser for the men. These proved too remote from the Silver Beach location, so two houses were rented in West Falmouth, about four miles from the theatre.

The University Theatre Guild theatre complex at Silver Beach.

As Ross made his way to Falmouth, *Variety* (11 June 1930) published yet another warning to young men about their idiosyncrasies and film careers:

Only he-men are wanted by the New York studios for chorus boys. Quite a close scrutiny of candidates. Each chorus boy is individually considered. If too pretty, dainty or over-marcelled, he is aired off the casting lists.

It has been discovered the average American film fans resent effeminate men in operettas, musicals, etc. Often the fans don't get the Broadway angle but take an instinctive dislike. Even though a male chorus line might have only a couple of geraniums, the fans quickly spot 'em.

Camera seems to intensify the effeminate mannerisms of the male crocheters, making them much more conspicuous than in stage musicals.

Although the article did not address Alexander's current career as a Broadway juvenile, it did encourage him to "butch it up" around the university lads and lassies who were frenetically preparing the season's opener, a forgettable comedy by Leslie Howard called *Murray Hill*. In the cast were Myron McCormick from Princeton, Henry Fonda from the University of Minnesota, and a new leading lady recently graduated from Smith College named Aleta Freel (née Freile) who "proved at once her right to join Margaret Sullavan and later Mildred Natwick in the front line of U.P.G. feminine talents. She was charming and pretty with a considerable potential of emotional depth" (Houghton 1951, 133). A Jersey City, New Jersey, debutante and daughter of a prominent physician, Dr. William Freile, Freel had achieved critical acclaim at Smith for her portrayal of Lavinia in Shaw's *Androcles and the Lion* and Margaret in J.M. Barrie's *Dear Brutus* and hoped to find the same success in Falmouth. In *Murray Hill*, Aleta Freel played Amelia, the surviving niece of the eccentric Tweedle Sisters; character actor and makeup artist Myron McCormick played the Tweedle family butler; and leading-man Henry Fonda, who had joined the company in 1928 and initially made more of an impression as a scene painter than as an actor, played Wrigley, a deputy-assistant mortician in love with Amelia.

Ross arrived at Silver Beach unannounced and immediately began to charm the company with his good looks, incomparable energy, and rowdy sense of humor. He helped Fonda paint scenery, he served patrons in the café, he played piano, sang, and acted in the post-show cabarets—he did everything with the company except act on stage. Houghton reported that everybody liked Ross and everyone wanted him to join the company. Only one thing stood in Alexander's way: he had never gone to college. Since Ross was an obvious talent and the company would benefit immeasurably from his participation, Charlie Leatherbee suggested an amendment to the rule that only college-educated individuals could be permitted to join the company. Virtually the entire company supported the amendment, with the notable exception of Bretaigne Windust who bristled at the idea of changing the rules. Even though he liked Ross and respected his abilities, Windust argued that the University Players Guild was created for university players and to abandon the requirement of a college education would cause irreparable harm to the organization. So adamant was he in this belief that he threatened to resign if Ross was admitted to the company. As a result, Leatherbee capitulated and the matter was dropped.

Neither disappointed nor discouraged, Ross made the most of his month in Falmouth. According to Houghton, "all summer long he lay on the beach, wandered over rocks and dunes, slept at the company men's house, participated in acts in the supper club, and made love to Aleta" (Houghton 1951, 140). If not legally or officially, at least from a practical perspective, Ross was done with his marriage and permitted himself to solicit and accept the attentions of someone else, in this case, the leading lady of the U.P.C. It should be noted that Houghton's use of the term "made love" did not necessarily connote the performance of a sex act; when I asked him about it, he told me that he meant the phrase in its traditional sense, the act of courtship. However, Henry Fonda, who claimed to know Ross the best, noted that he and Aleta had slept together (Fonda 1981, 57). In any case, the summer stay at Falmouth introduced Ross to Fonda and Freel, both of whom would play significant roles in his future.

On Tuesday 15 July 1930, Ross sent John Golden a telegram in reply to a package Golden sent him. The telegram read:

LETTER AND PLAY RECEIVED NO LIST OF QUESTIONS HOWEVER STOP THANKS AWFULLY TAKING CARE ON BAILEY ALSO MY CHECK PLEASE ADVISE IF AM EXPECTED AND WHERE IN NEW YORK SUNDAY DON'T WANT TO LEAVE A MINUTE SOONER THAN HAVE TO FIRST ACT ALL

LEARNED HOORAY HAVE DISCOVERED PERFECT
SIDNEY YOU WOULD BE NUTS ABOUT HER WORK
STOP YES PLAYS UKE AND CAN SING ENOUGH TO
GET BY PROBABLY STOP IMPOSSIBLE TO GET TO
PROVINCETOWN THIS WEEK SORRY LOVE AND
KISSES
  ROSS

The play in question is Hugh Stange's *After Tom*orrow scheduled to commence rehearsals in New York on Monday 21 July. Ostensibly, Ross is suggesting Aleta Freel for the leading-lady role of Sidney in the play. Also in evidence is Alexander's reticence to leave Falmouth any sooner than necessary, and his refusal of Golden's invitation to visit him in Provincetown during the week of 14 July. If thanking Golden for caring for his cat and sending him a check (presumably a final payment from the tour of *Let Us Be Gay*) does not indicate a more-than-professional relationship between the two, the invitation to gay-friendly Provincetown, and the valediction, "Love and Kisses," that closes the communication—whether it is meant seriously or ironically—certainly do.

In addition to Henry Fonda and Aleta Freel, during his stay in Falmouth, Ross found himself attracted to Myron McCormick, or more correctly, McCormick's hat. "I was up on Cape Cod with the University Players Guild," he said in an interview. "There was a college boy named Myron McCormick and he wore a remarkable hat." Ross asked for the hat but was refused. Subsequently the pair fought over the hat, but Ross failed to succeed in getting it. Nevertheless, on Saturday, 19 July, the night before he returned to New York City, Ross was given a going-away party by the U.P.G., during which he was presented with a going-away gift. No surprises there. It was Myron McCormick's hat!

7. John Golden's Broadway (2)

Ross Alexander was back in New York on 20 July ready to begin rehearsals for *After Tomorrow* on the following day at John Golden's 58th Street Theatre. Not wanting to return to his domicile on Bethune Street, Ross slept on a cot at Golden's theatre throughout the two-week rehearsal period. Early on Monday 21 July, Ross was introduced to Hugh Stange, author and director of the play, and his co-stars Penelope Hubbard, cast as Sidney Taylor, Alexander's love interest, and Donald Meek, as her long-suffering father Willie Taylor. For two weeks Alexander, Hubbard, and Meek, wandered through the slice-of-life comedy drama prior to a 4 August opening at the Apollo Theatre in Atlantic City, New Jersey. The story was a simple one: Pete Piper (Ross Alexander) and Sidney Taylor had been saving money so that they can get married, but when Sidney's mother abandons the family on the eve of her daughter's wedding, Willie has a stroke and the money saved is needed to pay his doctor's bills. The wedding is postponed and Willie recovers, holding on to the hope that his wife will return to him. He succeeds in getting Pete's mother, a grasping, weeping widow (Josephine Hull) to release her hold on the prospective groom by marrying an equally weeping widower, but when he discovers that his wife intends to sail to South America with her felonious lover (he embezzled bank funds), Willie dies.

The critical reaction to the play was reservedly positive on 5 August: "Received enthusiastically by a crowd that filled the Apollo," said the *Atlantic City Press*; "Superb cast—a heart throb in three acts," wrote the *Inquirer*; "A moving drama with a cast that should make it remembered 'After Tomorrow,'" judged the *Evening Bulletin*. In *Variety* (6 August 1930), George Weintraub provided, perhaps, the most insightful review noting that *After Tomorrow* is "very much of the safe and sound stock of the theatre which has been tied up with John Golden's name: clean, pawky, unpretentious play. There are several amusing situations, a number of gripping ones, though a trifle tearful, some canniness, much kindliness and a plot simple enough to be easily followed. . . . Only in [the] final curtain, by not bringing back the wayward woman, has Golden sheered from the familiar stage story. Such a popular theme needs only the actors who know fat parts and can set their teeth in them to pitch the humors high and tumble comedy after tragedy. First is Donald Meek, as the henpecked husband, who manages to be touching even in his most comical moments, and whose stricken man awakened sympathy and admiration. He is ably seconded by Penelope Hubbard and Ross Alexander as the young lovers acting brightly and with spontaneity."

Dissatisfied with the production and unimpressed with the reviews, Golden withdrew the play after a week in Atlantic City and placed Ross Alexander in another of his Broadway-bound productions, Frank Craven's *That's Gratitude*, starting rehearsals under the direction of the author on 11 August at the Little Theatre. Ross was cast as William ("Bill") North, "a good-looking young man of about twenty-four" (1, 44) who is engaged to marry Delia Maxwell (Myrtle Clark), the talented but homely daughter of Thomas ("Tom") Maxwell (George W. Barbier), an alcoholic businessman (in the ink business), but who is really in love with her pretty younger sister Lelia (Thelma Marsh). The opening scene of Act One, set in the living room of the Maxwell residence in Hutchinson, Kansas, pretty much lays out Bill North's predicament:

Lelia is discovered sitting on the lower end of the couch . . . her hands over her face sobbing. Bill is trying to comfort her and at the same time keep a watch out for any interruption.

Bill. Now, don't do that! I don't like to see you cry like that. Besides, your mother or Delia may come downstairs any moment. (*Lelia stops and tries to wipe away her tears.*) There, that's better. (*He gives a quick look upstairs.*) Now, listen to me, won't you? I do love you.

Lelia. (*Despairingly.*) Then why do you marry Delia?

Bill. I haven't yet, have I?

Lelia. (*Ready for another burst of tears.*) You haven't said you wouldn't yet, either.

Bill. I know. (*He takes a few steps away from her, and glances upstairs.*)

Lelia. (*With a slight blubber.*) And the announcements are out and everything!

Bill. (*Turning back to her quickly.*) I know. That's what makes it all the more difficult. That's why I'm asking you to have a little patience.

Lelia. If you think it's easy for me to be patient while you are making love to Delia—

Bill. I don't. . . . I don't like to kiss her at all. I don't feel right about the whole affair. Even when I *don't* kiss her. Pretending I love her when all the time it's you.

Lelia. Then why don't you tell them?

Bill. Because I've promised your father and I've promised Delia. I promised them long before I ever realized I loved you. (*Lelia sobs softly.*) I've always looked on you as a kid. It wasn't until you came home from school at Christmas that I realized you'd grown up. And then your father had everything set for Delia and me to get married. (*Lelia's sobs grow so loud that he gives an apprehensive glance toward the stairs.*) . . . Lelia, won't you please be patient for just a while longer. . . . We've got seven weeks yet before—you know—the—wedding. (*Another loud burst of sobs and more tears from Lelia.*) Shshshs! Please! (*He tries his best to quiet her, still with that anxious look to the stairs now and again.*) I'll try and find some way to tell your father and Delia.

Only don't say or do anything. Just leave it to me. . . . I'll start trying to do something right away.

Lelia. (*Rising.*) Because if you don't— (*Becoming a bit dramatic.*) if you *do* marry Delia, I'll never want to see you again!

Bill. Lelia!

Lelia. I wouldn't! I couldn't!— (*She runs for the stairs.*) Never—never—never—never! (1, 44–48)

To complicate matters, Delia is not thrilled about marrying Bill but neither of them wants to be the one to break the engagement that was arranged (and so beloved) by Delia's father.

Enter Robert ("Bob") Grant (Frank Craven) a small-time theatre promoter who once had rescued Tom Maxwell from a bad case of food poisoning and who has accepted Tom's invitation (as a token of appreciation) to spend a few days at the Maxwell residence. Delia is a very gifted singer with theatrical aspirations and would happily sacrifice marriage for a show-business career. Believing her voice is commercially viable, Bob encourages Delia's ambition and, with the help of a $7,000 loan from Bill, commits to casting her in his next theatre venture. The deal is carried out in a humorous pantomime scene (2, 120) while the unwitting Tom Maxwell proceeds to lecture Delia on the necessity of marrying Bill.

Six months have passed and Bob's musical play starring Delia is an acknowledged hit. When she returns to the Maxwell home before appearing at a local theatre, she is completely transformed in appearance: "*Delia appears on the landing. She is an altogether different Delia. Something has been done to her face—perhaps "lifted"—or perhaps she makes up well, but it is now quite a pretty face. Her hair is bleached to a beautiful blonde shade, and her gown is gorgeous. She poses a bit for [the family]*" (3, 169).

In the end, Delia runs off to study in Europe with fellow-actor and newly-minted husband Clayton Lorimer (Gerald Kent) leaving Bill free to marry Lelia after he collects the $7,000 he lent Bob to produce Delia's show.

Maida Reade, George Barbier, Ross Alexander, Myrtle Clark, Gerald Kent, and Thelma Marsh in Delia's transformation scene. Photo by White Studio © Billy Rose Theatre Division, The New York Public Library for the Performing Arts.

Bill. (*Going to Grant.*) You mean to say that you don't remember—right here in this room—my saying that if the show made money, I would expect to get it back?

Grant. No, I don't remember that at all. (*Then he grins.*) But I'll tell you the way I am. I wouldn't leave this house tonight with you feeling the way you do for twice seven thousand! Come on, let's fix it up. How would two thousand strike you?

Bill. Is that all you've got?

Grant. (*With a little shake of his head, as though he just couldn't understand this young fellow.*) It's all I can spare.

Bill. (*Slowly.*) I'll take that—on account—(*Then he smiles boyishly.*) On account of Lelia. But gee, Bob, I hope the show continues to make money.

Grant. (*Contentedly.*) Something tells me I'm going to have a good season, Bill. I think Delia is my mascot and if I collect—you do. (*He takes out his billfold and is counting out the two thousand as Lelia comes back down the stairs.*)

Lelia. What are you doing? Oh, look at all that pretty money!

Grant. (*Smiling.*) Yes, and if it weren't for you, Lelia, Bill wouldn't be getting this much!

Lelia. (*Holding out her hand, gaily.*) Well, then, where's my share?

Bill. (*Patting her.*) Your share is what Bob still owes me.

Lelia. (*Just a little anxiously.*) Is there enough, Bill, to—(*She smiles.*) You know?

Bill. (*Reassuringly.*) With what I have, yes.

Lelia. (*Glowing.*) Isn't that wonderful?

Bill. It is to me! (3, 181–182)

Thelma Marsh and Ross Alexander collecting money from Frank Craven.
Photo by White Studio © Billy Rose Theatre Division, The New York
Public Library for the Performing Arts.

That's Gratitude began a week's run at Brandt's Boulevard Theater in Jackson Heights on Monday 25 August to good reviews, followed by another week at Brandt's Carlton-Jamaica Theatre prior to a Broadway opening on 11 September 1930. Ross received fine notices on 12 September in the *Daily News* and *The Brooklyn Daily Eagle* and *Variety* (17 September 1930) singled out the pantomime scene between Alexander and Craven as "a capital bit of real humor and sentiment." In his syndicated column "At the Play," published in *The Philadelphia Inquirer* on 21 September, Robert Littell gave a special round of applause to Ross who, he felt, was "admirable as the young man in the case," and expressed thorough enjoyment in the play: "It was about time for something to come along as thoroughly funny, as neatly written and as uproariously acted as Mr. Craven's play, *That's Gratitude*, presented to us recently by John Golden. Our tongues have been pretty parched since the season began and it was very cheering to have at last a long, cool, silly, sparkling drink of the kind of comedy that decorates Broadway at best only two or three times a year."

Following 25 weeks and 197 performances on Broadway, *That's Gratitude* went on tour beginning on 9 March 1931 with a week's run at Brandt's Flatbush Theatre. The entire Broadway cast remained for the tour, including Allan Dinehart who had replaced Frank Craven as Bob Grant in December 1930. Following the Flatbush run, *That's Gratitude* moved to the El Capitan Theatre in Los Angeles for a month's stay before moving into the Blackstone Theatre in Chicago on Sunday 5 April 1931 and remaining there until 6 June. While many of the cast luxuriated at the Blackstone Hotel adjacent to the theatre, Ross chose to reside at his old stomping ground, the comfortable Lorraine Hotel. It may have been a question of finances since actors on tour were given a *per diem* or daily allowance to pay for their living expenses. The less money spent on hotel and food enabled actors to bank the portion of their daily allowance that remained. Still concerned about paying his hospital bills, Ross, who was never good at saving money, was not about to splurge.

By the middle of August, Ross was back in New York, still sleeping on a cot in Golden's theatre, and rehearsing a substantially revamped *After Tomorrow* that had been rewritten, cut, and elaborated by John Golden during his yearly winter sojourn in Florida. So extensive were the alterations to the play that Golden credited himself as co-author with Hugh Stange. On 20 August an open-to-the-students-of-dramatic-schools dress rehearsal was held at the Golden Theatre during which Ross wore Myron McCormick's "remarkable" hat. Nina Musset attended the rehearsal and described the hat incident in *The Brooklyn Daily Eagle* (27 September 1931): "At the dress rehearsal of *After Tomorrow*, [Ross Alexander] wore it and rehearsal ended. John Golden, the producer, did not tell him he was good or bad; he said only, 'Where is the hat?' then took it and put it away for safety in a chest until the evening of the first performance [on 26 August]."

Set in a basement apartment on Washington Heights, New York City, *After Tomorrow* continued to be the Depression-era drama that was produced in Atlantic City, with Pete Piper (Ross Alexander), Willie Taylor (Donald Meek), the henpecked husband, and his daughter Sidney (now played by Barbara Robbins). In Act One, Pete and Sidney dream of a hopeful future as Pete waits hopelessly to hear if he has landed a new job:

Sidney. Think what we could do with forty a week and my salary besides! We could grab that little flat we saw up on 215th. It's so little it would be easy to furnish. We've got my hope chest to start with. (*She motions to her little chest under the window.*)

Pete. (*With a faint grin.*) That's a hell of a start!

Sidney. Oh, I don't know. There're those bed-sheets from my grandmother, and that lace tablecloth'd look nice on the table.

Pete. If we had a table! (*They are silent for a moment, huddled close together, contemplating their helplessness. Pete continues.*) Fifty a month, wasn't it?

Sidney. *And concessions.* Gee, it's just a dream of a flat.

Pete. Yeah—just a dream!

Sidney. Well, why not? Why can't we dream? Maybe if we dream hard enough it might come true. (1, 26–27)

Ross Alexander and Barbara Robbins.

At the end of Act One Pete is informed that he has, in fact, secured the job he wanted and Act Two opens with wedding preparations underway. The entrance Pete makes, carrying varying necessities for the wedding out in the yard behind Willie's basement apartment, deserves examination for its comic as well as sentimental possibilities:

Pete. (*Calling from outside, as he kicks at the street door.*) Open the door! The groom has arrived!

Sidney. (*Running to the door.*) Hold your horses! (*She opens the door, disclosing the grinning face of Pete. The rest of him is hidden by an endless number of things. He has a suitcase, a can of red paint, a folding chair, a box containing the wedding cake, and even a wedding bell, wrapped in tissue paper.*) Good Lord, Pete! What on earth have you got there?

Pete. (*Staggering in.*) Kiss me, dumbbell! (*He smacks at Sidney, grins at Elsie, and starts unloading.*) How are you, mother? How's the old headache? Been doing a little shopping. This marriage thing's a serious business.

Sidney. (*Dryly.*) Sure you haven't forgotten anything?

Pete. Not a thing. When I put my mind on a job, you can gamble it'll be done right. Here's the suitcase with my things. And here's some more of that red paint for Willie. Did the fellow bring up those two-by-fours from the lumber yard?

Sidney. Yes, the yard's full of 'em.

Pete. (*Rattling on.*) Good! I brought this sample of the folding chairs. The caterer wanted too much for them so I got 'em for half price from the undertaker. The weddin' cake's in there. And the fellow told me it would be better if you let it get stale for another day. And here—take a good look at this! (*He tears the tissue paper from the wedding bell.*) That's what you asked for, wasn't it? There's your wedding bell, dumbbell.

Sidney. (*Rapturously.*) Oh, Pete, you got it!

Pete. Yes sir! That's the very contraption that they're gonna put the old ball and chain on us, under!

Sidney. That's a fine line of grammar.

Pete. Oh, don't get collegiate! What's grammar to a couple of passionate lovers like us? (2, 52–53)

Ross Alexander carrying things and wearing Myron McCormick's hat; Barbara Robbins, surprised. Photo by Vandamm Studio © Billy Rose Theatre Division, The New York Public Library for the Performing Arts.

Later in the act, Pete and Sidney reminisce about their long and awkward courtship:

Sidney. You've been wonderful, Pete, darling, to wait all these years for me.

Pete. I haven't waited a minute longer than you have. Remember the night I asked you?

Sidney. Do I? (*She presses her cheek to his.*) I remember how we planned it all—at Coney Island. (*Dreamily.*) Gee, I'll never forget—sitting on the sand for hours—watching the lights at Brighton Beach. (*She smiles, her shining eyes full of her love for him.*)

Pete. Yeah, and remember we heard the jazz band at Feltman's playing, "A Cup of Coffee, a Sandwich and You"? And then, I proposed to you—and I told you if you took me—that's about all you'd get? (*Sidney laughs happily.*) Then I made up that poem to you. Darned good, if I do say so. Want me to recite it to you?

Sidney. (*Firmly.*) No! (*Then, with a laugh.*) But you *will!*

Pete. You're right—as usual! (*He recites, proudly.*)
"Listen, Sidney, to your Pete,
I think you are awful sweet,
Honestly, I mean it, Syd,
You are just the candy kid.
If you marry me, we'll be one,
And I'll be a happy son-of-a-gun."

Sidney. (*Just a little wistfully.*) Oh, Pete! I wish you were a little more romantic!

Pete. (*Picking up the wedding veil.*) Fair Lady, your wish is granted! (*He puts the veil crookedly on her head, kneels in front of her, and with one hand on his heart and the other extended rigidly in the air, declaims:*) For one soft glance from thy limpid eyes, gladly will I clamp on my armor, mount my royal steed, grab my lance and ride forth to do battle for thy fair name!

Willie. (*Who has entered in time to hear the last few words.*) How would you like to grab that hammer and come out and go to work! (*He grins.*)

Pete. (*As he rises.*) Our next poem will be entitled, "Always get your hammer out." (2, 66–67)

Ross Alexander, Donald Meek, and Barbara Robbins. Photo by Vandamm Studio © Billy Rose Theatre Division, The New York Public Library for the Performing Arts.

However, to quote Lysander in *A Midsummer Night's Dream*, the course of true love never did run smooth, for, just as in the tryout the year before, Sydney's mother Elsie (Marjorie Garrett) runs off with her bank embezzling lover on the eve of the wedding and her father has a stroke, ending the second act on a somber and melodramatic note. As in the tryout, Willie is nursed back to health in the hope that his wife will return to him but dies after learning that she and her lover have sailed to South America, leaving Sydney sobbing and Pete trying to comfort her "*while he looks far into the distance, visualizing the future—and its freedom. The room is filled with Sidney's heartbroken sobs, while the music from the radio drifts to them . . . as the curtain falls*" (3, 121).

If the newspaper notices from the tryout failed to please John Golden, those after the Broadway opening did no better. In *The New York Times* (27 August 1931) J. Brooks Atkinson savaged the play claiming that "Life is bad enough for such people as the Taylors without gratuitous persecution by the theatre. They owe money right and left. They have grease spots on the tablecloth and roaches in the kitchen. Bad as things are, the theatre can make them worse. It can make a fiend out of a sullen mother, a bank robber and home-breaker out of a hapless roomer; it can toss in bad verse for comic relief, and strew the stage with bridal veils and wedding gifts only to make a tragedy blacker. Both the direction and the authorship have played fast and loose with *After Tomorrow* in the theatre. There is not a genuine character in it." Atkinson, however, enjoyed the performances, claiming that the actors "all have either talent or charm. As the wretched Willie Taylor, Donald Meek contributes the bald head, embarrassed giggles and worried optimism that have made him the perfect stage symbol of futile husbands. Barbara Robbins brings the vitality of youth to the part of the daughter, and Ross Alexander is likable and youthfully cynical as the swain. . . . But the ingredients of *After Tomorrow* are hostile. No band of actors could compound them into a genuine play."

Burns Mantle, writing in the *Daily News* (27 August 1931), was far less censorious of the play and even more complimentary of Alexander's work: "Nor has Ross Alexander, likable juvenile, done better work than he does as a self-sacrificing clerk who gives his all for the girl he loves." In *The Brooklyn Daily Eagle* (27 August 1931), Arthur Pollock echoed the praises for Alexander's work but found that "It is doubtful if *After Tomorrow* comes close enough to being fine art to overcome its somberness." Also finding the play lacking in popular and artistic appeal, *Variety* (1 September 1931) noted that "Ross Alexander gives the play another excellent performance. He is Pete, the youth who loves his girl wholly if with restraint. Pete has a sense of humor and he neatly scores the comedy points. There is a delicate spot in the last act when Sid, realizing the sex urge in her fiancé, timidly suggests they have a holiday together. But Pete gently explains his devotion does not call for any such measure. Young Alexander was recognized as a bright juvenile possibility two years ago, [when] he was cast for *Night Hostess*."

Appropriately chastised by the New York critics, Golden immediately attempted to "fix" the play, beginning with the ending which had reportedly left too many patrons shuddering and tearful. In the *Daily News* (6 September 1931), John Chapman wrote that "John Golden spent the latter part of last week, and will continue tinkering with new and happier endings of *After Tomorrow*. The problem centers about Donald Meek, and whether it will be a happier ending to have Meek die in the second act instead of the third, or to let him live throughout the play." No amount of reworking was able to resuscitate the play's poor showing at the box office and, in spite of its being optioned by Fox Studios as a talking motion picture, *After Tomorrow* closed on 31 October 1931 after 10 weeks and 77 performances on Broadway.

For Ross Alexander the experience marked a giant leap forward in his career. Suddenly he became part of the conversation usually reserved for more well-known actors. His picture appeared regularly in New York papers in connection with the play and in the October 1931 edition of *Broadway and Hollywood Movies*, he was the only actor mentioned in the short review-advertisement for *After Tomorrow*. On Sunday 4 October, a sketch of Alexander in the role of Pete Piper (still wearing Myron McCormick's hat) appeared in *The New York Times*, with the caption, "Ross Alexander, Who Is Making Something of a Name for Himself by His Performance in *After Tomorrow*, at Mr. Golden's Playhouse." Finally, on 2 November 1931, the *Daily News* reported:

When we caught a performance of John Golden's *After Tomorrow* last week, we felt sure that some cinema producer would soon find a place in filmdom for Ross Alexander, as charming a young actor as ever made a bright character out of a juvenile lead. Ross has been signed by Paramount. He'll make his film debut on completion of his present engagement. He's tall, slender and typically collegiate in type. Has had about five years' stage experience. Maybe when he gets to Hollywood, Paramount will lend him to Fox for his original role in a Movietone production of *After Tomorrow*. Minna Gombell, you know, will have the screen lead.

Ross Alexander did not get cast in the film of *After Tomorrow*. Charles Farrell, seven years older than Ross, was chosen to play Pete Piper. Ross did not begrudge him the role.

8. *The Wiser Sex*

Actually, Ross Alexander was not all that interested in appearing in films. Yes, he appeared enthusiastic in interviews and said a great many positive things in public, but what really drove him to accept a contract from Paramount Public Corporation was his divorce from Helen Burroughs-Smith. The couple had been living apart ever since Ross went out on tour with *Let Us Be Gay*, but they agreed to a divorce settlement only late in 1931 when Ross paid Burroughs's lawyer $10,000. In an interview published in *Movie Mirror* (October 1936) Ross told Katharine Hartley that he agreed to sign with Paramount only if they would give him a certified check for $10,000 in advance so that he could pay for his divorce. Much to his surprise, Paramount wrote the check. Suddenly, freed from a marriage contract, Ross found himself tethered by a film contract. Wary of a commitment as a "contract player" that allowed the film studio to assign him to whatever picture or task that was needed, Ross insisted on a rider to the standard contract that guaranteed him a bonus of $1,000 every time he stepped in front of a camera to make a motion picture. The request was rather extravagant coming from a newcomer, but his agent, William Morris, succeeded in persuading the studio that Ross was worth the money.

"I had a good reason for that," he confided to Hartley. "You see those contracts require you to do everything—make tests with other players, pose for publicity stills, advertising tie-ups, appear in benefits. From the length of those clauses you'd think that acting for pictures was the smallest part of it. And I wanted to be sure that when they did put me in a picture they'd think twice about the kind of part they were going to give me. It stands to reason that if they had to pay me an extra thousand dollars every time they gave me a part they wouldn't use me in little ones."

"The theory was all right," he continued, "but it turned out all wrong. Instead of thinking twice they thought three times and didn't use me at all. I made one picture on my contract in New York, before I came [to Hollywood]. That was a three-months' super-special called *The Weaker Sex*. Claudette Colbert was in it. And Lilyan Tashman. Franchot Tone. Douglas Dumbrille and William Boyd. And it was the *worst* picture ever produced! Ask Claudette if you don't believe me" (Hartley 1936, 114). She certainly agreed for, in his biography, *Claudette Colbert: She Walked in Beauty*, Bernard F. Dick remarks that "For an assembly-line production, *The Wiser Sex*, as the title implies, was at least not demeaning to women" (Dick 2008, 56).

Initially it had been reported in *The Film Daily* (4 November 1931) that Ross had been assigned to a picture entitled *Tomorrow and Tomorrow*, based on a play by Philip Barry and co-staring Margaret Armstrong and Vola Vale, but he was abruptly replaced by Arthur Pierson and hastily reassigned to the Claudette Colbert project. A young actor named Tad Alexander did appear in *Tomorrow and Tomorrow* and it is possible, though rather doubtful, that *The Film Daily* announcement confused Ross Alexander with a nine-year-old boy. In any event, at the Paramount Studios Building No. 1 located at 35-11 35th Avenue in Astoria, Queens, rehearsals for *The Wiser Sex* began on 1 December under the steady direction of Berthold Viertel, a fiery Austrian screenwriter and director who came to the United States in 1928 to work at Fox, and later at Paramount and Warner Brothers. Calling him Bergmann in *Prater Violet*, Christopher Isherwood described Viertel's idiosyncratic behavior during their collaboration on the 1934 British Gaumont film *Little Friend*:

"Let me tell you something, Master," he began, as he dropped my manuscript casually into the wastepaper basket, "the film is a symphony. Each movement is written in a certain key. There is a note which has to be chosen and struck immediately. It is characteristic of the whole. It commands the attention."

Sitting very close to me, and pausing only to draw long breaths from his cigarette, he started to describe the opening sequence. It was astounding. Everything came to life. The trees began to tremble in the evening breeze, the music was heard, the roundabouts were set in motion. And the people talked. Bergmann improvised their conversation, partly in German, partly in ridiculous English; and it was vivid and real. His eyes sparkled, his gestures grew more exaggerated, he mimicked, he clowned. I began to laugh. Bergmann smiled delightedly at his own invention. It was all so simple, so effective, so obvious. . . . Clouds followed the sunshine. Bergmann scowled grimly as he passed into philosophical analysis. He gave me ten excellent reasons why the whole thing was impossible. They, too, were obvious. . . . Bergmann sighed. "It's not so easy—" He lit another cigarette. "Not so easy," he muttered. "Wait. Wait. Let us see—" (Isherwood 1945, 47–48)

In New York, Viertel was Greta Garbo's constant companion and his old-world charm and charisma was not lost on Ross Alexander who found his eccentricities commensurate with his own. Apprehensive about working in a film, Ross hung on the director's every word, every gesture. Every direction he was given was accepted graciously and gratefully. Ross was charmed by Viertel and permitted himself to learn from him. According to John R. Allen, Jr., in a 6 November 2006 post in *Films of the Golden Age*, Alexander also credited Claudette Colbert with teaching him how to act on film. "Colbert carried the unusually shy and insecure Alexander, whose broad stage gestures, when translated to the medium of film, seemed overblown and mannered.

In a 1935 *Photoplay* interview, Alexander graciously acknowledged her assistance, stating that following her lead and accepting her hints about underplaying to the camera had enabled him to give a performance attractive enough to eventually lead to his Warner Bros. contract." Allen added that Melvyn Douglas, Colbert's co-star, also noted Ross's "nervous, high-strung and extremely sensitive nature" as well as his "inherent vulnerability."

Ross may have been unfamiliar with the process of filmmaking and the technique of film-acting on Paramount's Astoria "Main Stage," which measured 120 feet wide, 127 feet long, and 41 feet high, but he hardly had to stretch his histrionic imagination to incorporate the role of a tuxedo-wearing, wealthy playboy called Jimmy O'Neill in the production. Jimmie is a high-society admirer of Margaret Hughes (Colbert) whose fiancé, New York City prosecutor David Rolfe (Douglas) is more interested in racketeers than romance.

Harry Evans (William Boyd), Jimmy O'Neill (Ross Alexander), and Margaret Hughes (Claudette Colbert) in a publicity still.

Following an attempt by mobster Harry Evans to have Rolfe murdered, Margaret, her mother (Effie Shannon) and Jimmie go off on a cruise, leaving Rolfe to sort things out with his young and gullible cousin, Phil Long (Franchot Tone) who is infatuated with Claire Foster (Lilyan Tashman), a gold-digger and Harry Evans's moll. After Rolfe convinces Long that Claire is attached to Evans, Long takes Rolfe's gun and goes off to have it out with Claire. He finds Evans there, and in the scuffle between the two men, Evans is wounded in the arm and Long is killed. When Rolfe, who has been tailing his cousin, arrives at Claire's room, she tells him (under orders from Evans) that Long killed himself; but after she notifies the police, she accuses Rolfe of the crime.

Margaret returns from the cruise with her mother and Jimmy in tow, only to discover that her fiancé is on trial for murder and that Claire has managed to convince an entire male jury of her (albeit duplicitous) side of the story. Believing that a jury of the "wiser sex," i.e. women, would see right through Claire's theatrical machinations. Margaret hatches a plan to get to the truth of the matter. Under the watchful eye of Jimmy O'Neill, Margaret masquerades as a blonde gold digger named Ruby Kennedy, rents a room next to Claire's, and begins to chat her up over drinks and jewelry.

Jimmy O'Neill (Ross Alexander) and Ruby Kennedy (Claudette Colbert) in a publicity still.

113

Ruby and Jimmie invite Claire and Evans to a party, during which Evans comes on strong to Ruby, and Fritz (Robert Fischer), Evans's cook unwittingly draws attention to Evans's wounded arm. The next day, Fritz is discovered dead, Margaret (AKA Ruby) realizes that the second round discharged from Rolfe's gun is in Evans's arm, and Jimmie complains to Claire that he has lost Ruby to Evans. Claire rushes off in a jealous rage and, finding them together, she spitefully reveals that Evans was, in fact, Long's killer, bringing to a happy end a long, drawn-out melodrama.

Perhaps the decision by Paramount (announced in *Variety* on 8 December 1931) to close the Astoria Studio on 15 January 1932, a month earlier than expected, was responsible for the seemingly rushed and unfinished quality to the film when it was released. Certainly, Viertel was encouraged to wrap up the film quickly, and that meant long hours of retakes and rewrites for the cast. Ross kept everyone entertained by playing ragtime piano during the lulls between takes and kept everyone's spirits up by performing tricks of legerdemain and playing jokes on unsuspecting cast members and technicians. The tentative and nervous young man at the beginning of filming grew into a positive and encouraging team player who had confidence in his ability to charm and regale people. From a personal point of view, however, it was not all fun and games for Ross. On Christmas Eve, he learned of the death in Boston, and burial in Rochester, of his friend and mentor, Hugh Towne, who was only forty years old at the time. The shooting schedule made it impossible for Ross to visit his friend's grave.

New Year's Eve was a happier time for Ross as he accompanied Colbert and other members of the cast to the opening performance of *Savage Rhythm*, coauthored by Colbert's husband, Norman Foster, and Harry Hamilton, and produced by John Golden at his 58th Street Theatre. Since Ross was living at that theatre, he didn't have far to go to attend the premiere. He and his castmates behaved like the perfect audience in strong support of Colbert's husband, but despite their efforts, the play was savaged by the critics and only stayed on Broadway for twelve performances. In the week that followed, Ross and other cast members stayed for a few days on location at Plandome,

Long Island, a village in Nassau County that had been the home of the celebrated and influential husband-and-wife dance team, Vernon and Irene Castle. Filmed there during the winter rainy season were several exterior shots, including an automobile crash and, since wet and slippery weather was required, the desired effect was easily realized. *The Film Daily* (18 January 1932) announced that Melvyn Douglas had completed his role in *The Wiser Sex* and left for Hollywood to begin another project. William Boyd was done a week later; but Ross stayed on until the film wrapped during the first week of February.

During the second week of February Ross visited his parents in Rochester where he was treated like a celebrity and a favorite son of West High School, even though he never graduated. His folks were all agog to hear about his experience as a "film star" but he had little to say about *The Wiser Sex*. He spoke about Claudette Colbert and the debt he owed for her coaching and consoling him; he said that film making was a more grueling experience than theatre acting because the hours were long and there was little immediate gratification. On stage he was used to getting laughs and applause from a live audience; the camera was a demanding but silent audience in film and did not energize him. What energy he discovered in his performance came from director Viertel who kept reminding the cast that the political background of *The Wiser Sex* was almost an exact replica of the current Samuel Seabury investigation into corruption in New York's courts and police department—a commission created by Governor Franklyn Delano Roosevelt after he discovered that gangsters had infiltrated the New York political system. Such a comparison to contemporary politics made *The Wiser Sex* a timely and significant movie in Viertel's estimation, and Alexander's parents were impressed and proud that their son was a part of so important a venture. Ross was significantly less impressed with his own work on the film and turned the conversation to a happier experience: the 19 January 1932 premiere of Ernst Lubitsch's film *Broken Lullaby* (AKA *The Man I Killed*), written by Samson Raphaelson, a screenwriter and playwright who will figure prominently in Alexander's future Broadway career. The film starred Lionel

Barrymore and Nancy Carroll who was in the audience along with Ross, the cast of *The Wiser Sex*, and screenwriter and producer at Paramount Hector Turnbull, with whom Ross had become friends during his three-month stint at the Astoria Studio.

Ross managed very little rest or relaxation in Rochester; if he wasn't shuttled around town for personal appearances, friends he never knew he had visited his parents' Woodbine Avenue home to ask for his autograph. His father's leather business had taken a hit due to the Depression, so Alexander's attempt to turn the conversation from him to family matters invited more doom and gloom than he could manage. His mother who knew very little about his former wife Helen Burroughs moved from being surprised at their marriage to stoically accepting their divorce. For fear of being lectured about family values and the "right way" to behave, Ross rarely shared his emotional problems with his parents. To them he was a confident, well-liked, charmer who had optimized his talent and discovered success as an actor. They never realized—until the very end—how much he actually hated himself.

Leaving Rochester in mid-February, Ross boarded the Lake Shore Limited en route to Chicago, where he joined Hector Turnbull, Berthold Viertel, and Russell Holman, Adolph Zukor's assistant on the Paramount editorial council, aboard the Super Chief bound for Los Angeles. The travelers arrived on Sunday 21 February 1932 and were met by studio representatives who took Ross to his hotel adjacent to the 5555 Melrose Avenue Paramount Studios compound where he waited to be called on for work.

While waiting, Ross developed a friendship with gay publicist Jerry Asher who apparently became Alexander's confidante regarding his homosexuality. It is not known if Ross and Asher actually had any kind of physical relationship, but it was Asher to whom Ross confided the intimate details of his same-sex dalliances and Asher who so often assisted the studio in keeping that information away from the press. That is what he told journalists and biographers following Alexander's death, and because of his intimate relationship with Ross, there appears to be no reason to question his words, even though few studio records exist to verify his account. The paucity of documents surrounding Alexander's liaisons only seemed to verify Asher's claims since he categorically insisted that any and all evidence of same-sex behavior had to be destroyed.

Writing in *Modern Screen* (June 1933), Katherine Albert noted that "Hollywood is such a funny town. It is completely isolated—absolutely cut off from the rest of the world. That the President is having spectacular bills passed in Congress; that a famous senator is dead means very little. They don't read the papers, except the movie columns. They never listen to the news over the radio" (42) Asher gave Ross the A-list tour of that insular Hollywood: he introduced him to the recently reopened "very, very noisy" little Hollywood speakeasy and invited Miss America of 1925, actress Adrienne Doré, to dance with him at the Beverly Wilshire Hotel, the "smartest place to dance nowadays," encouraging Ross to be seen in public with her so that movie magazines might consider them an "item." Through Doré Ross was introduced to Joan Blondell who would later costar with him in *We're in the Money* at Warner Bros., and nineteen-year-old actor Tom Brown. Asher brought Ross to parties where he rubbed shoulders with the likes of Una Merkel, Clark Gable, Marlene Dietrich, Joan Crawford, Anna May Wong, Ramon Novarro, Jean Harlow, John Arledge (with whom he would appear in to films), and Bette Davis, who would become one of Alexander's real friends in Hollywood, and for whom, according to some film historians, Ross would nurture a boyish infatuation.

Alexander was still waiting for his next film assignment on 11 March when *The Wiser Sex* opened at New York City's Paramount Theatre. Publicity posters for the film erroneously listed Ross's name as Ross Hamilton, something that he initially bristled at, but later when the film was panned by the critics, he viewed as a blessing in disguise. Writing for *The Brooklyn Daily Eagle* (12 March 1932), Martin Dickstein gave the film a lukewarm review but praised the acting, suggesting that the best performances were given by Claudette Colbert, William Boyd, and Ross Alexander. The *Daily News* (12 March 1932) critic spent much time discussing Colbert's blonde wig and the clothes worn by the women in the film but did acknowledge that "Ross Alexander, Franchot Tone, Effie Shannon and Robert Fischer are among those who help out the principals." Faint praise, indeed! Mordaunt Hall, writing in *The New York Times* (12 March 1932) called the film "a somewhat clumsy melodrama, with dialogue that is beyond even the ken of the competent cast to make effective" and mercifully did not mention Ross.

Variety (15 March 1932) also made no mention of Ross but suggested that Claudette Colbert gave "probably the first second-rate performance . . . since she went into pictures." *The Los Angeles Times* (18 March 1932) declared that "Nobody is particularly outstanding although Miss Tashman gives, as usual, an interesting performance; Miss Colbert exerts a great deal of charm; Bill Boyd blusters and swaggers, and Melvyn Douglas is finished and smooth in his performance. You will be interested, no doubt, in Ross Alexander and Franchot Tone, both newcomers to the screen. Tone, particularly, although in an ineffectual role, stands out." *Harrison's Reports* (19 March 1932) called *The Wiser Sex* "dull and demoralizing. The story is illogical and there are several dirty situations," and the *Motion Picture Herald* (19 March 1932) remarked that "An audience at the New York Paramount seemed but fairly entertained by the effort, with general opinion holding that there was very little unusual about the story, little that is striking about the handling of it." The *Democrat and Chronicle* (30 March 1932), from Rochester, Ross's adopted hometown, noted that "Prominent in the supporting cast is Ross Alexander, who is cast as Jimmie O'Neill, a wealthy playboy friend of Margaret Hughes (Miss Colbert), with whom she goes to Europe after a break with her fiancé," and *The Courier-Journal* (19 March 1932), from Louisville, Kentucky, added that "Ross Alexander, who used to play here in stock, is hardly as screen 'pretty' as stage handsome but he does very well in a juvenile role."

Although Jerry Asher tried to convince Ross that "no press is bad press," the actor personally felt embarrassed by his association with *The Wiser Sex*. The film did not do well with the critics or at the box office, earning far less than even modest expectations. In the four-thousand-seat Paramount Theatre in New York, for example, where a weekly gross of $50,000–$60,000 was the norm, *The Wiser Sex* opened slow and failed to build to more than $35,000

(*Variety*, 15 March 1932). Ross tried to put his first failed effort in the film industry far behind him and enjoy the perks of living in Hollywood while waiting for his next assignment. He swam most days in the hotel pool and waited for the call. He toured the Paramount lot to acquaint himself with the technicians and stars at work in one or another of what he looked upon as gigantic sound stages, and he waited. He struck up a conversation with Cary Grant, flipped a coin or two with George Raft, accompanied Jeanette MacDonald on the piano, and learned a few witty remarks from Groucho and Chico Marx while he waited. It wasn't a bad life, actually, being paid to do nothing, but Ross was not wired to be indolent. John Milton's weighty aphorism, "They also serve who only stand and wait" was completely lost on him. Ross needed to—wanted to—work, so at the beginning of June 1932, he left Hollywood and rode a train back to New York.

9. Summer Stock

Returning to New York after several months in Hollywood was only a slight culture shock for Ross Alexander, felt most deeply in the area of where he was to live. John Golden came to his rescue by again welcoming him to sleep on a backstage cot in his 58th Street Theatre. Not long after his arrival on the East Coast, Ross was invited to play the principal role of the Overland Kid in Albert Bein's new play *Heavenly Express*, scheduled for a pre-Broadway tryout, beginning on 27 June 1932, with the Scarborough Players of Scarborough, New York. The blatantly allegorical play is based on the concept spoken by Luka in Maxim Gorky's *The Lower Depths*: "We are all of us tramps. I've even heard it said that the earth we live on is a tramp in the Heavens" (Bein 1940, frontispiece). It depicts the Overland Kid as an advance ticket taker for the Heavenly Express, a mystical railroad that transports hobos to railroad heaven. The transcendent nature of the play allows the Overland Kid to sing popular folk ballads ("The Wabash Cannonball" and "Big Rock Candy Mountain") and spin folk tales using a dialect indigenous to "bos." In Act Three, for example, he tells Granny about the fate of her son, Melancholy Bo:

Well—well—duh younger bo—a greenhorn fer right—he came traipsin' in t' duh jungles, fresh offa a freight—hongry an' lookin' fer food. Duh Melancholy Bo . . . offered him food—uh-huh—out'n his own share—which was small 'nough. Duh new bo took it widout sayin' t'anks. Den he walked over t' duh fire where java was bein' poured an' said "Gimme some." . . . He started t' go fer duh java—when t'ree boes standin' aroun' jumped at him, knocked his plate uh food down—an' began kickin' away an' punchin'—When up jumps duh Melancholy Bo from where he was sittin' an' swings right an' left, freein' duh new bo, puttin' him on his feet, pushin' him off, tellin' him to beat it, savin' his life while he hisself stood behin' t' tackle dese tough mugs. One uh dem brought out a razor . . . [and] marked him . . . But—but—he's talked about wherever boes gadder—'cause getting' marked fer savin' a life ain't so bad fer Melancholy, yer son, is it Granny? (3, 114–115)

Ross had been sent a copy of the play on 13 June and formal rehearsals began during the day a week later, while the Scarborough Players performed another play in the evening. The tryout for *Heavenly Express* lasted one week only since the Players' summer stock season required them to perform a different play each week. Even though his name continued to appear in the advertising for Paramount Publix Studios through November 1932, Ross felt free to pursue acting opportunities whenever and wherever they might materialize." If the film studio wanted to continue paying me for loafing around," he thought to himself, "that's their prerogative, so long as they permit me to pursue theatre work."

On 3 July, following the closing of *Heavenly Express* in Scarborough, New York, Ross moved to Red Bank, New Jersey, where the newly formed Monmouth County Players (billed as the "first permanent summer dramatic organization the Jersey coast has had in many years") had begun its season at the Elks' Auditorium on 2 July with Robert Emmett Sherwood's play *The Road to Rome*, staring Alice Brady, Jean Arthur, and McKay Morris, under the direction of William A. Brady, Jr. No sooner had Ross arrived at the Molly Pitcher Hotel in Red Bank to begin rehearsals on 5 July for Rachel Crothers's *Let Us Be Gay*, than *Variety* (5 July 1932) ran an article naming him among thirty-two actors in films "considered to have stood out on impressions made by frequent or telling appearances during the year, a number of whom give promise of future stardom." Others mentioned along with Ross included

Warren William, Ann Dvorak, Jimmy Durante, Guy Kibbee, George Brent, Bette Davis, Virginia Bruce, Cary Grant, George Raft, Melvyn Douglas, Helen Hayes, Maureen O'Sullivan, Ralph Bellamy, Wallace Ford, and Frances Dee. Ross Alexander was certainly in good company!

On 11 July, following a week of daytime rehearsals, *Let Us Be Gay* opened with Ross as Bruce Keen (the role he played on Broadway), Alice Brady as Kitty Brown, Jean Adair as Mrs. Boucicault, and Jean Arthur as Dierdre Lessing. Attendance was small because the summer heat filled the auditorium which was not equipped with fans or air-conditioning, but a review in the *Asbury Park Press* applauded the cast and singled out Ross saying, "Ross Alexander appears in the part he played in the original production and it goes without saying that he does well." While *Let Us Be Gay* was in production during the evening, Ross was in rehearsal for *Coquette*, the southern melodrama by George Abbott and Ann Preston Bridgers that had starred Helen Hayes on Broadway and featured Aleta Freel with the Monmouth County Players. Both actresses played Norma Besant, the coquette of the title, who exudes southern charm and flirtatiousness and sets her sights on Michael Jeffery, a "roughneck" who is "handsome, insolent, hot tempered and passionate" (Mantle 1966, 180), and played by Ross Alexander, Freel's real-life boyfriend. When Jeffery tries to avoid taking Norma to a dance because he doesn't own a dress suit, obviously a trumped-up excuse, she responds with the hauteur of a southern debutante:

Norma. I'm mighty sorry, Mr. Jeffery, that I've forgotten my pride so far as to throw myself at a man who doesn't—What are you laughing at?

Michael. You're just carrying on now, aren't you?

Norma. Carrying on?

Michael. You know you don't mean a word of that.

Norma. I think, Mr. Jeffery, it's about time for you to say good night.

Michael. I will in a minute. I don't belong with that crowd up at the Country Club. They sort of look down on me. . . . I know it's damned foolish to feel that way, but—If you'd like to go somewhere else with me sometime—

123

(*He gets no answer.*) Well, I guess I'd better say goodnight. (*He goes on out into the hallway. Norma stands a second, then runs after him.*)

Norma. Michael! Come back here. (*He comes.*) You needn't rush away like that just because you're turning me down. It's the first time that's ever happened to me, and I don't know but it's sort of interesting. But you are an awful stubborn, just the same. You're sure you won't come?

Michael. I told you I can't. (*Norma accepts defeat this time and changes the subject.*)

Norma. (*Quite seriously.*) What did you and Duke fight about this afternoon?

Michael. (*Reluctantly.*) He said something I didn't take a fancy to.

Norma. About me?

Michael. (*After a moment.*) Yes.

Norma. What was it?

Michael. I—If it's all the same to you, I'd just as soon not talk about it. (Mantle 1966, 151)

Of course, Duke had called Norma a "silly little coquette" and Michael thrashed him in defense of her honor. Norma appreciates Michael's gallant behavior but also wonders if the sobriquet might not really be true. In any event, against the wishes of her father Dr. Besant (McKay Morris) who believes Michael to be of wayward and lazy habits, Norma continues to court him and eventually becomes pregnant with his child. Michael insists on doing the right thing by her and convinces her to elope with him, a plan that leads to an explosive confrontation with Norma's father:

Michael. It seems to me with all this chivalry that's always being paraded around here, I might at least explain my side of the story. I never stood so much abuse from anybody.

Dr. Besant. If I didn't think it unbecoming to my years, you'd stand abuse of a different kind. . . .

Norma. Michael, you go now and let me talk to him—

Dr. Besant. If he doesn't go, I'll put him out. I'm not holding you blameless, Norma, but you haven't the slightest idea what's in the mind of a man like this fellow. And you can thank God that you've a father who'll protect you.

Michael. When she's married to me, you won't need to protect her.

Dr. Besant. My daughter will never marry you, not any *trash* like you! The sooner you get that through your head and take yourself away from here, the better for all concerned. . . .

Michael. Sure, I will, but I'll marry her just the same.

Dr. Besant. And you'll get out of this town too.

Michael. Oh, you own the town, too. I'll get out of town if I want to, and I'll take her with me. . . .

Dr. Besant. If you were anything of a gentleman, sir—

Michael. Oh, shut up, you God-damned old hypocrite! . . . I'm going to marry her. Get that through your head. And you can't stop me. If you had any sense, you'd be begging me to marry her, because we've lived together already, because we're just as good as man and wife now. Oh, hell. Now I reckon you'll shut your mouth for a while. (*To Norma.*) I'll come back this afternoon and get you. (*He rushes out. Dr. Besant stands transfixed.*)

Norma. Daddy, he didn't know. He lost his temper. Sometimes he gets like that.

Dr. Besant. Be still. . . . Of course, I don't have to be told that the things he said about you aren't true— (*No answer.*) Norma?

Norma. (*In terror of her father.*) No, daddy, no. (Mantle 1966, 162–163)

Self-righteously enraged and seeking to defend the honor of his daughter, Dr. Besant cold-bloodedly guns down Michael Jeffery and spends the entire third act of the play on trial for murder. Throughout the act Norma is fearful of being called as a witness on her father's behalf because her pregnancy clearly demonstrates that Michael was not lying about their relationship and that her father's defense, based on the belief that a "pure" Norma was maligned by a worthless lay-about, is a lie. In order to maintain the illusion that she is unsullied and thus protect her father's honor, Norma gallantly commits suicide. Ross has had his share of complicated romantic relationships in the theatre, but getting murdered for love provided him with a new opportunity to flex his acting muscles, and Ross took advantage of the situation.

Coquette opened on 18 July to another small but enthusiastic audience and excellent reviews for Aleta Freel and McKay Morris, but no mention of Ross Alexander, except in the credits. The *Keyport Enterprise* (21 July 1932) at least made reference to Ross as "a prominent young Broadway actor." Alexander certainly suited the part of a "handsome, insolent, hot tempered and passionate" youth and he had the talent to play a serious dramatic role; he was used to shouting at fathers (including his own) in romantic comedies and Michael Jeffery gave him the chance to do the same in a melodrama. It is unfortunate that we have no contemporary account of Ross in the role.

Benn W. Levy's popular four-character farce, *Springtime for Henry*, opened a week after *Coquette*. Since Ross had no role in the farce, he was not burdened by rehearsals during the run of the melodrama, and not saddled by performances the following week, while he was in rehearsal for Zoe Akins's gold-digger comedy, *The Greeks Had a Word for It*, playing the role of Dey Emery, a wealthy banker's playboy son. As might be expected, Dey wants to marry Polaire, a fortune-hunter *Follies* girl (Aleta Freel), but the wedding depends on her making a good impression on his father Emery Senior (McKay Morris). Since this is a comedy, Polaire fails to impress Emery Senior due to her devious and manipulative friend Jean (Rosalind Russell), who schemes to make Polaire appear to be a thief. Jean ends up almost marrying Emery Senior but the Polaire-Dey union does not occur, each blaming the other for their separation. In Act Four, the couple accidently meet on the day of Jean's wedding. Both had come to ask Jean to return a good-luck piece she had borrowed from Polaire:

Polaire. I came up here to have it out with her.
Dey. Go ahead; but you've got to listen to me first.

Polaire. Why? . . . What do you think you can say that's going to change anything now?

Dey. Whether it changes anything or not, I'm going to get a certain satisfaction in making you realize that I can't get you out of my mind—And I can't get it out of my mind that I lost my chance that day.

Polaire. I can understand that. You've just been a little boy with a big father, all your life. And that was your chance to make him listen to you. And you lost it.

Dey. I lost more than that. Will you ever forgive me?

Polaire. Sure; you're forgiven.

Dey. That doesn't mean anything—except that you don't care. But you did care for me—that day, didn't you?

Polaire. No; not really. Not for you. I just felt something. Then it got spoiled. You weren't to blame. You were just you. We all get a little coo-coo, sometimes. Marry a nice girl, Dey. . . . You're too much on the loose. Settle down, and forget there's such a thing as a wild party. You like horses. Get a horse. And a nice girl. There's no harm in you. I'd like to see you happy myself.

Dey. Are you through with me for good and all?

Polaire. Absolutely. . . . Believe me, Dey, it's up to you to turn into a nice prig and a good snob; because you were never meant to be on the loose—You mustn't turn into a gentleman bum—marrying tarts—and all that. *You're not good enough*. It takes a strong man to have any real fun in the world. Marry a nice girl, settle down, and get a horse. (4, 13–15)

The Greeks Had a Word for It opened on 1 August to a "fair-sized" audience and met with rave reviews for Rosalind Russell but only brief mentions for Ross Alexander and McKay Morris who "have parts which bring them on the stage for a brief time, but their roles are far from major" (*Asbury Park Press*, 2 August 1932). During the week's run, Ross and company rehearsed Philip Barry's pre-Depression comedy *Holiday*, the tale of Johnny Case (Ross Alexander), a charming, attractive Wall-Street Lawyer with good investments but no social pedigree, who falls in love with Julia Seton (Rosalind Russell), the beautiful eldest daughter of the wealthy and socially elite Seton family. The match is initially objected to by Julia's father, Edward Seton (John T. Dwyer) but when Case's Wall Street investments triple in value, Edward relents, believing that, in spite of his middle-class roots, Johnny has the business acumen that would add value to the Seton brand. Case, however, is an idealist who wants to retire after he has earned $25,000 ($365,164 in 2019 dollars) in order to live life while he is young enough to enjoy it. Julia and her father dismiss his idealism as a phase, and wanting to be married to Julia, Johnny is momentarily seduced to their way of thinking; but when he realizes the extent of the materialism into which he would be marrying, he balks:

Johnny. Julia—I'm sorry—but I can't stand it. . . . If we begin loaded down with possessions, obligations, responsibilities, how would we ever get out from under them? We never would. . . . Oh, my dear, we've got to make our own life—there's nothing to it if we don't—there's no other way to live it!—Let's forget wedding invitations and two weeks from Wednesday. Let's go now. Let's be married tonight.

Julia. I must decide now, must I?

Johnny. Please—

Julia. And if I say No—not unless you—?

Johnny. Then I'm going tonight, by myself.

Julia. (*A moment. Then*) Very well—you can go. Because I don't quite see myself with an idler for a husband.

Johnny. (*A silence. Then Johnny speaks slowly.*) I suppose the fact is, I love feeling free inside even better than I love you, Julia. (3, 102–104)

Throughout the play Johnny enjoys witty repartee with Linda Seton (Aleta Freel), Julia's younger sister and a dreamer in her own right. Feeling trapped in the materialism of the Seton brand, Linda quickly falls in love with Johnny and defends his idealism:

Linda. (*Turns to Julia.*) You've got no faith in Johnny, have you, Julia? His little dream may fall flat, you think—yes! So it may! What about it? What if it should? There'll be another—the point is, he *does* dream! Oh, I've got all the faith in the world in Johnny. Whatever he does is all right with me. If he wants to sit on his tail, he can sit on his tail. If he wants to come back and sell peanuts, Lord how I'll believe in those peanuts! (3, 107)

The play ends with Linda leaving to follow Johnny and the curtain falls leaving the audience in the hope that Johnny will realize that Linda is the Seton with whom he is really in love.

Holiday opened on 8 August to positive reviews, with Aleta Freel and Rosalind Russell again receiving top honors and Ross Alexander cited as giving a credible performance (*The Daily Record*, 2 August 1932). At the end of the run, on Saturday 13 August, Ross Alexander, Aleta Freel, Rosalind Russell, and other members of the Monmouth County Players were guests of actor Gavin Muir and his wife at a party they hosted in honor of film star Rod La Rocque whose many credits included the role of Bob Brown in the 1930 film adaptation of *Let us Be Gay*. A month earlier Ross and Aleta attended a "Polo Night" celebration of the Montmartre Friday Supper Club along with Jean Arthur and the Gavin Muirs. Like the character she played in *Coquette*, Aleta Freel was the daughter of a well-known socially elite family and used to exclusive parties and social gatherings; like the character he portrayed in the same play, Ross Alexander was less comfortable in social situations. Out in Hollywood, he attended parties in an attempt to improve his opportunities as a film actor; in New Jersey, where his performances gained him little renown, Ross mixed with the upper crust as an appendage on the arm of Aleta Freel.

On 15 August, the Monmouth County Players presented the world premiere of a first play by playwright Rosemary Casey entitled *Love Is Not Important*. Advertised as a "brilliant high comedy of the Philip Barry school" (*Asbury Park Press*, 13 August 1932), the play cast Ross Alexander as wealthy polo player Henry Warren who proposes marriage to Diana Westlake (Rosalind Russell), an actress on tour with a play written by her ex-fiancé Arthur Franklin (McKay Morris). Diana had discovered another woman's nightgown in Franklin's apartment and, being a temperamental actress, she raised the proverbial roof and broke their engagement. As soon as she accepts

129

Henry Warren's proposal of marriage her former fiancé (who has continued to be in her life as the author of her play) reappears, contrite and hopeful that she will take him back. The denouement of such a well-worn plot is in no way a surprise, and once again during this summer season, Alexander plays the romantic interest of a woman who spurns him. Only in *Coquette* did his character find true love, but then again, he was murdered in that play.

Advertisement for *Love Is Not Important* in the *Asbury Park Press*,
13 August 1932.

In giving a positive notice to the production, Houston Brown, writing in *The Daily Record* (16 August 1932) praised the play and singled out the performances of Rosalind Russell and McKay Morris. About Ross Alexander he only had this to say: "Other members of the cast, with the possible exception of Ross Alexander, did not distinguish themselves but diligently applied themselves to the task before them." The *Asbury Park Press* (16 August 1932) noted that Ross "does his part very well, yet there seemed to be something lacking in his playing last night. Perhaps after a few performances he'll take to it as he has to other roles." *The Daily Register* (17 August 1932) also singled out Rosalind Russell and McKay Morris but added that "There are excellent parts also for Aleta Freel, Ross Alexander, [and] Gavin Muir."

On Sunday 21 August, Ross left the Molly Pitcher Hotel and Red Bank, New Jersey, after an undistinguished season of summer stock. Perhaps the most notable aspect of the summer was in the hotel register where Ross and Aleta both gave their local address as Jersey City, New Jersey. Perhaps that is one reason why local gossip whispered that they were married. Evidently local whispers became a general roar, for New Jersey newspapers ran with the item.

10. Back on Broadway

No sooner had Ross Alexander left New Jersey than he was in production for a Broadway-bound sex farce imported from Vienna called *The Stork Is Dead* (AKA *The Stork*, and *Not Yet*). Written in German by Hans Kottow and liberally adapted by Frederic and Fanny Hatton, the play had tried out for a week in Bayonne, New Jersey, beginning 6 October 1930 without success. A.H. Woods, the producer of sex farces such as *Parlor, Bedroom and Bath* (1917), *Up in Mabel's Room* (1919), *Getting Gertie's Garter* (1921), and *A Kiss in a Taxi* (1925), decided that *The Stork Is Dead* deserved a second attempt at Broadway and put it in rehearsal at the Apollo Theatre during the last week of August.

Ross Alexander was cast in the principal role of Comte Rene de Gaumont, a dissolute young libertine who enjoys romancing women. The first act opens with the count rising from the bed on which his mistress, Lola Faubert (Ninon Bunyea), is lying, only to tell her that he must dress for his wedding to a young, rich, and virginal society girl, Suzanne Bridier (Ethel Norris), whom he is marrying for her money. Lola who is hot and spicy threatens to reveal their affair to Suzanne's father, Lucien Bridier (Mark Smith), an automobile manufacturer, unless Rene agrees to be celibate for the first three months of his marriage. If he fails, he must pay her a third of the dowry his bride brings him and the wealth he has just received from his cousin Paul (Fred Stewart). Suzanne was raised in the convent so it is easy for Rene to invent reasons why he will not sleep in the same bed with her. When she presses him about their duty to have children, the count explains that they cannot have children because "the stork is dead," an excuse that causes the young mademoiselle to wear black in mourning.

As time passes, Suzanne's parents begin to worry that Rene is not behaving toward his bride the way a proper husband should and take matters into their own hands. In an attempt to instruct her daughter in the ways of seducing a man, Madame Didier (Nana Bryant) tells her to walk around the house in her underclothes, a scheme that finally drives the count into his wife's arms. Moreover, Madame has the living room sofa (where Rene had been sleeping) removed so that the husband has nowhere else in the house to sleep except in his wife's bed. Just as Rene and Suzanne get set to live happily ever after, Lola reappears, primed to reveal all to Monsieur Bridier, but cousin Paul comes to the rescue by making her an offer she cannot refuse—a proposal of marriage to a wealthy man.

The Stork Is Dead opened under the direction of A.H. Van Buren at Werba's Boulevard Theatre in Jackson Heights on 12 September before a large and enthusiastic audience that, according to Arthur Pollock in *The Brooklyn Daily Eagle* (13 September 1932), gave unmistakable evidence that it was having a good time. Of the play, Pollock noted that "*The Stork Is Dead* has the great virtue of getting better as it goes along. At the end of the first act one wonders why Al Woods ever thought it worth the trouble of producing. . . . At the beginning of the second act, however, we meet the count's young wife, played by Ethel Norris. She is cute and wide-eyed and clever. The thing begins to seem more natural, less forced . . . . A little delicacy now and then would make *The Stork Is Dead* twice as indelicate and therefore as many times more effective, and a better cast and more suave direction would enhance its value as entertainment." Pollock found Ross entirely unsuited to his part in Act One but much more comfortable in his role in the two following acts.

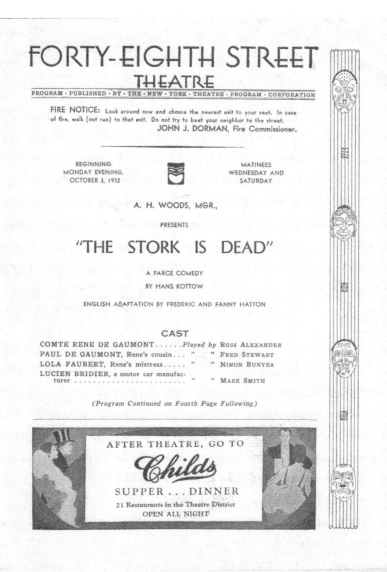

FORTY-EIGHTH STREET
THEATRE
PROGRAM · PUBLISHED · BY · THE · NEW · YORK · THEATRE · PROGRAM · CORPORATION

FIRE NOTICE: Look around now and choose the nearest exit to your seat. In case of fire, walk (not run) to that exit. Do not try to beat your neighbor to the street.

JOHN J. DORMAN, Fire Commissioner.

BEGINNING
MONDAY EVENING,
OCTOBER 3, 1932

MATINEES
WEDNESDAY AND
SATURDAY

A. H. WOODS, MGR.,

PRESENTS

"THE STORK IS DEAD"

A FARCE COMEDY

BY HANS KOTTOW

ENGLISH ADAPTATION BY FREDERIC AND FANNY HATTON

CAST

COMTE RENE DE GAUMONT	......Played by	Ross Alexander
PAUL DE GAUMONT, Rene's cousin...	"	" Fred Stewart
LOLA FAUBERT, Rene's mistress.....	"	" Ninon Bunyea
LUCIEN BRIDIER, a motor car manufacturer	"	" Mark Smith

(Program Continued on Fourth Page Following)

Program of *The Stork Is Dead* at the Forty-Eighth Street Theatre.

135

After a week at the Boulevard Theatre and further rehearsals and rewrites, *The Stork Is Dead* opened on Broadway at the Forty-Eighth Street Theatre on Friday 23 September 1932. The audience, although sober, chortled and guffawed merrily and was thoroughly entertained by what Brooks Atkinson called "the old musty formula" by which the word "night" becomes "a roguish leer and every actor looks as mischievous as he can be. Here is the heavy comic lead choking and coughing and wiggling his chops, and here is the ingenue speaking of wicked topics in tones of high soprano innocence" (*The New York Times*, 24 September 1932). Ross, fortuitously, was not mentioned in Atkinson's review, but he was called out again by Arthur Pollock (*The Brooklyn Daily Eagle*, 24 September 1932) who still insisted that he was miscast in the role of the libertine. In the *Daily News* (24 September 1932), Burns Mantle seemed to agree: noting that *The Stork Is Dead* is "competently played in its chief roles," he determined that "Ross Alexander is a clean minded juvenile even with a dirt-smeared part." As for the play itself, Mantle continued: "Disrobing scenes, disrobing suggestions, naked minds and nude suggestions. Not subtle, any of it. A little funny, some of it. Not for the sensitive or the easily shocked, any of it." *Variety* (27 September 1932), however, found that "Ross Alexander did very well as Rene," even though it panned the play, claiming that "Naughty but not so nice is *The Stork Is Dead* which completed a week of disappointments on Broadway." John Mason Brown, writing in the *New York Evening Post* (24 September 1932) argued that "The indications were many last evening that there was something dead on the stage of the Forty-Eighth Street Theatre. According to the Hattons, it was only a stork. But somehow I suspect them of being wrong."

Perhaps most telling of the professional and critical attitude regarding *The Stork Is Dead* was the fact, reported in *Variety* (27 September 1932), that on opening night, producer A.H. Woods went to watch another play! After running three weeks to poor business, *The Stork Is Dead* passed away mercifully, much to the relief of the cast, on 15 October. Two weeks later, Ross found himself among the New Jersey elite at a large dinner party at the Mayfair Yacht Club, sponsored by Aleta Freel's parents to announce the engagement of their daughter Doris to Stuart Bennedict, a native of Montclair, New Jersey. The affair reminded Ross of the second act of Philip Barry's *Holiday*, and he felt as ill at ease as Johnny Case did among the New York City elite in the play. But, like Johnny, Ross earnestly endeavored to fit in as Aleta's escort. Evidently Ross was currently residing with her at her family's home in Jersey City because New Jersey newspapers continued to refer to Ross as her husband. In November, however, the press began reporting that Ross and Aleta were engaged; even Walter Winchell in his syndicated column, "On Broadway" claimed that "Ross Alexander, recently in *The Stork Is Dead* flop, and Aleta Freel, ingenue, are looking for a parson" (*The Post-Star*, 29 November 1932).

Just days after the engagement fête Ross was announced as the male lead in *Honeymoon*, a four-character comedy by George Backer and former music critic Samuel Chotzinoff beginning rehearsal on Monday 7 November under the direction of Thomas Michell in preparation for a 5 December tryout at the Broad Theatre in Philadelphia. Ross was typecast as Sam Chappmann, a wealthy young American playwright on his honeymoon in Paris with his bride Joan (Rachel Hartzell). As soon as they arrive at the home of their unconventional friend, Mrs. Leslie Taylor (Katherine Alexander), a recent a divorcee, they begin to bicker, with Sam immediately behaving in a fashion that is dictatorial and bull-headed and Joan responding in a manner that is resentful and pig-headed. Sam goes off to London to see a dress rehearsal of his highbrow play *Plethora* produced by the English Stage Society, but Joan, who cannot even pronounce the name of the play much less know what it means, opts to fly off to Nice to meet an old admirer (who owns a film studio) in an attempt to make her husband jealous. She succeeds in her efforts to make Sam anxious and the distraught husband flies back to Paris only to regale Mrs. Taylor about his marital troubles in her boudoir at 3:00 A.M. One thing leads to another with the strait-laced young bridegroom and the world-weary divorcee falling into bed together as the curtain falls on Act Two. The following morning, Joan reappears repentant from her assignation and is easily forgiven by her condescending husband who, wisely, keeps his own dalliance a secret. Also concealing the scene in her boudoir, Mrs. Taylor sends Sam and Joan off to finally have their honeymoon together, instead of with their friends.

The Philadelphia Inquirer (6 December 1932) praised Katherine Alexander as "delightful throughout" and decided that Ross Alexander and Rachel Hartzell "were convincing in their bickerings." The *Courier-Post* (6 December 1932) called Katherine Alexander a triumph and one-half of the saving grace of the production. Ross Alexander, who "carries his role well and naturally," was judged to be the other half of the saving grace of the play. *Variety* (13 December 1932) added that "Ross Alexander was a highlight as the very young husband" and gave the following notice of the play:

It impresses as a nice little play, with an even chance of being made into something more substantial if the right kind of work is done on it. As presented here first, and as seen again Saturday night, it wouldn't have a chance on Broadway, but there is the groundwork of a modest hit hidden somewhere in its system. . . . Play is being radically rewritten here, especially its second act. In fact, another character, previously only referred to, has been written into the action . . . and by the end of the week the management expects the show to be greatly strengthened. . . . Where *Honeymoon* erred mostly was in its windy dialog; sharpening and clarifying certain passages were the real needs.

Hobbling on through mixed reviews, poor attendance, and daily rewrites that reminded Ross of his experience in *The Ladder*, *Honeymoon* finally opened on Broadway at the Little Theatre on 23 December, with director Thomas Mitchell joining the cast as Bob Taylor, Leslie's ex-husband. In the rewrite, Bob tries to persuade Leslie to marry him again, guilting her into believing that their divorce was not entirely his fault. She feels sorry about that and, when Sam (in the famous boudoir scene) pulls out a gun, explaining that he had considered suicide because of his marital troubles, he and Leslie bond over the discovery of their mutual feelings of responsibility and guilt. They embrace not out of lust, as in the earlier iteration of the play, but out of empathy, and instead of falling into bed, the couple decide to go out and dance the night away.

Katherine Alexander and Ross Alexander in *Honeymoon*. An advertisement
in *The Brooklyn Daily Eagle*, Sunday 19 February 1933.

Critical reviews of the revised production appeared on Christmas Eve
and, as expected, some were naughty and some were nice. Percy Hammond
in the *Herald Tribune* (24 December 1932) did not rave about the show but
provided the positive *buzz words* subsequently used in *Honeymoon* advertising:
"The authors are urbane, the characters eloquent, the players magnetic, the
play witty." Burns Mantle in the *Daily News* (24 December 1932) wrote that
both Katherine and Ross Alexander had a naturalness and charm "that are
immediately disarming and technically sound" and argued that any comedy
with them in the cast "is pretty certain to offer compensations that justify any
evening spent in a playhouse." Writing in *The New York Times* (24 December
1932), Brooks Atkinson was rather less effusive, calling the play "bewildering
and dull" and "a pedestrian example of worldly playmaking" while admitting

that it did have its goods points, among which was the acting of Rachel Hartzell and Ross Alexander who "attack the parts of the honeymooners with considerable spirit." He did also find a third-act exchange between Sam Chapman (the new spelling of Alexander's character name) and Bob Taylor to be especially amusing:

When the two gentlemen are lounging round in a meditative mood, one of them inquires of the other at random, "Do you speak Swedish?" "No," is the answer. "Neither do I," says the interlocutor; and after a thoughtful interval he sums the whole thing up. "Hard to find anyone who speaks Swedish," he concludes. When you come to think of it, that's true.

The critic in *Variety* (27 December 1932) also found the episode diverting and singled out Ross Alexander for giving "an excellent account of himself as Sam Chapman, loquacious and cocksure of himself until the affair with Leslie." Arthur Pollock of *The Brooklyn Daily Eagle* (24 December 1932) didn't like the play which, "fashioned without skill makes rather heavy going. The dialogue is utterly devoid of that light touch so necessary to comedies of the sort and the characters live and act with very inadequate motives. The authors go on and on without ever quite making their points." Regarding the performances, he found that "Katherine Alexander, Rachel Hartzell, and Ross Alexander do their best. Perhaps it is the fact that Thomas Mitchell hasn't to talk so long as they that permits him to seem more successful."

On 9 January 1933, *Honeymoon* moved from the Little Theatre to the Vanderbilt Theatre at 148 W. 48th Street, slashing the top ticket price from $3.30 to $2.20, and cutting actors' salaries by nearly thirty percent. The show had been doing average Depression business but that proved insufficient to pay for running expenses; by lowering operating costs, and making tickets more affordable, *Honeymoon* managed to squeak by through February by taking in only $3,000 or less a week. Unfortunately, Chapman's highbrow play, *Plethora*, was the only thing about the production that suggested an overabundance and on 25 February, after playing ten weeks to meager box office receipts, *Honeymoon* finally gave up the ghost. It may have been some comfort to Ross Alexander that he was still advertised in the February 1933 issue of *Photoplay Magazine* as under contract to Paramount Publix Studios, though he was still waiting for them to tell him to report for work!

On Monday 27 February, only two days after the closing of *Honeymoon*, Ross and Katherine Alexander returned to the Vanderbilt Theatre to commence rehearsing *The Party's Over*, another Depression-era comedy written and produced by Daniel Kussell (formerly a librettist for musical comedies) and directed by Howard Lindsay (who would later join forces with Russell Crouse to write the long-running *Life with Father* and the Pulitzer-Prize-winning *State of the Union*). Ross was cast as Martin Phillips, an "irresponsible, breezy, vain" young lad, "whose one ambition is to be a radio crooner. In spite of his egotism, he is wholesome, well-bred, and lovable" (Kussell 1933, Description of Characters). He is in love with Phyllis Blakely (Peggy Conklin), the daughter in a household supported financially by her elder brother, Bruce Blakely (Harvey Stephens)), a successful businessman in love with divorcee Patricia Henley (Katherine Alexander). Even though their parents, Theodore (George Graham) and Sarah Blakely (Effie Shannon), have shirked their parental responsibilities, they still strive to remain the nominal heads of the family. Theodore is something of a Lothario who dresses like a dignified dandy and Sarah allows her interest in patriotic genealogy and work for the D.A.R. to interfere with her interest in her children. Add to this family mix another younger son, Clay Blakely (Geoffrey Bryant), a student at Yale who is stubborn, selfish, ungrateful toward his elder brother who supports him financially, and in love with Betty Decker (Claire Trevor), a waitress at a lunchroom in New Haven.

In Act One, Martin enters the Blakelys' living room with the announcement that he is getting an audition to sing on the radio and fills the room with spontaneous exclamations of "Hey, Hey" in various timbres representing radio voices. The character of Martin prompted Ross to explore and mimic the characteristic vocal patterns of radio celebrities as well as their idiosyncratic exclamations. The "Hey, Hey" of *The Party's Over* will resurface in 1936 as "Oh, Ho" in *Here Comes Carter*.

When Phyllis tries to flirt with him, he frustrates her by repeatedly referring to his audition, until she finally cracks and he capitulates:

Phyllis. Now, Martin, if you mention that audition again, I'll strangle you. Kiss me, darling. (*Passionately clings to him.*)

Martin. (*A little nervous, although he is more composed than Phyllis, looks over his shoulder to see if anyone is coming.*) Honey, what I wanted to say, was, as soon as I click, we'll get married.

Phyllis. (*Still holding on to him, with her head on his shoulder.*) I know that was what you wanted to say, but I don't want to wait for any clicks. . . . If you wanted me, nothing would matter.

Martin. Yeah, but what are we going to do, live in a tent?

Phyllis. You're going to broadcast, aren't you?

Martin. Sure, but—that's what I'm telling you. When I'm all set, then everything will be right, but until then, what are we going to do, sit in the park, and winter coming on?

Phyllis. Oh, Marty, you take all the joy out of living. Now listen, we won't have to worry. Bruce won't let us down. He'll see us through until you get going. (1, 18–20)

A series of passionate kisses from Phyllis inspires Martin to suggest that they elope immediately, but just as spontaneously he gets cold feet.

Martin. I'm not crabbing, but if this audition doesn't come off, and Bruce doesn't go for the idea, where are we?

Phyllis. We'll be together.

Martin. (*Without enthusiasm.*) Yeah?

Phyllis. (*She throws her arms around his neck and kisses him.*) Listen, Sweet, we'll take the tube to Jersey City, and in an hour we'll be married, and then—

Martin. Yeah, I know.

Phyllis. You don't know. We can keep it a secret until we want them to know. Oh, honey, I want you so— (*Kisses him longingly.*) And you want me too— (*Kisses him again.*) Let's hurry, darling.

Martin. Oh, Phyl, did you—did you bring along some money?

Phyllis. Of course, silly.

Martin. Hey, hey— (*Exits with Phyllis.*) (1, 22)

While Phyllis and Martin are off getting married, Bruce refuses to continue to pay for Clay's tuition at Yale, arguing that he shows little aptitude for college and only wants to live at Yale to be close to a girl. Mrs. Patricia Henley arrives at the Blakely residence so that Bruce can accompany her to the boat on which she will sail to Paris in order to get a divorce from her wealthy estranged husband George. As Bruce is about to leave with Mrs. Henley, Clay receives a phone call from Betty and pleads with Bruce to talk to her. Earlier Clay begged Bruce to give him $200, and the phone call would explain to Bruce the reason why. Mrs. Henley goes off to the boat alone while Bruce, feeling completely responsible for what goes on in the family, stays to answer the call.

Ross Alexander and Peggy Conklin in Act Two, scene one of *The Party's Over*. From an advertisement in the *Daily News*, Sunday 30 April 1933.

Martin and Phyllis reappear in Act Two, scene one, in bed on their wedding night at a New Jersey hotel. As in Act One, Phyllis wants nothing but to talk and make love to Martin, but as he is wearing earphones and listening to the radio, the road to lovemaking is fraught with poor reception.

Phyllis. Isn't it exciting, darling—

Martin. If I can't sing better than this pelican, I'll give it all up.

Phyllis. (*Ignoring him.*) Well, if we're found out, I'll just show them the license and this— (*Holding up her third finger, displaying wedding ring, with proud toss of her head.*) Why, I'm a very much married woman. (*Smiles longingly at Martin. Phyllis takes license out from pillow.*) I have a license, a wedding ring, and a husband—Well, wasn't Santa Claus good to you, young woman?

Martin. I wish you'd listen to this bird flat his B. Get a load of him, sweet . . . this crooner actually smells. . . . (*Tearing earphones from his head in disgust.*) If this is what they want, I give up. (2, 1, 2)

The scene continues with a discussion about when to break the news to Bruce and the family and what to do in the event he refuses to help. Phyllis restores Martin's confidence that everything will work out and, replacing his earphones, he contemplates a big radio contract with an equally large paycheck completely ignoring Phyllis's attempts to make him listen to her. Ultimately, she achieves her goal because the radio stops working. Martin, frantically trying to fix it, cries out: "This should happen to me on my honeymoon" (2, 1, 4) and orders Phyllis to call down to the desk to report a broken radio. She thanks God for small miracles as the scene ends.

Ross sits offstage for the rest of the act, during which Clay decides to marry Betty (who is pregnant—hence the need for $200) and Phyllis reveals to her family that she is married and pregnant. Bruce disapproves and refuses to support Martin, but agrees to speak to someone with connections in the radio business to help him get an audition. The act ends with Bruce sending a cable to Mrs. Henley in Paris, telling her that because of important business issues requiring his attention, he will not be able to join her as planned. As at the end of Act One, Bruce's commitment to the support of his family trumps his commitment to the woman he desires to marry.

Act Three opens on Martin, wearing his pajamas and dressing gown in the living room of the Blakely home, several weeks after the end of Act Two. Leisurely reading the newspaper and finishing his breakfast, he is in conversation with Beulah (Georgette Harvey), an African-American maid, who has just brought him his marmalade:

Martin. Oh, Beulah, like a good girl, turn on the radio for me. Dial number fifty-five.

Beulah. No, suh.

Martin. What do you mean, "No suh"?

Beulah. The radio ain't workin'.

Martin. Why, I had it on until early this morning.

Beulah. And that's why it ain't workin' now. I heard the old gent'man say you kept the house awake most the night, and this morning he took one of the tubes out and says, "He'll be damned if yo'–all will keep him up no mo'."

Martin. Always clowning. (*Beulah starts to leave.*) Wait a minute.

Beulah. Wot yo'–all want? I got my Sunday dinner to cook.

Martin. Now listen, Beulah. You've heard me sing and you've listened to those fellows on the radio.

Beulah. Yes, sir—mos' all las' night—

Martin. I want your honest opinion. How do you think my voice compares with those you've heard on the radio?

Beulah. I think yo're all rotten.

Martin. A fine critic. (3, 2)

Evidently Beulah's assessment is identical to the one Martin receives from Bruce's associate who didn't like Martin's voice and argued that he had no chance of a career in radio. Martin rebounds from the criticism saying, "well, it's only one man's opinion" (3, 4), and exits as Clay enters with Betty, now his bride, hoping that Bruce will afford them the same courtesy as he

145

did with Phyllis in allowing her husband to live in the family house. Bruce, however, will have none of it and orders them out of the house—a command Betty is eager to obey since she is nervous about meeting the family, who inauspiciously arrive as Clay and Betty are leaving.

A few days later, Bruce's business is about to go bankrupt unless he gets a substantial loan; Mrs. Henley, having returned from Paris, appears at Bruce's office and tells him that if he were penniless at four o'clock, she would marry him at five o'clock. Bruce suddenly decides that his commitment to Mrs. Henley trumps his commitment to his freeloading family and when the loan he was hoping for finally comes, he refuses it. Scene three opens on a game of Bridge played by Clay and Betty against Martin and Phyllis. Since Martin is the dummy hand, he is playing the ukulele, which antagonizes Father (Theodore) Blakely:

> **Father**. Stop that music. I can't think. (*Martin stops.*)
>
> **Phyllis**. Aw, dad, don't be a pill.
>
> **Clay**. Amusing yourself is taboo around here.
>
> **Father**. You don't call that amusement?
>
> **Martin**. This is my swan song, Dad.
>
> **Father**. Your what?
>
> **Phyllis**. Haven't you heard, dad? Martin's going in the movies.
>
> **Martin**. Listen, sweet, you'll have to get some photographs taken—you know, wife of a movie star at home—baking pies—planting geraniums—sewing on tiny garments—hot dickie dee doo.
>
> **Father**. How soon are you going in pictures?
>
> **Martin**. As soon as I take my [screen]test. (3, 29)

Bruce enters and tells his family that he is bankrupt and that they are now all on their own, with the exception of his mother for whom he managed to put aside a bequest. Mrs. Henley appears to rush off with Bruce to be married, leaving the curtain line to Martin who enters and speaks to Father Blakely: "Oh, Dad, Mother wants you. There's a meeting of the parasites" (3, 34).

146

The Party's Over had been scheduled to open at the Vanderbilt Theatre on 22 March 1933, but due to extensive redecorations in the theatre, the opening was postponed until the 27th. Ross thoroughly enjoyed playing Martin Phillips since the role traded on all of his theatrical strengths and many of the reviews shared his enthusiasm. Burns Mantle (*Daily News*, 28 March 1933) found Ross Alexander and Peggy Conklin "paired as two saucy impertinences eloquently representative of the most persistently parasitical of all younger generation types. They play these two right up to the exclamation point in both parts." The play, he suggested, "pleasantly reflects a phase of life among the parasites during the closing days of the disappearing depression. And it did . . . create a lot of laughter last night." Arthur Pollock (*The Brooklyn Daily Eagle*, 28 March 1933) said succinctly: "Katherine Alexander, Ross Alexander, Peggy Conklin, Harvey Stephens, Effie Shannon, George Graham, Geoffrey Bryant, Claire Trevor all do nicely with their roles. The audience liked them and the play too. It will probably prosper." Similarly, in *The Brooklyn Citizen* (28 March 1933), Alvin J. Kayden wrote that "The cast of *The Party's Over* cannot be overpraised." The *Variety* (4 April 1933) notice, however, was less effusive, suggesting that "As a spring presentation, *The Party's Over* is fair diversion with doubtful chances of registering." Nonetheless, Ross, as the would-be radio crooner was judged to be "diverting early in the going in a part that had most of the comedy chances." The *Barnard Bulletin* (7 April 1933) was particularly laudatory toward Ross, writing, "A most hearty pat on the back should be rendered Ross Alexander for his work as Martin Phillips, the young radio hopeful who spends his marriage night with a pair of ear receivers clamped on his head. That certain husky exuberance in his voice and the infectious good cheer which he manages to put into his 'hey, hey's' are by themselves worth the price of admission."

Notably, on 7 April 1933, the Cullen-Harrison Act, legalizing the sale in the United States of beer with an alcoholic content of 3.2 percent, went into effect, thus marking the beginning of the end of Prohibition. Ross celebrated the event by organizing a block party for the casts of shows that were playing on 48th Street, including *The Party's Over* (148 W 48), *Saturday Night* (137 W

48) and *Three-Cornered Moon* (138 W 48). As Ross described in an interview in the *Oakland Tribune* (23 August 1936), "That night after the show I organized a party to celebrate the return of beer. We had lots of fun and somebody [Henry Fonda] suggested that the parties ought to be continued. So, we rented the lower floor of an old building [a pub on West Forty-First Street] that was being used for a speakeasy, put in a beer tap and had a party once a week from then on. We served beer and steak sandwiches, and I broiled the steaks." In his biography of Jimmy Stewart, *Pieces of Time* (1997), Gary Fishgall adds that for a dollar, partygoers got all the beer they could drink and hobo steaks—huge slabs of beef cooked with salt on both sides (58). Alexander's actual method consisted of covering steaks with an inch layer of wet salt and holding the meat close to the flame until the salt hardens and lifts off the meat. Then, turn and do the same for the other side. In his memoir *So Far, So Good* (1994), Burgess Meredith recalled that the clientele of the club included Margaret Sullavan, Ruth Gordon, Barbara O'Neil, and Myron McCormick. "One night I wandered in to find a weird concert in progress. Jimmy Stewart was behind an accordion, with Dick Foran providing harmony. As an ex-boy tenor, I was invited to join them—it didn't require much prodding—and that was the beginning of the Stewart-Meredith partnership" (102). Fishgall added that guests also included actresses Helen Hayes and Katharine Cornell as well as clarinetist Benny Goodman who was kept tooting night after night until he couldn't pucker (58–59). In addition, *Modern Screen* (23 June 1936) reported that during this time, Ross belonged to a club comprised of six young Broadway hopefuls who would meet for lunch every week. The member who had received the best "break" theatrically that week would treat. There were many weeks, however, when all six members bought their own lunches. The other members of the club were Henry Fonda, Jimmy Stewart, Brian Donlevy, Owen Davis, Jr., and Elisha Cook.

Six weeks after it opened, *The Party's Over* lived up to its name and closed on 6 May 1933. The play was good enough to have been purchased by Harry Cohn for Columbia Pictures (at the cost of $17, 500—$255, 614 in 2019 dollars) but not good enough for an extended run on Broadway. Ross watched as Harvey Stephens left for Hollywood to repeat the role of Bruce Blakely in the film version followed by Claire Trevor (Betty Decker) who had earned a six-months contract with Fox. With his own ultimately disappointing attempt at a film career firmly in his memory, he wished his colleagues all the best of luck and hoped that they could navigate the studio system better than he. Stephens, who had actually made his film debut in *The Cheat* (1931) opposite Tallulah Bankhead, ultimately did not reprise his role in the film; Stuart Irwin was cast instead. Nevertheless, Stephens had a lively film and television career that extended through the 1960s. Claire Trevor likewise had an extensive film resume, beginning with *Life in the Raw* (1933) and ending with *Kiss Me Goodbye* (1982), in addition to a notable television guest-starring career.

After the demise of *The Party's Over*, Ross (who had been living with Aleta Freel at her parents' home in Jersey City) accompanied Aleta to the Westchester Playhouse at Mount Kisco, New York, where she had been invited by producer Frank Day Tuttle and director Monty Woolley to join the resident company that included their friends Henry Fonda, Mildred Natwick, and Margaret Sullavan, Fonda's ex-wife. *Fonda: My Life* (1981) paints a lively picture of that summer in Mount Kisco:

The company lived together in a beautiful sprawling inn called the Kettle House. The inn had a large dining room, two tables with linen placemats, crystal goblets, silverware, and good china. Tuttle had inherited a fortune from his father and preferred luxurious surroundings. . . .

Now, on July Fourth, as they sat in the dining room, ten people at a table, Tuttle said to Fonda, "Let's do the fireworks again this year." Fonda agreed. During dinner the leading man carried his beaten-up felt hat from actor to actor, taking up a collection. They needed only about twelve dollars. The men dug into the pockets of their white duck trousers. The women snapped open their change purses. Dimes, quarters, a dollar bill now and again. Then Fonda reached Sullavan [who had recently signed a three-year movie contract at $1,200 a week]. He held the hat before her. She shook her head no. He thought she was being facetious. He moved his hat closer to her shoulder. Sullavan shook her head more vigorously.

"You mean you're not going to put in anything?" Fonda asked in a stage whisper. Sullavan refused to answer. Instead she munched another bite of her salad.

Tuttle observed that though Fonda continued around the table, "You could see he was smoldering." At last he turned to Ross Alexander and said, "Christ! And with the money some people are making."

Sullavan didn't wait ten seconds. She pushed back her chair, picked up a goblet of ice water and poured it over Fonda's head. (83)

Ross Alexander did not remain in Mount Kisco long after the Fourth of July because he was called to replace Henry Hull in the lead role of *Under Glass*, a play in tryout at the Mariarden Theatre in Peterborough, New Hampshire, beginning 17 July 1933. The play, by George Bradshaw and Eva K. Flint, also featured Jane Bramley and Brian Donlevy in principal roles and told the story of newlyweds who argue so violently (shades of *Honeymoon*) that they agree to a trial separation, during which the husband appropriates his father-in-law's mistress, and the wife goes to Reno. Instead of a divorce, of course, a reconciliation is reached and the newlyweds live happily (if contentiously) ever after. During his stay in Peterborough, Ross befriended William H. Mayo, the ex-president of United States Rubber, a wealthy patron of the theatre at the Mariarden Theatre, and one of the backers of *Under Glass*. Mayo, who was a self-styled bachelor, performed in a number of plays at the theatre and was well-regarded as an actor. *The Boston Globe* (19 October 1933) even suggested that he planned to "take a part in *Under Glass* when it should open in New York City." Given Alexander's propensity for attracting wealthy older men, it would be easy to imagine a romantic relationship between him and the bachelor Mayo. Of course, no one who was present in Peterborough at the time has commented on such things and it was publicist Jerry Asher who, years after the fact, brought Ross's assignations with older men to light.

Immediately following the week's run of *Under Glass* which had been a huge success in New Hampshire, Ross was off to Dennis, Massachusetts, where a new John Golden and Charlotte Armstrong play, *Two Can't Be Happy* (AKA *Love Is Not All*, *Nobody but You*, and *Alone Together*) was scheduled to try out at the Cape Playhouse on 28 August under the direction of Golden and Alexander Dean, the artistic director of the theatre. Ross was cast as John Spratt, Jr. who meets Marnie Peebles (Elizabeth Love) on a six weeks' cruise and falls in love at first sight. They cannot seem to find any privacy aboard ship due to the presence of a bevy of curious passengers, including John Sprat, Sr. (John Doyle); John Junior's sister, Stella (Dorothy Vernon); her playwright husband, Paddy Driscoll (Porter Hall); Mrs. Erminie Weddle (Hildur Ouse), a gushing widow; Hortense Roach (Dortha Duckworth), a middle-age lady eloping with a voluble Spaniard, Louis Arroyo (Roman Bohnen); Cora Gilly (Barna Ostertag), the officious daughter trying to stifle the enjoyment of her father, Felix Gilly (John Daly Murphy), an old man out for a fling with the young and fetching Magnolia Reeves (Emma Bunting); a distracted ship's captain, Captain Trudgeon (Boyd Davis); and the usual variety of ship's officers and stewards. As a result, John and Marnie hide away in a lifeboat so that they can spoon in private. A well-timed tropical storm manages to detach the lifeboat from the ship and sets it ashore on a desert island (not unlike Henry De Vere Stacpoole's 1908 novel, *The Blue Lagoon*). John and Marnie marry one another based on their memory of a traditional marriage ceremony; but, a year and a half later, tired of living like castaways and bored with each other, the no-longer-newlyweds bicker constantly and agree to live apart (as in the play *Under Glass*). Evidently John has proved to be an inefficient Robinson Crusoe and the eventual presence of a baby only causes more stress for Marnie and more tension between her and her useless husband. Once they are rescued, the couple realize that marriage can only be success if there are distractions—hobbies, pastimes, recreational pursuits, entertainments, and the company of friends.

Reviewing the production, *Variety* (5 September 1933) determined that "The idea is promising, but it has not been fully developed here. Of the three acts, the second alone, with its amusingly contrasted scenes, its suggestion of a parody on *The Admirable Crichton*, and its mingling of sentiment and

151

comedy, seems ready for professional use. The other two acts are rambling, inconclusive, and burdened with an excess of unimportant characters. The play as it stands calls for extensive rewriting, pruning and redistribution of emphasis."

Following the week's run of *Two Can't Be Happy* at the Cape Playhouse, Golden and Armstrong went sullenly back to the drawing board, and Ross returned to rehearsing *Under Glass*, announced for a 23 October opening, directed and produced by William B. Friedlander for the newly formed New York Plays Corporation. Five days prior to the advertised premiere, Alexander's friend William H. Mayo, one of the backers of the play, committed suicide by shooting himself in the head. News reports cited despondency over years of ill health as the cause. Whether it was out of respect for Mayo, or simply because the play was unready, the Broadway opening of *Under Glass* at the Ambassador Theatre was postponed until 30 October when a more polished version of what had been previewed in New Hampshire faced the New York City critics.

Ross Alexander in *Under Glass*. Publicity photo in the *Daily News*, 31 October 1933.

Ross reprised the role of Tony Pell, the young and inexperienced husband, married to the virginal Stephanie ("Steve") Schuyler Pell, played by Ethel Barrymore Colt, daughter of the "First Lady of the American Theatre," Ethel Barrymore, in her first leading role. As in the New Hampshire iteration, set in the New York City living room of Stephanie's father William Schuyler (Boyd Irwin), Tony and Pell separate, and Tony takes a mistress, the actress Mari Fielding (Leona Maricle), formerly the lover of his father-in-law, and moves out of his house. While Stephanie is in Reno securing a divorce, Tony's friend John Douglas (Robert Keith) carries on an epistolary courtship with her, at the same time she is wooing the affections of Edward B. Ransome (Harry Shannon), her divorce lawyer. To rankle Tony, Stephanie accepts both men's proposal of marriage, but after she returned from Reno, she reveals that she has no intention of marrying either of them. As she and Tony continue to spar, Mari enters and, using lines from the dramatic roles she has played, attempts to lure Tony back to their apartment. Watching from the upstairs landing, Stephanie counters by throwing down a pair of Tony's pajamas, and Tony follows her into her bedroom. Having waiting all night for Tony to reappear, Mari reveals that she is in love with Tony and will entrap him, pretending to be pregnant if necessary, in order to win him back. She, however, completely underestimates Stephanie's ability to manipulate men in the final scene of the play:

Tony. (*Breaking.*) Steve—you're not going to let me go?

Steve. What do you think?

Tony. (*He takes her in his arms.*) Oh, darling, can't you see, can't you hear, can't you feel—I love you—I love you, every inch of me—I want you—there's no one else in the world for me, no one. And there never will be. Oh, Steve! (*He kisses her. A long kiss. They break. She turns away.*)

Steve. (*Forcing it out.*) It's too late.

Tony. Damn! (*Mari enters in a Vionnet gown with a fur coat over her arm.*)

Mari. Well, I'm ready. It didn't take me long, did it?

Steve. (*Blowing her nose.*) No—you were quite fast. . . . My dear, you look perfectly lovely.

Mari. Do you like it? It's Vionnet. Are you ready, Tony? . . .

Tony. In a moment.

Mari. Well, Stephanie, goodbye—I've had a lovely time.

Steve. I'm so glad. If I ever have another husband, I'll ask you over. . . . Goodbye.

Tony. It's been nice knowing you. (*Mari is in the doorway.*)

Steve. Thank you. (*She smiles at him.*) It's been nice knowing you too. And I hope we can see each other sometime—and always remain friends.

Tony. Oh, Steve—

Steve. Goodbye—and Tony— (*She hesitates.*) I wish you all the success and happiness and love that we almost had—Oh—

Tony. Steve! Steve! (*He rushes to her and picks her up in his arms.*) Darling—darling—what's the matter?

Steve. Goodbye, Tony—never mind, never mind, goodbye.

Tony. What is it? Steve—

Steve. It's nothing I want to bother you about—go away, Tony—

Tony. Tony. Oh, darling, tell me— (*She whispers in his ear—happily.*) What? Oh, God, Steve—oh, darling, why didn't you tell me before. (*She waves over Tony's shoulder to Mari.*)

Steve. I only just found out myself.

Tony. You can't send me away now.

Steve. (*She puts her arm around his neck.*) No, darling. I never meant to— (*A pause. He buries his head in her bosom. Mari stands in the door and shakes her head.*)

Mari. Well—I'm damned.

Curtain. (3, 26–28)

In *The New York Times* (31 October 1933), Brooks Atkinson wrote that "As the versatile Tony, Ross Alexander gives a jaunty performance," but regarding the play as a whole he determined that "the difference between a sophisticated and a distasteful comedy is largely a matter of style. When the style of the writing and acting is slovenly, the fun can sound pretty sordid. It does in *Under Glass*." In *The Brooklyn Daily Eagle* (31 October 1933), Arthur Pollock was generous in his criticism of Ethel Barrymore's daughter but dismissive of the rest of the cast. The playwriting he determined "seldom succeeds in getting beyond the tepid point, for [the authors] have neither the wit nor the agility for the brewing of light entertainment." With the headline, "*Under Glass* Is a Feeble Farce" (*Daily News*, 31 October 1933), Burns Mantle began his review of the "rambling and incoherent yarn, flightily directed by William Friedlander, who produced it, and nervously acted by its young people." One of the "young things," however, he noted, "is played by Ross Alexander, a comely and capable lad." Later, on 12 November, in a syndicated article, "Does New Play Called *World Waits* Debunk Admiral Byrd," Burns Mantle recalled *Under Glass* and called Ross "one of the theater's defter juveniles."

Variety (7 November 1933) wrote that "*Under Glass* has the elements of smartness in the sense that it reflects that type of intelligence associated with sophisticated, wealthy New Yorkers. But somehow the writing doesn't keep pace with the idea, impression being it isn't effective enough to make the Broadway grade." However, the opinion regarding Ross was much more positive: "Ross Alexander is the lively, loquacious Tony. He's a good-looking juve who has been around for several seasons. Talent scouts somehow passed him up, but after the *Glass* premiere, a flock of 'em went back-stage to talk over Hollywood with him." *Under Glass* closed on 4 November after only a week on Broadway, but by the end of the run, Ross Alexander had been cast in another film.

11. *Social Register*

Under Glass closed on Broadway on 4 November 1933. Ten days later Ross Alexander was out in Astoria in the cast of *Social Register*, a film based on the 1931 play by Anita Loos and her husband John Emerson, starring the popular silent film actress Colleen Moore, and produced and directed by Marshall ("Mickey") Nielan, a prominent actor, writer, and director of the silent film era. Nielan and Moore were old friends who had worked together in a number of films, including *Dinty* (1920), *The Lotus Eater* (1921), and *Her Wild Oat* (1927). Moore had temporarily left the industry after the advent of sound pictures and Nielan's well-known addiction to alcohol had made him unreliable and difficult. *Social Register* was the first of seven planned talkies to be produced by Nielan's newly formed company, Associated Film Productions, and released by Harry Cohn and Columbia Pictures.

Ross was cast as Lester Trout, a saxophonist who freeloads off of the appropriately christened Patsy Shaw (Colleen Moore), claiming to have lost his job and feigning sickness. Patsy, a Broadway chorine, had won a scavenger hunt at a party thrown by Robert Benchley (himself) by stealing a necktie from the home of wealthy socialite Henry Breene (John Miltern). Breene's son Charlie (Alexander Kirkland) retrieves the tie and becomes smitten with Patsy, so much so that in the third month of their courtship, he presents her with an expensive diamond bracelet. Against the advice of her chorus-girl friends, Patsy, always the easy mark, lends the bracelet to Trout so that he can pay off his debts. Now that Patsy has a rich steady boyfriend, Trout expects to drain her dry.

Charlie's mother, "Maggie" (Pauline Frederick), hoping to sever the romantic relationship between her elitist son and a chorus girl, invites Patsy to a posh party where she is sure to make a fool of herself. Instead of making a fool of herself, however, Patsy ends up entertaining the sophisticated guests who find her more charming than the vocal quartet singing tiresome English glees. Even the alleged ultra-conservative family patriarch Jefferson Breene (Charles Winninger) does not oppose Patsy's relationship with Charlie since, under the alias, "Jonesie," he is having an affair with Gloria (Margaret Livingston) one of Patsy's roommates. Still intent on breaking up the couple, Maggie instructs the family lawyer Albert Wiggins (Edward Garvie) to pay Trout $5,000 to lure Patsy to his Long Island shack and arrange to have her sleep there overnight. Trout sends Patsy a telegram claiming to be deathly ill, knowing that she will immediately rush to his aid, and as soon as she arrives, he manages to cajole the sympathetic and big-hearted Patsy into nursing him through the night. Charlie discovers her whereabouts and appears, unannounced, the next morning, at Trout's address, where it appears that Patsy has been unfaithful to him.

Ross Alexander, Colleen Moore, Alexander Kirkland in 'Social Register,' opening at the Temple Sunday.

Charlie finds Patsy alone with Lester Trout. Advertisement in *The Ithaca Journal*, 5 May 1934.

Charlie breaks up with Patsy, allowing the parasitic saxophonist to sweep in and convince her to marry him. Almost immediately after she is married, Patsy discovers the $5,000 check from attorney Wiggins and realizes how severely she has been manipulated. She confronts her husband about the check before tearing it to pieces and demands an explanation. Unable to disentangle himself from the plot to keep Patsy and Charlie apart, but still attempting to manipulate his wife's sympathies, Trout admits to what he was paid to do. Patsy subsequently forces Charlie's mother to confess her involvement in the plot by threatening to give the entire story to the newspapers. Maggie breaks down and implores Patsy not to disgrace her, to which the ever-sympathetic Patsy agrees. Charlie Breene begs Patsy's forgiveness, which is again freely given, and following their reconciliation, he orders Wiggins to annul Patsy's very brief marriage to Lester Trout.

Colleen Moore and Ross Alexander in "Social Register" at Arcade Thursday.

With check in hand, Patsy confronts Trout. Advertisement in the *The Paducah Sun Democrat*, 11 March 1934.

Ross enjoyed working with Colleen Moore, Charles Winninger (the Captain Andy of *Show Boat*) and Alexander Kirkland (Dr. Fergusen in Sidney Kingsley's Pulitzer-Prize-winning *Men in White*); Ross found that he and Kirkland shared many of the same tastes in theatre and they spent many an evening together discussing Lee Strasberg, Harold Clurman and Stella Adler. He also discovered that they shared similar sexual attractions which made for a lively working relationship. Additionally, Ross felt privileged to be around the well-known piano duo, Jacques Fray and Mario Braggiotti, and the much-loved vocalist with the Paul Whiteman Orchestra, Ramona. Both the piano duo and Ramona performed musical numbers at Robert Benchley's party in the film. Margaret Livingston was Paul Whiteman's wife, so the band leader was often in attendance at the studio and Ross appreciated the opportunity of getting to know him as well.

According to *The Film Daily* (16 November 1933), production of *Social Register* got under way on Tuesday 14 November at the Eastern Service Studios in Astoria, Queens. A week later, the same publication released an update of the film's progress:

> Eastern Service Studio Notes: A varied assortment of bright colored berets adorn the heads of Mickey Nielan, Cameraman, Merritt Gerstad and the entire technical staff on the production of *Social Register* . . . [Associate producer] William de Mille set the fashion with his navy blue top piece, and to add more color to the general atmosphere Neilan provided a dozen of the funny little hats for his crew . . . Colleen Moore putting [Prop master] Dan Doran on the scout for furniture for her miniature doll house which is her greatest hobby . . . [Assistant director] Harold Godsoe hiding behind dark glasses to evade the extras . . .(*The Film Daily*, 24 November 1933)

Because his alcoholism was not a secret to the cast and crew, Neilan sought to make the filming process as enjoyable and hassle-free as possible.

Ross had a great time playing the parasite and romantic antihero, especially after Regina Crewe, Motion Picture Editor of the *New York American* wrote on 25 November 1933: "The brilliant Mickey [Nielan] has Colleen Moore for his star, and in the cast are Pauline Frederick, Alexander Kirkland, Margaret Livingston, Charles Winninger, and others including Ross alexander, a youngster curiously overlooked by the movies until now, who may prove to be the film 'find' of the year."

Filming of *Social Register* was completed on 6 December after which Ross and many of his fellow actors continued their stage careers. Colleen Moore returned to her home in Los Angeles and sued David O. Selznick, producer at MGM for $1500 rent due on her residence which he occupied from 6 November 1933 to 6 December 1933, while she was in the East filming *Social Register*. Prior to the release of the film on 10 March 1934, Jerry Wald wrote in *The Hollywood Reporter* (1 February 1934): "With the majority of the motion picture producers always on the lookout for new 'stars-to-be,' how come they've all passed up Ross Alexander and Frank Parker of the air waves? Alexander, who is by no means bad on the eyes, can out-act most of our present 'top' male attractions, while Parker, who sings sweet songs for sponsors, is the 't-d-h' type (tall, dark and handsome). You can thank me for the tip." Obviously, Alexander was being noticed by Hollywood columnists even before the film had opened. After *Social Register* was viewed, however, Ross was not mentioned in mainline reviews except as a cast member, and the movie was universally savaged by the critics. *Harrison's Reports* (24 March 1934) began its review: "Poor! The story is trite and the action slow. Although the heroine is a sympathetic character it is not enough to hold the interest, since most of the other characters and their doings arouse an apathetic feeling in the spectator." The reviewer continued, "Nothing novel is presented in the story, which is poorly directed, and the performances are ordinary. Colleen Moore struggles with a part that is wholly unsuited to her" and concluded that the film was "Unsuitable for children, adolescents, or Sundays." *The Film Daily* (18 August 1934) wrote that "A weak story, awkwardly unfolded handicaps this one," and *Variety* (9 October 1934) proclaimed that "this trite development of a none too bright stage play has all the signals against it. . . . Story, based on a conventional appeal, has no real suspense, and the picture is overboard on footage. Camera work seldom reaches the average level and the rest ranges from poor to bad. Direction is generally good but there's nothing to direct."

Both Ross and the film did merit a positive reaction, however, in *The Paducah Sun-Democrat* (14 March 1934) from Paducah, Kentucky. Writing that the movie "without qualification can be termed a one hundred percent audience picture . . . *Social Register* is rightfully described as an hilarious comedy, although it is properly balanced with a touch of romantic drama. . . . Ross Alexander, recruited from the Broadway stage, gives promise of developing into a film star of the first rank." Since *Social Register* proved to be a disaster at the box office, one might question the validity of the claim that it was "a one hundred percent audience picture," but it is difficult to be dismissive of the comment about Ross Alexander since it had been echoed in major outlets. The charismatic lad with the dark curly hair and striking blue eyes had managed to charm theatregoers in Boston, Nashville, Chicago, Philadelphia, and New York, so shouldn't he have had a similar effect on audiences throughout the United States through the medium of moving pictures? His first two outings in the film industry produced two failed films and no new prospects so Ross returned to what had always been his comfort zone, the legitimate stage. He felt ill-equipped to be a film actor: he did not believe himself handsome and rarely thought he photographed well; he found his "hot-potato-mouth" voice difficult to modulate and unattractive on film; and, perhaps most of all, he resented the fact that he was ultimately out of control of his performance. Without consulting him, the director and film editor decided how he would appear in the final footage, and he had to smile and pretend that everything the audience sees is what he had intended. At least onstage, Ross received the immediate gratification of an honest audience response to his work. Doing a film, there were no laughs, no applause, just the white noise of the machinery to propel him. Why he would continue to seek a career in a medium that seemed antithetical to his aesthetic instincts is the subject of the second part of this book; but now we rejoin Ross Alexander as he and John Golden renew their collaboration on Broadway.

12. John Golden's Broadway (3)

As early as March 1933, it was announced that John Golden had purchased the rights to Samson Raphaelson's play *The Wooden Slipper* for production during the 1933–1934 season with Ross Alexander in the leading male role. By mid-October, however, John Golden was in rehearsal with *A Divine Drudge*, a dramatization by Golden and Vicki Baum of her novel *And Life Goes On*, and the *Daily News* (13 October 1933) announced that *The Wooden Slipper* had become the property of producers Charles Hopkins and Raymond Moore who planned to put the play into rehearsal as soon as their production of Rodney Ackland's *Strange Orchestra* opened on 28 November 1933. Because *Strange Orchestra* closed after its initial performance at a loss of their entire investment, Hopkins and Moore sold the rights to *The Wooden Slipper* to Dwight Deere Wiman who placed the play into rehearsal, under the direction of the author, on 11 December, the week after *Social Register* completed filming.

At the end of the first week of rehearsal Ross appeared in Gilbert W. Gabriel's syndicated article, "Many Good Players in Stage Year," where he was called "one of the most cheering and buoyant of the younger comedians," an early Christmas present from a columnist to kindle Alexander's holiday spirits—not that they needed kindling. Ross thoroughly enjoyed working on *The Wooden Slipper* primarily because the author/director gave him free reign with his role, allowing him to improvise stage business that provided comedy as well as pathos. Ross portrayed Andre Lebrun, a proud, artistic chef who has been jilted by his girlfriend Antoinette (Alice Reinhart) for a "distinguished, somewhat portly, middle-aged man" (Raphaelson 1934, 12). On board the Orient Express in Budapest, bound for Paris, Andre meets Julie Zigurny (Dorothy Hall), the homely, untalented daughter of the famous theatrical Zigurny Family, whose fiancé has fallen in love with her beautiful, gifted actress-sister Ina (Ruth Altman). The two commiserate passionately:

Andre. You never went through what I'm going through. Nobody ever did—Nobody. Tears and blood and death. . . . My sweetheart—'Toinette—my treasure. Two years we have known each other. I was unhappy every day, every night. It was marvelous—Ten days ago she left Paris. Going to visit relatives in Budapest—that's what *she* said—There are no relatives—no relatives at all—It was a man—And I bought her a magnificent traveling bag—for her holiday. . . . I got to Budapest one day too late—but I'll get them in Paris. I'll cut her throat from ear to ear.

Julie. (*Stiffens. She leans toward him.*) Kill them both!

Andre. By the eternal, I will! . . .

Julie. And then you can look at them—dead at your feet.

Andre. It'll be wonderful—wonderful! —And then—

Julie. (*Reaching the heights.*) And then—you can kill yourself!

Andre. (*Recoiling.*) Kill myself! Are you crazy? What about my career?

Julie. Your career? (*Deeply envious.*) You have a career!

Andre. Of course, I have a career.

Julie. How wonderful.

Andre. Now that you mention it—it *is* wonderful to have something to live for. (*Pause.*)

Julie. Then you can't kill her, can you?

Andre. I suppose not.

Julie. That's too bad.

Andre. Yes—It's hell when you have to sit—and do nothing—and kill no one. (1:3, 40–41)

Andre reveals that he is a cook, "the son of the son of the son of the chef to Louis the Fourteenth" (1:3, 42), who, if it were not for his youth, would be world-famous. Impressed by his bravado, Julie (giving her name as Jenny Schmidt) tells him that she is looking for work as a kitchen maid and Andre offers to help her acquire a position in Paris.

Act Two finds Andre and Julie/Jenny working together in the kitchen of Count Longare's Parisian home. As might be expected, the kitchen maid is falling in love with the self-absorbed chef who finally sees the signs and asks:

Andre. Are you—are you perhaps personally interested in me?

Julie. Do you want me to be?

Andre. I don't think so.

Julie. Then I'm not.

Andre. (*Sternly*.) Jenny—don't lie to me.

Julie. (*Her voice breaking*.) I'm not lying.

Andre. What are you crying for?

Julie. I'm not crying. (*But she is*.)

Andre. (*Coming close to her*.) Would you perhaps like me to kiss you, Jenny?

Julie. No.—Would you like to? (*Suddenly Andre kisses her. When the kiss is over, he stares at her a moment. Julie looks back at him anxiously. Abruptly he walks away from her a few steps, then turns and stares at her from a distance, then he comes over to her again, hands clasped behind his back. Julie trembles*.) Was it—no good? (*Andre stares at her a moment in silence, then he paces away from her again, arms clasped behind his back, and toward her again. He pauses in his pacing*.)

Andre. Well! I'm surprised—All I can say is—I'm surprised! (*Julie stares at him happily*) (2:1, 55–56)

When Mortimer Pavlicek (Paul Guilfoyle), a wealthy devotee of the

Zigurny Family and prospective suitor to Julie, persuades her to go on stage in the lead role of a play he insists on producing in Budapest, Andre realizes that Julie/Jenny is more than a mere kitchen maid saying, "A lady—! I knew there was something wrong with her from the minute I met her!" (2, 2, 68). After three months of extensive study and rehearsal, the day for Julie's theatrical debut arrives, and with it comes Andre to the Zigurny residence with the announcement that he is opening a restaurant in Paris and the offer of employment for Julie as a cashier. His view of Julie as a good dish washer does not sit well with Otto Zigurny (Montagu Love) who sees the cook as mere comic relief and demands his immediate withdrawal from the premises. Andre leaves the house but attends Julie's premiere. Prior to his altercation with Otto, Andre has a telling piece of business in which, entering the room, "*He carries his hat in his hand. He looks around and is somewhat puzzled that the room is empty. Shyly, he feels the brocade on a chair. He takes a biscuit from a dish, tastes it, drops the rest of it back in the dish, and empties the dish in the waste basket. He sits with more confidence*" (3:1, 76).

Julie's debut, not unexpectedly, receives a hostile response from the audience as well as members of her family who finally must admit how completely unfit for the stage she is. Andre, on the other hand, is mesmerized by Julie's performance and finds her the most glamorous woman in the world:

Andre. From your first entrance I was spellbound. Oh, I may be an insignificant cook, but I know greatness when I see it. . . . To think you were in the same kitchen with me for six months! It couldn't have happened. It's like a dream . . . I love you, I've always loved you—Julie.

Julie. Go on, Andre.

Andre. But I'm a cook.

Julie. You're Andre.

Andre. You're right. I *am* Andre. I left the old place—Do you know the corner of Rue de Rivoli and Avenue des Anges?

Julie. I know it very well.

Andre. That's where my restaurant is going to be. "Andre's."

Julie. Do you need a cashier?

Andre. (*Shaken.*) I—I see—For a moment I thought you meant it—but it's all right—I deserve it—

Julie. No, Andre. I mean what I'm saying. What's a career to me, if you love me? What do I care for fame, for applause, for millions of people, when I can have you?

Andre. These beautiful hands in a kitchen. No, no.

Julie. Listen, Andre. Let's take the first train to Paris. We won't even read tomorrow's newspapers—so they'll never stand between us. Will you marry me, Andre?

Andre. (*Embracing* her.) Oh, Julie!

Julie. Jenny to you! (3:2, 84–85)

Ross Alexander and Dorothy Hall in *The Wooden Slipper*.

On Friday and Saturday, 29 and 30 December, *The Wooden Slipper* gave two public previews at the Ritz Theatre prior to a scheduled 1 January 1934 opening. Audience reactions during the previews indicated that more work was required before the play could officially open and the premiere was moved to Wednesday 3 January. Brooks Atkinson, writing in *The New York Times* (4 January 1934) had only good things to say about the cook and Ross Alexander: "[Raphaelson's] Paris cook is a delight, for Andre is no humble servitor of the classes. He thinks of himself as an artist. He talks with rapture about his genius with sauces. He swaggers around his kitchen like a lord of creation. There is nothing else in the play that is so delightful. . . . It is fortunate for all of us that Ross Alexander plays the part of the inspired cook. For Mr. Alexander has not only an engaging personality, but an infectious sense of humor and considerable skill as an actor. Every scene in which he appears begins to ripple with comedy and expectancy." Burns Mantle, in the *Daily News* (4 January 1934) echoed Atkinson's view saying "the cook, as Ross Alexander plays him is much the most attractive human in the cast." Complaining about the author's stage direction and dragging dialogue, Mantle continued, "Ross Alexander, on the other hand, evidently doing his own directing of Ross Alexander, makes so amusing and splendid a fellow of the proud cook that he saves many a scene." In *The Brooklyn Daily Eagle* (4 January 1934), Arthur Pollock noted that "Ross Alexander is the young cook. Mr. Alexander is never animation itself and that nice voice of his ought really someday to get life into it, but he plays more persuasively than ever he has before." *The Hollywood Reporter* (9 January 1934) declared that "Ross Alexander is simply a joy in the role of the chef, and by comparison with the rest of the company and the lines given them it's a little hard to figure out whether he had all the best lines to say or whether he really managed to say them better than the rest." In addition, the *Motion Picture Herald* (12 February 1934) cited that "Ross Alexander was good—the one bright spot" in the production.

Although Ross received some of the finest notices of his career, *The Wooden Slipper* was found to be lacking in wit and lightness and a "lack of determination to be one thing or the other and through the unevenness of its tempo and moods, turns out to be a whatnot that sounds as though it were a poor translation" (*The Hollywood Reporter*, 9 January 1934). Because of the mixed reviews—generally good for the cast, generally poor for the play—Dwight Deere Wiman closed it after 5 performances on Saturday 6 January. The following week Ross Alexander began rehearsals at the Theatre Masque for John Golden's production of Anne Morrison Chapin's *Broken Doll*, a project that reunited Ross with Barbara Robbins, his leading lady in *After Tomorrow*, and John Golden who staged the play assisted by Edward T. Goodman.

In the play, retitled late in rehearsals as *No Questions Asked*, Ross was cast as Sonny Raeburn, a dipsomaniac who encounters Noel Parker (Barbara Robbins) on the Staten Island Ferry climbing over the guard rail in an attempt to kill herself because she is pregnant and her fiancé, Richard Gorham (Milo Boulton) refuses to marry her until he gets his mother Mrs. Goham (Kate McComb) to consent. Very drunk, Sonny complains about someone attempting suicide right in front of him:

Sonny. Not even out of the harbor and someone's got to jump overboard. It's an outrage. I'll speak to the captain. . . . I can't stand people who commit suicide—do you hear? It makes me sick. So don't do it again—not when I'm around. . . . I'm a nervous wreck and you have to come out and commit suicide right under my nose. That's no rest cure. (*Noel turns and starts away blindly.*) Don't go away mad. Wait. I want to tell you something. (*He detains her and imparts his news proudly.*) I've got a suicide complex. Had it for years. What do you think of that? Makes an amateur out of you, doesn't it? But never mind—Let's have a drink. Where's the bar. (Prologue, 9–10)

Sonny and Noel go to Tony's Bar, get very drunk, and, on a whim, decide to get married.

Act One follows three months later in a luxuriously furnished duplex apartment in New York City, where Noel has managed to keep Sonny sober, charming, attractive, and witty at a society party on the premises. We learn that he is a successful architect living with his wealthy mother, Pet Walsh (Spring Byington), but his sobriety is extremely fragile and by the end of the act he is falling-down drunk again because Noel, having had to endure a parade of grasping relatives and an ex-fiancé in her home, was too busy to attend to him.

In Act Two, Sonny escapes the watchful eye of Miss Kubee (Dorothy Vernon), a nurse hired by Doctor Stern (Joseph King) to look after him and leaves the house only to encounter Mrs. Gorham who fills him with lies about Noel's behavior with her son, Richard. Suffering *delirium tremens*, Sonny staggers home and confronts Noel about what he has learned from the woman:

Sonny. Do you know an old woman called Gorham?
Noel. Sonny—
Sonny. Do you?
Noel. Yes. How did you—
Sonny. Shut up. Do you know her son?
Noel. Yes, but—
Sonny. When did you see him last?
Noel. Sonny—
Sonny. When?
Noel. Tonight. Sonny let me—
Sonny. Where?
Noel. He met me in front of [my sister] Hat's and I drove him over to New York.
Sonny. You've been living with him.
Noel. No—I—
Sonny. You have. His mother just told me—downstairs—this very minute—she told me all about you—you've been living with him all the time. Didn't I catch you myself the other night—sneaking out?
Noel. Oh, my God!

Sonny. You telling me what to do, when I should breathe, when I could have a drink, when I could say yes or no, and me letting you get away with it, when all the time—

Noel. No—no—Sonny—You don't understand. It was a long time ago. I'll explain everything.

Sonny. You don't have to. You're running away with him tonight. His mother said so.

Noel. No—no. I'm not, Sonny—

Sonny. I'll say you're not—(*He jerks gun from pocket and fires twice at her. Noel runs toward him. They grapple and fight all over the room, each trying desperately to get the gun. Pet runs downstairs screaming—the gun goes off again and Sonny crumples up on the floor, the gun falls from Noel's hand.*) (2, 31–33)

Sonny, who was shot in the arm, recovers in Act Three, but the scene over the gun which ends Act Two proves to be too much for the pregnant Noel. She faints causing her pregnancy to be revealed to Sonny who still holds on to the belief that she is carrying on with Richard Gorham. After she disabuses him of that misconception, Sonny apologizes for trying to kill her, only to learn that Noel is only sorry that he failed in the attempt. There is a note of tenderness in his admission that Noel was the one person in the world he's been able to get along with—that he found "something that hadn't been presented by an indulgent mama," but feeling vulnerable and hurt, he lashes out again at his wife: "And you were just making a sucker out of me. Oh, well, to Hell with you!" (3, 34). In response, Noel reminds him of the invitation to go to Russia to supervise the building of one of his architectural designs, but he is contemptuous of the opportunity:

Sonny. Russia? What for? I might not like the liquor over there. (*He lifts the cup. She catches his hand. He stares at her.*) What a lousy trick! (*Suddenly he throws the whiskey in her face and walks away. She slowly wipes it away with her handkerchief. After a moment he speaks in a shaky voice.*) I don't want to get drunk. It wouldn't help a bit. I'd only feel worse.

Noel. When you get to work someplace else—you'll forget all about me.

Sonny. (*Shakes his head.*) I've got just enough brains to know I can't make the grade alone.

Noel. Then could you stand my going with you? (*No answer.*) I haven't got any place else to go.

Sonny. When my shoulder got better I could knock you about a bit. I'd like that.

Noel. I'd like that too, Sonny. I'd like that better than anything in the world.

Sonny. I want to so much—I could almost do it now. (*He starts toward her, his right arm lifted, he sways weakly. She catches him.*)

Noel. You'd better wait.

Sonny. You'll stick around?

Noel. As long as you'll let me. (*Curtain.*) (3, 35)

By the time *No Questions Asked* opened at the Theatre Masque on Monday 5 February 1934, the final scene had been adjusted to allow Sonny to accept Noel's baby as his, with no questions asked, but, even with a sympathetic and optimistic ending, the play earned only mixed reviews from even the most indulgent critics. Again commending Ross Alexander's work, though finding it squandered on his role, Brooks Atkinson (*The New York Times*, 6 February 1934) determined that "the author feels pretty chipper about the whole business, molds a play as though she were making mud pies and concludes her study of contemporary manners with a pat of good-fellowship on nearly everyone's back. At the end you feel that a dipsomaniac and the mother of a prospective illegitimate child ought to have something stouter than a few stereotyped phrases with which to combat the future. . . . When the curtain falls the only point of which you can be certain is that the play is done. . . . *No Questions Asked* is manufactured on the principle of artful dodging. When a melodrama is written with candor it can be enormously entertaining. When it is assiduously collected out of the shed of spare parts it tempers one's respect for the theatre."

Arthur Pollock (*The Brooklyn Daily Eagle*, 6 February 1934) found that "Ross Alexander plays the young drunk entertainingly, too. He is growing rapidly as an actor." Of the play, however, he wrote that "the best that can be said for *No Questions Asked* is that not a little of its dialogue is worthy of a better play. Anne Morrison Chapin is the author. If she had done the dialogue and someone else the plot the result might have been happier, and Mr. Golden, too." Burns Mantle (*Daily News* 6 February 1934) personally did not like the drama but admitted that "when at the end of the play Ross Alexander, playing the hero, asserts his right to accept the responsibility of paternity and no questions asked it is easy to understand the applause of those emotionalists who approve." About Ross in the role of a dipsomaniac, Mantle wrote, "Young Mr. Alexander is also good at being manly without making too much of a fuss about it, and being drunken without overdoing it. He acquired something like tremens with a very short devotion to the bottle, but there was no time for extensive detail." *The Hollywood Reporter* (9 February 1934) noted that "Ross Alexander plays Sonny Raeburn amusingly" and "the play with all its faults provides enough meat for Hollywood to go to work on—and turn out a considerably better picture than it is a play." *Variety* (13 February 1934) concluded that "Ross Alexander again scores, this time as the boy who likes his likker but likes his bride even more." The review also noted that the "writing is mixed and at points over-written. Plot is along melodramatic lines, but there is a comedy vein that really counts." Even so, "reviewers seemed in doubt about the play's chances."

No Questions Asked opened during a snowstorm in New York City so business was light for the first week of the run. By the second week, the city had dug itself out of the snow, but business remained poor at the Theatre Masque where the play closed on Saturday, 17 February, after only sixteen performances. Ironically, on the following Tuesday, Ross appeared on the 6 P.M. broadcast for the Stage Relief Fund over Station WJZ, a CBS affiliate in New York City, to solicit donations to help the elderly, the indigent, and the under-employed members of the theatrical profession. Three days later, on 23 February 1934, the *Democrat and Chronicle* published an *Associated Press*

175

article by Mark Barron citing the results of a poll among New York theatre critics to name the best players on Broadway during the 1933–1934 season. Although George M. Cohan and Helen Hayes walked away with the top honors, Ross Alexander received prominent mention even though he had not appeared in a hit that season. Other actors who received notice included Lloyd Nolan, Osgood Perkins, Alexander Kirkland, Roland Young, and Douglas Montgomery. Again, Ross was in good company. During the first months of 1934 Ross was often seen luncheoning at the Algonquin Hotel, famous for the "Round Table" luncheons frequented by producers, writers, and critics in the Pergola room. While not a member of that illustrious gathering, Ross was variously seen in the company of Helen Hayes, Katharine Hepburn, Miriam Hopkins, Laura Hope Crews, and Roland Young (*Modern Screen*, 3 March 1934).

No Questions Asked marked the end of Alexander's Broadway career as well as his association with John Golden. Over the next two years the two would infrequently keep in touch, and, although Ross would express a sincere desire to work with him again, life would move him in a direction that made their collaboration impossible. In the year and a half since he appeared in *The Stork Is Dead*, Ross performed in seven plays and a film—all critical and financial flops. The six plays on Broadway netted a total of 180 performances, less than the number of performances in the individual runs of *The Ladder*, *Let Us Be Gay*, or *That's Gratitude*. The theatre had not been unkind to him, however, for even in flops his work was noticed by important New York critics who supported his talent and applauded his development as an actor. Ross wasn't satisfied, however. He felt that he had more than paid his dues and deserved a more tangible recognition for his work than a scrapbook filled with good reviews. Still, never having had to struggle to find work, Ross was ill-equipped to pound the pavement in search of the indescribable moment when his career would finally take off. Instead, he waited, expecting that elusive opportunity to fall into his lap. Fortuitously, he didn't have long to wait.

ACT TWO
Hollywood

13. *Flirtation Walk, Gentlemen Are Born*, and *Maybe It's Love*

No sooner had *No Questions Asked* closed than Ross was signed by MGM on a six-week option for $850 a week. Having the promise of a regular salary, Ross Alexander married Aleta Freel at the home of her sister Doris, now Mrs. Stuart Benedict, in East Orange, New Jersey. Alexander's best friend Henry Fonda served as his best man. Three different accounts of the wedding give three different dates—ranging from 19 to 21 February—which comes as no surprise since New Jersey newspapers had claimed the couple were married as early as 1932 and later reports would suggest that they had been married in 1924. As noted earlier in these pages, Ross met Aleta during the summer of 1930 in West Falmouth, Massachusetts, where she had debuted with the University Players as Henry Fonda's leading lady in Leslie Howard's comedy *Murray Hill*. The daughter of Dr. William Freile and his wife Williammena, Aleta was born on 14 June 1907 in Jersey City and raised as an elite New Jersey debutante who summered in France during her college years at Smith, from which she graduated with honors in 1928.

Following a summer with the University Players, Freel spent the winter with Muriel McCormick's company of players that inaugurated the Palm Beach Playhouse in Florida on 13 January with A.A. Milne's *Mr. Pim Passes By*. She returned north to summer at the Westchester Playhouse at Mount Kisco, New York, where her roles included Linda Seton in Philip Barry's play *Holiday* and Mary in A.A. Milne's *Michael and Mary*. She made her Broadway debut in Valentine Davies's melodrama *Three Times the Hour* on 25 August 1931, produced and directed by Brock Pemberton (and Antoinette Perry). Although the production was a twenty-three-performance flop, reviewers were kind to Freel and she was subsequently cast in Norman Krasna's Hollywood comedy *Louder, Please*, which opened on 12 November 1931 under the direction of George Abbott. After that show closed early in 1932, Freel joined Charles Winninger in the cast of Chamberlain Brown's revival of *The Music Master* opening at the Riviera Theatre on 4 April 1932 followed by roles in a variety of significant stock productions, including Benn W. Levy's *Springtime for Henry* at the Croton River Playhouse, Hammon-on-Hudson, New York (4 July 1932); a variety of plays also featuring Ross Alexander produced by the Monmouth County Players at Red Bank, New Jersey (July-August 1932); Allen Scott and George Haight's comedy *Goodbye Again*, produced by the Theatre Unit (formerly the University Players Guild) at West Falmouth (August 1932); and a tour of *Springtime for Henry* at the Blackstone Theatre, Chicago (December 1932), Garrick Theatre, Philadelphia (January 1933), and Boulevard Theatre, Jackson Heights (February 1933).

On 6 March 1933, Freel reappeared on Broadway as Marjorie Gray in the Theatre Guild's production of Maxwell Anderson's Pulitzer-Prize-winning play *Both Your Houses*, after which she appeared in Sutton Vane's *Outward Bound*, Laurence E. Johnson's *It's a Wise Child*, and Haight's *Goodbye Again* during the summer at the Westchester Playhouse. She returned to Broadway on 21 September in Elizabeth McFadden's thriller *Double Door* which played 143 performances at the Ritz Theatre before moving to the Chestnut Street Theatre in Philadelphia on 22 January 1934.

The above expostulation of Aleta Freel's theatrical resume is more than simply a fatuous digression because it is important to understand the pedigree of Alexander's bride. She was a beautiful socialite who was also highly regarded as an actress. Ross enjoyed being accepted in high society and was certainly proud to have Aleta by his side, but, like the character he played in *Holiday*, he didn't want to be a socialite. Whether it was Ross's middle-class upbringing or the inclination of a parent to believe that a good-looking and charismatic young man was marrying his daughter for her money or her social connections, Aleta's father never completely embraced the match. Perhaps he disapproved of Ross's behavior toward Aleta while he resided in the family home in Jersey City: Ross was often subject to rants that left Aleta in tears, but there was never any evidence of physical violence, and his brown moods were always followed by apologies and kisses. Aleta tolerated her husband's behavior because she enjoyed being part of a "power couple" in the theatre and in high society. Ross was a catch and she had caught him: he made her feel more beautiful and more talented.

Ross and Aleta left for Hollywood the day after their wedding and arrived in California on 26 February 1934. According to *The Hollywood Reporter* (27 February 1934), Ross was scheduled to make tests for a term contract at MGM in Culver City and Aleta was set to test at Warner Brothers in Burbank. While they waited to be tested, Ross and Aleta settled into a modest 1582 square-foot, three-bedroom home at 7357 Woodrow Wilson Drive in the Hollywood Hills. The main house, built in 1920, was reminiscent of a hunting lodge with river stone walls and exposed ceiling beams on the ground floor, and a master bedroom that featured unobstructed views of the "Hollywood" sign and the surrounding canyon. In addition, the 8,816 square-foot lot included a one-bedroom guest house or domestics' residence, a two-car garage, and a private yard.

On March 26, 1934, *The Hollywood Reporter* announced that Ross was being tested "for one of the top spots in the Constance Bennet starrer, *The Green Hat*. Company figures the youngster may be another Robert Montgomery." In an interview published in *Movie Mirror* (October 1936), Ross gave a play-by-play account of his screen test:

Metro signed me on a six-week option at $850 a week. I married again and came back [to Hollywood]. That time they did get around to making a test of me. But even that wasn't until the sixth week. Afterwards the front office called me in. One of the executives said: Did you see your test, Mr. Alexander?" I said I had. "Then tell us, if you were a producer, what would you pay that actor?" "About fifty cents a week," I answered. "That's what we think!" he said. . . . The trouble with them was that they didn't have the heart to tell me what was the matter. I knew, but I wasn't going to tell them. I look like the west end of a horse going east! And don't think I think I'm kidding when I say that! (114)

Evidently a sufficient number of MGM executives disagreed with Alexander's assessment because it was announced in *Variety* (27 March 1934) that MGM had "pacted" Ross for what would amount to the next three months of waiting to be given an assignment. During that time Ross and Aleta settled into their new home and engaged African-Americans Cornelius Stephenson and his wife Elta as their chauffeur and cook.

If the motion picture establishment Ross returned to was different from the Hollywood he experienced in 1932, it was likely because of the more strenuous observance of the Motion Picture Production Code (MPPC), a series of moral guidelines that had been proposed in 1927 and formally adopted in 1930, but only loosely enforced until 13 June 1934 when the Production Code Administration (PCA) was established, requiring that all films released on or after 1 July 1934 be approved by the PCA prior to their release. The studios adopted this form of self-censorship to ward off censorship by the US government and to replace censorship that had existed in individual states. Generally speaking, the MPPC ordained that no motion picture would be produced that would lower the moral standard of the audience: crime, sin, and evil must never be portrayed sympathetically; proper moral values should be presented in scenes of daily life; and no law should be mocked or the violation of which sympathetically portrayed. Specifically, brutal killings must not be presented in detail; methods of crimes should not be presented in detail; illicit drug trafficking must never be presented; the use of liquor (when not required by plot or characterization) must not be shown. In order to preserve the sanctity of marriage, adultery may not be presented in an attractive fashion; scenes of passion must be moderated or not shown at all; seduction or rape must only be implied, never depicted explicitly; sexual perversions, white slavery, miscegenation, venereal diseases, and scenes of actual childbirth are forbidden; and children's sex organs are never to be exposed. Vulgar subjects, obscene gestures, words, jokes, or suggestions, and profanity are forbidden. Complete nudity must never be shown; disrobing scenes should be avoided; and indecent exposure is forbidden. No religion, no ministers of religion, or religious practices may be ridiculed or treated comically. Bedroom scenes must be treated delicately and tastefully; the flag of the United States must be treated with respect and the history and peoples of other nations must be treated justly. In short, the movie business had embraced a kind of political and social correctness that made pre-code films like *The Wiser Sex* and *Social Register* ancient history. Ross may have appeared on Broadway in plays that would have violated the newly enforced production code—*The Stork Is Dead, Honeymoon, Under Glass,* and *No Questions Asked* come immediately to mind—but plays of that ilk would no longer be in Alexander's future on the silver screen.

In early June, near the end of his contract with MGM, and less than two weeks prior to the establishment of the Production Code Administration, Ross was called for a screen test at Warner Brothers for a role in their new West Point musical film, *Flirtation Walk*, written by Delmar Daves and Lou Edelman and staring Dick Powell and Ruby Keeler. Evidently his test was successful for on 5 June 1934, Ross was given a contract with Warner Brothers slated to begin on 4 June and continue for a period of fifteen and two-thirds weeks, for which he would be paid $400.00 per week for the first two and two-thirds weeks (which overlapped with the remainder of his MGM contract), and $500.00 per week for the remaining thirteen weeks of the term. The studio maintained the right to extend employment for an additional period of twenty-six weeks at $700.00 per week and subsequent extensions of fifty-two weeks at regular salary increments.

Typical of motion-picture contracts of the period, the studio required that the actor "act, pose, sing, speak" or otherwise perform in the projects of the studio's choosing, and could (without additional compensation) enlist the actor to make personal appearances and phonograph recordings, and to be photographed for publicity purposes, all at the studio's discretion. The studio also mandated that the actor would render services solely and exclusively to the studio and grant the studio sole and exclusive right to the use of his name and likenesses; moreover, the studio had the right to lend, rent, or transfer the services of the actor to any other reputable producer. Additionally, the studio contract included a "morals' clause which was of special interest and concern to Ross. It read:

> The Artist agrees to conduct himself with due regard to public convention and morals, and agrees that he will not do or commit any act or thing that will tend to degrade him in society or bring him into public hatred, contempt, scorn, or ridicule, or that will tend to shock, insult or offend the community, or ridicule public morals or decency or prejudice the Producer, or the motion picture industry in general, and that he will not do or commit any act or thing that will tend to injure his capacity to at all times fully comply with and perform all of the terms and conditions of this agreement, or which will tend to injure his physical or mental qualities. (United Artists Corporation: Series 1.2: Warner Brothers Scripts. Box 185, folder 7.)

Finally, the studio reserved the right to lay off the actor without pay for a period of three weeks (consecutively, or aggregately) out of every thirteen weeks during which the actor is employed, ultimately guaranteeing the actor (if the layoff option is exercised every three months) forty weeks of paid employment.

Alexander's signature was still drying on his Warner Brothers contract when he was spirited off to West Point, New York, with members of the cast of *Flirtation Walk*, including Pat O'Brien, John Eldredge, Henry O'Neill, Glen Boles, and John Arledge to join director Frank Borzage, technical advisor Colonel Timothy J. Lonergan, star Dick Powell, and an assortment of sound, electrical, and wardrobe screen workers who had arrived earlier. Ross and company arrived three days prior to the military academy's graduation exercises, in time to familiarize themselves with the Army routine, and to steep themselves in the West Point traditions before shooting began on 11 June 1934. According to *The Brooklyn Daily Eagle* (20 June 1934), at West Point, the men were taken to the military academy's barber shop to be clipped and shorn in the appropriate cadet manner, receiving special "kay-det" haircuts, which are part of West Point regulations for dress and deportment.

The *Oakland Tribune* (1 July 1934) added that the actors' uniforms were made in West Point's own shops by members of the academy's tailors and the boots, sabers, and rifles were all authentically West Point. While the director and crew recorded the sights and sounds of the academy on 14 June, the cast was given a holiday in New York City during which Ross and other devotees of prize-fighting, Dick Powell and Pat O'Brien, attended the Max Baer-Primo Carnera match at Madison Square Garden, which went to eleven rounds before Baer was proclaimed victor and the World Heavyweight Champion. Even though the actors had only a few lines to speak when filming of the West Point sequences continued, it was reported that Warner Brothers sent them to the academy in the interest of the authenticity which the War Department required. O'Brien, for instance, has only a brief scene, just outside the academy gates (Shot 205, near the end of the film), but the studio believed that his actual presence would have the effectiveness of truth which "sets" on a sound stage don't always produce. On Monday 18 June, the cast and crew left New York to return to California where filming continued at Warner Brothers Studios in Burbank.

In *Flirtation Walk*, Ross played Oscar "Oskie" Berry, the garrulous, good-natured roommate at West Point of Dick "Canary" Dorcy (Dick Powell) who, while stationed in Hawaii, had fallen in love at first sight with Kit (Ruby Keeler), the daughter of General Fitts (Henry O'Neill). To complicate matters,

Kit is engaged to her father's aide, Lieutenant Biddle (John Eldridge). Since Dorcy is only an enlisted man, he applies to the academy to become an officer and a gentleman in order to compete with Biddle for Kit's affections. Oskie provides much of the comic relief in the film, more by his line readings than from the lines themselves, some of which never made it from the script to the screen because of Alexander's ad libs and paraphrasing, and, at least in one case, because of censorship by the PCA. The original exchange between Oskie and Dick was written:

Dick. Come on, Oskie, snap into it or you'll be late for parade again.

Oskie. (*Gets up with a weary sigh.*) That's the trouble with this place. The fellows are all right—the food ain't bad and the femmes'll do but for the last three years all I've done is dress and undress.

Dick. (*By this time, Dick is putting on his full-dress hat. Smiling.*) Write a letter to the Superintendent and he'll get you a valet. (Daves and Edelman 1934, 53)

In the released film, however, the exchange runs as follows:

Dick. Come on, Oskie, snap into it or you'll be late for parade again.

Oskie. (*Gets up with a weary sigh.*) That's the trouble with this place. The fellows are all right—the food ain't bad and the femmes'll do but for the last three years all I've done is parade.

Dick. (*By this time, Dick is putting on his full-dress hat. Smiling.*) Write a letter to the Superintendent and he'll get you a bicycle.

Evidently the suggestion of Ross dressing and undressing was considered too provocative by the censors who feared that women might faint at the thought. It all sounds rather ridiculous in hindsight, but audience members, even in the more permissive 1920s and 30s were wont to experience heart failure and the "vapors" when presented with titillating stimuli!

The plot thickens when General Fitts becomes Superintendent of West Point, bringing both his daughter and her fiancé to the academy, much to the distress of Dorcy who, having been hurt by Kit in an earlier encounter, prefers to distance himself from her, even when she approaches him openly. Unable to understand his roommate's behavior toward a beautiful woman's advances, Oskie explodes in his longest diatribe in the film: "I've seen a lot— I've visited *lunatic* factories—I've seen a guy feedin' th' front of his dress shirt to gold *fish*—I knew a gal who thought I was her dream man—what I mean is, I've seen plenty of *Nuts* in my time—but . . . (*Overflowing.*) But when the Goddess of Love herself says to you: (*Mimicking Kit.*) 'Aren't you the chap I met—in Hawaii?' An' you say: 'Pardon, gal, you've got the wrong guy.' It's time for me—(*He goes dramatic.*) Well, there's nothin' left to live for. . . . Goodbye— roommate—a long farewell" (Daves and Edelman 1934, 59).

When it comes time for the cadets to produce the traditional Hundredth Night (from June) Show, Oskie, Spike (John Arledge), Eight Ball (Glen Boles), Chase (John Darrow), and a chorus of military cadets try to convince Dorcy, the chairman of the show committee, to write Kit into the show. When he objects, he is impeached, Oskie becomes chairman in his place, and Kit is persuaded by the cadets to appear in the production. The image below depicts Kit's presence at the first reading rehearsal of the show. Although Oskie, Spike, and the rest of the cast are shown mooning over her, there is an obvious musical-comedy-style tension between Kit and Dorcy.

Dorcy (Dick Powell), Kit (Ruby Keeler), Oskie (Ross Alexander), and Spike (John Arledge) at the first reading rehearsal of the Hundredth Night Show. Courtesy of Photofest.

In the musical, which is based on the (then ironically comic) premise that "women become officers in our army *and give all the orders*" (Delmar Daves and Lou Edelman 1934, 72), Ross acted the role of Lieutenant Quibble, aide-de-camp to General Whynot (Ruby Keeler). The two carry on like two vaudevillians with painfully droll material and obvious digs at Lieutenant Biddle, aide to General Fitts:

Quibble. I am your aide, General.

Kit. My aid to what?

Quibble. Your aide-de-camp, General.

Kit. Well, we're not going camping for a while. Sit down.

Quibble. Yes, General.

Kit. (*Inspecting him with approval.*) Lieutenant Quibble, you're a very personable young man.

Quibble. Thank you, sir—ma'am—General.

Kit. Do you happen to be engaged or married—or anything?

Quibble. No, General.

Kit. In that case, consider yourself semi-engaged to me. It'll make things so much simpler.

Quibble. Thank you very much, General. (*Spike enters, gives him a note.*) . . . It's from the Academic Board. They ask a conference with you, General. . . .

Kit. Tell 'em they're fired. Tell 'em to go back to the army where they belong.

Quibble. (*Stunned.*) But . . . without the Academic Board who's going to discipline the Cadets, General?

Kit. There isn't going to be any more discipline. Those nice Cadets are starved for Beauty and a Woman's Touch. They're going to get it. (Daves and Edelman 1934, 87–88)

Dorcy enters with a Cadet Chorus to voice complaints ("No Horse, No Wife, No Mustache") and after two numbers ("Mr. and Mrs. Is the Name" and "Flirtation Walk") choreographed by Bobby Connolly in Busby

Berkeley fashion, Kit and "Canary" have made up. That is, until after the show, when Kit's wedding to Lieutenant Biddle is announced. Dorcy sneaks out after curfew to confront her about the impending marriage, and, in spite of Oskie's fervent efforts to whistle a warning to him, Dorcy is discovered by Biddle who convinces him to resign from the academy to save Kit from further embarrassment. After submitting his resignation, Dorcy is visited by Scrapper Thornhill (Pat O'Brien), his former sergeant, who has come to West Point to see him graduate. A speedy denouement follows: West Point denies Dorcy's resignation; Biddle acknowledges Kit's affection for Dorcy and steps aside; and Dorcy graduates, with Kit and a tearful Scrapper watching on the sidelines.

During the third week of filming *Flirtation Walk*, *The Film Daily* (28 June 1934) announced that Ross Alexander had been cast in *Just Out of College*, a Warner Brothers film set to begin production in July while Bobby Connolly rehearsed and shot the musical sequences for the army picture. For a week beginning on 3 July, Connolly was scheduled to film the Hawaiian number on arguably, at that time, the biggest set constructed at Warner Brothers. *Picture Play Magazine* (November 1934) provided a first-hand account of the routine:

> The climax of our visit to Burbank came when we were allowed to enter the secret set of a transplanted Hawaiian jungle, complete to the last swaying palm tree. Bobby Connolly, the dance director of many a *Scandals* and *Follies* in New York, was in charge here. He was rehearsing a hundred fetching hula maidens in the intricacies of a hip-waving native dance. Shredded skirts were everywhere; a stringed orchestra sobbed seductively in the background; bushy-haired Hawaiians paddled strange boats in the tropical pond in the middle of the setting. . . . The full moon blazed through the jungle, leaving a trail of silver across the water. The guitars strummed, the maidens swayed and as Mr. Connolly said "Give it to 'em!" the shredded skirts followed in a veritable

symphony of motion, the native boys chanted a distinctly Broadway Hawaiian tune, and the cameras turned.

Outside the stage it was noon, and hot. Inside it was moonlight at midnight, on a beach near Waikiki. This one setting captured the magic and glamour of the movies as completely as any single setting I've ever seen.

The trees were shellacked, I was told, to give them the appearance of wetness. The Hawaiian girls were from Glendale, Santa Monica, and Hollywood, but the men were real Islanders. Make-up men refurbished the girls' brown bodies after each take. Between scenes instead of resting, two or three girls continued their torsos tossing accompanied by the plaintive plunking of a guitar. It was very picturesque, a cross between a *Follies* finale and a Florida boom.

We found at Warners that a lively studio will always have its spell of fascination. There is probably nothing more diverting in the world than a film factory hitting on all twelve. (55)

Following the Hawaiian routine, Connolly prepared and filmed the military wedding number which was reported to have employed some four hundred dancers and staged "No Horse, No Wife, No Mustache" and "Flirtation Walk" after Ruby Keeler arrived in Hollywood on 28 July. No sooner had Keeler arrived on the West Coast than Ross joined her and Dick Powell to break ground for Powell's new home in Brentwood, each ceremoniously turning a spade full of dirt for photographers and reporters in an obvious publicity event created by the studio. Director Frank Borzage and choreographer Bobby Connolly also posed for the cameras with spade in hand as did actors Pat O'Brien, Henry O'Neill, John Eldredge, Glen Boles, Quinn Williams, and John Arledge, all members of the cast of *Flirtation Walk*.

On 22 July, the night before he began shooting *Just Out of College*, Ross and his wife attended a surprise birthday party for musician and bandleader

Harmon O. Nelson, hosted by his wife, actress Bette Davis. Davis, also on the Warner Brothers roster, was a good friend of the Alexanders, and, at times when Nelson was off on tour with his band, she persuaded Ross to escort her to soirees at the Bath and Tennis Club in the Cheviot Hills neighborhood of Los Angeles, creating yet more photo opportunities for studio publicists and gossip columnists.

Ross Alexander and Bette Davis at the Bath and Tennis Club.

Written by Eugene Solow and Robert L. Johnson, *Just Out of College* depicted the story of four college friends who had high hopes of finding successful careers in New York City upon graduation. They soon discover that, even with a college education, during the Depression, jobs are scarce and applicants are many. Tom Martin (Ross Alexander} wants to become an architect but has to settle for part time work filing blue prints; his roommate, Bob Bailey (Franchot Tone), intends to be a journalist but just manages to sell the occasional story for a subsistence wage. At a lunch counter they jovially celebrate their achievement:

> **Tom**. Pot roast for me—and a fish for my nephew!
>
> **Bob**. No! Wait a minute! (*Pushes Tom's hat over his ears.*) You cock-eyed carpenter, we're celebrating! (*To Counterman.*) Filet mignon—for two!
>
> **Tom**. (*Emerging from under his hat.*) Hey! What kind of job did you *land?*
>
> **Bob**. (*Hesistantly.*) Well, I don't get paid until my stuff's accepted—
>
> **Tom**. (To *Counterman.*) Change that order, Bud! Filet magnon for one—and an order of tripe! (Solow and Johnson 1934, 21)

Smudge (Dick Foran) (his surname was originally "Johnson" in the screenplay but, because of its use as a slag term for penis, "Johnson" was changed to "Casey" in the film) aspires to become an athletic coach, commensurate with his success as a star athlete in college; but soon he discovers that he has to settle for work as a prize fighter and truck driver to make ends meet. Fred Harper (Robert Light) is the most successful of the foursome because he goes to work for his father, a prosperous stockbroker, who pays him $20.00 a week ($380 in 2019 dollars).

Tom's girlfriend Trudy Talbot (Jean Muir) moves to New York to be close to him and shares an apartment with Susan Merrill (Ann Dvorak), a librarian who meets and falls in love with Smudge. At their home they host a weekly Sunday breakfast for Tom, Bob, Smudge, Fred, and his sister, Joan (Margaret Lindsay), with whom Bob is in love. Soon, Tom and Trudy announce their wedding which is a simple affair at the ladies' apartment, with Tony (George Humbert), their Italian landlord, serving muscatel and playing the wedding march on his accordion. Tom, his college friends and their girlfriends line up in the hall and form a procession leading to Mr. Gillespie (Arthur Aylesworth), a "funny little man in a black derby" who wryly officiates at the ceremony:

Mr. Gillespie. (*Dryly, rapidly.*) By the virtue of the authority invested in me as Justice of the Peace of the Borough of Manhattan, State of New York, I pronounce you man and wife. Three dollars please. (Solow and Johnson 1934, 57)

(From left right) Smudge (Dick Foran), Susan (Ann Dvorak), Bob (Franchot Tone), Joan (Margaret Lindsay), Tom (Ross Alexander), Trudy (Jean Muir), and Mr. Gillespie (Arthur Aylesworth) in the wedding sequence.

No sooner has the celebration begun than an elderly little man (Herbert Heyward), who lives below them, enters "in his shirt sleeves—unshaven—his eyes red-rimmed."

Tom. (*Comes into scene.*) Oh, hello! (*Snapping his fingers.*) Say—I'm sorry—I forgot about your wife—

193

Little Man. (*Speaking very shakily.*) No, no, that's all right— (*He passes a trembling hand across his stubbly chin, blinking.*)

Trudy. (*Comes into scene.*) We've been shouting and stamping on the floor—and your poor wife—

Little Man. May I come in—for a minute? It's a little bit lonesome down there.

Trudy. Of course! You come right in and join us! (*She takes him by the arm. They move into the room.*)

Little Man. Just for a minute—very lonesome— (*He blinks, seeming very dazed.*)

Tony. Maria! Whatsa so steenge wit de muscatel?

Trudy. (*Kindly.*) You must be all in, working days, sitting up every night with your poor wife. How's she feeling tonight? Is she asleep?

Little Man. (*Sits.*) She's comfortable—at last, thank you. She just passed away—Please go right ahead with the party—(*He passes a shaking hand across his chin and starts to cry. There is dead silence as they all look at him in horror.*) (Solow and Johnson 1934, 58–59)

Reversals of expectations continue throughout the film. Fred's father commits suicide because of his involvement in the failure of the First Atlantic Trust, leaving his family destitute and driving his daughter Joan to accept the marriage proposal of wealthy industrialist Stephen Hornblow (Charles Starrett) to keep the family afloat. Smudge and Susan marry only to find themselves both out of work. Desolate and desperate, Smudge steals ten dollars from a pawn shop in order to put food on the table and is shot dead trying to escape. Sent to report on the incident, Bob recognizes his old friend but keeps his name out of the article claiming that "Nobody knows him." Dejected and bitter, Bob goes to Tom and Trudy's apartment where he is greeted by a jovial Tom who is celebrating the birth of his son:

Tom. (*Wrapped up in his own feelings and still oblivious to Bob's near collapse.*) I've got everything I want!

Bob. (*Very low.*) Yeah—sure you have—a wife, a kid, and a lot of debts. How are you going to live?

Tom. We'll make out somehow—everybody does. Give me a chance! I haven't even *started!* We'll be all right!

Bob. Sure—and in seventeen years, after wearing and worrying yourself to death, you'll have enough, if you're lucky, to send your kid to college. So what?

Tom. I wouldn't swap horses with John D. Rockefeller or anybody else in the world! You don't need money to be happy.

Bob. Maybe not—Ask Fred how he feels about it. All washed up before he started, because—yeah—I guess old man Harper was right—If it doesn't figure in dollars and cents—it doesn't figure any other way.

Tom. You're crazy! Harper jumped out of a window because he *couldn't* figure any other way—!

Bob. (*Suddenly bursting out with it—hysterically.*) And *Smudge*—what about *Smudge*? One of the swellest, straightest guys that ever lived—laying on a slab right this minute in the morgue! (*Breaking down and sobbing.*) What for? What *for*? What did *he do*?

Tom. What are you *talking* about? Are you *crazy*?

Bob. (*Leaping to his feet—hysterically.*) Sure, I'm crazy! Smudge—one of the nicest guys that every lived—!

Tom. (*Taking a firm grip on Bob's arm.*) Calm down, Bob, or I'll sock you in the jaw! Tell me what happened!

Bob. They shot him down in the street—like a dog—because he was hungry! (*Suddenly bursting into violent laughter.*) *Because he was hungry!* Tell me who's crazy now! Ask Susan! See what she says. (*He rushes across the room and out of the door.*)

Tom. (*Running after him—in the doorway.*) Bob! (*He stands there— stunned—in the doorway. The pounding of Bob's feet on the stairs and the outside door slamming are the only reply.*) (Solow and Johnson 1934, 114–115)

Franchot Tone and Ross Alexander, performing a dramatic scene.

In the end, Susan leaves New York City and returns to her family in Des Moines; Joan cancels her engagement to Hornblow in favor of a life with Bob, and Tom and Trudy contentedly accept a life in poverty.

Shooting for *Just Out of College* was completed on 20 August 1934 and, by the time it was in the cutting room, the title was changed to *Gentlemen Are Born*, which had been the title of a Dick Powell-Josephine Hutchinson film that was subsequently rechristened *Happiness Ahead*. Between 23 July and 20 August, Ross had been subject to the schedules of two films, on call every day for one or the other, and sometimes both. Because he was a "contract player" at Warner Brothers, he did not earn an additional salary for the double. What he did secure was the studio's admiration for his work and an extension of his contract for twenty-six weeks, at $700.00 per week.

Although it was technically Alexander's second film, *Gentlemen Are Born* was released first, on 17 November 1934, eleven days prior to the 28 December opening of *Flirtation Walk*. Reviews of each film were favorable to Ross. A *Motion Picture Daily* (3 November 1934) preview of *Flirtation Walk* suggested that "Ross Alexander again demonstrates his abilities, which point upward," and, in regard to the same preview, *The Los Angeles Times* (6 November 1934) noted that "Ross Alexander again brightens a number of scenes." About *Gentlemen Are Born*, the *Oakland Tribune* (11 November 1934) wrote that "The picture has its moments but in the main suffers from an undertone of futility. [Dick] Foran, a new personality, reveals interesting promise and Ross Alexander, also new to the films, should develop into a favorite." The *Daily News* (23 November 1934) reported that "Franchot Tone and Ross Alexander manage to put over one difficult scene with telling effect," and *Variety* (27 November 1934) stated: "Ross Alexander is more sharply typed. He is quite familiar (as a type) in real life with a slightly self-conscious element to his good fellowship and humor. He is clean-cut and personable but no Prince Charming." *Picture Play* (February 1935) decided that *Gentlemen Are Born* "is, in fact, a fairly attractive film, missing its possibilities because it is superficial. Fans will like Mr. Alexander, a newcomer, for his glib breeziness."

Ross Alexander with his adoring wife, Aleta, at the Los Angeles premiere of *Flirtation Walk.*

197

Flirtation Walk received its premiere on 28 November 1934—at the Hollywood Theatre in Los Angeles and the Strand Theatre in New York City—a day after Jack L. Warner, Ross Alexander, Dick Powell, and fifty singers, appeared in a special variety show on radio station KFWB, designed to promote the film. Among those in attendance at the premiere were Ross Alexander and his wife Aleta; Ruby Keeler and her husband Al Jolson; and Dick Powell. The *Democrat and Chronicle* (29 November 1934) wrote that "Ross Alexander, the Rochester actor, stands out with a singularly appealing personality and a sure knack for spontaneous comedy. He brightens and vitalizes a scene instantly." *Variety* (4 December 1934) advised that "Ross Alexander, as Powell's roommate will be liked. He was at the Strand the week ahead of *Flirtation* in another picture, and these two standout performances suggest that he will do okay for himself in the film colony. Personable young men with a knack for light comedy and horseplay always fit. Alexander looks like a comer." *The Independent Exhibitors Film Bulletin* (11 December 1934) reiterated that sentiment with "This chap, Ross Alexander substantiates the promise he held out by his fine work in *Gentlemen Are Born*. He is a 'comer.' Watch him!" In addition, *Screenland* (February 1935) voted Alexander's performance in *Flirtation Walk* one of the month's best (along with Frederic March in *We Live Again,* Loretta Young in *The White Parade,* Frank Morgan in *There's Always Tomorrow,* and Anne Shirley in *Anne of Green Gables*). Even though Ross understood that, in films, he had to dial down his theatrical energy and fulsome line readings, he nevertheless managed to be the liveliest actor in every scene he played. Moreover, he made every actor in the scene look good, especially the stars whom he was hired to support. Ruby Keeler, who would do three films with Ross, raved about working with him, and Jack L. Warner, his producer, was so confident in Alexander's abilities that he sought to groom him as a matinee-idol leading man. There were, if we are to believe publicist Jerry Asher, some red flags regarding Alexander's extracurricular sexual activities, but so long as he remained a fan favorite, the studio methodically kept Ross free from scandal and bad publicity.

Before Ross had completed shooting *Flirtation Walk* and *Gentlemen Are*

Born, *The Los Angeles Times* (17 August 1934) announced that he had been chosen to play the male lead opposite Gloria Stuart in *Half Way to Heaven*, the film adaptation of Maxwell Anderson's 1927 play *Saturday's Children*. By the time shooting began under the direction of William McGann in the autumn of 1934, the title had been changed to *Maybe It's Love*. As written by Jerry Wald, Harry Sauber, and Lawrence Hazard, the film unveiled the story of Rims O'Neil (Ross Alexander), a vivacious twenty-five-year-old employee at the firm of A.J. Mengle, Steamship–Freight Brokerage who dreams of managing the new Havana Office, much to the surprise and unspoken displeasure of Bobby Halevy (Gloria Stuart), a secretary at the same firm. Adolph Mengle, Sr. (Joseph Cawthorn), "an excitable old German who unconsciously murders the English language," has other plans for Rims, however. He wants him to take Adolph Mengle, Jr. (Philip Reed) under his wing and teach him the steamship business. Junior, in turn, "a typical rich man's son who likes the company of women in preference to his studies in college," is far more interested in Bobby than the business. Rims suspects that he has been dating her under the guise of working late at the office, even though she *has* actually been working late. When he sees Junior taking her home after one such extended workday, he confronts them:

Rims. Working late with Old Man Mengle, eh?

Junior. Now listen, O'Neil—

Rims. You keep out of this. This is between her and me. (*To Bobby.*) So you thought you were putting something over on me, huh? You couldn't go out with me—you had to work. I catch on—Of course, I haven't Young Mengle's purchasing power—

Bobby. You've said about enough.

Rims. Yeah? You ain't heard nothin' yet. From now on it's just business with us.

Bobby. That suits me perfectly.

Junior. But listen, O'Neil—

Rims. I told you to keep out of this. I'm not blaming you—you didn't drag her out. If she didn't want to go out with you, she wouldn't.

Bobby. That's a fine way to talk in front of Mr. Mengle.

Junior. Oh, don't mind me—go right ahead—I'll try and enjoy it.

Rims. (*Shouting.*) I'm doing the talking here.

Bobby. (*Just as loud.*) But I refuse to listen. (Wald, Sauber, and Hazard 1934, 38–39)

Observing the feisty relationship between Rims and Bobby and hoping that he might still have a chance with her, Junior convinces his father to send Rims off to Havana to run the new office. Although Rims is elated to have the job, he is uncomfortable leaving Bobby alone with Junior, and Bobby is distressed at the thought of Rims going so far away. Her overbearing sister, Florrie Sands (Ruth Donnelly), educates her in the ways of persuading him to stay and even getting him to marry her. Following her advice to the letter, Bobby becomes Mrs. O'Neil and Rims is fired from his job after leaving Mengle, Sr. without a foreman in Havana.

Ross Alexander and Gloria Stuart in conflict in *Maybe It's Love.*

The marriage eventually turns sour over Rims's inability to live on a budget, his gambling, and his complaining about the parasitic presence of Bobby's family who regularly show up at dinner time but rarely chip in to pay for the food. On the occasion of their six-month anniversary, Rims buys a second-hand Chevrolet as a surprise for Bobby, but what might have been a romantic drive for the couple becomes a clown act at a circus with Bobby's family piling into the car and Willy Sands (Frank McHugh), Bobby's brother-in-law, telling Rims how to drive. After Rims leaves the automobile in disgust and goes drinking, Willy takes the wheel and wrecks the car, creating another tense situation between Rims and Bobby's family:

Rims. I'm feeling fine right now. Just good enough to tell you what I really think—

Florrie. You're a fine specimen! The kind we should preserve.

Willy. We'd have a good start. He's pickled already.

Rims. And I'm tired of listening to your comic relief. Get out all of you—

Florrie. Come, Willy—he's a madman—

Willy. I'm plenty mad myself. (Wald, Sauber, and Hazard 1934, 90)

Florrie (Ruth Donnelly), Willy (Frank McHugh), Bobby (Gloria Stuart) and Rims (Ross Alexander) in an advertisement for *Maybe It's Love* in the *Daily News*, 10 February 1935.

Bobby, who has, incidentally, returned to work at Mengle's firm, takes as much exception to her husband's mistreatment of her family as he does to her going back to work, particularly given his concern over her relationship with Junior Megle:

Bobby. What harm is there in a wife going back to work? We need money.

Rims. (*In a loud voice.*) I'm the man of this house! I can make enough for you and I. We'll do all right if you keep that family of yours away.

Bobby. (*Burning.*) Now, listen to me! If you think I'm going to let you insult my family, order them out of my house—you're crazy! Who do you think you are?

Rims. (*With a sneer.*) Just the sap who didn't take the boat to Havana—just the sap who asked you to marry me and allowed your family to say yes. But they're not going to run my life. If you want them, go to them; but they're not going to come here. That's the way I feel about it and you can take it or leave it. (*He rushes out of the room. Bobby looks after him, bewildered.*) (Wald, Sauber, and Hazard 1934, 91–92)

Mengle, Sr. offers Rims another opportunity to travel to Havana, but he again misses the boat because he and Bobby have reconciled and installed a new bolt-lock on their door.

Just as *Maybe It's Love* was being readied for production, syndicated columnist Sidney Skolsy reported that "The Ross Alexanders have separated and Mrs. Alexander is now in the east preparing to get a divorce" (*Chicago Tribune*, 28 September 1934). Ross never mentioned the separation in interviews but the six months he and Aleta had spent in California had been difficult for them both. Ross was trying to fit into the role of a "contract player" and do what he is told without complaint—not an easy task for him; Aleta had yet met with no success in her screen tests and continually ached to return to the East where her career had blossomed. It is no surprise that tensions were high in that household, but it is surprising that no other columnist ran with the story. Evidently the studio executives managed to hush it up on the

West Coast and Dr. Freile had enough clout to have the story buried in New Jersey. It is also noteworthy that the couple's reconciliation a short time later was also kept out of the press.

Ross Alexander and Gloria Stuart, Film Partners Series, No. 5.

Maybe It's Love opened to decidedly mixed reviews, with the *Motion Picture Herald* (24 November 1934) suggesting that "While there is nothing great in cast, story or production value of this picture, there is plenty of reason to assume that it should prove better than satisfactory average entertainment for the run of the mill picture fan." Faint praise, indeed! Calling it "a somewhat inconsequential little film," the *Oakland Tribune* (16 December 1934) noted that "Alexander's work in this production realizes the promise his former appearances have shown," and *Modern Screen* (31 December 1934) wrote that "this little picture will please the fans despite the fact that it is given a cheap production and the photography is scarcely better than fair. . . . Granted that the dialogue is frankly wisecracking and aimed directly at the masses; that Joseph Cawthorn, good actor that he is, purposely overplays; that, as a thespian, Gloria Stuart makes a real beauty, and that Ross Alexander is consistently miserable, you're *still* in for some good rowdy fun."

Harrison's Report (January 5, 1935) spoke at length about the automobile sequence and concluded that, since the film had earned the status of "Class A Suitability," it was judged suitable for children, adolescents, and Sundays. *The Boston Globe* (25 January 1935), in turn, spent ample time discussing Ross: "The picture also served to present Ross Alexander, who scored such a hit in *Gentlemen Are Born*, and in *Flirtation Walk*, in his first starring role. Mr. Alexander is an amusing purveyor of humor, and his two previous performances in motion pictures have been both refreshing and convincing. But as Rims, the poor boy desperately in love with Bobby, who has too many relatives, he is not quite so convincing. One suspects however, the fault lies not with Mr. Alexander, but with the persons who adapted the play for the screen. It takes a bit of genius to make amusing the plight of two young people very much in love with each other, who are confronted with in-law troubles, jealousy, and financial difficulties." *Movie Mirror* (February 1935) published Alexander's picture under the title (printed in bold lettering) "Watch For This Man!" and concluded that "Under the very eyes of such seasoned picture-stealers as Dick Powell, Ruby Keeler, and Pat O'Brien, this talented newcomer carried off the highest film honors." *Hollywood* (February 1935) was apologetic saying, "Sorry we can't be enthused over this one. It is a slangy, wise-cracking picture, badly put together.... There isn't anything to rave about in this picture."

Photoplay (February 1935) admitted that "Ross Alexander makes the young husband an extremely interesting person, but the picture on the whole is frankly dull." The *Daily News* (10 February 1935) conceded that "Warner Bros. have at least succeeded in squeezing every drop of comic juice out of the photoplay's situations. But what is even more important is the appearance again in films of that rising young juvenile, Ross Alexander. Although Ross appears on the handbill second to Gloria Stuart, the fact remains that he dominates the action of *Maybe It's Love*. Pitted against the seasoned Miss Stuart, and the picture stealing pair of Frank McHugh and Ruth Donnelly,

Alexander's success is a success in spades. The boy is going places, no mistake."
The Brooklyn Daily Eagle (15 February 1935), on the other hand, called the
acting, "only fair," the direction, "pretty ordinary," and the movie, "a picture
that is easy to forget." The *Motion Picture Herald* (30 March 1935) said, "This
is a surprise picture. Pleased better than a lot of the much advertised specials.
. . . The cast means very little to my patrons and the title was not much at
the box office but it sure pleased those who came." On 6 July 1935, the
Motion Picture Herald added that "Ross Alexander has built himself plenty of
patronage since his performance in *Flirtation Walk*. Young folks here would
go to see him no matter what the picture might be."

Maybe *It's Love* did not do well at the box office and was thus considered
a failure by studio executives. Ross may have earned a fan base of significant
proportions but his days of acting the lead male role suddenly became few
and far between. He was quick to learn that, in the movie business, one is only
as good as his/her last picture.

14. *A Midsummer Night's Dream*

On 27 November, barely a week after *Maybe It's Love* had been completed, Ross Alexander was announced in the cast of *A Midsummer Night's Dream*, a spectacular film production of Shakespeare's comedy, produced by Jack Warner and directed by the world-famous German director, Max Reinhardt. How Reinhardt came to direct a "high-brow" Shakespearean film at Warner Brothers is the stuff of Hollywood legend that began in July 1934 when *The Los Angeles Times* reported in a banner headline: "Reinhardt Play Booked."

> *Midsummer Night's Dream* to Be Staged by Famed Producer This Fall, State Chamber Announces. Max Reinhardt, world-famous producer and actor, with a cast of twenty-one European thespians, ballet dancers and musicians, augmented by California artists of stage and screen, will give twenty performances of Shakespeare's *A Midsummer Night's Dream* at the Hollywood Bowl and at the Greek Theater in Berkeley from September 19 to October 19.
>
> That was revealed at the State Chamber of Commerce headquarters here yesterday when officials of the State chamber announced the successful termination of many months of planning on the part of outstanding Californians to present the Reinhardt players in the first of a series of annual cultural festivals in this State.

Reinhardt especially well known in Los Angeles for his production of *The Miracle* in 1926, will present *A Midsummer Night's Dream* in the English language, the first time he will have produced the play in that tongue in America, his former production of the drama in New York having been given in German. Mendelssohn music will be employed in the accompaniment.

The production has been underwritten by a group of Californians looking toward the establishment of California's leadership in America's cultural endeavors. Under the chairmanship of J.B. Levinson, San Francisco patron of music and dramatic art, a special committee of the State Chamber of Commerce made a careful study of the opportunities presented to California by a Reinhardt production. (13 July 1934)

A soon as the project was announced Reinhardt contacted his son, Gottfried, who had been trying to establish a career in Hollywood, and urged him to secure a number of film stars for the principal roles in the production, including Charlie Chaplin (Bottom), Greta Garbo (Titania), Clark Gable (Demetrius), Gary Cooper (Lysander), John Barrymore (Oberon), W.C. Fields (Thisbe), Wallace Beery (Lion), Walter Huston (Theseus), Joan Crawford (Hermia), Myrna Loy (Helena), and Fred Astaire (Puck) (Reinhardt 1979, 297). Max Reinhardt's expectations may have displayed a misunderstanding of the availability of major Hollywood stars but they did express his high-level approach to the production: everything was to be magical, larger than life, and performed with sublime artistry.

When Reinhardt arrived in Hollywood on 5 September, a mere twelve days before the premiere, the actors who had been cast by Reinhardt's assistant director, Felix Weissberger, included John Lodge (Theseus), William Farnum (Egeus), William Henry (Lysander), George Walcott (Demetrius), Walter Connolly (Bottom), Sterling Holloway (Flute), Francesca Braggioni and Jacqueline de Wit (Hippolyta), Olivia de Havilland and Gloria Stuart (Hermia), Philip Arnold (Oberon), Julie Haydon (Titania), Mickey Rooney (Puck), and Nini Theilade (First Fairy).

Cast members of *A Midsummer Night's Dream* at the Hollywood Bowl.

Ross Alexander and his wife Aleta were among the fourteen thousand in attendance at the 17 September premiere of *A Midsummer Night's Dream* at the Hollywood Bowl, a spectacle, the likes of which the film community had not experienced in live theatre. The Los Angeles Philharmonic Orchestra, led by Einar Nilson, underscored the production with music by Mendelssohn, and the bowl itself was transformed into a magical forest above which thousands of lights sparkled as stars. The premiere was the social event of the autumn in Los Angeles and drew a substantial audience from the moneyed elite as well as the film community. Reinhardt's production drew such rave reviews from the local newspapers that four days later, on 21 September, Jack Warner agreed to produce a film version of the Reinhardt production. A week later, *The Film Daily* (29 September 1934) announced that William Dieterle, one of Reinhardt's protégés in Europe and currently a director at Warner Brothers, would function as Reinhardt's assistant in the filming of *A Midsummer Night's Dream.*

In October Reinhardt and Dieterle began testing actors for the film. Perhaps because of the sensational reviews he earned playing Puck on stage, Mickey Rooney was the first announced performer for the picture. In fact, the *Motion Picture Daily* (12 November 1934) indicated that "the only two people definitely set for the cast are Mickey Rooney, borrowed from MGM, who will portray Puck, and Bronislava Nijinska, famous European dancer." Nijinska, sister of the celebrated dancer Nijinski, was hired to choreograph the ballets in *A Midsummer Night's Dream.* Other credits mentioned in the article included a screenplay (adapted from Shakespeare) by Charles Kenyon and Mary McCall, Jr.; original Mendelssohn music would be arranged by Erich Wolfgang Korngold; art direction by Anton Grot; and costumes by Max Ree.

By the end of November, eighteen roles in *A Midsummer Night's Dream* had been cast by Warner Brothers, with *The Los Angeles Times* (27 November 1934) providing the list: Ross Alexander as Demetrius; Olivia de Havilland as Hermia; Mickey Rooney as Puck; James Cagney as Bottom; Jean Muir as Helena; Joe E. Brown as Flute; Dick Powell as Lysander; Hugh Herbert as

Quince; Donald Woods as Oberon; Ian Hunter as Theseus; Frank McHugh as Snout; Otis Harlan as Starveling; Grant Mitchell as Egeus; Anita Louise as Titania; Hobart Cavanaugh as Philostrate; Eugene Pallette as Snug; Arthur Treacher as Ninny's Tomb; and Nini Theilade as the First Fairy. By 19 December when shooting began, Veree Teasdale had been cast as Hippolyta, and Donald Woods had been replaced by Victor Jory in the role of Oberon.

Not all of Warner Brothers players were thrilled to be cast in *A Midsummer Night's Dream*. Dick Powell believed that he was completely miscast as Lysander and struggled to get out of his contractual obligation to perform in whatever the studio bosses determined. Eventually he was persuaded by Reinhardt that Shakespeare was not entirely highbrow and allowed for clowning and comic line readings, but his performance ultimately displayed his discomfort with the Shakespearean text. Ross Alexander as Demetrius fared better, perhaps, because he had fewer lines to interpret, though even he appeared uncomfortable in the costume and makeup which he feared made him appear effeminate. Nevertheless, having already dealt with a famous German director, Berthold Viertel, on *The Wiser Sex*, Ross had little trouble working with Reinhardt or Dieterle. He did what he was told and offered as much understanding of the role of Demetrius as he was given in the few lines of text.

Ross first appears as Demetrius in procession, led by Theseus, duke of Athens, and Hippolyta, queen of the Amazons, making gestures to get Hermia's attention. He is obviously in competition with Lysander for Hermia's affections. During the "Welcome Song" that follows, Demetrius scorns the longing looks radiating from Helena and continues to pursue Hermia, who noticeably prefers Lysander, even though her father is determined that she should marry Demetrius. Lysander celebrates his victory with Hermia by humming several bars of Mendelssohn's "Spring Song" and Demetrius continues his passionate pantomime as Hermia and Lysander escape into the magical forest. He follows them into the forest, pursued, in turn by Helena who pleads her affection for him in a scene in front of Oberon who is hiding in the trunk of a tree.

211

Ross Alexander, Victor Jory, and Jean Muir in *A Midsummer Night's Dream*.
Courtesy of Photofest.

Oberon responds to their plight by applying a potion to Demetrius's eyes, putting him to sleep so that when he awakens, he will fall immediately in love with the first woman he sees. The same situation befalls Lysander. Suddenly both men find themselves in love with Helena, with Demetrius actually speaking Shakespeare's lines: "O Helen, goddess, nymph, perfect, divine! / To what, my love, shall I compare thine eyne? / Crystal is muddy. O, how ripe in show / Thy lips, those kissing cherries, tempting grow!" (2.2.140-143). He subsequently resigns his affection for Hermia, in favor of Helena: Lysander, keep your Hermia. I will none. / If ever I loved her, all that love is gone. / My heart to her but as a guest-wise sojourned, / And now to Helena is at home returned, / There to remain" (2.2.172-176). However, since Lysander is no longer in love with Hermia, the quartet remains disarranged.

Jean Muir, Ross Alexander, Dick Powell, and Olivia de Havilland in *A Midsummer Night's Dream.*

Demetrius and Lysander go off to fight with swords while Puck, imitating their voices, leads them through the forest: "Up and down, up and down, / I will lead them up and down. / I am feared in field and town. / Goblin, lead them up and down" (3.2.418-421). The following image shows Mickey Rooney as Puck, imitating Lysander's voice, to magically manipulate Ross Alexander in pursuit through the forest.

Mickey Rooney and Ross Alexander in *A Midsummer Night's Dream.*

Ultimately, Demetrius goes back to sleep, and dreams of the faithful Helena who falls asleep beside him. Puck applies the love potion to Lysander, already asleep in the forest, so that when he awakens, his gaze will immediately fall on Hermia who lies sleeping next to him. When the couples awake the next morning, the lovers are properly matched and leave the magic forest.

The scene changes to the palace of Theseus, a splendid one-hundred-thirty-five-foot-wide Italian Baroque construction, where a large crowd has gathered to celebrate the marriage of Theseus to Hippolyta. Hermia's father continues to pester the duke of Athens about the marriage of his daughter, but to no avail, for Theseus overrides his wishes and decrees that the loving couples—Demetrius and Helena, Lysander and Hermia—shall be married that very day. The image below displays the three loving couples at Theseus's palace: Hermia and Lysander stage right (audience left) of Hippolyta and Theseus (raising his goblet in a toast), Demetrius and Helena stage left (audience right). Note the opulence of the meticulously detailed costumes.

JeanMuir and Ross Alexander in *A Midsummer Night's Dream.*

Olivia de Havilland, Dick Powell, Verree Teasdale, Ian Hunter, Ross Alexander, Jean Muir in *A Midsummer Night's Dream.*

215

The following image reveals the palace of Theseus from the back of the room, exposing the vastness of the space filled with courtiers, attendants, lords, and ladies assembled for the nuptial festivities. The staging of the ensemble is extremely active with various groups in conversation focusing away from the dais, while others stand at attention facing into the center of the room, and still others direct their gaze toward Theseus and Hippolyta, following the same path as the camera. The image below is an enlarged detail depicting Demetrius and Helena in the stage left (audience right) portion of the scene. Note again the extremely detailed costumes worn by the ensemble.

Long shot of Theseus's palace, from the rear of the crowd.

Detail, showing Ross Alexander and Jean Muir.

216

The above description of Ross Alexander's activities in *A Midsummer Night's Dream* does not take into account the fairy aspect of the film, the massive forest with hills and dales and an actual lake that was constructed on Warner Brothers' Studio 8, or the sterling efforts of the comedians preparing "Pyramus and Thisbe" for the wedding celebration. James Cagney as Bottom, who, in the guise of an ass became the object of Titania's infatuation, had the greatest number of extended speeches in the film, and Joe E. Brown as Flute acting the role of Thisbe, perhaps, the finest comic business; but even though the fairy spectacle and the rehearsing comedians managed a great deal of screen time, neither interacted with the romantic plot of the film. Joe E. Brown recalled that "Some of us were certainly not Shakespearean actors. Besides myself from the circus and burlesque, there was Jimmy Cagney from the chorus, and Mickey Rooney and Hugh Herbert from burlesque. At the beginning we went into a huddle and decided to follow the classic tradition in which Herbert and I were brought up. I really believe that Shakespeare would have liked the way we handled his low comedy and I'm sure the Minsky Brothers did. The Bard's words have been spoken better but never bigger or louder" (William Birnes and Richard Lertzman 2015, 99–100).

Actors typically arrived at the studio at 6:00 A.M. to get into costume and makeup, a more intricate affair in *A Midsummer Night's Dream* than that to which Ross had been accustomed. Used to wearing street clothes or army uniforms in his previous pictures, Ross was initially uncomfortable with his costumes and makeup but such discomfort was far more secondary than the embarrassment he shared with many of the cast over his unfamiliarity with Shakespeare. He spent hours with Stanley Logan, the dialogue director on the film, in an attempt to make sense of his rhymed dialogue, and to intone it in such a way that it sounded natural and not stilted. Even though Logan echoed Reinhardt's belief that the Shakespearean play was a comedy and should be played in a low-brow comic style, Ross was unconvinced since much of his dialogue was poetic and not designed for laughs. He chose not to follow the lead of Dick Powell who tossed off his lines with the speed and sass more characteristic of a "Screwball Comedy" than Shakespeare. In the

October 1935 issue of *Hollywood*, Jean Muir (Helena) gave a candid account of rehearsals in early December even before the cameras began to roll:

"It was awfully funny . . . the way Dick finally got into his stride in *The Dream*. . . . The first five days of rehearsal were pretty bad for everyone. We were all worried and felt out of place in our parts before the camera. Some of us had worked with Reinhardt on his production of *The Dream* when it was given last summer in the Hollywood Bowl. Those of us who had knew how kind and how patient Mr. Reinhardt was and we were not exactly scared . . . but Dick, who hadn't been was. He hadn't seen the Bowl performance either.

"Somehow, it hadn't dawned on him that *The Dream* was a comedy and a ribald one at that. The first day he came out on set, his face was deadly serious, his hands rather shaky. He read his part in a monotone, accompanied by what he considered to appropriate Shakespearean gesture. He was nervous because he was confronted with a new problem.

"Reinhardt rehearsed and rehearsed one simple little scene. No one was criticized, no one scolded. But somehow Dick couldn't seem to get the hang of it. I noticed, though, that Mr. Reinhardt was gradually jostling Dick around the scene until he came pretty near to the right approach. Then, on the fifth day, in the middle of a particularly difficult version of the scene, Dick's face lighted up and he shouted at the top of his lungs, 'I GET THE IDEA . . . YOU CAN GAG IT!' . . . the idea that *The Dream* was sort of a slap-stick comedy had at last percolated through the wall of uncertainty which surrounded Dick.

"After that there was no more confusion. Dick romped through the play like a kid just let out of school. He LOVED it! He ran off with all his scenes! He was GRAND! Mr. Reinhardt beamed on him like a proud papa. Dick's enthusiasm was contagious. We were all the better for it. Somehow in finding himself he made all more at ease; we all did better work." (51)

Ross appreciated Muir's positive spin on the rehearsal process, but he was still uncomfortable with Dick Powell's approach to Shakespeare, even though it had been sanctioned by Reinhardt. He believed that Henry Jewett's interpretation of Shakespearean comedy was more grounded and honest than the vaudeville style of play—though he had to admit that *A Midsummer Night's Dream* was a very different comedy than *Much Ado About Nothing*, and who was he to disagree with the great Max Reinhardt!

Because he was served with an injunction by A.A. Haendler, head of a Paris theatrical agency, to restrain Reinhardt from working on *A Midsummer Night's Dream* because he allegedly broke a contract to direct a production of *Die Fledermaus* in London, Reinhardt was not allowed to appear at the studio for the first week of shooting. Instead, William Dieterle directed the filming and continued to direct morning shots, even after Reinhardt was exonerated of the charge and allowed to return to work. Reinhardt did not enjoy working at 8:00 A.M. when filming typically began; instead, he worked with the actors in the afternoon and evening and slept late while Dieterle photographed the scenes he directed the night before. According to the *Oakland Tribune* (17 March 1935), although Reinhardt spoke very little English, he was able to detect the least mispronunciation, the misplacement of a word, or the most minute change in an actor's lines from the first to last speech in *A Midsummer Night's Dream*. Before each scene he called the actors together and went over the lines to be spoken and, assisted by Dieterle, he described the blocking of the scene and set out to discover the core action of the event in order to develop the dramatic moment to its fullest potential. Even though Reinhardt allowed the actors a certain amount of freedom in their movements, in order that they would appear completely natural in their performance, he managed their behavior in even the smallest detail.

Max Reinhardt on the set of Theseus's Palace in *A Midsummer Night's Dream.*

Before the palace set had been constructed, the magic forest was completed on Warner Brothers' Stage 8, a description of which was reported by *The Los Angeles Times* on 23 December 1934:

The wood (designed by Anton Grot) filled Stage Eight entirely and burst onto the adjoining street, over which a grass-covered runway extended clear to the roof of the carpenter shop. The wood is the most remarkable [setting] in Hollywood annals, a synthetic reinforced paradise of silver birches, willows, great oaks, ferns, flowers, brooks and stones, with backdrops to give the perspective of distance.

On a greensward, Mme. Bonislava Nijinska was instructing the fairies-to-be, elves, pixies, gnomes and the like in the graces of the dance. Lights flared suddenly, evil eyes in a dark forest, as electricians tried out *apparati*. A voice thundered intermittently from an invisible loudspeaker. Associate director William Dieterle, frowning prodigiously, was trying to make a camera test of a prancing unicorn.

When it became clear that the forest set could not be lit properly by cinematographer Ernest Haller, he was replaced with Hal Mohr who shortened slightly the heights of the trees, sprayed them with aluminum paint, and covered them with cobwebs and tiny metal particles to reflect the light. According to studio reports, the production eventually consumed sixty-seven tons of trees, 1500 pounds of rubber, 600,000 yards of cellophane, and 650,000 candles. Mme. Nijinska's rehearsals were often visited by Hollywood choreographers Busby Berkeley and Bobby Connolly who wanted to watch her methods. Their presence caused a major distraction to the young women in the dancing chorus, who, understandably, wanted to audition for the gentlemen by dancing "full out" rather than in rehearsal mode as Nijinska required. Eventually, Berkeley and Connolly were barred from Nijinska's rehearsals.

Although work on *A Midsummer Night's Dream* proved to consume the entirety of the actors' lives, reports emerged from Hollywood revealing that Ross spent his free time taking his wife to one or another of Hollywood's more upscale restaurants. During the early days of rehearsal in December, one such establishment presented him with a bill for $60 ($1,125 in 2019)—just for dinner for two with Rhine wine. Ross demanded a receipt from the waiter, and throughout the eleven weeks of production of *Dream*, he continued to flaunt the bill in front of his costars to forewarn them of what they might expect if they decide to frequent the establishment. In addition, on New Year's Day 1935, Ross and the cast of *Dream* feted the Alabama football team at Warner Bros. studio as a prelude to their participation in the Rose Bowl Game. The *Oakland Tribune* (2 January 1935) provided a detailed account of the festivities:

After touring the studio and watching [rehearsals] for *A Midsummer*

Night's Dream and Busby Berkeley making spectacular scenes for *Gold Diggers of 1935*, the team and members of their official party were guests of Jack L. Warner at luncheon. Joe E. Brown, the most athletically inclined of all Hollywood's stars, acted as master of ceremonies, and entertained the visitors with some amusing stories. Al Jolson sang "Mammy" and received an ovation. Dick Powell, who hails from Arkansas, discovered that seven of the Alabama team also are natives of that State, and one of them is an old friend. Dick sang "Happiness Ahead" and "Mr. and Mrs." From his latest hit, *Flirtation Walk*. Winifred Shaw, vivid newcomer to pictures, also sang several numbers, and Olive Jones, another Warner starlet, played the piano.

In addition to Ross Alexander and the players already mentioned, the Alabamans were greeted by Warner's contract players, including Anita Louise, Frank McHugh, Pat O'Brien, Warren William, Donald Woods, Jean Muir, Errol Flynn, Henry O'Neill, Maxine Doyle, Grace Ford, and Ross's childhood playmate, Phil Regan.

Early in January while Ross was busy rehearsing and filming his scenes for *A Midsummer Night's Dream*, he was selected by *The Boston Globe* (7 January 1935) as one of the new up-and-coming "names" in filmdom, along with Fred Astaire, Fred MacMurray, Robert Donat, Cesar Romero, Elsa Lanchester, Rosalind Russell, Paulette Goddard, Clair Trevor, and Alice Faye, among others. After only three released pictures at Warner Brothers, Ross had become part of the conversation that included him in a list of potential Hollywood stars. The *Lebanon* (Pennsylvania) *Daily News* (2 February 1935) reinforced Alexander's position as a "comer" in Hollywood with an essay on "scene stealing" that focused on Ross's performance in his three released Warner's pictures. Because it is highly illustrative of the actor's abilities, the article is presented in its entirety below:

The subject of today's effusion is a young actor whose likeness has recently appeared on several local screens—and for those in the class who haven't already sighed and turned their heads, let us hasten to wager that when we say actor, we mean actor—not Gilded Youth or Adonis Incarnate or Man of 1,000 Faces or America's Boyfriend or anything but actor, plain actor.

The name this rare avis goes by is Ross Alexander. He is not yet a star. So far as we know, his opinions on art, wimmin and The New Deal have not yet been broadcast through the nation. BUT, if this department were dispensing medals for the most successful picture stealer of the year, the first and shiniest of the lot would go to young Mr. Alexander, with all the good will this department could muster and of which he'd naturally have no need.

Do we hear some worthy member of the class interrupting to ask, "What is a picture stealer?" Well, the easiest answer would be Ross Alexander. If in saying this, however, we still fail to make ourselves clear, let us put it that a picture stealer is a genuine actor (or actress) whom the official stars of the piece—nice looking boys and girls, usually, trying to get along and managing very well without our sanctions, thank you—are occasionally somewhat embarrassed to find in their midst.

To elaborate a little: Do you remember *Flirtation Walk*—the slightly odd little number at the Colonial, some time ago, in which we learned how it's Mrs. Al Jolson who makes Generals and how the best place to get hints on putting on musical shows is West Point? We assume, for the sake of policy, that you do. And, do you remember also, cavorting in it, the aforementioned Mrs. Jolson, complemented by Messrs. Dick Powell and Pat O'Brien? No doubt, you do. But what you remember best, we'll wager, is the dark young man, vaguely suggestive of an electrically charged horse hair, who played Powell's roommate and gave a sudden, blunderbuss lift to the business on his every appearance, without so much as a by your leave. Well, that young man was Ross Alexander, may his tribe increase.

And then do you remember *Gentlemen Are Born* at the Capitol a week or so ago? Maybe you missed this one, but you shouldn't have, for it was one of the better pictures of the month. And in it, as you may have guessed, was this same Mr. Alexander. This time, however, he had some competition. The official lead, that is, was Franchot Tone who in his Theatre Guild days was generally conceded to be the most promising young actor on the American stage, and who in this effort was more like his old self of that happy period than he has been since he packed his makeup kit for Hollywood.

223

This time, as we were saying, Mr. Alexander had some competition. But was he downhearted? He was not. Nor had he any reason to be. For every time he had a couple of lines, something of the same sort happened as happened previously in *Flirtation Walk*: The proceedings took on added color; a sense of direct emotional contact with the audience was achieved, and when the final closeup faded and the lights came up, it was that infinitely appealing, slightly comic, unsettlingly anxious young figure, waiting in the hospital corridor for the return of his wife from the operating room—Ross Alexander again— whom we thought of.

Well, we might go on like this indefinitely, of course, but though the spirit is willing, space is precious and anyhow we believe we've made our point— which is (a) that Mr. Alexander is one of the most fearsome scene stealers we've ever come across and (b) it follows, a swell actor. Before taking leave, however, we might say that neither we nor Mr. Alexander himself are going to be responsible for the roles he subsequently draws. His current picture, for example, is a mild little creampuff called *Maybe It's Love* that wouldn't be worth two cents without him and that even he can't make it worth much than three. And the one in which he is now working is the Warner Brothers' conception of how *A Midsummer Night's Dream* should go, in which he will probably be buried under a million dollars' worth of Reinhardt. Yet we do not see why either of these things should make us step any more cautiously. Because after all Ross Alexander has given every evidence of being the real thing, and come what may (and come plenty may in Hollywood, as we all know) that fact, having once been established, has got to stand.

Not to be completely overshadowed by her husband's Hollywood successes, Aleta Freel had become a founding member of a permanent producing organization on the East Coast called the Stage Association. Accordion to the *Daily News* (8 January 1935), the members, all graduates of the University Players at West Falmouth, Massachusetts, included Leslie Adams, Henry Fonda, Burgess Meredith, Norris Houghton, Charles Leatherbee, Joshua Logan, Myron McCormick, Mildred Natwick, James Stewart, and Bretaigne Windust. The new organization had offices in the

St. James Theatre and claimed that it had "no 'messages,' no program of propaganda" but simply wanted to present its members in plays that show them to good advantage. Although the Stage Association did little to advance Freel's career, either in film or theatre, it did manage to keep her connected to her East Coast friends and associates who continued to provide emotional support for her artistic dreams.

After eleven weeks of production, *A Midsummer Night's Dream* completed filming on 9 March 1935 at the cost of $1,380,000, according to Warner estimates, at least $250,000 over budget. Documenting the archive materials in the Turner Classic Movie database, Frank Miller reported that while the visual aspect of the production looked spectacular on film, misfortune continued to threaten *A Midsummer Night's Dream*. A trained bear that appeared throughout the film died unexpectedly; two of the smaller sets designed for the production burned down; and, perhaps, worst of all, on 13 January—barely a month after filming began—Mickey Rooney broke his leg while tobogganing at Big Bear Mountain, forcing him to remain in Hollywood Hospital from 14 January through 9 February, during which George Breakston, who understudied Rooney in the stage version of *A Midsummer Night's Dream* and who performed the role of Puck when the play's touring schedule moved beyond California, stood in for Puck in the long shots and recorded the offstage lines spoken by the character. Once Rooney returned to the set, he had to complete the film wearing a full cast disguised with foliage and hidden by holes cut into the barks of trees. In more active scenes, he was moved around on a tricycle by stagehands camouflaged to fade into the sylvan undergrowth.

A 9 October premiere at the Hollywood Theatre in New York City was announced with the entire cast and creative crew advertised in attendance. Press previews were used to great advantage, with Delight Evans announcing in *Screenland* (October 1935) that "The most important preview in screen history has just been held, and I want you to be among the first to know about it. . . . This occasion was a secret and exclusive preview of Max Reinhardt's screen production of *A Midsummer Night's Dream*, produced by Warner

Brothers—the same producers who gambled on talkies and won. This time they are taking a greater gamble—on Art. I hope they win again; and I think they will, because thanks to their acumen in lavish casting, to Reinhardt's supervision, and to one Will Shakespeare, they have not only attained Art, but They Got Entertainment! To say I was thrilled with *A Midsummer Night's Dream* is the height of understatement. It is an incredible, eerie adventure in pure fantasy: a dream of dazzling beauty, a rowdy circus, an enchanting spectacle, a robust, earthy riot" (13). *Modern Screen* (October 1935) added that "we were delighted to find that all the Warner players took their Shakespeare quite calmly. They read their lines as if they were actually conversing and didn't once rave and gesture all over the place. This was particularly commendable in the younger players—Dick Powell, Jean Muir, Ross Alexander and Olivia de Havilland, whom we think you will consider a find" (8). With excellent advance publicity stirring up interest in the film, *A Midsummer Night's Dream* sped along to its 9 October premiere at the Hollywood Theatre, described by the *Motion Picture Daily* (10 October 1935) as "one of those kind of openings that would make the Metropolitan Opera House manager burst a shirt stud with pride. Broadway hasn't seen anything like it—not since the depression, anyway, and memories grow hazy beyond that."

In the audience at the premiere, Ross and Aleta were surrounded by dignitaries and celebrities from all walks of life, the likes of which impressed even Aleta who had grown up in elite society. Attendees included Albert Einstein, who had recently applied for citizenship in the United States, Edward G. Robinson, Joan Crawford, Franchot Tone, Adolph Zukor, founder of Paramount Pictures, Mrs. James Roosevelt, mother of President Franklyn Delano Roosevelt, Will H. Hays, administrator of the Production Code, Deems Taylor, composer and music critic, Lily Pons and Kirsten Flagstad, opera singers, Rudy Vallée, crooner, Fannie Hurst, novelist, and Daniel Frohman, Broadway producer, as well as members and officers of the English Speaking Union, one of the oldest and most important international societies in the world and, for which, the premiere served as a benefit performance.

The Hollywood Theatre in New York City, hours before thousands of spectators crowded the entrance for the premiere of *A Midsummer Night's Dream*.

The reviews that followed all agreed that the production was beautiful, artistically crafted, and auspiciously photographed, the *Motion Picture Daily* (10 October 1935) perhaps saying it best: "In its breath-taking photography, shot through filmy and lace-like filters; in the arrangement of the ballet, heightened by the mechanical and technical wizardry of the camera; in its beautifully arranged and brilliantly played musical accompaniments, *A Midsummer Night's Dream* represents a new level in artistic and production standards." However, the same publication introduced the aspect of the film

227

that most came under fire: the actors' performances. "In its acting, supplied by virtually the entire roster of Warner stars and featured players, the spectacle ranges from the excellent to something less." The *New York Post* (10 October 1935) added that "the curious result of this casting is a jumble of good and bad and indifferent acting; and there is not one dialogue scene which is not marred or ruined by at least one of the players. Dick Powell, whose Lysander is in evidence for most of the picture easily outstrips all the other players in total wreckage. "

Quoting critic Malcolm Johnson, the *Motion Picture Daily* (11 October 1935) continued: "To put it brutally, this cast, as a whole, does it badly. The players with few exceptions are as though suddenly seized with stage fright in awe of their material. . . . They stumble, usually at headlong pace, through their lines, reciting them without conviction, like parrots. They seem to have no feeling for the meaning of the words, of the poetry." Quoting London critic Eileen Creelman, the journal reported that "in only two instances have the directors, Max Reinhardt and William Dieterle, been unfortunate in their selection of players. The vulgar grimaces of Dick Powell and Ross Alexander are decidedly distressing." Quoting another London critic, William Boebnel, however, the opinion was reversed: "It would be engaging . . . to comment on the fine performances of Ian Hunter, Olivia de Havilland, Ross Alexander and Jean Muir. But then all the acting was good, even though one or two actors were ill chosen."

Andre Sennwald in *The New York Times* (10 October 1935), added that, although, Mickey Rooney's performance as Puck "is one of the major delights of the work . . . In the other important roles the film is uneven in performance and suggests flaws in Mr. Reinhardt's reading of the play. . . . The distraught lovers are a study in scrambled moods. While the two maidens, Jean Muir and Olivia de Havilland, immerse themselves in excesses of tearful passion, their consorts, Dick Powell and Ross Alexander, prance about in an excess of good humor and delight in informing the audience what hilarious fellows they are." Kate Cameron in the *Daily News*, however, observed that "The cast works with beautiful harmony under the master's direction. . . . Dick Powell and Ross Alexander are good as the quarreling lovers, Lysander and Demetrius."

Variety (16 October 1935), complaining about the casting of Dick Powell and the annoying grimaces of Mickey Rooney, echoed the sentiments of other reviews and insisted that the film runs too long. In its elite road-show guise, *A Midsummer Night's Dream* ran 133 minutes, including a six-minute overture and ten-minute intermission. "Trimmed by at least twenty minutes *Dream* would be greatly improved as entertainment." In addition, *Variety* made a dramatic statement about the importance of the film:

Whether the production, costing around $1,300,000, will justify itself commercially, is a question. It's a selling job and a big one. No other film of the current season has attracted as much discussion and public interest among intellectuals and in the press. It has been heralded as the concrete answer from Hollywood that a new era in films is here. As a matter of fact, *Dream* proves nothing of the kind. But it does emphasize that the screen, as a form of expression, need never hesitate to tackle the most difficult jobs of translating a lovely idea from stage or literature. No one who witnesses the spiders weave the bridal veil for Titania will forget this short scene of consummate loveliness. Hence, *Dream* may be said to be a fine prestige picture not only for Warners but for the film industry as a whole. And that's why it should get the full cooperation of the business.

As time passed, *A Midsummer Night's Dream* opened in cities including Los Angeles, Philadelphia, Toronto, Cleveland, Pittsburgh, Washington, D.C., and Boston, initially doing excellent business at every screening. The more cities that saw *A Midsummer Night's Dream*, the more did the picture earn mixed reviews. Calling the film an incomparably "valiant achievement," *The Boston Globe* (9 November 1935) wrote that "Dick Powell and Ross Alexander are not as wholly successful. They are a little too consciously winning, too comic in their love battles. It would seem more suitable should these same young men play their parts with more intensity, instead of striving for laughs." Writing in *The Brooklyn Daily Eagle* (1 December 1935), John Reddington asked: "Is it to be Reinhardt's *Midsummer Night's Dream*, which, for all its ingenuities, its passages of visual poetry, does so little with the audible magnificence of the text? And is one who is convinced that Reinhardt has magnified and intensified the range of the camera merely to ignore the amateurishness of Dick Powell, Ross Alexander and Jean Muir?" A week later, on 8 December 1935, Charles Collins, writing for the *Chicago Tribune*, added: "The roles of Lysander and Demetrius, young men of the four-sided love story, are to me a flaw in the general scheme of things—an error not of conception but of execution. Reinhardt wanted them to be light fantastic fellows, high comedians of amorous exploits; but apparently, he could not find in Hollywood a pair or youths of sufficient skill in acting for this difficult technique. Most of the time Masters Dick Powell and Ross Alexander appear to be kidding their love affairs. The Powell lad is sometimes arch, sometimes cute, sometimes merely fresh, and he never convinces me that he is a proper object for Hermia's romantic infatuation."

In October 1936. *A Midsummer Night's Dream* returned to New York City for a popular-priced run at the Strand Theatre. Winston Burdett's review of the production in *The Brooklyn Daily Eagle* (5 October 1936) proclaimed that "the forest scenes come closest to recapturing the mood of the poet, not when Mr. Reinhardt's fairies make their twenty-yard leaps across a brook or when Oberon and Titania sail into the night suspended on cords of steel, but when the camera works its magic more simply by a stray shot of the sleeping forest. The players, James Cagney, Joe E. Brown, Victory Jory and Ross Alexander, give performances which are, by their own lights, excellent but they have not been transformed overnight into accomplished Shakespeareans, least of all in the matter of reading their lines."

The finest reviews Ross earned in *A Midsummer Night's Dream* came from West High School in Rochester, New York, that announced, "To Honor Film Player: Comment on Ross Alexander Smith, a former West High School pupil who plays an important role in the film. *Midsummer Night's Dream* will be a feature in Tuesday's [26 November 1935] issue of the *Occident News*, West High School paper." Ross was impressed that the school considered him one of their own, even though he did not graduate. He knew, of course, that words in a high school newspaper do not have a great deal of power with studio executives or critics at large; still, he enjoyed the magnanimous gesture of approval from his high school fans.

In spite of the occasional kind review and the overwhelming support of his high school fans, however, Ross viewed *A Midsummer Night's Dream* as a personal failure on every level. He hated the costume and makeup; he disagreed with Reinhardt's direction; he felt that he should have spoken up more often to challenge directorial decisions. At the same time, Ross didn't want to be labelled a "difficult" actor who refused to trust his fellow-performers and directors; but, when an actor honestly believes that every choice being made for him is wrong, how can he succeed? Obviously, the majority of reviews for *A Midsummer Night's Dream* proved that Ross was correct in his original misgivings about the vaudeville approach to the film. Such a style may have been appropriate for the low comedians performing *Pyramus and Thisbe*, but the lovers, he felt, needed more substance, even if their squabbles were immature. The fact that he had neither the experience as a Shakespearean actor nor the education as a Shakespearean scholar to support his instincts cast Ross into a deep depression, from which he emerged determined, in future projects, to voice his opinions more vigorously and more selectively bestow his trust.

It was obvious to Ross that *A Midsummer Night's Dream* would do little to help his career in "A" movies for, almost immediately after shooting wrapped on the Shakespeare film, he was assigned to a pair of "B" films, the first starring Zazu Pitts, and the latter with Joan Blondell.

15. *Going Highbrow* and *We're in the Money*

Shortly after *A Midsummer Night's Dream* completed shooting in March 1935, Ross and his wife welcomed Henry Fonda to Hollywood and insisted that he and his cat, George, stay with them until he could find a place of his own in Beverley Hills. Fonda had come out West to star in Fox's film adaptation of his latest Broadway success, *The Farmer Takes a Wife*, co-starring Janet Gaynor, and directed by Victor Fleming who would go on to direct *The Wizard of Oz* and *Gone with the Wind*. What Fonda found at the Alexanders' home on 7357 Woodrow Wilson Drive seemed less like a private residence than a miniature farm, with goats and ducks, herded by Mr. Watson, an English bulldog and Itchy, the cat, who, wary of interlopers in his private dominion, greeted Fonda and George with cautious indifference. Fonda wondered why Ross didn't hire a farmhand to take care of the animals, but Alexander wouldn't even consider the possibility. He believed that he understood the whims and idiosyncrasies of his animals better than anyone else.

As he noted in his autobiography, Fonda quickly discovered that the fun-loving couple he knew at Falmouth and Mt. Kisco had become domesticated into what appeared to be an almost passion-less marriage of convenience, far removed from Hollywood's reach in the sparsely populated hills through which wound Woodrow Wilson Drive (Fonda 1981, 96). In addition, as William H. McKegg observed a month before when he visited the Alexanders, Fonda noticed that the couple had few friends from the film industry. Certainly, Ross was friendly with members of his casts but the only Hollywood "star" who was a regular guest at the Woodrow Wilson address was Bette Davis. McKegg also noted that he found in his visit to Ross Alexander "just the sort of call any fan would enjoy. Nothing was overdone or exaggerated. Ross is friendly. He has the stage actor's directness. While talking, he'll move one of his arms in circular fashion, as if stirring up his speech, or dragging himself forward by each sentence" (McKegg 1935, 79).

One of the stories Ross told McKegg—and one he was fond of repeating—involved a man who, while out driving, saw a farmer plowing a field with a bull pulling the plow. Seeing that the farmer was having great difficulty, the man stopped the car and got out to speak to him. "Don't you know," he asked the farmer, "that in these modern days, you don't have to have a bull pull a plow? There are horses for that, and better yet, there are tractors." Thanking the man for his concern, the farmer replied: "I have a horse to pull this plow and I also have a tractor, but I want to teach this bull that there is something else in this world besides pleasure." The "no pain–no gain" mantra of hard work Ross learned from his forebears had stayed with him, even when his life and career seemed to be in the ascendant.

While staying with the Alexanders, Fonda discovered that Ross and Aleta had a fascination for aviation, which, they explained, began on a flight to a local resort, during which the pilot permitted each of them to handle the controls. Much to Fonda's surprise, they told him that their goal was to achieve a hard-to-get transport pilot's license. No longer amazed by any of the Alexanders' interests, Fonda also noted their affection for the children of a Chinese family who had recently lost their father. The Alexanders' gardener served as surrogate father to the children and Ross and Aleta became a doting uncle and aunt who gave them the run of the household (and the farm animals) and took them to screenings of Ross's films. Yes, Ross and Aleta had become domesticated, even though each was determined to pursue a career. Because she felt that separation was fatal to a marriage, Aleta spent more time in Hollywood than she might have liked. The newly created Stage Associates organization demanded her presence in New York City but, given the rumors of her husband's alleged infidelities with Hollywood starlets, she was afraid to go East for any extended period. At the time, she was unaware that the rumors were simply studio publicity stunts, planted to associate Ross with the feminine flavor of the month and dispel any whispers of his homosexuality. As Aleta's opportunities in Hollywood dwindled into failed screen tests, she felt that her only chance of a career could be attained three thousand miles away from her husband. Such knowledge ultimately proved to poison the marriage.

At 6:00 A.M. on 13 March 1935, Ross reported to Warner Bros. to begin shooting *Social Pirates* (AKA *Crashing Society*, and released as *Going Highbrow*). In addition to Ross who was chosen to play Harley Marsh, the "young, good-looking scion of an impoverished, aristocratic New York family who falls in love with Sandy, a pretty waitress who knows all the answers and is 'adopted' by the Upshaws because they need a daughter to make a debut," June Martel acted the role of Sandy and Guy Kibbee and Zazu Pitts played the social climbing, *nouveaux riches*, Matt and Cora Upshaw. Edward Everett Horton rounded out the principal characters as Augie Witherspoon, "an eccentric comedy character who has managed the Marsh estate and successfully ruined it, but still remains friend and advisor to Harley Marsh" (Edward Kaufman and Sy Bartlett 1935, *Cast of Characters*).

We first meet Harley Marsh (to whom the script refers as Dick Powell) in an early scene with Augie Winterspoon:

Harley. Look, Augie—you managed the estate into a complete coma— First, with that synthetic rubber plantation, then, all those other wide-eyed schemes. It's a wonder you haven't put our money into developing a squirt-less grapefruit

Augie. Squirt-less grapefruit? A brilliant idea!! I must make a note of it.. .. Harley! I have it! .... A brilliant inspiration! A coup de grace.

Harley. (*Wearily.*) Now what?

Augie. The idea came to me like a flash—and when a Witherspoon gets an idea—

Harley. (*Dryly*) It's a miracle....

Augie. Now listen to this— (*Picks up newspaper and reads.*) "Mr. and Mrs Matt Upshaw, who will occupy the Presidential Suite at the Waldorf, arrived today from Genoa after purchasing a rare Tintoretto in Rome. The record price of — (*Throwing paper on desk.*) The rest doesn't matter.

Harley. (*Matter-of-factly.*) Nothing matters.

Augie. (*Still fired up.*) No, nothing matt— (*He reacts and thunders.*) Of course, it matters! It's downright silly for them to go abroad to buy a painting when *you* have a gallery full here.

Harley. What for?

Augie. For a fortune! They have *money*—your mother has none; your mother has *paintings*—they have *none*. Put the two together and what have you?

Harley. (*Clowning wearily.*) A headache. (Kaufman and Bartlett 1935, 13–14)

Eventually Harley realizes the efficacy of Augie's idea and agrees to persuade his mother (Nella Walker) to sell her paintings.

Meanwhile, Matt Upshaw has developed a friendship with Sandy who works as a waitress in a coffee shop and refuses to believe that Matt is a millionaire. Following an amusing rendition of the "Sextet" from Donizetti's *Lucia*, in which Harley and Augie take part, Augie, dangling a $50,000 retainer in front of Mrs. Marsh, convinces her to sponsor the debut of the Upshaw's daughter, in spite of Harley's objections. Since the Upshaws have no daughter, Matt persuades Sandy to play the part as Millicent, the niece of an old friend.

On Fifth Avenue, Harley happens to see Sandy trying to extricate her shoe from a grating on the sidewalk. He falls in love with her at first sight, and in something of a daze, he walks toward her and tips his hat.

Sandy. Well, if you persist in standing here, you might be of some use. If you'll hold these bundles, maybe I can get my shoe loose. (*Before he has a chance to realize what is wrong, she dumps the bundles in his arms and once more proceeds to wiggle her foot. This doesn't help, so she reaches down and tries to loosen her foot with her hand. For the first time, Harley sees what is wrong.*)

Harley. Oh, now, that's too bad.

Sandy. (*Coldly as she looks up from her position.*) Isn't it?

Harley. On Fifth Avenue, too.

Sandy. (*Still looking up from her stooped position.*) Carry this grate around the corner and I'll be on Fifty-Seventh Street.

Harley. (*Disregarding her iciness.*) If you'll hold the bundles, I think I can extricate you.

Sandy. (*As she straightens and holds her arms out for the bundles.*) All right, smarty—extricate. (*He gladly hands her the bundles and stoops down to help her. With a firm hold on the counter of her pump, he wiggles it sideways several times and his hand slips causing it to run up her silken ankle. NOTE: Censorship angle. Avoid anything suggestive in the above scene. Don't let Harley's hand slide up Sandy's leg.*) I get it—the pawing type!

Harley. (*Embarrassed as he rises.*) I'm awfully sorry—my hand slipped.

Sandy. So I noticed.

Harley. If you'll step out of your shoe, I think I can get it loose. (Kaufman and Bartlett 1935, 56–57)

In his efforts to free the shoe, Harley manages to break off the heel:

Harley. I—I—I really don't know how to apologize.

Sandy. (*Burned up.*) You don't know how to do anything else. . . .

Harley. (*Apologetically.*) Isn't there some way that I can show you how sorry I am?

Sandy. (*Curtly, as she starts to get into the [limousine waiting for her.]*) Sure. — Go back and lay down beside the heel. That'll make it a pair! (Kaufman and Bartlett 1935, 58)

The next time Harley encounters Sandy, she is appearing as Millicent at her "coming out" party. He accidentally steps on her foot and causes her dress to be caught by the French doors as she tries to exit. Outside, the heel of her shoe gets caught in the small, round spigot of the garden sprinkling system, and, once again, in trying to extricate the shoe, Harley breaks off the heel.

Harley. You know you don't really dislike me so much.

Millicent. If I had any way of walking through the ballroom without any shoes on, I'd show you how much I like your company. (*Harley glances around and sees a pair of rubber books nearby, left by the gardener.*)

Harley. Would rubber boots do? (*He picks Millicent up in his arms and carries her to a canopied garden swing and sets her down. He then gets the boots and brings them over to her.*) Wasn't it thoughtful of your gardener to leave these here? You remind me of Cinderella.

Millicent. (*Begins to laugh.*) Of course. Just my size. . . . (*Harley puts the boots on her and she presents a cute, grotesque appearance with her evening gown and the rubber boots.*) (Kaufman and Bartlett 1935, 80–81)

What Harley had hoped would be a romantic conclusion the scene becomes ironically comic when he closes his eyes and Millicent starts wrapping a garden hose around his shoulders:

Harley. (*Ecstatically.*) You darling!

Millicent. Are you bathed in happiness?

Harley. I'm about to be.

Millicent. You think not!? (*She turns on the nozzle of the hose full in Harley's face and as the water splashes over him and he jumps up with an exclamation,*

Millicent hobbles awkwardly away in the rubber boots, leaving Harley trying to extricate himself from the hose.) (Kaufman and Bartlett 1935, 82)

Ross Alexander and June Martel in the "boots" scene from *Going Highbrow*.

Following the "boots" scene Harley confesses to Augie that he loves Millicent so much that he would rather have nothing to do with her if there were a single suspicion on her part that he was only interested in her for her money. To ignite the romance between Millicent and Harley, Augie hires actor Sam Long (Gordon Westcott) to pretend to make love to Millicent, as a catalyst for Harley's jealousy. The scheme works because almost immediately, Harley asks Matt Upshaw for Millicent's hand in marriage. When it is revealed that Millicent is a penniless waitress, Harley is thrilled beyond belief, knowing that she would never consider his interest in her to be mercenary. Coincidentally, Sam happens to be Sandy's estranged husband, who invites a punch in the nose from Hartley after claiming that he "won't give [Sandy] a divorce because she's nothing but a —" (103). Later Sam is willing to agree to a divorce for $10,000 but Augie purloins a letter that proves that Sam was a bigamist when he married Sandy, so their marriage is invalid, leaving Sandy free to marry Harley. Matt, Hartley, and Augie descend on the coffee shop where Sandy is working to tell her the news.

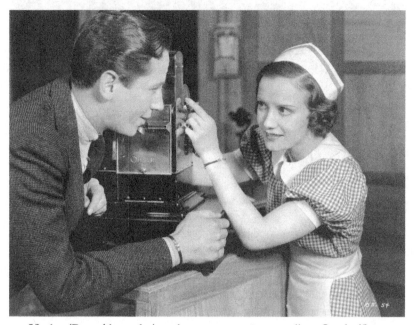

Harley (Ross Alexander) at the counter trying to talk to Sandy (June Martel).

Ross follows Sandy into the kitchen of the coffee shop where he explains that she was never actually married to Sam Long. Taking her in his arms, he upsets the tray she was carrying and it crashes to the floor. The sound echoes throughout the coffee shop causing Matt and Augie to rush into the kitchen where they find Harley and Sandy in a long embrace.

Going Highbrow completed production on 1 April 1935. Two days later, in his "I Cover Hollywood" column, Lloyd Pantages advertised that Zazu Pitts was frightened half to death when Ross Alexander kissed her during the filming of one of her scenes, just because she hadn't been told that it would happen. "Well, I declare!" she exclaimed and pushed Alexander away, to the roaring delight of the entire company. It seems that she had remarked to the director, Robert Florey, and to her film husband, Guy Kibbee, that she had always been a "kiss-less actress." *The Montclair* (New Jersey) *Times* (16 April 1935) explained that "The next scene called for the various characters— Edward Everett Horton, Kibbee, Miss Pitts and young Alexander, to be very excitedly happy over a situation. This was Florey's chance. He privately instructed Ross Alexander to seize Zazu at the height of the excitement and give her a resounding smack. Alexander followed instructions to the letter. But the scene had to be cut because the kiss was not only too loud for the sound-track, but Zazu's scream was far too shrill. After the excitement had died down, and Miss Pitts had joined rather wanly in the laugh at her expense, she consented to Florey's suggestion that it be done over again and left in the picture as a comedy touch."

Augie (Edward Everett Horton), Harley (Ross Alexander), Sandy (June Martel), and Matt (Guy Kibbee) in the final scene of *Going Highbrow*.

While *Going Highbrow* was in the editing room, being prepared for a 6 July 1935 release, Paramount Pictures requested the loan of Ross Alexander to appear in two of their upcoming pictures, *Accent on Youth* and *The Big Broadcast*. During the first two weeks of April, Ross began working on

241

the scripts of those films in anticipation that Paramount's request would be honored by Warner Brothers. On 15 April, however, it was announced that Jack Warner refused to lend Paramount the actor because Warner Bros. wished to give Alexander the male lead opposite Joan Blondell and Glenda Farrell in *Serves You Right* (AKA *We're in the Money*), a comedy by F. Hugh Herbert and Brown Holmes, scheduled to begin production on 8 May, under the direction of Ray Enright. A week prior to the filming of *We're in the Money*, *The Boston Globe* (2 May 1935) announced that Ross Alexander had been voted the favorite actor by the students of Natick High School in the annual "What's What Contest" sponsored by the school newspaper, the *Sassamon*. From the very beginning of his career, much of Alexander's fan mail had come from teenage girls and boys and the voting at the high school demonstrated just how popular Ross had become with teenagers.

In *We're in the Money*, Ross played C. Richard Courtney, another upper-class young man (though far from impoverished as in the previous film) who masquerades as a chauffeur, "Carter," in order to escape process servers long enough to avoid the breach of promise suit brought against him by Claire LeClaire (Anita Kerry). His timing is important since in a few weeks a state law prohibiting the trial of breach of promise suits will be put into effect. The film begins with Carter and his sweetheart, Ginger Stewart (Joan Blondell), locked in a deep embrace in a secluded corner of a public park. Their romantic moment is interrupted by the honking of a car horn, which Ginger explains is her Aunt Emma calling her. As she arrives at the honking automobile, we discover that Aunt Emma is, in reality, her partner Dixie Tilton (Glenda Farrell) and that the two women are process servers employed by Homer Bronson (Hugh Herbert), the often-befuddled lawyer representing Miss LeClaire. We soon discover that Bronson desperately needs the women to deliver subpoenas to witnesses in the breach of promise case because the tough-looking process servers he had originally hired had met with accidents and failed in their efforts to serve wrestler Man Mountain Dean (himself), Courtney's bodyguard, singer Phil Logan (originally Phil Ryan in the screenplay) (Phil Regan), Courtney's friend, and Butch Gonzala (Lionel

242

Stander), owner of the night spots where Courtney and LeClaire committed their alleged indiscretions. The following image depicts the scene in Bronson's office in which the men are seen covered with bandages—one with his arm in a sling—one on crutches—one in a plaster cast.

Dixie (Glenda Farrell), Ginger (Joan Blondell), Claire (Anita Kerry), three unnamed hooligans, Max (Hobart Cavanaugh), and Bronson (Hugh Herbert) in *We're in the Money*.

Because Ginger and Dixie hope to get out of the process-serving business, they agree to take on Miss LeClaire's case for $1,000, enough money for them to start a new life. The scene changes to the Courtney mansion where Stephen Dinsmore (Henry O'Neill), C. Richard's financial advisor is reprimanding him for his behavior toward Miss LeClaire which has caused her to sue him for half a million dollars. As Dinsmore proceeds to advise Courtney to take his yacht out for a trip "While LeClaire cools her heels, and I cool off her attorney," Courtney receives a phone call from Ginger causing the scene to change abruptly to the park, where the couple are discovered in another "big kiss," interrupted once again by the horn-honking of the irrepressible Aunt Emma, calling Ginger back to work.

The first subpoena the women deliver is to singer Phil Logan at the Club Royale. The image below depicts a working shot of the scene with Ginger and Dixie in evening gowns seated at a table, right of center, and Logan standing beside the table. An orchestra can be seen at the rear of the shot, in front of which are cameras, director, and crew. Extended over the center of the image is a large boom microphone.

Work image of the Club Royal sequence in *We're in the Money*.

The women manage to serve the unsuspecting Logan in front of the nightclub audience that laughs and applauds thinking that the entire routine was some kind of joke on the singer.

Next Ginger and Dixie successfully serve a summons to Man Mountain Dean during his wrestling Match with Chief Little Wolf (himself) and to Butch Gonzola, who falls prey to Ginger's seductive technique of serving the subpoena just as he is ready to make love. The last individual to be served is Courtney, who, assisted by Homer Bronson's offer of a ride to the docks, flees his apartment and hides out on his yacht with Dinsmore, his finance man. Once Courtney is on board, Bronson discovers his identity and summons Ginger and Dixie to the dock, where he has charted a motor boat to ferry the women out to Courtney's yacht. As they approach the vessel, Ginger decides to jump into the water in the belief that someone on the boat would hear her cries for help and rescue her. She is rescued and, much to her amazement, discovers that Carter is, indeed C. Richard Courtney, a realization that compels her to slap him back and forth with the wet subpoena, which Courtney ascertains is a summons. She is abruptly tossed back into the water, but this time it is Courtney who jumps in after her and returns her to his yacht:

> **Ginger.** Think I was going to drown myself and then sue you?
>
> **Courtney.** I don't pretend to know anything about your intentions anymore—
>
> **Dinsmore.** (*Approaches, shaking his head sadly.*) I wish you two people would make up your minds.
>
> **Ginger.** I've made up mine! (*She jumps overboard again. Courtney shrugs.*)
>
> **Dinsmore.** After her—quick!
>
> **Courtney.** Let her go! — She won't drown!
>
> **Dinsmore.** The summons isn't legal until she gets back and signs the certificate of service. We've got to keep her on the boat. (*Courtney is already jumping overboard.*) (Herbert and Holmes 1935, 88–89)

Joan Blondell and Ross Alexander in the water-rescue scene from *We're in the Money.*

The above image presents the third water rescue scene, with Courtney dragging Ginger back to the yacht.

There follows an extended scene in Ginger's room on Courtney's yacht. To gain access to Ginger, who had refused to speak to him, Courtney masquerades as his Cockney steward (Charles McNaughton), but Ginger quickly realizes the deception, and the following scene ensues:

Ginger. I'm only surprised you didn't sneak in disguised as an avocado salad!

Courtney. I wouldn't try to fool an old fooler like *you*! . . .

Ginger. You get out—and stay out—or I'll put a permanent stop to you. (*He doesn't move, only grins. Ginger picks up a vase and throws it at him. It barely misses him, and shatters against the wall.*)

Courtney. One Italian vase—eight hundred dollars! (*Ginger, getting madder, picks up the first thing her hand comes to, and throws, again barely missing Courtney as he ducks.*) Silver military brushes—one hundred dollars—and they just missed parting my hair! (*Ginger, even madder, throws a lamp at him.*) Tiffany lamp—forty-seven fifty—you're slipping!

Ginger. Slipping nothing! — I hate you more every second! (*She heaves a cigarette box which barely misses his ear.*)

Courtney. I begin to believe you. Jade cigarette box—six hundred dollars!

Ginger. (CLOSE SHOT. *Picking up a cut-glass decanter.*) Here's where you get convinced! (*She lets the decanter fly. There is a klonk from off—then the thud of a body falling.*) Darling! (*She rushes out of the scene. CLOSE SHOT. Courtney lies on the floor. Ginger rushes in and bends over him.*) Carter, honey—I didn't mean it— (*Takes his head in her lap.*) Sweetheart—speak to me— (*Frantically pleading.*) Say something, Carter darling—*say something*!

Courtney. (*His eyes fluttering.*) Cut-glass decanter—two thousand dollars!

Ginger. I'm so sorry! — I didn't mean a thing I said or threw!

Courtney. I know, Ginger—we were all mixed up!

Ginger. (*Ruefully.*) I certainly straightened you out—on the floor!

Courtney. I needed it! — I shouldn't have blamed you because *I* turned out to be a lot of things you couldn't know I was!

Ginger. It was *my* fault. — The whole mess!

Courtney. No—I blame myself—for it all.

Ginger. Well, if you'll forgive you—I'll forgive me! (*They smile at each other—and kiss.*) (Herbert and Holmes 1935, 94–96)

Dinsmore (Henry O'Neill), Courtney (Ross Alexander), Ginger (John Blondell), Dixie (Glenda Farrell), Clair (Anita Kerry), and Justice of the peace (Harlan Briggs) in *We're in the Money*.

The couple tears up the subpoena and decides to get married, a fact Ginger intimates in a cablegram that reads, "C. RICHARD COURTNEY FORMERLY MY CHAUFFER. STOP. MEET ME AT PIER WITH EQUIPMENT FOR CRUISE AND SILK STOCKINGS I GAVE YOU LAST CHRISTMAS. STOP. MUCH LOVE, GINGER" (97). Dixie and Bronson, however, interpret the cable as a trap set for Courtney in order to serve him with a summons when he docks. Ginger tries to convince him that she had nothing to do with the summons but Courtney does not buy it. When his case finally goes to trial, believing that Bronson has photographic evidence against him, Courtney agrees to marry LeClaire to spite Ginger, who he believes romanced him in order to advance LeClaire's case. It turns out that the photograph of Courtney and LeClaire in a compromising position is a composite picture created by Bronson to persuade the jury and not real evidence. When news of Courtney's marriage to LeClaire reaches Ginger and Dixie, they race after him to stop the wedding at the home of the Justice of the peace (Harlan Briggs). When the Justice asks "If any man can show cause why they may not be lawfully joined together, let him now speak, or else hereafter forever hold his peace" (122), Ginger, Dixie, and Homer stop the ceremony, explaining how Courtney has been framed by a composite photograph. The above image depicts the scene.

Courtney sarcastically welcomes the news:

Courtney. Now I can marry *you*, can't I?

Ginger. *No!*—You *can't*—I just did this to get even for getting you into this frameup.—Now that we're *even*—I don't ever want to see you again!

Courtney. Well, that goes for *me*, too.

Ginger. Thank you—and you're welcome. (Herbert and Holmes 1935, 128)

They go their separate ways until they are discovered together on a park bench where they rekindle their affection as the film ends.

Production for *We're in the Money* extended from 8 May through 12 June 1935, although Ross had completed his scenes by 4 June 1935 when *The Brooklyn Daily Eagle* announced that Hal B. Wallis, in charge of production at Warner Bros., believed that Ross Alexander would eventually "make the marquees of the nation, and without any long delay." Wallis continued, "Alexander is a young actor brought to Hollywood from New York. His work in *Flirtation Walk* marked him as a performer of exceptional promise. Since then his roles have been increasingly important and he has never failed

248

to give an excellent account of himself." Another news article published in *The Montclair Times* (7 June 1935) investigated how film actors spend their time between takes, other than talking to interviewers, changing clothes, replenishing makeup, repairing wigs, conferring with the director, studying lines, or posing for still pictures. It was reported that "Ross Alexander will go into a corner and reel off his lines for the next scene to his [African-American] valet, [Henry], who holds the script for him. When this is done, he usually will be thinking up some 'rib' on one of the others on the set."

Later, on 9 June 1935, the *Daily News* carried a syndicated story about the already infamous dunking scene in film:

"Blondes don't like to be dunked," Limey Plewes, property boy, explained, "we'll probably have trouble. A cast and crew [were] on [their] way to Los Angeles harbor to film certain sequences of *We're in the Money*. Joan Blondell was to be dunked like a doughnut. "Once wouldn't be so bad," said Limey. "But the script calls for three separate and different dunks. With retakes and all, she'll be in and out of the water most of the day. We'll have our hands full.

Miss Blondell seemed calm enough. In fact, she was found asleep in the back seat of her car. "It's funny," he continued, "but brunettes dunk much easier than blondes. Kay Francis, for instance, or Dolores Del Rio. They don't mind water a bit. "Just why does she have to be dunked three times?" "Well, that's the scenarist's idea," Limey explained. "She is chasing a guy to give him a subpoena, or something. She follows his yacht out into the ocean on an outboard motor. It runs out of control and she jumps overboard. That's one dunk. Then she serves a summons to Ross Alexander and he pushes her in. That's two dunks. Then Ross feels sorry for her and goes after her. When he sees how pretty she is and tries to make love to her, he shoves her under. That's three dunks. As a matter of fact, I'll probably have to push her overboard myself the second time. I'm outside the camera angle. Blondes are like that. They don't like to be dunked."

Not long after *We're in the Money* found its way to the cutting room, reviews began to come in for *Going Highbrow*. The *Motion Picture Daily* (24 June 1935) found the film "a pleasing comedy melodrama" and the performances "generally good." *The Philadelphia Examiner* (6 July 1935) determined that Ross Alexander gave "a rather spotty performance, with evidence of embryo talent," but complained about Robert Florey's direction that "wasted good talent on what might have been a fast-moving comedy of real worth." *Harrison's Reports* (13 July 1935) claimed that "the story is inane; nevertheless, some of the situations are laugh provoking if not exciting. There is really not one situation that will remain in one's mind. Nor do the characters do anything to arouse one's sympathy since most of their actions are ridiculous." Other newspapers, such as *The Boston Globe* (19 July 1935) found the film to be "an infectious comedy which proves to be excellent hot weather entertainment." Writing in *The Brooklyn Daily Eagle* (23 August 1935) John Reddington noted that "A juvenile new to me, Ross Alexander, is actually youthful, and possessed of an ingratiating personality as well as a pleasant baritone voice, for which a use is found in the course of the film. *Going Highbrow* is hardly earth-shaking comedy, but it does its job of entertainment unpretentiously, now and then amusingly." Writing also about *We're in the Money*, Reddington observed that "Mr. Alexander, who also is the juvenile in another Warner Brothers film at the Brooklyn Strand, does his work here as effectively, though he is more suited for comedy than the dramatics that are an occasional part of his job in *We're in the Money*."

Variety (4 September 1935) claimed that, in *Going Highbrow*, "Ross Alexander, the juve, needs better camera angles, but effects a fairly satisfactory lead. He's from legit. . . . Alexander handles the two songs in the film [by Louis Alter and Jack Scholl]. Just fair. The duets with [Edward Everett] Horton offer some laughs, however." The *Motion Picture Herald* (7 September 1935) observed that, "replete with unusual situations, gravitated by the amusing sequence of events and cast with the full appreciation of comedy this picture should appeal to those audiences who like their comedy straight. In essence the picture relates the age old theme of the small town couple finding themselves at middle age with more money than they know what to do with, trying to break into New York society and willing to pay and pay to achieve their goal. . . . There is no reason why the whole family wouldn't enjoy the picture."

Writing about *We're in the Money*, the *Motion Picture Daily* (18 July 1935) suggested that "Loaded with hokum and crammed with slapstick reminiscent of the Keystone cop era, this picture should fill the bill as an adequate laugh getter and should set well with audiences who like their entertainment lighter and funnier." The *Motion Picture Herald* (27 July 1935) concluded that "Funnier than any of the previous features in which Joan Blondell and Glenda Farrell have been teamed up as get-their-man maidens, here is a rip-roaring, laugh-in situation comedy. Fast moving farcical treatment embellishing every word, gesture and bit of action, in which much old-fashioned hokum is combined with plenty that's new and novel, it's the type of funfest that can be presented to patrons with the iron clad promise that the whole is one scream of merry mirth." The *Democrat and Chronicle* (10 August 1935) was less enchanted with *We're in the Money*, but found that "the young Rochester actor, Ross Alexander, does all that opportunity permits, which is enough to cause one to hope he soon gets something better." *The New York Times* (22 August 1935) was even less enraptured and concluded that "nothing short of desperation at the lack of story material could have prompted the producers to drag in three comedy chase scenes, especially when two bore all the earmarks of having been taken from the stock-shot shelves. In short, the new Warner effort leaves Broadway's entertainment sector no better—if not a little worse—than it found it." Wanda Hale, writing in the *Daily News* (22 August 1935), however, found the film a "hilarious, if slapstick, film version of the gentle art of 'evading service,' as hounds of the law call it," and judged Ross Alexander, "delightfully, romantically impressive."

Ross had little time to ponder the mixed reviews and consider how they impacted his career, for as soon as he had completed work for *We're in the Money*, he was on his way to Annapolis, Maryland, to join director Frank Borzage, Dick Powell, Ruby Keeler, Lewis S. Stone, Dick Foran, and John Arledge in another military, musical adventure called *Anchors Aweigh* (AKA *Classmates*, and *Dress Parade*, but released as *Shipmates Forever*) in production at the United States Naval Academy.

16. *Shipmates Forever* and *Captain Blood*

By the end of the first week in June, Ross Alexander had arrived in Annapolis, appropriately coiffed and fitted in regulation Navy attire, and ready to participate in traditional initiation activities, including strength tests, swimming, boating, and marching, in addition to climbing the seemingly endless elliptical staircase to the room he shared in the film with three other plebes. No sooner had Ross settled into the Navy routine in Annapolis than Hollywood columnist Louella Parsons announced that he was cast in a detective film to star James Cagney based on a magazine story by Richard Wormser entitled "You Have to Learn Sometime," about a sleuth who has to go to college in order to protect a college youth from kidnappers. The film was advertised as a vehicle for Cagney and Alexander as late as 28 September 1935, but never made.

During the month's stay in Annapolis, followed by five weeks in Hollywood, interspersed with trips to the Navy flagship, "Pennsylvania," at San Pedro Bay (where fourteen battleships, two aircraft carriers, fourteen cruisers, and sixteen support ships were based), Ross was given plenty of screen time in Delmer Daves's screenplay for *Shipmates Forever*, even though his activities were mostly tangential to the main story of a New York City nightclub crooner, Richard "Dick" John Melville III (Dick Powell), who, under duress, proves to his father, Admiral Melville (Lewis Stone), that he could graduate from the Naval Academy, even if he had no intention of accepting his commission. Dick is in love with June Blackburn (Ruby Keeler), a dancer whose father and brother were killed during their service in the Navy. While Dick and June are somewhat sour on the Navy, Lafayette "Sparks" Brown (Ross Alexander) from Arkansas, Johnny "Coxswain" Lawrence (John Arledge) from Texas, and Slim "Cowboy" Lincoln (Eddie Acuff) from Arizona are normative characters who breathe life into the moribund cloud that hangs over Dick throughout the film. The trio first encounter Dick on their way into the Naval Academy when Dick's friends (and orchestra) give him an embarrassing sendoff that immediately exposes how out of step he is with the other plebes.

Once Alexander, Arledge, Acuff, and Powell are settled in dorm room number 3305, Ross takes it upon himself to read a list of regulations about the storage of their belongings shelf by shelf in their lockers as the others, to some extent, follow his instructions. The ironic tone that Ross instinctively brings to the detailed instruction adds comedy to what could have been a dry, academic recital of Navy rules. Ross subsequently expresses his habitual trope throughout the film: "Where's the radio? Gotta have a radio," another major source of comedy, particularly when he reveals that he has constructed a radio in his bed that turns on when he lays down. During an ensuing dining-hall sequence, Ross performs the childish rituals of using his hand to wipe a smile off his face and, when upperclassman Gifford (Dick Foran) taps his water class, he pretends to be a railroad engineer pulling the cord to announce the "Choo Choo" of an oncoming train. The actions are puerile to be sure, but Ross performs them without comment and with the good will of a midshipman following tradition.

After Powell decides to take a single room (something frowned upon by the Navy) in order to focus on his studies without distraction, the remaining roommates pray to a small image of Tecumseh, the "God of 2.0" for success in the term exams, another traditional ritual at the Naval Academy. The full-size image of the great native-American warrior had been given to the Naval Academy in 1866, after being salvaged from an old Civil War ship, the Delaware, that had been sunk at Norfolk to prevent it from being captured by the Confederate Army. On the eve of the exams, instead of asking Dick Powell for help in his studies, Arledge prays to the full-sized bust of Tecumseh in the Yard at Annapolis; but his prayers go unanswered and he is forced to leave the Academy, an event met with somber reaction from Alexander, Acuff, and Robert Light, in the role of Ted Sperling, the midshipman who replaced Powell in room 3305.

Having aced his exams, Powell is forced to accept roommates during his final years at the Academy, so he returns to his old room and joins Acuff, Light, and Alexander, who has finally been blessed with a real radio. The traditional "Ring Dance" follows in Annapolis during which Ross's girlfriend, Martha Merrill, slips the Academy's ring on his finger, and other couples follow suit; all but Keeler and Powell, who refuses to wear the ring. However, on board the battleship to which the midshipmen are assigned prior to graduation, Powell puts the ring on his finger while Ross conducts a choral rendition of a song sung by Powell at his nightclub, "Don't Give Up the Ship." During battle maneuvers, Ross is assigned to the big guns where he manipulates the direction of the canon by means of a scope and wheel; Powell and Arledge find themselves in the engine room, where a fire breaks out and consumes Arledge who remained behind in an attempt to stop the blaze and badly burns Powell while trying to save Arledge's life. When Ross, Acuff, and Light visit Powell in the infirmary, Ross is particularly gratified when he sees the ring on Powell's finger. Following the graduation ceremony, Ross jovially tries to explain to Merrill that Naval regulations forbid his marrying her before two years had passed, and good spirits effervesce until Powell and Keeler visit Arledge's grave where the film abruptly ends.

Midway through shooting in Annapolis, severe weather closed down production permitting columnist Harold W. Cohen to offer a detailed account of the goings on among the actors and staff when the cameras aren't rolling:

Annapolis is like Atlantic City when it pours, nothing to do but play indoors. Eddie Acuff . . . has been late in reporting on the set almost every day. [Assistant director] Lew Borzage warns him he must be on time in the future. So, this morning, he's up at six o'clock. "Just my luck, he grins later, "it has to rain the one morning I would have been Johnny-on-the-spot.". . . Johnny Arledge decides to spend the afternoon in Washington—he's never been there. "How was the trip," you ask him upon his return. "Swell," drawls the smiling Texan, "three cocktails at the Mayflower [Hotel], two at the Willard [Hotel] and one look at the Capitol.". . . A pretty girl at one end of the room eyes Ross Alexander. "Maybe she doesn't know I'm a married man," the good-looking juvenile stammers." . . . It's three o'clock. The phone rings. It's for Powell. They want him to get ready since the skies show promise of clearing. A moment later and the rain comes down harder than ever. Dick returns his makeup kit in the trunk. There will be no work today, that's certain. . . .

Everybody talks about the cooperation the Naval Academy has been giving the troupe. A week ago, Powell was permitted to march at the head of a parade of newly-commissioned ensigns, boarding waiting boats on Chesapeake Bay. He met President Roosevelt, talked to the chief executive for several minutes. "A great guy" was his (Powell's) only comment. There's a reason for this cooperation. Admiral Sellers will tell you. The Academy wants everything just right; it means good will for both the school and the navy. "You movie people," he laughs, "certainly cause a flurry. There hasn't been so much excitement around here since the boys beat Army.". . . It's growing dark. A red tint to the sky promises a clear day tomorrow. Everybody is happy. It means Hollywood again by the middle of next week. All they'll miss here are Carvel Hall's mint juleps. (*Pittsburgh Post-Gazette*, 22 June 1935)

During his time in Annapolis, Ross Alexander picked up a great deal of navy information and slang, producing a noticeable effect throughout his daily conversation, in which now rang a pronounced nautical twang (*The San Francisco Examiner*, 10 October 1935). Marcia Ladson of Rockville,

Maryland, said that she and some friends met Ross on the street in Annapolis, during lunch hour, while he was filming *Shipmates Forever*. He was already late in returning to work but took the time to invite them to the gymnasium to watch him work, and gave them meticulous directions to get them there (*Hollywood*, November 1935). Alexander also went on record, saying that the United States Naval Academy provides a tougher course than the United States Military Academy. "I was in West Point only two weeks, but Annapolis has already taken me more than three—and I'm not through yet" (*Kentucky Advocate*, 28 October 1935).

On 19 July 1935, when Ross was back in Los Angeles, Dwight Franklin sent Jack L. Warner a memo that read: "Don't you think Cagney would make a swell Robin Hood? Maybe as a follow up to the *Dream*. With the gang as his Merry Men. [Frank] McHugh, [Allen] Jenkins, {Ross] Alexander, [Hugh] Herbert, etc. Entirely different from the [1922 Douglas] Fairbanks picture. I have a lot of ideas on this if you are interested." (Behlmer 1985, 44). *Robin Hood*, of course, was made by Warner Bros., though without Cagney and Alexander.

During days off in July, Ross frequented swimming parties sponsored by castmates or friends thereof. One such party in Bel-Air was attended by journalist Caroline Somers Hoyt who wrote about it in meticulous detail in the April 1937 edition of *Movie Mirror*. The event was sponsored by a famously beautiful Russian princess whom Aleta had met during her time spent among the elite society of New Jersey. Ross and the rest of the guests arrived wearing swim suits but Aleta wore a blue linen sports dress complemented by a big white linen hat. From the moment of their arrival, it was obvious that Ross and Aleta had had an argument and that Ross had no interest in hiding the fact. The hostess greeted the couple genially but expressed disappointment that Aleta did not appear in swimming attire. As Aleta started to explain, Ross interrupted her saying, "Lady Astorbilt chose to be contrary today!" Aleta graciously ignored her husband's remark and said, "Yes. You see, I am not at my best in a bathing suit. Seriously, I have a little cold and thought I'd rather not swim today." The hostess hastened to reassure her that she needn't swim, but Ross was stubbornly unconvinced, saying, "You didn't have such a cold that you couldn't sit up reading until one o'clock this morning." This dramatic scene was disrupted by new arrivals, as the entire swimming party congregated around the pool.

Ross's resentment knew no bounds and at every opportunity he continued to spit barbed remarks at his wife, and even swimming in the pool, he tried to splash water in her direction. Finally, coming out of the water, soaking wet, he proceeded to sit on the arm of Aleta's chair, allowing the water from his body to spot (and ruin) her dress. "Ross, look what you're doing," Aleta cried. "I'll show you what I'm doing," he responded with a cruel and wild look in his eyes. He pulled off her hat and threw it into the pool. As Caroline Somers Hoyt recalled:

> She was a thoroughbred, though—slender, blonde Aleta Alexander. She tried to smile and, as a woman will, she rummaged in her bag for a comb to smooth her hair, disarranged when her hat was jerked off. But her hand trembled so she could scarcely hold the comb, and the tears just wouldn't stay back. And then Ross changed. He changed almost as a Mr. Hyde changes into a gentle Dr. Jeckyll. Suddenly and completely. He dropped on his knees and put his arms around her, ardently, with a gesture the more sharply tender because he first hastily wiped the water from his arms that he might not further spoil the little linen frock. "Darling, my darling, I'm sorry! Please don't cry! Please!" His voice broke. . . ."I could kill myself for making you cry." . . . It was almost an hour later when they rejoined us, Aleta, radiant, and Ross radiant, too. And all the rest of the evening he never left her, except to get something for her. He was a cavalier any girl would have thrilled to command. He paid court to her, worshipped her for all to see. (101–102)

Prior to the 1 August end of shooting for *Shipmates Together*, a boxing match was filmed between Dick Powell and Dick Foran, the upperclassman who took it upon himself to give plebe Powell as much trouble as possible. In addition to forcing him to sing the entire 100 verses of "Abdul Abulbul Emir," and coercing him to entertain the girlfriends of the upperclassmen, Foran was matched with Powell in the Academy's annual interclass boxing tournament. The image below depicts Powell in his corner, coached by Ross Alexander and John Arledge. Although Dick Powell knocks Foran out in the third round, the match was cut from the final print of the film.

John Arledge, Dick Powell, and Ross Alexander in *Shipmates Forever*.

Preview reviews for *Shipmates Forever* began appearing in September with the *Motion Picture Daily* (18 September 1935) determining that "For the great mass of American youth, Cosmopolitan [William Randolph Hearst's film company, in collaboration with Warner Bros.] has here a colorful, tear-jerking, heart-appealing story. It is fine, upstanding Annapolis entertainment with names, plot, singing and dancing, all splashed with star-spangled hurrah. ... The depth of feeling injected by Frank Botzage, director, makes the story believable and clean cut in motivation, balancing pathos, laughter and romance with telling effect. Supporting performances reflect ace endeavors by John Arledge, Ross Alexander, Eddie Acuff, Robert Light and Dick Foran. . . . It is charted for highs at the box-office." The *Motion Picture Herald* (28 September 1935) noted that "In character, the entertainment appeal of this picture is universal. It is something to hold the interest and attention of every class of patron. Besides its theme and production values, it offers much that is novel to engage showmanship interest."

Once the film was open to the public, however, reviews were aggressively mixed. *The Los Angeles Times* (10 October 1935), for example, found the film "entertaining and at times stirring. It leans to the sentimental rather inordinately in some scenes, but apparently moves its observers to tears. The picture presents a strong group of character types. Ross Alexander, Eddie Acuff, Richard Foran, John Arledge and others win a great deal of attention." While *The Boston Globe* (12 October 1935) found the cast excellent and singled out Ross Alexander for his "amusing performance as Sparks," it found many of the pranks played and ideas spouted by the young cadets more along the lines of a high school fraternity than the nation's Naval Academy, an opinion echoed by *The Pittsburgh Press* (19 October 1935), arguing that "The entire business is childish for that matter. To be sure here is an authentic insight into the daily life, the woes and the innocent amours of the midshipmen at the Naval Academy. There are formations, bugle calls, drills, exposition of traditions, customs, etc. of the embryonic bosses of our sea-going war dogs. That part of it you might find interesting. But the inane fiction injected about the crooner with the top admiral for a father, its painful attempts at humor, its shameless bids for the customers' tears, its lusterless dialog and its stereotyped story, in my opinion rate it as about the most feckless of these films dedicated to the Army and Navy forever. . . . With nary a reservation, I recommend *Shipmates Forever* to all eighth-graders." The *Harvard Crimson* (18 November 1935) concurred, arguing that "Ross Alexander is amusing, but his part is not sufficient to justify the rest of the picture. *Shipmates Forever* is a dull combination of saccharine romance and big-navy propaganda; if you really must go, take your maiden aunt from the D.A.R."

On the other hand, the *Oakland Tribune* (13 October 1935) found *Shipmates Forever* "the best of the Navy cycle to date. . . . To offset a dash too much of sentimentality hither and yon, the film offers some very amusing incidents; some tense minutes, too. Woven into the plot is so much music [by Frank Crumit, Al Dubin, and Harry Warren] you'll be surprised; and probably pleased." *Variety* (23 October 1935) notably mentioned that "Ross Alexander figures importantly as a light comic" and found that "The peacetime military service theme, a forte now on the Warner lot, gets a thorough and brisk going over in *Shipmates Forever*. It has most of the ingredients of previous similar successes, including practically the same story with only the names changed, but it also contains the best assets of its predecessors and should do satisfactory business." *The Los Angeles Times* (27 October 1935) also noted that "Ross Alexander has his way with audiences, as usual, or in this case, what there is of an audience," but concluded that *Shipmates Forever* "is not up to the usual Dick Powell-Ruby Keeler offering. . . . It is just a trifle at best, pleasant superficial and not especially interesting."

To insure good attendance at the 16 October premiere of the film at the Strand Theatre in New York City, a parade involving 150 sailors and junior naval reservists took place before the performance, ending with the sailors standing at attention at the front of the theatre which was decorated by a fastidiously detailed six-foot miniature replica of the front part of a U.S. battleship. The yardarm of the mast had blinker signal lights built on each end, and the crow's nest was also fitted with blinker lights; under the prow were painted green and white waves to suggest the realistic movement of a ship through water. Navy flags were posited in front of the theatre and the entire building was covered with navy pennants and flags. Rear Admiral Yates Sterling, Jr., commandant of the Third Naval District, Headquarters at New York City, and of the Brooklyn Navy Yard, was in attendance along with his entire staff at the premiere, which was dedicated to the U.S. Navy.

The Strand Theatre at the premiere of *Shipmates Forever*.

All the panoply ahead of the film did not prevent the critic from *The New York Times* (17 October 1935) from emphasizing its flaws: "Briskly directed by Frank Borzage, and strong in its supporting cast, the new photoplay is less aggressively sanctimonious in its treatment of the service than most of the other Warner Stars-and-Stripes pictures. Although its story is routine, its humorous moments are many, its romantic interest not too obtrusive and it manages to be entertaining most of the way.... All of which does not hide the fact that *Shipmates Forever*, on a strictly story basis, has been heard somewhere before.... If you can overlook the obvious familiarity of the pattern, the new photoplay may be recommended. Certainly, it is the best of the recent naval cycle. It moves rapidly despite its long running time—about an hour and a half—and Ross Alexander, Eddie Acuff, Lewis Stone, Dick Foran, Robert Light, and Mr. Arledge, especially the latter, turn in performances which tend to make one overlook Mr. Powell's occasional attempts to be lachrymose and Miss Keeler's studied winsomeness."

Writing in the *Courier-Post* (16 November 1935), Ida Hermann noted that the film's "formula plot, which holds up before jaded fans like ice cream left in the sun, will hurt its chances for popularity. The cast, as a whole is excellent. It is their antiquated assignments which leave little to the imagination. Here and there lines sparkle. That is when Ross Alexander comes on the scene as a radio-infected youngster. His naturalness, talent, charm and individual sense of humor should stamp him as one of the better Hollywood juveniles." It is certainly telling that Ross is consistently mentioned as one of the bright spots in *Shipmates Forever*, particularly by reviewers who find the film lacking. John Reddington, another critic who liked Ross better than the film as a whole, produced, perhaps, the most perceptive review of *Shipmates Forever* in *The Brooklyn Daily Eagle* (6 November 1935):

"It seems to me that the script is more than a little unfair to the joys of crooning, which, I hazard, are as much compensation for a good crooner as a direct hit at sea would be for a Navy man. After all, it can hardly be said that Powell is not adept at the business of crooning and the father (Lewis Stone) might have shown a bit more tolerance for the boy's real ambition without violating his self-respect as a father and an officer. However, the chief strain on the credibilities of the audience is the element in the story which has Powell as the honor man in his class, but a poor mixer. Certainly neither contention is supported in Powell's good-natured features. . . . There is a pleasant performance by Ross Alexander, but the only real character portrayal in the film is accomplished by Johnny Arledge as a young boy who flunked out of the Academy and loses his life in an effort to win his way back in again. *Shipmates Forever* is no more than a vehicle for its featured players; if you like them, you will like it."

On 5 August 1935, four days after *Shipmates Forever* completed filming, Ross was at work on another spectacular naval film, *Captain Blood*, written by Casey Robinson, adapted from Rafael Sabatini's 1922 novel *Captain Blood: His Odyssey*, and helmed by the challenging Hungarian-born director, Michael Curtiz. Cast as Jeremy Pitt, a ship's navigator in the service of Lord Gildoy (Dennis D. Auburn), Ross appears on horseback at the beginning of the film, galloping to the residence of Doctor Peter Blood (Errol Flynn), to entreat him to come to the aid of his master. The following image depicts Pitt, shabbily dressed with torn sleeves, standing at the door of Blood's house in conversation with the doctor who, due to the late hour, is in his dressing gown.

Ross Alexander and Errol Flynn in *Captain Blood*.

Once he has tended to Lord Gildoy, who happens to be a rebel against the Catholic King James II of England (Vernon Steele), Blood (and the rest of Gildoy's household) is arrested by Captain Hobart (Stuart Casey) and taken to the great hall in Taunton Castle where he, Pitt, Wolverstone (Robert Barrat), Hagthorpe (Guy Kibbee), Ogle (Frank McGlynn, Sr.) and others are indicted and found guilty of the crime of treason. Instead of being hanged, however, the group is sent to the colony of Port Royal in the West Indies to be sold as slaves. Colonel Bishop (Lionel Atwill) is given first refusal of the slaves by the colony's Governor Steed (George Hassell), but Bishop's niece, Arabella (Olivia de Havilland), asks her uncle to buy the entire lot, if only to keep them from the dangerously unhealthy mine trade of Dixon (Reginald Barlow). Bishop buys Pitt, Wolverstone, and others but he is not inclined to put up with Blood's temperament, so Arabella takes it upon herself to buy him and consign him to slave labor, until she discovers that Governor Steed is in need of a doctor who can relieve his gout. She arranges for Blood to treat him and he quickly becomes the Governor's house physician—a step up from the slave labor endured by the others.

Blood convinces Steed's previous quacks, Doctor Bronson (Hobart Cavanaugh) and Doctor Whacker (Donald Meek) to finance his escape from Port Royal, and in the slave hut, he explains to the other captives that Honesty Nuttall (Forrester Harvey) is on the lookout for a small boat, on which they can escape. The following image is a publicity shot of Jeremy Pitt (Ross Alexander), Peter Blood (Errol Flynn), and Wolverstone (Robert Barrat) cautiously peering through the grate of the slave hut.

Ross Alexander, Errol Flynn, and Robert Barrat in *Captain Blood*.

Under the guise of tending to Jeremy's injured leg, Blood conveys to him further plans of the escape:

Blood. (*Casually and quietly*.) I have just been with Nuttall at the boat.
Pitt; (*Eagerly*.) Yes? . . .
Blood. And the stores and equipment are all stowed away on board. . . .

I told Nuttall we will get to the boat by midnight. Jeremy, we must not fail tonight! (Robinson 1935, 57–58)

Colonel Bishop, suspicious of Blood's activities, interrupts Blood's dialogue with Pitt, sending Blood off to tend to the Governor's gout, and conducting Pitt to the whipping post where he is tortured in an attempt to force him to divulge Blood's secret plans. On his return from ministering to the Governor, Blood finds Pitt strapped to the whipping post, limp and unconscious.

Blood. Jeremy! In God's name what has happened?

Pitt. (*Half-delirious.*) Water! Water! (*Jeremy reaches for a pannikan of water, which has been placed on the ground before him, just out of his reach. Blood picks it up and places it at Pitt's trembling lips. Pitt gulps it noisily.*)

Blood. Easy, lad.

Pitt. I didn't tell him! I didn't!

Blood. Tell him what, Jeremy?

Pitt. About—you know—our plans. Oh God, my back! (*Blood looks at Pitt's back and the sight of it makes him draw a sharp intake of breath. He glances at* CLOSE SHOT: *A whip lying on the ground.* CLOSEUP: BLOOD *and* PITT.)

Blood. Who did this?

Pitt. Bishop.

Blood. Bishop!

Pitt. (*Again with pathetic pride.*) I didn't tell him! (*He raises his head at something he sees off scene.*) Peter, is that a boat standing in at the bay?

Blood. (*Following his look.*) Yes, Jeremy. An English ship. But tell me—

Pitt. I wondered if I was still out of my mind. I've been seeing boats sailing in and out. But ours will never sail—not now—or if it does, you'll sail without me.

Blood. (*An attempt to hearten him.*) Nonsense. And get lost on the ocean without our navigator? (Robinson 1935, 68–70)

Once again Colonel Bishop interrupts the scene between Blood and Pitt. What is particularly notable about the sequence is the presence of hair under Alexander's armpits, unusual because the Warner makeup department invariably shaved actors' armpits if they were exposed during filming. In *Dark Victory*, a biography of Bette Davis, author Ed Sikov explained: "Flynn wasn't afraid to offend his directors and producers, not to mention Jack Warner himself, with his chronic lateness and unpredictability, nor was he reluctant to pick fights on the set, the most notorious of which was his refusal on the set of *Captain Blood* to let the makeup department shave Ross Alexander's hairy armpits for Alexander's spread-eagle flogging scene because he, Flynn, took too much sexual pleasure in them offscreen, a point Flynn pursued loudly and in the most colorful language until the director, Michael Curtiz, backed down and left Alexander's armpits alone" (Sikov 2007, 133). Oddly, Alexander's armpits were the chief concern of the production crew, not his safety while being lashed by a ten-foot bullwhip in the hands of Joe Cody, a professional whose whipping is actually painless to the victim, a characteristic that makes Cody useful to the movies. According to the *Daily News* (16 September 1935), as soon as the director shouted, "Cut," "Ross Alexander accepted his tormentor's invitation to join him in a glass of beer. Joe Cody smilingly dismissed Ross's expression of amazement at his skill with the whip. 'Oh, that was easy,' said Joe. 'I keep in pretty good practice all the time. That wasn't nearly as tough as snapping a cigarette out of a guy's mouth, or plucking a handkerchief from his pocket, with the old bullwhip.'"

An interoffice memo, dated 10 December 1935, to executive producer Hal Wallis from writer and supervisor Robert Lord also took issue with the whipping scene and other scenes of violence in the film:

> Dear Hal,
> Why do you have so much flogging, torturing and physical cruelty in *Captain Blood*? Do you like it? Does Mike [Curtiz] like

it or do you think audiences like it? Women and children will be warned to stay away from the picture—and justly so.

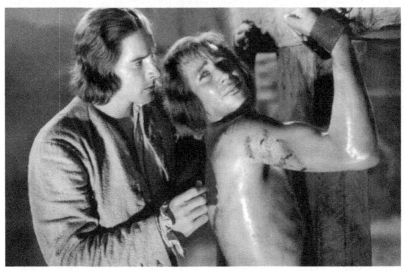

Errol Flynn and Ross Alexander at the whipping post, lateral view.

Errol Flynn and Ross Alexander at the whipping post, anterior view.

Evidently, director Curtiz did like the edgy violence in the film, for Lord's memo had little effect on the final cut.

Just as Colonel Bishop threatens to beat Blood in submission because of his ministering to Pitt, a "terrific rolling thunderclap of cannon fire drowns his voice on the last word and shakes the very air" (71). In the confusion caused by the attack on the colony by the Spaniards led by Don Diego (Pedro de Cordoba), Blood manages to release Pitt. With the rest of the slaves (and Nuttall) they escape Port Royal by taking possession of Don Diego's vessel and ultimately save the colony by destroying the other Spanish ships. As a token of gratitude, Colonel Bishop offers to have some portion of their sentence remitted but, in reply, the slaves toss him into the water, forcing Bishop to exclaim: "Peter Blood, I'll make you pay for this if I spend my life doing it" (92).

Ross Alexander climbing the ropes and Robert Barrat on deck in a publicity shot for *Captain Blood*.

Now that Blood and his crew have no choice but to become pirates of the Caribbean, Blood draws up a series of Articles of Agreement, with the able assistance of Jeremy Pitt, who, with a quill, writes what Blood dictates on a scroll of parchment. The importance of Pitt in the hierarchy of the ship's crew is established by the fact that he, Blood, and Wolverstone dine together regularly, during which they decide on strategy, targets, and ports of call. At one such meal, Pitt protests that "The men are set on putting in at Tortuga. Their gold is burning holes in their pockets" (105), so Tortuga—a safe haven for pirates—it is, where Blood meets and enters into a precipitous partnership with French pirate, Levasseur (Basil Rathbone), who subsequently captures an English ship and takes, as prisoners, Lord Willoughby (Henry Stephenson), an agent of the new King William, and Arabella, returning from a visit in England.

Pitt, Wolverstone, Hagthorpe, and Blood appear at the island of Virgen Magra, where Levasseur had docked with his prisoners and, seeing that Levasseur's captives included Arabella, Blood offers to buy her for a substantial portion of pearls. Not willing to part from her that easily, Levasseur challenges Blood to a duel, during which the French pirate is killed. Offended by Arabella's disdain after he saved her from Levasseur, Blood decides to take her to Port Royal, even though her uncle, now the Governor of the colony, would immediately arrest him and the rest of his crew:

Pitt. Peter—! The English fleet is at Port Royal! Colonel Bishop—!

Blood. Sweet merciful heaven! Haven't you ears?! Set the course for Port Royal! (136)

Blood's decision does not set well with his crew who refuse to carry out the order.

Wolverstone. It's hard to lay tongue to the right words—

Hagthorpe. I'll lay tongue to the words! We won't sail to Jamaica! Them's the words!

Ogle. Aye! . . .

Wolverstone. When you risked your neck in a duel over that petticoat that was your business. But now it's our necks you're risking and I say not for her or a dozen like her!

Nuttall. I've a great affection for my neck. I've no wish to hear it cracked by a hangman's knot! . . .

Pitt. We've been with you from the first, Peter. We've got the right to— (*This brings Blood sharply around.*)

Blood. You , too, Jeremy? (*Pitt hangs his head, abashed. For a moment there is silence.*) All right, lads. . . . You've told me we're not sailing to Jamaica— there's nothing more to be said. . . . Good night. (*He starts away.*)

Wolverstone. Hold on! (*Blood stops.*) Where *are* we sailing?

Blood. (*Mildly.*) Why that's for you to tell me—since I'm no longer running this ship. . . . As Jeremy said, you've got the right. You've been with me from the first. You've been loyal and true. You've followed me into every tight hole men can follow another.

Pitt. And you brought us out! . . .

Blood. I've no right to ask you to follow me in this. I see that now. The girl is my concern, not yours.

Wolverstone. (*Bellowing in rage.*) Are we to stand by, then, and see the little twit laugh at our Captain?!

Blood. There's Bishop's fleet. We might be paying a high price to keep from being laughed at.

Hagthorpe. We're not yet such lily-livered scum as to be afraid of Colonel Bishop! . . .

Blood. (*To men.*) You'd better think carefully. Yonder lies Jamaica and straight we sail for it—

Hagthorpe. (*In ecstasy.*) And straight we sail for it! (Robinson 1935, 142–145)

By the time Blood's ship reaches Port Royal, the colony is under attack by French ships. Lord Willoughby tries to convince Blood to remain and fight in service to the King of England, but the thought of serving King James II is met only with diatribes from the crew:

Blood. But this concerns you, too, my lads. What do you say to serving the King?

Pitt. (*Fiercely*.) I'd sink the ship with all hands before I'd serve him! (153)

However, when Willoughby reveals that King James has been replaced by King William and his wife Mary, who have issued pardons for Blood and his men and offered them commissions in the Royal Navy, Blood and his crew are anxious to fight the French.

Errol Flynn, Ross Alexander, Guy Kibbee, and Robert Barrat, on their way to Port Royal in *Captain Blood*.

Ross reappears as Jeremy Pitt in a short scene with Arabella, after the ship's ladder has been let down and a small boat has been readied to take her to safety. He is hurrying her toward the top of the ladder:

Pitt. It's Captain Blood's orders. You're to be put ashore in the safe keeping of these men. The ship's no place for a woman in time of battle.

Arabella. I want to talk to him.

Pitt. The Captain's busy. (*He bundles her over the side of the ship and starts her down the ladder.*) (Robinson 1935, 158)

After that brief exchange, Pitt disappears among the combatants in the sea battle over Port Royal. Although Blood's ship sinks at the end of the mêlée, he and his men ultimately succeed in protecting Port Royal from the French. Blood becomes affianced to Arabella and is appointed Governor of the colony in place of Colonel Bishop, who in his desire to chase the pirate Blood, left the colony unprotected from invasion by the French.

Much has been written about the volatile relationship between Flynn and Curtiz as well as the director's flagrant disregard of producer Hal Wallis's angry memorandums. The following image depicts a publicity shot of a somewhat more playful rivalry between star and director as Errol Flynn leads his pirate crew against Michael Curtiz leading members of the U.S. Navy in a tug of war, refereed by Olivia de Havilland.

Members of the U.S. Navy, Michael Curtiz, Olivia de Havilland, Errol Flynn, Guy Kibbee, Robert Barrat, Ross Alexander, and the rest of the pirate crew, in a tug of war. A Warner Bros. publicity shot.

Two of the memos from Hal Wallis to Michael Curtiz, issued in September 1935 are especially notable. The first, dated 9 September concerned the dailies between Errol Flynn and Olivia de Havilland: "The dailies in the garden, between Blood and the girl—generally—were good. He plays the scene at the carriage very well . . . and if you will work with the boy a little, and give him a little confidence, I know he can be twice as good as he is now, but the fellow looks like he is scared to death every time he goes into a scene. I don't know what the hell is the matter. When he has confidence and gets into a scene, he plays it charmingly" (Behlmer 1985, 24). Curtiz's approach to Flynn had been unapologetically autocratic and he took every opportunity to ridicule his work in front of the entire cast. Curtiz believed, like Edward Gordon Craig that actors should be *Übermarionettes*, puppets whose gestures and line readings are created and moulded by the director. For seasoned professionals like Ross Alexander, such a directorial approach was not unusual; but for a neophyte like Errol Flynn, it was hard going. Curtiz's biographer, Alan K. Rode, however, reveals that "Flynn quickly tired of Curtiz's autocratic demeanor and channeled his frustration into mastering his performance. As the second month of shooting began, his line readings exuded more authority . . . Flynn improved so quickly that before the end of the production schedule, Curtiz was authorized to reshoot a number of the actor's earliest scenes in order to improve the picture" (Rode 2017, 178–179).

The "big blowup" between Wallis and Curtiz, however, involved the director's complete indifference to Wallis's commands regarding costuming, dated 30 September 1935:

I have talked to you about four thousand times, until I am blue in the face, about the wardrobe in this picture. I also sat up here with you one night, and with everybody else connected with the company, and we discussed each costume in detail, and also discussed the fact that when the men get to be pirates that we should not have "Blood" dressed up.

Yet tonight, in the dailies, in the division of spoil sequence, here is Captain Blood with a nice velvet coat, with lace cuffs out of the bottom, with a nice lace stock collar, and just dressed exactly opposite to what I asked you to do.

I distinctly remember telling you, I don't know how many times, that I did not want you to use lace collars or cuffs on Errol Flynn. What in the hell is the matter with you, and why do you insist on crossing me on everything that I ask you not to do? What do I have to do to get you to do things my way? I want the man to look like a pirate, not a molly-coddle. You have him standing up here dealing with a lot of hard-boiled characters, and you've got him dressed up like a God damned faggot. . . . When the men divided the spoils you should have had him in a shirt with the collar open at the throat, and no coat on at all. Let him look a little swashbuckling, for Christ sakes! Don't always have him dressed up like a pansy! I don't know how many times we've talked this over. (Behlmer 1985, 24)

When *Captain Blood* proved to be a hit, Wallis bowed to the fact that Curtiz was right to ignore his "suggestions."

According to the *Motion Picture Herald* (23 November 1935) *Captain Blood* required the construction of two highly detailed seventeenth-century war galleons which strained the capacity of one giant stage; a Jamaican slave plantation filled a second stage; a third stage housed the palace of King James II and the inner rooms of the mansion belonging to the Governor of Port Royal; and a fourth stage was occupied with a pirate tavern on Tortuga. In addition, extending along Vitagraph Lake for one-quarter mile, was a minutely-detailed reproduction of the colony of Port Royal as it existed in the seventeenth century. Fred Jackman, in charge of special effects for the film noted that the cost of building three miniature ships came to a total cost of $3,300, while the cost of building the two ships to scale amounted to $120,000. Jackman continued to suggest that no actor got nearer the ocean

275

than a few days of location work at Laguna Beach. No real ships were used, and even the colony of Port Royal and the island of Virgen Magra were, for the most part, in miniature. He concluded that "The dramatic action laid aboard ship was filmed on one of the stages where the main deck of the ship was recreated. When the ship was at sea, ordinary sky backings and process backgrounds took care of the background—A relatively small set, built around the studio tank, took care of the few intimate shots of the principals at the town's waterfront. Port Royal was twice bombarded, once by the Spanish and once by the French, but the bombardment was carried out in miniature. Some of the latter scenes, thanks to a combination of miniature and various composite processes, even showed real people in the village being crushed by the fall of the miniature buildings. . . . Which should give you some idea of the magic you saw in this picture" (*Democrat and Chronicle*, 27 February 1936). Not only were replicas of buildings and ships used in the picture. Actors also had mannequins dressed liked them for use in long shots and certain action scenes. The image below displays Ross Alexander and Robert Barrat standing beside their duplicate dummies.

Ross Alexander, Robert Barrat, and doppelgangers in *Captain Blood*.

As in *Shipmates Forever*, Ross Alexander's participation in *Captain Blood* was that of a "sidekick," but unlike his work in the previous film which added color and comedy to the proceedings, Alexander's efforts in *Captain Blood* were more intrinsically connected to the plot of the film. According to Jeffrey Meyers, Ross was paid $5000 ($93, 744 in 2019 dollars) for 56 days of shooting (Meyers 2002, 118). Although most of the press coverage and reviews of the film focused on newcomers Errol Flynn and Olivia de Havilland, individually and collectively (due to their on-screen chemistry), Ross received good press, especially from one of his greatest supporters, gossip columnist Louella Parsons, who wrote in her syndicated column, published 6 August in *The San Francisco Examiner*, that "Ross Alexander is one of those actors who will achieve a hit some day that will be heard around the world. He did pretty well in *Flirtation Walk* and he has been slowly but surely building himself a public, but the boy so far hasn't had the big break that we all are waiting for. He may get it as Jeremy Pitt in *Captain Blood*, one of the important featured roles." Critic Vernon Peck, Jr.'s review, "*Captain Blood* Entertains at 'Cal,'" suggested that "Ross Alexander and Guy Kibbee receive a chance to demonstrate the worth of their talents in a more serious role than that [to] which they have been accustomed" (*The Petaluma Argus-Courier*, 2 March 1936); the *Democrat and Chronicle* (17 January 1936) noted that "our own Ross Alexander does one of the better supporting roles in fine fashion;" and *Modern Screen* (29 February 1936) determined that "Next to Flynn's outstanding performance there are excellent portrayals by Olivia de Havilland, Ross Alexander, Guy Kibbee, Basil Rathbone and Forrester Harvey." The *Daily News* (26 December 1935) added that "Robert Barrat, Ross Alexander, Guy Kibbee and Frank McGlynn make excellent friends and companions in bonded exile to Dr. Peter Blood," a sentiment echoed by *Variety* on 1 January 1936 and *The Los Angeles Times* on 1 and 5 January 1936. In March 1936, *Photoplay* indicated that "Olivia de Havilland, Lionel Atwill, Ross Alexander, Guy Kibbee, Basil Rathbone, to mention but a few, were outstanding."

Errol Flynn, his wife Lili Damita, Aleta (Freel) Alexander, and Ross
Alexander at the premiere of *Captain Blood*.

The final weeks of production for *Captain Blood* were devoted to reshoots
of earlier scenes between Errol Flynn and Olivia de Havilland. Although the
film wrapped on 29 October 1935, Ross's scenes had been completed two
weeks earlier, permitting him to begin production on *Backfire* (released as
Boulder Dam) on 21 October.

17. *Boulder Dam* and *Brides Are Like That*

Early in October 1935, even before he had completed his role in *Captain Blood*, Ross Alexander was advertised as having won the lead in *Backfire*, Warner's epic film about the construction of the Boulder Dam. What was particularly newsworthy at the time was the fact that Ross had been cast in a role for which James Cagney, Edward G. Robinson, and William Gargan had, at various times, been named. Assigning it to a comparative newcomer, executives at Warner Bros. demonstrated their longstanding trust in Alexander's abilities and box-office appeal and made good their documented boasts that the actor was "the screen's fastest rising star." Or that was the spin on a production that turned out to be a glorified B movie. Frank MacDonald, low on the totem pole of Warner directors, was given a month and a less than adequate budget to film the screenplay by Sy Bartlett, Ralph Block, and Laird Doyle (uncredited), from a story by Dan M. Templin. Actress and dancer Ann Dvorak, who had been involved in a score of well-documented disagreements with Jack Warner, had been cast as Alexander's love interest in the film, but having to withdraw because of "illness," she was replaced by Patricia Ellis who was a singer, not a dancer. By 18 October, the role in question, originally billed as "Tamara Navara and Don Hennessey, The World-Famous Dance Team" became "Tamara Navara, Prima Donna of the Blues." Mort Dixon and Allie Wrubel quickly cobbled together a vocal number, "Long Gone Baby," for her to impress her adoring audience of dam builders, and her family's nationality was changed from Italian (originally "Garnelli") to Scandinavian ("Vangarick"). Director MacDonald and cinematographer Arthur L. Todd left on 15 October for the border between Nevada and Arizona to take shots of the Boulder Dam which had been dedicated two weeks earlier on 30 September 1935 by President Roosevelt, and filming at Warner's studios began on 21 October, with a completion date scheduled for 20 November.

In *Backfire* (AKA *The Cinch*, released as *Boulder Dam*), Ross played Rusty Noonan, a hot-tempered, womanizing garage mechanic at Detroit's United Taxi Company with a gift of gab, but no tact. An early scene cut from the final print, between him and Miss Trainor, who works in the office of the taxi company, displays the womanizing aspect of his character:

Rusty. Well, if it ain't Ice Box Kate!

Miss Trainor. (*With a look of sincere resentment.*) Do you know what time it is?

Rusty. (*Looking at clock.*) Sure, if that sour look on your beautiful puss hasn't stopped it.

Miss Trainor. You'd better start getting here on time.

Rusty. I didn't get much sleep last night. Had a lot of fun though—but maybe I'm making you jealous.

Miss Trainor. Jealous? Listen, I wouldn't go out with you again if I had to stay home for the rest of my life. But I'm giving you a tip, if you don't wise up, you're going to be looking for a job.

Rusty. Honey, there's two things I never take serious, and that's why I always have 'em—jobs and dames.

Miss Trainor. You're late enough now—go on in.

Rusty. About tonight—what time shall I pick you up?

Miss Trainor. I went out with you once and I learned all I wanted to know about you, and that is—you're just all wrong.

Rusty. Now don't give me that sweet sixteen serenade: "I thought you were different."

Miss Trainor. I sort of feel sorry for you, Rusty. You really *do* think women are all that sort. (Bartlett, Block, and Templin, 17 October 1935, 2–3)

Rusty's hot temper is in evidence when he challenges Wilson (William Pauley), his boss, to a fight after he is fired for insubordination and chronic tardiness:

Wilson. I want to give you a tip. You're going to go through life losing jobs if you don't change your attitude.

Rusty. (*A mean look coming into his face, and he walks back.*) Maybe you'd like to change it for me.

Wilson. Look, kid, you're asking for trouble. Scram before you get it.

Rusty. Listen, I don't like you. And I think I ought to do something about it, so square off.

Wilson. You asked for it, Noonan. (*The two men square off and start fighting. Wilson drives a fist into Noonan's middle, and as he doubles over, smashes him on the jaw. Noonan goes down, but gets up. Noonan feints with his left to Wilson's middle. As Wilson's hands drop to protect, Noonan crosses a right to Wilson's jaw. Wilson drops, his head cracking on the hollow floor.*)

Rusty. (*Standing over him.*) Come on, get up—I'm still asking for it. (*Wilson does not move, Rusty moves him with his foot.*) What are you waiting for, you big tub, smelling salts? (Bartlett, Block, and Templin, 17 October 1935, 8)

Seeing that Wilson is dead, rattled, Rusty runs away and, after a series of unrewarding stopovers, he ends up in the outskirts of Las Vegas, near the border between Nevada and Arizona where the Boulder Dam is under construction. Tamara Navara, the stage name of Ann (AKA Della in the screenplay dated 18 October 1935) Vangarick (Patricia Ellis) takes an interest in him and invites Joe Callahan (the name Rusty gave as his own) to spend time with her and her family. In a short while, Rusty becomes domesticated, as indicated by the scene in which he and Ann shell peas in the Vangarick kitchen.

Rusty. (*Opens a pod and inspects its contents.*) There's six in this one.

Ann. Will you stop takin' the census on those peas and start shellin''em.

Rusty. Aw, a guy can't have any fun with you around. (Bartlett, Block, and Templin, 18 October 1935, 46)

Ross Alexander and Patricia Ellis, shelling peas in *Boulder Dam*.
Courtesy of Photofest.

Although Rusty has found a family that has immediately embraced him, he has had no luck in finding employment. His hot temper and feeling of entitlement make him unwilling to wait for a job at the dam to open up, a reality he reiterates to Ann when she presses him about getting a job: "I told you I won't crawl back there and ask for a job if they were diggin' nuggets out of it, and I won't" (18 October 1935, 51). However, after hearing Pa Vangarick (Egon Brecher) and his cronies glorify working on the dam, Rusty swallows his pride and gets a job with former acrobat Ed Harper (Eddie Acuff) scaling on the dam's construction crew, where he quickly manages to become the hardest working scaler on the site.

As Rusty and Ann become involved in a relationship, Lacy (Lyle Talbot), another dam worker with a romantic interest in Ann, begins to wheedle Rusty about his resemblance to someone he knew in Detroit. So long as Lacy cannot recall his face, Rusty feels safe in Ann's company, but even she becomes the cause of his inner turmoil:

Rusty. I've been around—plenty. And even as a kid, I'd worked out all the answers. And now, I got a question, and the answer don't fit.

Ann. What's that, Joe?

Rusty. I ain't braggin', but I've had plenty of girls, lookers and smart dames. I had dames all figured out the same way as I had booze—they was swell when the party was goin' on, but they was a headache the next day. And I figured any guy that was in love was exactly like a drunk—he couldn't handle his booze.

Ann. (*With just a suggestion of pique.*) What's this gotta do with me?

Rusty. You're the one that's got me all balled up. When I think of you— you know how you sort of day dream—I always think of comin' home to you, after work—not leavin' yuh, after a party.

Ann. And you don't like that?

Rusty. I like to think of it. But somehow, that ain't me. I — I don't know whether I could live it.

Ann. (*Stands up angrily.*) Well, don't wear out that tired mind of yours worrying about it, because I'm not so sure I could stand it either.

Rusty. (*Standing by her and taking her by the shoulder.*) You're sore? . . . I — I was —gee, maybe it ain't no compliment, but—but that's the first time I ever told anybody I loved them. (Bartlett, Block, and Templin, 18 October 1935, 80–81)

Back at work, Rusty jumps on a runaway dynamite truck, going eighty miles an hour, and tosses the dynamite into the water before the vehicle crashes head on into a wall. Both the driver and Rusty jump off in time to save themselves and Rusty (or Joe as he is known) is celebrated as a hero by the other workers. In addition, he enjoys an ironically comic exchange with a worker who inquires if he is all right: "Rusty: I dive off a truck goin' eighty miles an hour into a rock pile and you ask me if I'm hurt—I ought to punch you in the nose—*of course I'm hurt*" (Bartlett, Block, and Templin, 28 March 1935, 89). The big boss of the project, Agnew (Henry O'Neill), promotes Rusty to construction boss and, as the image below suggests, the entire Vangarick family exudes pride in Rusty's achievement.

Stan Vangarick (George Breakston), Pa Vangarick (Egon Brecher), Ma Vangarick (Eleanor Wesselhoeft), Peter Vangarick (Ronnie Cosbey), Ann (Patricia Ellis), and Rusty (AKA Joe) (Ross Alexander) in *Boulder Dam*.

Embolden by the good-fellowship of his co-workers and his recent promotion, Rusty proposes to Ann and the two become engaged. A celebratory turn at the local bar becomes sinister when Lacy finally recalls Rusty's true identity and threatens to reveal all to the sheriff (Olin Howlin) unless he leaves town, alone and for good, within the next twenty-four hours. Believing that he has no choice in the matter, Rusty abruptly picks up his things and moves out of the Vangarick home, leaving Ann a note: "I want to marry you, I love you, and I was on the level about what I said. Taking a run out this way is something I can't help. If you love me, believe me and don't ask questions. Joe" (Bartlett, Block, and Templin, 18 October 1935, 111).

Back at work on the dam, Lacy's life is endangered by a broken carrier cable that leaves him hanging precipitously over the dam wall. Unconcerned for his own safety, Rusty rescues him in exciting Hollywood fashion, jumping on a trolley that is slowly being lowered down to where Lacy is hanging. Holding on the hook cable of the trolley, "Rusty's new position has brought him almost parallel and on the same plane with Lacy. The wind is swinging them both. With a contra motion of his body, Rusty retards his swinging until he and Lacy are swinging toward each other. With a hasty gesture he reaches out and grabs at Lacy, misses. On the return swing he catches Lacy around the neck with his arm and simultaneously Lacy lets go of the cable and wraps both hands around Rusty's body. The two men dangle in midair" as the trolley pulls the men to safety (Bartlett, Block, and Templin, 21 October 1935, 120).

Having been rescued by his rival, Lacy sees no reason to reveal Rusty's past to the authorities. Instead, Rusty reveals all to Agnew and the local sheriff who convince him to return to Detroit and accept his punishment, with the Boulder Dam Company and his fiancée standing by him:

Rusty. I'm going back whether they want me or not. Nobody's ever going to hold anything over my head anymore.

Agnew. (*Agnew's fist hits the table, with emphasis and pleasure.*) Good man, Callahan—and you aren't going to face the music alone. The young lady isn't the only one that's going to stick by you. The company will. You'll have the best lawyers, but more than that you'll have the lives of those men you saved that day in the truck and Lacy's to testify in your defense. You aren't the same man that slunk out of Detroit, you're a new one—one for whom justice demands leniency. And, Callahan, believe me—you'll get justice. (*Smiling.*) And when it's over, there'll be a job, a better job, waiting for you, because you deserve it. (Bartlett, Block, and Templin, 21 October 1935, 127–128)

The expression of solidarity moves Rusty to tears as the film ends with Rusty and Ann finding hope and trust in each other's eyes.

Not long after filming began, Ross lost a tooth due to an especially tough steak while dining at a Hollywood restaurant. He was speedily fitted with a replacement by the studio dentist and no close-ups were affected. A week later, in early November, as Ross was filming fight scenes and other physically demanding activities for *Backfire*, his parents arrived at his Woodrow Wilson address, for an extended stay, during which they were invited to witness Ross taking the most thrilling ride of his life. Perched on a small platform on the end of a seventy-foot boom, he was swung from the ground sixty-five feet up the side of vertical rock wall built in one of Warner's production stages. There he took his place on a ledge with a group of daredevil workmen, formerly employed at the real Boulder Dam, to create the scene. Although one of the former employees at the dam had previously been dressed and made up to look like Ross, the actor chose to scale the wall himself. According to the *Republican and Herald* (7 March 1936), Alexander was later made an honorary member of the "Hellcat Crew" by members of that organization who had appeared in the scene with him. The "Hellcat Crew" was composed of the most courageous workmen who constructed Boulder Dam. Alexander's mother was terrified by the stunt and her pained reactions as Ross was vaulted into the air would have botched a take were it not for Alexander Ross Smith, Sr., who provided her with a handkerchief to muffle her cries. When the cameras weren't rolling, Ross could be seen instructing his co-stars, Patricia Ellis and Lyle Talbot in the fine art of spinning tops. Admitting that he was the top-spinning champion of the sixth grade at public school in Brooklyn, Ross used the time to demonstrate and teach a varied repertoire of spins, including the "double-back spin," the "up-and-over twirl," the "two-finger throwback," and the "Alexander Special."

Prior to the 7 March 1936 general release of the film (called *Boulder Dam* as of 1 January 1936), scheduled to coincide with the 1 March 1936 official opening of the real Boulder Dam, the *Motion Picture Daily* (19 February 1936) and *The Film Daily* (25 February 1936) previewed the movie and praised its cast, singling out Ross Alexander and Patricia Ellis, and director, Frank MacDonald, for making the film "a fast-moving affair which holds one's interest throughout." Following the general release, however, reviews as usual were mixed. The *Daily News* (28 March 1936) began its review, "One shudders—this one does, anyway—to think what would happen if Boulder Dam were as indifferently constructed as this film bearing its mighty name." Nevertheless, it concluded that "Ross Alexander's faun-like personality saves the role of Rusty. Patricia Ellis's stylized beauty suffices as the torch-singer and Lyle Talbot makes the villainous Lacy agreeable in the story that hasn't much to offer except occasional shots of the colossal dam project." *The New York Times* (30 March 1936) was less charitable, suggesting that Patricia Ellis rushed "through her duties as a soft-hearted Las Vegas nightclub singer as if she envisioned a nice glass of hot milk and a good long sleep at the end," and Ross Alexander, "whose screen appearances in the last year number a mere half dozen or so, seems a bit tired of it all, too, in spite of the fact that *Boulder Dam* is his first staring vehicle."

Variety (1 April 1936) called the film "A fairly exciting programmer which spots Ross Alexander as a worker and hero in the construction of the Boulder Dam, The background is novel and the story has enough to get by but lack of names and general box office strength will keep the takings down." Claiming that Ross "is far more likable in [*Boulder Dam*] than in *Brides Are Like That*," the romantic comedy he made subsequently, *Variety* concluded that in *Boulder Dam*, "The story is never potent, but manages to hold the attention. Its dialog is fair. Parts for Alexander and the girl (Patricia Ellis) as well as some others are written in the laborer's tongue, with plenty of slang and "aints" but not very colorful. The dialect work of Egon Brecher and [Eleanor] Wesselhoeft is a bit strained. Miss Ellis just fair."

In *The Brooklyn Daily Eagle* (24 April 1936), however, Winston Burdett wrote: "I could not help sympathizing with Ross Alexander, the recalcitrant hero, who replies to the raptures of his fellow workers with a blunt "So what?" For a while it seemed as though Mr. Alexander was going to hold out against the dam, but eventually the argument that it is to be the biggest yet has him out there grilling with the rest. And in this way he becomes quite a hero and the Warners complete another sermon on the bliss of hard labor and the glory of big enterprise. . . . Against a background of jagged precipices and the yawning river canyon, you see Mr. Alexander perform two striking feats of heroism: he catches a runaway truck loaded with dynamite and he saves Lyle Talbot from the arms of death as he dangles several hundred feet above the Colorado on a lurching cable. . . . The boy-girl side of the story is a very juvenile business, indeed, and the script is literally ridden with wisecracks. But Mr. Alexander has an attractive personality, a good voice and a gift of gab, and he manages to take all in his stride." In *The Pittsburgh Press* (26 June 1936), Florence Fisher Parry agreed, suggesting that "Young Ross Alexander has been worked pretty hard lately, and I have seen him in a number of roles, all consistently well played. He is improving rapidly and is being groomed for the juvenile stardom which he shows definite signs of deserving."

With a headline that states *"Boulder Dam* Is Movie That Appeals to All: Ross Alexander Makes Hit in Leading Role," Mae Tinée began her review in the *Chicago Tribune* (14 July 1936). She continued, "The picture at the Oriental is one of the most downright enjoyable movies that's visited town in a long while. . . . You'll go for young Ross Alexander. There, quoth the critic, is a boy to be classed with Robert Taylor! Same sort of innate charm and good breeding. Plus ability. Background there, I'm sure. His Rusty Noonan is an adroit and appealing characterization. A fine sense of fitness keeps this boy from overplaying his hand. Nice looking chap, too. . . . Dialog clicks. Direction tops! Photography? Immense! It seems to me that *Boulder Dam* should appeal to right near everybody." In addition, the *Motion Picture Herald* (29 August 1936) noted that "We were agreeably surprised in this picture. It being far superior to what we had been led to believe. Besides furnishing some very excellent shots of the dam, it had a better than ordinary story which was well acted and produced. Play this one."

As usual, Ross Alexander had little time to pour over reviews, good or bad, for even before he finished shooting *Boulder Dam*, he was advertised as the male lead in yet another Warner Bros. film, *Red Apples*, co-staring with

Anita Louise, the fairy-queen, Titania, in *A Midsummer Night's Dream*. As early as October 1934, Louella Parsons had written in her syndicated column:

> One thing that makes this motion picture business of ours so exciting is the prospect of a new find. Ross Alexander made a hit in his very first picture, *Gentlemen Are Born*. Then he played in *Flirtation Walk* and Jack Warner is so completely sold on him now that he is giving him the lead in Barry Connor's play, *Applesauce*. But before you fix the name *Applesauce* in your memory, let me tell you that Ben Markson, who is adapting the story, has changed the title to *Red Apples*. If Jack's prophecy comes true Alexander will be among the biggest ones next year at this time, so let's keep an eye on him. (*The San Francisco Examiner*, 16 October 1934)

Given the vicissitudes of Hollywood, it should not be surprising that Warner's prophecy had yet to come true for Ross Alexander, nor that it took over a year to bring *Red Apples* (AKA *Applesauce, Every Girl for Herself*, released as *Brides Are Like That*) to production. Stardom in Hollywood (and on Broadway, for that matter) often arrives when it is lest expected, and Ross would have to wait for another year before his "big break," which, without a doubt, was not abetted by his participation in *Brides Are Like That* which began filming Ben Markson's screenplay on 18 November 1935, under the direction of William McGann.

In the film, Ross portrays Bill McAllister, "a cheerful, likeable young ne'er-do-well, with a great gift for flattery," in love with Hazel Robinson (Anita Louise), "a sweet, simple girl," whose father, John Robinson (Gene Lockhart), is "an apple commission merchant, with a quarrelsome determination to be the boss of his family," and whose mother, Ella (Kathleen Lockhart), "always says the wrong thing at the right time in her husband's opinion." Bill's uncle, Fred Schultz (Joseph Cawthorn), who too often ends up paying Bill's bills, is "a rich apple grower with a terrific grouch over his nephew's laziness," and a business rival of John Robinson. Dr. Randolph Jenkins (Richard Purcell), "a successful young surgeon of the Babbitt type, also in love with Hazel," manages to get engaged to her on the very day Bill had planned to propose with a ring he had charged to his uncle. When Bill discovers that his proposal had come too late, he congratulates Jenkins and proceeds to lecture him subtly on happiness:

Bill. Don't you know what happiness is?

Dr. Jenkins. Quit your kidding, Bill.

Bill (*Very earnestly.*) I'm not kidding—I'm serious. You know, you're going to marry one of the sweetest little girls in the world. And I'm not saying this on *that* account. I'm saying it because it's something that every prospective husband ought to know. . . . Happiness doesn't mean acquiring things, having people give you things, or doing things for you—that isn't happiness. Happiness is doing nice things for people, giving *them* things— saying nice things to make them happy. Why, that's the only real happiness there is in this world, Doc. . . . In other words—happiness is just like a kiss— the only way you get any good out of it yourself, is to give it to somebody else.

Dr. Jenkins (*With a condescending air.*) All right, Bill. You stick to your applesauce and I'll stick to hard work and common sense, and we'll see which one of us makes the most money.

Bill. No—let's put it another way. You stick to your hard work and common sense, and I'll stick to my applesauce, and we'll see which one of use makes the most happiness.

Dr. Jenkins. All right, that's a go. (Markson 1935, 32–33)

At the Fifth Annual Thanksgiving Night Ball at the Green Valley Country Club, Bill appears dressed "as a gallant of the type of Captain Miles Standish, a plume in his hat, a sword at his side, and the habiliments of a romantic figure" (38) while Hazel is dressed as a "demure" Priscilla Mullins, and Dr. Jenkins "wears a severe Pilgrim costume" (36). The following image displays Bill, Hazel, and Jenkins seated at table, with Tom Carter (Joseph Crehan), "an executive of the Apple Growers' Association and a friend of

Bills," and Jones (Robert Emmett Keane), a jeweler, standing behind them in a publicity photo.

Ross Alexander, Joseph Crehan, Anita Louise, Robert Emmett Keane, and Richard Purcell in a public shot from *Brides Are Like That*.

Irritated because her fiancé categorically forbade her to allow Bill to visit her, and enraged by a conversation she overheard between the two men, in which Bill painted a cynical picture of marriage in order to encourage Jenkins to cancel the wedding, Hazel breaks their engagement. Bill suddenly reappears and pleads: "Oh, Hazel, I love you! I'm yours! You can boss me for the rest of my life if you'll only marry me. I can't get along without you. . . . Will you marry me, darling?" to which Hazel, still infuriated by Bill's cynicism, replies, "No, indeed, Mr. McAllister" (69a).

Since *Brides Are Like That* is a romantic comedy, Bill and Hazel eventually make up and marry, much to the consternation of her parents who wonder how Bill will support his wife financially. Even though the couple live on very little money and occasional handouts from Hazel's family, Bill's sunny

291

personality and philosophy of happiness keeps them warm. Coming home and finding his wife in tears over burning the biscuits, Bill immediately goes into action:

Bill. (*He has been looking around, spots the burnt biscuits on the table and registers that he knows what she is crying about.*) Oh, sweetheart, before I forget it, I'm going to ask you to do me a favor. I met Dr. Thompson today and I was telling him I had a slight—a very slight attack of indigestion. And he suggested a remedy that you could mix up for me very easily— He asked me what I was going to have for dinner, and I told him that my wife had promised to make me some biscuits. And he said, "Biscuits! The very thing.". . . Yes, sir, biscuits! He said, "Have your wife put some of those biscuits in the oven and burn them till they are as black as your hat."

Hazel. (*Looking up, startled.*) What?

Bill. Yes. He said, "What you need is carbon in your stomach. And there's no carbon in the world as good as burnt biscuits." And he said, "Don't be afraid to eat them. Eat plenty of them."

Hazel. Did he, Bill?

Bill. Yes. So, will you leave some of the biscuits in the oven until they're burnt to a cinder, honey?

Hazel. (*Backing away to arms length—holding his hands.*) Why, Bill. Isn't that the funniest coincidence! I did burn all the biscuits—every one—as black as you want them, I guess!

Bill. (*Delighted.*) You did? Isn't that the lucky thing? (*Kisses her.*) Everything you do is lucky. Just the right thing—always. (Markson 1935, 90–92)

Additionally, Bill reveals that he sold their automobile and has paid all of his outstanding bills with the money from the sale. The news is not altogether happy for Hazel who had promised her father that she would talk Bill into working for him selling insecticide for apple trees, or else leave him. Since the salesman job required having an automobile, obviously now Bill cannot accept it, and Hazel is worried about keeping her promise to leave Bill if he doesn't take the job. Uncle Fred appears, demanding that Bill make good his debts, followed by the Robinsons who insist that Bill take the job offered. In *deus ex machina* fashion, Bill announces that he has invented a way to ship raw apples in a "cheap thermos box . . . any distance in any kind of weather—hot or cold—and they'll stay crisp and fresh indefinitely" (107). Excited about Bill's discovery, Schultz and Robinson agree to give Bill a fifty percent interest in their apple companies. The image below presents the final scene of the film, with Fred Schultz (Joseph Cawthorn), Bill McAllister (Ross Alexander), Hazel Robinson (Anita Louise), John Robinson (Gene Lockhart), all standing, and Ella Robinson (Kathleen Lockhart), seated.

Joseph Cawthorn, Ross Alexander, Anita Louise, Gene Lockhart, all standing, and Kathleen Lockhart, seated, in the final scene from *Brides Are Like That.*

Shortly after production began, Ross's continuous filming schedule began to catch up with him. His normally robust physique, unused to illness, was felled by a bout with the flu that kept him out of the studio for nearly a week. On 28 November 1935, while Ross was sick in bed, his butler, William

Bolden, was driving his car when he became involved in an automobile accident. He struck an automobile driven by R.A. Asay of Tulare, California, and caused the passenger in that car, twenty-year-old Frank Barrier, to suffer a broken nose and minor cuts about the face and head. Some days later, Mark Turk, Barrier's guardian, brought suit against Bolden and Alexander for damages sustained during the accident. Four months later, on 30 March 1936, a petition for compromise in the suit was granted when the court authorized Mark Turk to accept $150.00 ($2,793 in 2020 dollars) in settlement for injuries sustained by Frank Barrier during the accident.

By the end of November 1935, when Ross had recovered sufficiently from the flu to return to work, his wife had failed in yet another screen test, causing her to fall into a deep depression. Life in the film capital had never felt rewarding for Aleta whose success was on stage and whose close friends (including Anne Morrow Lindbergh) were in the East. Because she felt that she had given up her career for that of her husband, she began to accuse him of not appreciating her sacrifice and leaving her to fend for herself while he ran the fast track to stardom. From Alexander's perspective, Aleta became insufferably needy and jealous of how he spent any time that he was away from her. She believed every studio rumor of a liaison between her husband and his co-star, completely oblivious of the reality that such gossip was good for publicity and, in some cases, designed to conceal any speculation of Ross's same-sex activities. In addition, Alexander's bipolar treatment of her at home and in public did not do much to persuade her that her sacrifice was not in vain.

On his part, Ross was perfectly happy to let Aleta go back East and enjoy a profitable Broadway career, meeting together whenever their schedules permitted. He knew a great many professionals who had successful bi-coastal marriages, but Aleta would have none of that. She believed that separation was death for marriage, so it was clear that she and Ross were at an impasse in their relationship. They had separated earlier for several months, during which Aleta returned to her family home in New Jersey. Whether she had been unable to find work on the New York stage, or was counseled by her parents, Aleta returned to Ross but the problems that had led to the parting originally were reawakened.

What Aleta needed, on Friday 6 December 1935 when, during a moment of pique, she threatened to move back to New Jersey to pursue a theatre career, was her husband to say, "Oh, don't go. I need you to be here." What he did say, exhausted from a twelve-hour day at the studio and out of patience with her, was, "Well, for God's sake go back and quit nagging me about it." After the couple went to bed, Aleta rose and went to the gun rack and picked up a .22 rifle and walked out into the yard. At the inquest on 12 December, Ross recalled: "She rushed out of the room and a few seconds later I heard two shots. I ran into the dining-room and called William Bolden, the butler, to turn on the yard lights. With Bolden following me I ran around the house and stumbled over my wife's body, pitching to the ground. Her rifle lay beside her. She was still gasping and I called an ambulance and had her moved to the Cedars of Lebanon Hospital where she died the following morning" (*The Los Angeles Times* 13 December 1935). It is instructive to note that in earlier reports of the shooting, Ross puts a slightly different spin on the event. In the *Chicago Tribune* (8 December 1935) and *The Philadelphia Inquirer* (8 December 1935), Alexander describes the event: "After we retired last night my wife arose and went to the gun rack and took up a .22 rifle. . . . We had been quarreling over a trifling matter. She was irritated over some screen tests in which she failed recently. I heard a shot, but I thought she was bluffing. Then I heard another shot." One wonders why Ross, knowing of his wife's despondency and the possession of a rifle, would be unconcerned to hear the initial gunshot. The *Daily News* (7 December 1935) reported that "Alexander was hysterical when police arrived and could not give a coherent story," and on the following day, the same newspaper announced that Aleta "fired the fatal shot through her temple while her husband slept," a report that was echoed in *The New York Times* (8 December 1935). *The Record* (9 December 1935), from Hackensack, New Jersey, added that "Alexander admitted that he and his wife had a 'small family spat' just previous to the shooting but said that he did not think it played any part in his wife's sudden actions."

Because he was informed of his daughter's death by Alexander's business manager, Vernon D. Wood, instead of Ross himself, and believing that there were diverse accounts of the tragedy (including whether the weapon used was a rifle or pistol), Dr. William Freile demanded an inquest to discover the truth of the matter. He knew that Ross had battered his daughter emotionally throughout the marriage and could believe that, at any moment, Alexander's emotional aggression could lead to physical violence. At the inquest, Dr. Freile sat in the front row and shook hands with his son-in-law prior to his giving testimony, another slightly different explanation of the events: "We were sitting on the bed discussing her failure to obtain work in the pictures and she kept saying she wanted to go to New York. When I lost my temper and told her to go on home, she got up without a word and left the bedroom. A few minutes later I heard a shot and, before I could move, a second shot. I ran out and called our Negro butler, William Holden, and said to him, 'I think Mrs. Alexander has done something foolish.' We ran into the yard and I stumbled over Aleta, lying on the ground moaning. Bolden said, 'Don't look Mr. Alexander" (*The San Bernandino County-Sun*, 13 December 1935). Ross also testified that his wife was familiar with guns and was a good shot.

Dr. William Freile and Ross Alexander at the inquest.

After a brief deliberation, the six-man coroner's jury returned a verdict of suicide. Dissatisfied with the verdict, many friends and relatives of Aleta Freile persuaded New Jersey Governor Hoffman to intervene in behalf of a more extensive inquiry into the case. Hoffman contacted California Governor Merriam but made it clear that it was not his intention "to interfere with any investigation in your state," nor "to suggest the extent of the inquiry," but that he would appreciate "any legal action pursued in the case by legally constituted officials" (*The Daily Record*, 16 December 1935). No further action was taken.

Aleta's suicide deeply affected Ross Alexander, though not necessarily for the reasons one would expect when faced with the loss of a loved one. What brought Ross to tears was not the discovery of his wife clinging to life or her last gasp of breath as she died. What grieved him the most was his own behavior leading up to her suicide. Not the argument; they had argued regularly throughout their marriage. Ross felt little guilt about that. It was his inactivity following the argument that Ross kept turning in his mind. He saw Aleta go to the gun rack and take away a .22 caliber rifle. Why didn't he stop her then? What did he expect she would do with a rifle at that time of night? It isn't likely that Aleta engaged in target practice at bedtime. Why didn't he follow her and take the gun away from her—and, having seen her with the rifle, why was he stunned and immobile when he heard the first shot? These questions raced through Ross's mind, tormenting him with the possibility that he actually wanted her to die, that his own self-absorption prevented him from—what? Could he really have prevented Aleta's suicide by being more attentive to her actions that night? Logical and illogical answers so crowded his brain that his only recourse was to shut out all feeling and return to work.

The day following his wife's death, Ross was back at the studio filming scenes for *Brides Are Like That* which he continued to do through the following week, taking time out for the inquest on 12 December, and on 16 December, to accompany Aleta Freile's body to Jersey City where she was buried in New York Bay Cemetery on 18 December, following funeral services at the home of her aunt, Dr. Eva Freile. Immediately after the burial, Ross flew back to Los Angeles, where he completed his work on *Brides Are Like That* and experienced "a shivery escape from being asphyxiated while he slept and . . . might not be alive today if it hadn't been for his bull terrier, Mr. Watson. Alexander, who has been ill, lay down on the bed to rest, and went to sleep. A draught blew out the gas heater in his room and he lay breathing in the fumes. The terrier's frantic barks saved the day" (*The Evening News*, 21 December 1935). Given Alexander's behavior after the death of his wife, the accident may well have been the first of several suicide attempts on his part, a subject that will be addressed more fully in Act Three of this text.

Ross had been advertised as loaned-out for the romantic lead in *Everybody's Old Man*, a Twentieth Century-Fox film, scheduled to begin production on 9 December 1935, but due to the recent death of his wife, Ross was replaced by Norman Foster and given time off to spend the holidays with his parents in Rochester. There at his familiar home at 433 Woodbine Avenue, Ross took the opportunity to decompress from months of continuous filmmaking that enabled him to earn $30,124.00 in 1935 ($564,787 in 2019 dollars), an enormous amount of money to a boy who never finished high school.

While visiting his parents, Ross agreed to be interviewed by the *Democrat and Chronicle* during which he announced that his next film project would be *Nowhere*, a remake of *Young Nowheres*, a 1929 film based on the story by I.A.R. Wylie, starring Richard Barthelmess and Marion Nixon, and directed by Frank Lloyd. The remake was to be written by Abe Finkel and Harold Buckley, directed by William Clemens, and costarring Beverly Roberts. When asked to compare his experience in film with that on the stage, Ross refused, saying, "I was through six flops on Broadway, and so I know the stage fairly well. I once drew twelve weeks' pay in two years down in New York. The stage means one technique and the screen another. It's simply a matter of learning all over again. One thing the movies do for you, however. Once in a while you can go into a projection room and get a glimpse of how lousy you are. On the stage you can never see yourself" (26 December 1935).

During a moment of reflection early in the new year, Ross sat down and

wrote John "Unk" Golden a letter, the first communication between them
since he left New York for Hollywood:

> Sunday [5 January 1936]
>
> Dear "Unk"—
>
> This letter has been a long time getting written, but then,
> chief among my many faults is, "never do today what you can put
> off 'till tomorrow."
>
> It's been two long years since I cast off the cloak of self-
> respect and joined up with the "West Coast Cloak and Suiters,
> Inc." However, "life among the savages" has had its brighter sides.
> I've been eating regularly and I haven't had to ask "Dixie" for a
> raise. Out there there's no one to ask!
>
> Often, I have longed to come back and do a show but I'm
> damned if I think I could remember two hours' worth of lines.
> I was disappointed that your new show [*Tomorrow's a Holiday*]
> didn't get a better reception from those wolves in top hats that
> masquerade as critics. God knows what they'll like next.
>
> I came East to Rochester to be with my folks for Christmas.
> After all that far-famed California sunshine the snow was quite a
> shock. I've been shivering for two solid weeks. Friends of Mother's
> have been wondering if I got St. Vitus dance out on the coast.
>
> All this drivel has been leading up to what I really have
> wanted to say for two years. The years I spent with you are among
> the happiest times I've ever known in my short and eventful life.
> I can certainly wish I were able to go back and enjoy them all
> again. My thanks to you, Unk, for having given me a chance in
> my "favorite occupation."
>
> Kindest regards,
>
> Ross

On 8 January, Golden replied, drawing attention to Aleta's suicide with his characteristic tact and gentleness: "I felt very badly about that recent trouble and I hope that as far as you're concerned that it didn't cause you too much anguish." While his phraseology might appear strange, addressed to a friend who had discovered his wife dying from a self-inflicted bullet in their back yard, since Ross made no mention of the event in his letter, Golden had no sense of how he was processing his grief and was offering his condolences in sincere but rather general terms. By the time he replied to Alexander's letter, ten of the actor's films had been released, but Golden was only diplomatic in his assessment of his work: "I've seen you in one or two pictures and I am sure that if you keep trying you will accomplish the fine things that I know are inside of you." Encouraging, certainly, but the phrase, "keep trying," hardly denotes praise. He goes on to say, "I had a couple of my old kids in here the last day or two—Nydia Westman and Una Merkel—and they were as welcome as you would be if you walked in tomorrow." Before signing off, Golden responded to Alexander's heartfelt expression of gratitude with a rather formal acknowledgement: "Of course, Ross, I appreciate heartily the nice things that you say about our experiences together and lets both look forward to the time when we may have more of them."

The raw warmth of Ross's letter does not find its equal in Golden's reply, nor should it, given Golden's long career as a producer, director, writer, and collaborator, where he has been forced to choose his words carefully and present himself as rational rather than emotional. That a warm spot still burns in his heart for Ross is clear, even after a two-year absence. Otherwise, why would he have replied to Ross's letter so quickly upon receiving it? To read more into Golden's reaction is mere speculation.

By the time Ross returned to Hollywood early in the new year, reviews of *Brides Are Like That* began to appear. The *Motion Picture Daily* (17 January 1936) determined that "The picture is good, wholesome family entertainment and should score well with general audiences." Of the performances, "As teams, Alexander and Miss Louise, and the Lockharts, use the situations furnished by the plot to establish themselves in the front rank of comedy performers."

In the *New York Herald Tribune* (23 March 1936), Richard Watts, Jr., noted that "Ross Alexander is a boy Pollyanna, with overtones of Peter Pan, in [this] frail, amiable and commonplace little screen comedy. . . . Mr. Alexander, who is an engaging light comedian, plays the glib hero pleasantly, which is no small achievement, for the character is a bit trying on occasion." *Time* (30 March 1936) admitted that "William McGann's well-paced direction and the amiable acting of young Ross Alexander, whose mannerisms have not yet had time to crystalize as irritatingly as Robert Montgomery's make *Brides Are Like That* a satisfactory, if not particularly exciting example of inexpensive program comedy." The boffo *Daily Variety* notice, published as an advertisement for the film in the *Motion Picture Herald* (7 March 1936) boasted that *Brides Are Like That* "Comes as near perfection in sprightly, heart-warming comedy, as the average diversion seeker will find. And if it doesn't return handsomely on the investment it will be because of inadequate selling. . . . For Ross Alexander and Anita Louise, and for Director McGann, the picture certainly marks hightide. . . . Alexander's boyish, ingratiating personality will endear him to women particularly, young and not so young, and he plays the role of the applesaucer, who believes honeyed words are worth more than gold, with delicate skill and persuasive romantic manner. Part should put him in high demand, especially for pictures appealing to youth." The April 1936 issue of *Photoplay* gave Ross all the credit for the success of *Brides Are Like That*, saying, "Ross Alexander turns on all the volts of his personality to make this familiar little story hum. It's his first major part as the ne'er-do-well windbag who fools his critics in the applesauce business. Anita Louise is lovely as his trusting sweetheart and Gene Lockhart and Joseph Cawthorn are funny—but it's Ross's show. You'll like it."

Even William Gilmore's negative review in *The Brooklyn Daily Eagle* conceded that "At least it can be said of Ross Alexander that he has verve. . . . It is faint praise indeed to say that he is somewhat more of a person in this picture than Anita Louise. Nevertheless, he remains the chief reason why you might, supposedly, like this film." In a follow-up notice of the picture in *The Brooklyn Daily Eagle* (27 March 1936), Gilmore wrote:

Ross Alexander is proof that there are other heroes than the strong, silent kind. He is proof that the man who will send his wife five pound boxes of candy when all the bills are unpaid, who can react with inspired tact when she burns the biscuits, and who can think of no higher activity than kissing her pretty little nose for the rest of his days has a box office appeal which threatens the national conception of maleness. For which I am sorry. Whatever might happen to such a bounding idiot in real life he is safe in the hands of the Hollywood script writers (in this case inspired by the original play) who turn him into a mechanical genius at the last moment in order to save the economic situation which has resulted from his lovable improvidence. Ross Alexander is the kind of hero that brings out all the mother in you. And there seems to be enough of the mother in the American public to keep a swarm of such adolescents going for years. If you are of such stuff as these films are made of you will dote on Ross Alexander, thinking him just the cutest bit of ebullient masculine charm you ever came across. . . . *Brides Are Like That* poses the situation of a happy-go-lucky youngster whose feet can't bear to remain too long on the ground worrying about supporting a young wife used to the better things in life. Thus, we have a comedy of the difficulties of young wedded bliss, as Hollywood, in a homey mood, conceives them. Unless Mr. Alexander's mile-a-minute chatter is sufficiently palliative music for your ears you will find the whole setup a bit boring.

Two days later, the same newspaper published an interview with Ross Alexander in which he stated that he did not consider his dramatic role in *Boulder Dam* as difficult as the part he played in *Brides Are Like That*—a so-called "easy role" in an "easy picture" every scene of which, Ross avowed, he completed in "drenching perspiration." He explained that "Light comedy is difficult, chiefly because of one thing—tempo. The humor seems effortless only if a certain pace is maintained throughout the picture. In one way it is easier to play comedy on the stage than on the screen; for on the stage it is possible to adjust this tempo to the audience. That is impossible in film work" (*The Brooklyn Daily Eagle*, 29 March 1936).

In an earlier interview with syndicated journalist Leo Baron, Ross spoke out against the theory that touring with one-a-week stock companies provides excellent training for careers in film. "Working in stock, where the play is changed every week, gives one a tendency to run through a part in a more or less slipshod manner. A role is never really learned to perfection. It's only studied. Bits of action become stereotyped and mechanical and are used in virtually every other play. The legitimate first run play, on the other hand, keeps a young actor on his toes, and gives him an opportunity to create his own role to suit his individuality. Screen work is much the same way. One is always doing something new, and not a rehashing of last year's success." Changing the topic, Ross mentioned that Henry Fonda was his closest friend in Hollywood. They had met when Fonda was doing stock for the University Players in Falmouth, Massachusetts, and remained friends through their respective Broadway and early film careers. When Baron asked him what he thought of Fonda as an actor, Ross replied sincerely, "I couldn't answer that. I've never seen him on the stage or screen" (*The Decatur Daily Review*, 9 December 1935). About that, Ross swore he was serious!

Act Three
The Aftermath

18. *I Married a Doctor, Hot Money,* and *China Clipper*

In her landmark study, *On Death and Dying* (1969), Elizabeth Kübler-Ross identified five universal stages of grief and loss experienced by patients who are dying and, by extension, anyone dealing with bereavement. They are: Denial and Isolation; Anger; Bargaining; Depression; and Acceptance. Not everyone experiences the five stages in the order presented above, but Kübler-Ross makes a compelling argument that everyone suffering the loss of a loved one undergoes each of the five stages (1969, 176, 189; 1992, 104). Ross Alexander was no exception. His stoic denial and isolation, immediately following his emotional collapse at the discovery of Aleta's body, carried him through the inquest and burial and allowed him to finish work on *Brides Are Like That,* playing a character so bright and jovial that no one would guess the tragedy in his personal life. Denial carried him through the holidays in Rochester where he allowed no expressions of grief to appear in newspaper interviews or in his private correspondence with John Golden. Suppressed emotions always have a tendency of exploding, and explode they did when, during the second

307

week in January 1936, Ross returned to 7357 Woodrow Wilson Drive in the Hollywood Hills, hoping that production would soon begin for *Nowhere*. As soon as he entered the house shared by him and Aleta, Ross immediately re-experienced the events of the night of 6 December. Again, he saw Aleta take the rifle from the gun rack; "Why didn't I stop her?" again roared through his brain. The gun shots echoing in his head so overwhelmed him that he had to be controlled by his valet, who believed that he might do himself harm.

Alexander's close friend, Henry Fonda, was contacted, in the hope that he could help Ross through this rough patch. Not missing a beat, Fonda and his roommate, Jimmy Stewart, hopped into their automobile and arrived at Alexander's doorstep, intent on removing him from Woodrow Wilson Drive and taking him to their house on 233 S. Carmelina Avenue, next to Greta Garbo's home in Brentwood. Fortunately, Ross's fondness for, and tolerance of animals was a plus, because Fonda's house also accommodated thirty feral cats, all named George. While in Brentwood, Ross enjoyed the sport of kite-flying, a passion for which he shared with Henry Fonda. He was introduced to songwriters Hoagy Carmichael and Johnny Mercer, and a vocal quintet calling themselves the "Merry Macs," a group of New York harmonizing vocalists who had recently relocated to Los Angeles. In his memoir, Fonda indicated that Ross "gave up women for port, and drank bottle after bottle. He was rocked, obviously, and he had a real guilt feeling, because I'm sure he knew. I don't think she left a note, but he must have known why she did it" (Fonda 1981, 103). Fonda promulgated the belief that Ross had been having affairs and Aleta killed herself because of that. He never suggested that Ross might be interested in men, even though he claimed to be Alexander's closest friend. Given the "Don't Ask, Don't Tell" attitude toward homosexuality in the film industry at the time, it is possible that Ross never outed himself to Fonda; and, if he did, it is improbable that Fond would have made that admission public. Of course, some will argue that the non-mention of same-sex relationships indicates that they didn't actually exist, but that would fly in the face of contemporary accounts that, without bias, acknowledged Alexander's homosexuality.

After spending some weeks in Fonda's flea-infested home in Brentwood, Ross returned to Woodrow Wilson Drive and began filming *I Married a Doctor*, a new film version of the Sinclair Lewis novel, *Main Street*, starring Pat O'Brien and Josephine Hutchinson, written by Casey Robinson, and directed by Archie Mayo. It was something of a surprise to Ross to be reduced to a supporting role in the film after he had been the star in *Boulder Dam* and *Brides Are Like That*, but he didn't complain, since the studio continued to promise him starring roles in upcoming projects, including *Nowhere*, and *Love Begins at Twenty*, co-starring Anita Louise, and written by Tom Reed, and the celebrated screenwriter Dalton Trumbo. In February 1936, Dalton Trumbo was advertised in *The Los Angeles Times* (26 February 1936) as the author of the new screenplay for *Nowhere*, but the film was postponed indefinitely, though it remained on Warner Brothers' schedule of "Coming Releases" through 20 January 1937. *Love Begins at Twenty* was released on 22 August 1936 without either Ross Alexander or Anita Louise.

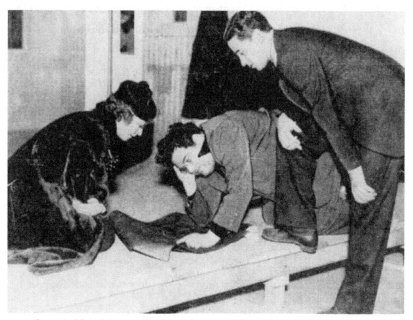

Joseph Hutchinson, Archie Mayo, and Ross Alexander, on the set of *I Married a Doctor*.

309

To a small mid-western town, Doctor Will Kennicott (Pat O'Brien) introduces his new wife, Carol (Josephine Hutchinson), a woman from Chicago, who is immediately disliked by the local women because she charms their husbands, and subsequently disliked by the men because she thinks the town is ugly and should be beautified. Carol feels alienated from the townspeople and even her husband who continues to side with them against her. The only friend she has is Erik Valborg (Ross Alexander), an artist who lives on a farm with his parents Nels (Robert Barrat) and Bessie Valborg (Hedwiga Reicher), and whom she meets while she is out hunting with her husband. Carol appreciates Erik's drawing and encourages him to draw what he knows, to which Erik replies: "Why should I draw what I despise?" Erik leaves the farm and moves to town, taking a job in a tailor shop. The pair unite as the only artistic faction in a town full of churls, and together they create a visualization of what the town might look like according to Carol's beautification plan. It goes without saying that the town council quickly votes down Carol's proposal, with a great many innuendos about her spending so much time at night with Erik. When asked to comment, Dr. Kennicott fails to support his wife and bows to the will of the council.

Defeated, Carol and Erik walk along a lengthy expanse of railroad tracks, during which she advises Erik most adamantly to leave town and find a good teacher. Erik replies that it will be another year before he has saved up enough money from his job at the tailor shop to leave. Carol asks if he can tolerate another year in a town he despises, and he replies that he can tolerate anything if Carol is there. Their conversation is interrupted by Kennicott driving by the tracks, and Carol and Erik accept his offer to drive them back to town.

During the ride, Kennicott mockingly remarks that his pants need mending, throwing shade on Erik's employment and standing in the town's hierarchy; and, once Erik has been delivered to his place of employment, Dr. and Mrs. Kennicott continue to argue over the doctor's lack of support for his wife.

Ross Alexander, Josephine Hutchinson, and Pat O'Brien in a publicity still
from *I Married a Doctor.*

On Thanksgiving Day, Carol takes a basket of food to the tailor shop,
hoping to meet Erik there. He is so taken with her that he almost allows a
heated iron to burn through a pair of trousers. When he burns the tip of his
finger, Carol offers him first aid, claiming that she enjoys doing things for
him. He becomes so possessed of her that later on the same day, he rushes
in to Kennicott's office and tells him that he loves his wife and that he feels
certain that she loves him. When he is pressed to reveal how he knows that
she loves him, he replies that she shows her affection in a million different
ways, even if she hasn't actually said "I love you." Kennicott advises Erik to
forget her, in the same way that he will forget they ever had this conversation.

In an interview with syndicated columnist Jimmie Fidler, Ross confided
that acting is often a matter of clever strategy. In the scene in which he
confessed to Kennicott that he loved his wife, Ross revealed that it was
necessary that he appear excited to the point of apoplexy. Time and again he
attempted the scene, but apoplexy is not easily attainable. He admitted that
he finally achieved the effect "by knotting his necktie so tightly that the blood

flow was retarded. This brought perspiration to his forehead, made his eyes pop out, and dilated his nostrils. Simulated apoplexy to perfection" (*Wilkes-Barre Times Leader*, 19 May 1936)!

Later that Thanksgiving, Kennicott and his wife travel over the snow in a horse-drawn sleigh, on their way to the Valborg farm where Nels Valborg has had an accident and needs to have his left arm amputated in order to survive. Carol is not welcome in the Vaborg home because she is blamed for Erik's leaving the farm causing them to lose half their crop because the elder Valborg is too old to work it all by himself. Moreover, now that Nels has only one arm, Erik is needed more than ever and more blame is heaped upon Carol.

A week later, Kennicott appears at the tailor shop and tells Erik that he is only concerned with the happiness of his wife. If she, indeed, loves Erik, he would not stand in their way. Instead, he advises him to run away with her. However, if she does not love him, Kennicott advises Erik to go away and stay away permanently. With or without Carol, Erik needs to get out of town. Full of excitement, he rushes to the Kennicott house and announces that they're free—free to go away together, free from Kennicott's hold on her as a husband, free to live together happily as man and wife. Caught completely off guard, Carol scolds Erik for saying such things to a married woman but also realizes that her actions may have made the wrong impression with him. She admits to loving him as a friend, but nothing more than that, and apologizes sincerely for having hurt him. Completely blind-sighted by Carol's response, Erik runs off to get very drunk.

Not only is Erik very drunk, he is driving an automobile with a female passenger. Unable to control the car when approached by an automobile going in the other direction, Erik's car flips over. The female passenger emerges alive, but Erik is sent to Kennicott's medical practice where he ultimately dies. Realizing that everyone in town now blames her for Erik's death, Carol decides to return to Chicago in spite of Kennicott's preachy monologue the gist of which is "There are Main Streets everywhere; the faults one finds in every town across the country are just due to human nature." Once Carol is gone, the town residents vote to implement many of her ideas to beautify the town and hypocritically claim to miss her. Every afternoon, Doc Kennicott goes to the station to meet the afternoon train from Chicago in the hope that Carol will return. After a passage of time, she appears on the platform and Carol and her husband are reunited, both having learned a great deal about the human condition.

Josephine Hutchinson and Ross Alexander, in their final scene together in *I Married a Doctor.*

An important and tragic subplot between the Kennicotts' maid, Bea Sorenson (Louise Fazenda) and Miles Bjornstam (Ray Mayer), a handyman shunned by the townsfolk, is interwoven throughout the main plot. Bea and Miles fall in love and move to a shack away from town. When Carol brings the couple a Thanksgiving dinner, Bea is ill and confined to bed. Later in the film, when the women of the town finally take it upon themselves to visit Bea—something she had hoped they would do—a grieving Miles announces that she has died, and chastises the ladies for taking so long to visit. Although the subplot had little direct effect on the main action of the film, it did further the characterization of the townspeople and their failure to embrace those among them who were "different."

Alexander's role in *I Married a Doctor* was something of a departure for him. He had had serious moments in earlier films (*Gentlemen Are Born, Captain Blood, Boulder Dam*) but never was he written to die because of an unrequited love affair, or to die in so selfish a way, speeding while drunk in an automobile, with a young lady passenger. It is one thing to be suicidal on his own time, but to drag an innocent passenger along is inexcusable. Evidently, the studio felt the same way, by allowing the young lady to survive the crash and permitting Ross to die. In addition, *I Married a Doctor* marked a change in Ross's personal behavior. Previously, in every film, Ross arrived on time at the studio, ready to get into makeup, and excited to work. From this point on, Alexander's work ethic completely changed: he showed up for calls late or hungover; he behaved uncharacteristically belligerent on the set; and, more often than not, he appeared unprepared for the day's filming. In addition, his traditional joking around with cast and crew suddenly had an edge to it, no matter how hard he tried to mask the dark thoughts that rattled his mind since the death of his wife.

No sooner had Ross begun filming *I Married a Doctor* than Warner Brothers' producer Hal Wallis announced that Ross Alexander, was among the studio's upcoming stars "facing the outstanding year of their careers." Also included in the list were Errol Flynn, Olivia de Havilland, Jean Muir, Anita Louise, Patricia Ellis, and Ian Hunter, for whom Wallis said that the studio had even better things planned during the coming year to propel them on the road to stardom (*The Brooklyn Daily* Eagle, 27 January 1936). Moreover, the *Motion Picture Herald* (1 February 1936) revealed that Ross had joined that rarified gang of Hollywood celebrities who become the center of excitement whenever they appear at luncheon or dinner spots where they are constantly sought by autograph hunters. Not to be ignored, gossip columnists began to follow Ross to Sardi's, his favorite dining establishment, reporting that, before Valentine's Day, he was seen there with actresses Phyllis Brooks and Valerie Hobson in the Continental Lounge, serenaded by Charles Bourne at the piano, while, a week later, he had lunch there alone!

By the end of February, *I Married a Doctor* was in the cutting room and

Ross, Archie Mayo, and Guy Kibbee were among those invited to a stag party hosted by Pat O'Brien at his home in Brentwood Heights to celebrate the completion of the picture. In *Movie Classic* (March 1936), Ross was advertised as co-star with Anita Louise and Gene Raymond in *Every Girl for Herself,* another alias for *Brides Are Like That,* which, incidentally, did not feature Gene Raymond. The magazine might have meant Gene Lockhart, or the film, *Love Begins at Twenty,* which had been earmarked for Ross and Anita (though, again without Gene Raymond), the provocative title of which was not lost on columnists. Evidently the studio's publicity department was anxious to keep Ross and Anita in the headlines because gossip columnists fully embraced the hint of romance between them when Ross accompanied Anita to a concert by classical guitarist Andrés Segovia: "Ross Alexander's attendance at the Segovia concert with Anita Louise caused lots of comment. It's said the young man usually votes for nightclub entertainment, but the harp-playing Miss Louise must have a strong influence" (*The Los Angeles Times,* 1 March 1936). Even still, the same article reported that Ross and actress Isabel Jewell "seemed mutually interested" at the Guild Ball. If nothing else, Warner Bros. was peddling Ross as a ladies' man.

On 5 March 1936, Ross attended the eighth annual Academy Awards at the Biltmore Hotel, where he rubbed shoulders with Lionel Barrymore, Frank Capra, Cecil B. DeMille, Clark Gable, Stan Laurel, Mervyn LeRoy, Jack Oakie, Cesar Romero, Robert Taylor, Barbara Stanwyck, and Bette Davis, among others. Two of Alexander's pictures, *A Midsummer Night's Dream* and *Captain Blood* had been nominated for Best Picture but neither won. *A Midsummer Night's Dream* did win the award for Best Film Editing and Best Cinematography but *Captain Blood,* which had been nominated in five categories, did not take home a trophy.

A week after the Academy Awards, Ross was arrested for public intoxication in front of the Trocadero Café where the actor was engaged in a heated dispute with a parking lot attendant, whom, it was rumored, Ross had approached for sex. Although it is impossible to confirm because the cause of the argument seemed less important to the police than Alexander's inebriation, a sexual motive was not improbable. Ross was placed in a holding cell for several hours before being released on bail set at $100. He was arraigned a week later on 17 March, when he pleaded guilty to violating the county drunk ordinance and was fined $25.00 by Justice C.D. Holland of Beverly Hills. Fortunately, Ross did not have to report for work the next day with a hangover, but at the end of March he was back in front of the camera, not for *Love Begins at Twenty*, as he had expected, but for *There's Millions in It* (released as *Hot Money*), written by William Jacobs, and directed by William McGann, who had previously helmed the romantic comedies *Maybe It's Love* and *Brides Are Like That*.

In *Hot Money*, Ross portrays Chick Randall, a brilliant, fast-talking, recently-released-from-prison promoter who is approached by his friend Willy (Andrew Tombes) and Willy's financial backer, Max Dourfuss (Joseph Cawthorn) to market a miraculous gasoline-substitute formula invented by Dr. David (Paul Graetz) who wants a million dollars in cash for his invention. Though at first unwilling, Randall becomes passionate about the product after he sees a demonstration and convinces money-man Dourfuss that, to raise the amount of money Dr. David wants for his formula, the corporation needs to rent large and well-appointed offices, hire secretaries and salespeople, and establish a board of directors comprised of four nondescript vagrants whose names are similar to famous wealthy men: Hank Ford becomes Henry Ford (Frank Orth); Joe Peter Morgan becomes J.P. Morgan (Cy Kendall); Eddie Biddle becomes Edward Biddle (George Andre Beranger); and Gus Vanderbilt becomes Augustus Vanderbilt (Joe Cunningham). Once all of the above has been taken care of, Randall gathers his salespeople, demonstrates the product, and delivers an impassioned motivational address:

Randall. I don't know how many of you men realize it or not, but you have just been witness to a miracle—a twentieth-century miracle. You have seen a hundred-and-twenty horse-power motor run on water. Do you get the significance of what I'm saying? Run on water—water taken right from the hydrant—fifteen gallons of it to fill this tank. Of course, to that fifteen gallons we add a pint of Doctor David's concentrate, and we have produced a gasoline substitute better than the best gasoline refined today. This substitute costs us but one cent a gallon. We shall be able to sell gasoline to the world for two cents a gallon—gasoline for two cents a gallon—get yourselves into that picture. You are going to sell stock in that company. Think you can do it? . . . Here is a gasoline company bigger than Standard Oil and all the other oil companies of the world put together. The amount of stock that is available at the inaugural price of five dollars is limited. When that's gone there won't be any more. You men who sell it to your friends will do them a good deed— you'll bring happiness and wealth to thousands besides yourselves. You can tell the lucky customer that meets up with you that Prosperity isn't around the corner—It's right here. Knocking at their door. Now, boys, get out and tell your customers just that. (Jacobs 1936, 51–52)

Randall hires pretty Grace Lane (Beverly Roberts) as his secretary and immediately becomes smitten with her, even though she is initially suspicious of Randall's "get-rich-quick" racket.

Willy (Andrew Tombes), Chick Randall (Ross Alexander), and Grace Lane (Beverly Roberts) in a publicity still from *Hot Money*. Courtesy of Photofest.

317

After seeing a demonstration of the product, however, Grace changes her attitude toward Chick and his ideals and even expresses a willingness to invest her own money in the company stock.

Grace. I've heard you say often that you want to make a lot of money for the fellow that's put his savings in your company. I think you mean it. Anyway, you've sold me.

Randall. Lady, I could sing—that's how good I feel, hearing that from you. Grace—care if I call you Grace— (*As she indicates "no" by shaking her head.*) Swell name, Grace—My mother's name. Grace, you must have known for a long time now that I have been very much "that certain way" about you.

Grace. (*Drawing away from him—a bit frightened.*) No, I hadn't—

Randall. Everybody around this joint has—That's why everything with this company has to be on the up-and-up—the way you'd want it to be.

Grace. What have I got to do with it?

Randall. (*Smiling—with a twinkle in his eye.*) Well, a few years from now—when our Junior is going to school— (*As she looks at him in amazement.*) I'd hate to have the kids point a finger at him and say that his father and mother were connected with a company that—

Grace. (*Interrupts him.*) Now, hold on Mr. Randall—You called me "Grace" for the first time just a few moments ago, and already we have a Junior in school—You *do* work fast.

Randall. Yes, I do.

Grace. How old is Junior?

Randall. Going on seven.

Grace. What grade is Junior in?

Randall. High fourth.

Grace. Junior works fast also.

Randall. Takes after his father.

Grace. Good day!

Randall. (*Grabs her by the arm and draws her close to him.*) Where are you going?

Grace. (*Facetiously*.) I'll see you tomorrow at Junior's graduation.

Randall. No, you won't—You'll see Junior's papa right now! (*He draws her close—takes her in his arms and gives her a tonsil-wrecking kiss.*) (Jacobs 1936, 69–71)

Willy (Andrew Tombes) center, holding soap, Chick Randall (Ross Alexander), Max Dourfuss (Joseph Cawthorn, and Forbes (Addison Richards), in the dry soap scene from *Hot Money*.

As the sale of stock in the company soars, the amount of available formula to use in demonstrations dwindles. To acquire more of the mixture, Dourfuss goes off in search of the mercurial doctor, who, apparently, has disappeared. He returns empty handed except for a piece of paper, on which the doctor's scribblings appear to be a formula, which he discovered among the doctor's clothing discarded by a river, leading Dourfuss and his partners to believe that the doctor committed suicide. Randall hires a chemist, Professor Kimberly (Robert Emmett Keane) to decode the formula, and places what is left of the gasoline mixture into a fancy bottle in his office. The formula that was left among the doctor's clothes turns out to be a very effective dry soap, and the remaining gasoline mixture is accidently swallowed by Dourfuss, who mixed it with a spritz of seltzer water thinking it was scotch. Delegates from the

Better Business Bureau descend upon the company, desirous of witnessing the miracle gasoline alternative, but Randall has nothing to show them except for the pieces of dry soap that Willy brings in, which Randall plays up as a miscommunication between him and the chemist. The committee from the Bureau express great interest in the bar of soap about which their spokesman, Forbes (Addison Richards), tells Randall, "We think you've got something in this soap" (101).

An apple cider salesman, who has been trying to gain an audience with Randall throughout the second half of the film, turns out to be Dr. David, and his jugs of cider, the gasoline concentrate. The gasoline conglomerate buys the rights to the formula for ten million dollars, enabling Randall to pay Dr. David his million dollars in cash and give his stockholders hefty dividends, and prove to Grace that he and the venture were legitimate.

Late in March, while Ross was filming *Hot Money*, *I Married a Doctor* was previewed at Warner's Hollywood Theatre. Uncharacteristically, Ross attended the preview alone and sat apart from the cast who had gathered in the center of the audience. The character Ross played had been an outsider, uncomfortable among the folk that peopled his town, who fell in love with the town doctor's wife, and who had nerve enough to go to the doctor and claim her for his own. The scenes between Ross and Pat O'Brien were written in a highly melodramatic fashion, but Ross felt sure that the film's audience would appreciate the sincerity of his performance and find the young man naïve and unworldly rather than foolish. What he didn't expect was the audience's breaking into laughter during a serious and sympathetic scene—but laugh they did and Ross crumpled down in his seat, hoping that he wouldn't be noticed in the audience and remained that way until everyone was out of the theatre. Katharine Hartley, in her article "Ross Alexander the Great" explained:

> To be laughed at is the worst thing that can happen to
> an actor. Even though Ross knew it was not his fault—not
> anyone's—and that that particular scene would be omitted at the

final cutting before the picture's release (that is what previews are for) still it hurt. Then, as if that were not enough, Ross was summoned to do the same part on the air for *Hollywood Hotel* [on Friday 3 April 1936, on radio station KFRC at 6:00 P.M. on the west coast; and over the CBS-WNAC network at 9:00 P.M. on the east coast]. . . .

I happened to be there that day. I sat next to him in the control room during rehearsal. The dread of being laughed at again must have been uppermost in his mind. But he never let on. Only his high color, his nervousness, and his pacing up and down gave him away. "Nervous?" someone asked. "Oh no, I've done radio before. I was on the *Collier's* hour steadily several years ago." The boy who had slid down under a seat to avoid recognition only a few days before was now disclaiming any remembrance of the episode. (*Movie Mirror* Vol.9, No.5 [October 1936], 63)

However the preview audience reacted to the melodrama of Ross's performance, the *Motion Picture Herald* (4 April 1936) found that "Marked by exceptional performances on the parts of Pat O'Brien, Josephine Hutchinson, Ross Alexander, Louise Fazenda, and Ray Mayer particularly, and by all the others of the cast in general, the show undoubtedly possesses entertainment quality for word-of-mouth advertising. . . . Sober in character, though not without plenty of comedy, the picture has the quality to stir the more serious emotions. Sold as a feature that hits right home, that sometimes is ironic in its picturization of bigotry and the unwillingness to understand or sympathize, it can be given unusual attention." Reviews that followed were similarly complimentary to Alexander's work: the *Daily News* (19 April 1936) noted that "Ross Alexander gives a fine performance, as the misunderstood artist," and *The New York Times* (20 April 1936) concluded that "Pat O'Brien, Miss Hutchinson and Ross Alexander carried [the film], naturally, as the three principals of the triangle, but they had some valuable assistance from Louise Fazenda, Ray Mayer, Margaret Irving, Robert Barrat and several of the others as small-town daguerreotypes." Although Winston Burdett, writing for *The Brooklyn Daily Eagle* (20 April 1936), noted that "it is hard to think of anyone who would have been more happily cast than Mr. Alexander in the role of the impetuous youngster," *Variety* (22 April 1936) disagreed and suggested that "Though he turns in a polished job, Ross Alexander is miscast as the young Swedish farmer. Glib English and other mannerisms are entirely out of place for this character." *The Harvard Crimson* (8 May 1936) agreed that "Ross Alexander as Eric is quite uncalled for; since his last role he has managed to put still another hot potato in his mouth." That notwithstanding, the paper gave the film a positive notice. Although *Modern Screen* (2 June 1936) called Alexander's characterization of the youth who longs to rise above his environment "faultless in its understanding," Wood Soanes, never one of Alexander's fans, gave him another bad notice in the *Oakland Tribune* (23 May 1936) writing: "In his direction, Archie Mayo has done competent work in the selection of small-town types with one exception, and that an important one. Warners still labor under the impression that in Ross Alexander they have an actor of rare talent and Alexander continues to let them down. This time it is in the important role of the clod-hopper artist who messes up the Kennicott's lives."

Early in April, Ross purchased a ten-acre ranch at 17221 Ventura Boulevard in Encino, California, where his neighbors included Ruby Keeler, Al Jolson, Ann Dvorak, Edward Everett Horton, and Louise Fazenda. According to *The Los Angeles Times* (13 April 1936), on his ranch, Ross planned to create a sportsman's paradise, installing two badminton courts, a swimming pool, tennis court, baseball diamond, basketball court, and a shooting and archery range. The following image is a photograph of the Spanish-styled house on his estate.

Around this same time, Ross was advertised as the lead in a film about professional hockey (one of his personal favorite sports) called *The Shrinking Violet*, co-starring June Travis, with Sybil Jason and Dick Purcell, a screenplay by George Bricker, and scheduled to begin production in June. In addition, Ross was among the founders of an organization called the Old New York

Club comprised of stage actors who were lured to Hollywood following their success on Broadway. In addition to Ross, the club included Owen Davis, Jr., James Stewart, Brian Donlevy, and Elisha Cook, Jr. They plan to meet once a month, and the actor getting the best break over the period between meetings gets to dine for free.

Ross Alexander's home at 17221 Ventura Boulevard, Encino, California.

After he completed filming *Hot Money* at the end of April, Ross Alexander made a hurried trip to downtown Los Angeles and bought $275 worth of equipment for his miniature railroad, sprawling through the front room of his new home in Encino. Ross had become a miniature railroad aficionado at Christmas 1932; when his friends gamely inquired what he wanted for Christmas, his reply, "An electric train," was taken as a joke, characteristic of Ross's idiosyncratic sense of humor. When Christmas arrived, however, there was Ross on the floor of his living room, connecting pieces of tracks and coupling miniature railroad cars together behind a handsome electric engine, ready to take a winding jaunt through the little village that surrounded the railroad. Over the years, both the village and the railroad had outgrown the living room at Woodrow Wilson Drive and portions of Alexander's collection had to be stored in a rented studio not far from his home.

No sooner had Ross acquired his railroad equipment than his father arrived at his doorstep, the result of a promise he made his son that as soon as he had his first starring role in pictures, he would make the trip from Rochester to Hollywood to visit him. Since Ross had starred in *Boulder Dam* and *Brides Are Like That*, it was time for the elder Alexander Ross Smith to make good his promise. Interestingly, Alexander's father brought with him the leather strap which often had been used to discipline his young son since, according to Ross, his father did not believe in "sparing the strap and sparing the child" (*The Philadelphia Inquirer*, 1 May 1936); and since his father was in the leather business, there was always a new strap available when the old one wore out.

Among the points of contention between father and son was Alexander's penchant for buying clothes. Named one of Hollywood's best-dressed film stars, Ross spends at least $1000 a year on clothes (that's $18,487 in 2020 dollars). His secret of economical fashion-plating is to buy only the best, and take good care of it. His closets reveal a total of twenty suits; he buys four or five new tailor-made suits every year at a cost of $100 each. He has two full dress suits, at $300 each, which he has had for two or three years, altering them somewhat to address changes in style. Hats and shoes run Alexander between $150 and $200 yearly, and shirts, slacks, ties, scarfs, and overcoats, bring the total expenditure up to $1000. In an interview with *The Mercury* (4 May 1936), Alexander recalled: "When I'd go shopping with my parents and they'd ask me to select a suit, invariably I'd pick out one that cost twice as much as the average. They'd point out to me that I could have two of the other suits for that price. But I'd tell them that if I couldn't have the one that was made of good materials and correctly tailored, I'd rather get along with what I already had." Even in 1936, Alexander's father still could not understand his son's reasoning. Another issue Mr. Smith found exasperating was the way Ross coddled his livestock. "Why must Minnie and Maude (Ross's two pet goats)," his father asked, "be on an exclusive diet of cigars?" Ross admitted that they eat the equivalent of three boxes of cigars a day, but since he could afford to buy the cigars, why should he not give them what they want! Papa

Smith's argument that Minnie and Maude are only animals did not go down well with his son.

After his father departed, Ross took the opportunity to go camping in the Canadian woods where, according to the *Times Herald* (15 May 1936), he was lost for four days, subsisting only on a diet of wild berries. A former boy scout, he attempted to light a fire by friction for two days without success but, on the third day, he discovered a match in his hip pocket. He was eventually rescued by a searching party who located him by the smoke from his fire. He was speedily returned to Hollywood where he showered, shaved, and began filming his role in *China Clipper*, a tribute to the first long-distance airline in the United States, written by Frank Wead, with additional dialogue by Norman Reilly Raine, and directed by Ray Enright, who had previously directed Ross in *We're in the Money*.

The film reunited Ross with many of Warner Bros. regulars including his recent co-stars, Beverly Roberts and Pat O'Brien who played Dave Logan, an importer working for James Horn (Joseph Crehan), who has just returned from failing to make a business deal because of his late arrival in Shanghai. Realizing the need for speed and punctuality in the world of business, and inspired by Lindbergh's successful flight between New York and Paris, Dave Logan quits his job as an importer in order to create a commercial airline system, in spite of the objections of Horn and his wife, Jean "Skippy" Logan (Beverly Roberts). Arguing that "when a man believes in something, that's what he ought to do," Dave enlists his war buddies, wise-cracking pilot Tom Collins (Ross Alexander) and aircraft designer Dad Brunn (Henry B. Walthall), in the creation of a passenger airline between Philadelphia and Washington, D.C., financed by B.C. Hill (Addison Richards), who pulls out when that project loses $98,000. Dave, Tom, and Dad decide to start an airline running mail between Key West and Havana, but when Department of Commerce Inspector (Kenneth Harlan) grounds the plane because it is not equipped to land on water, delivering a compelling argument, Dave manages to convince the inspector to allow them to fly (see image below).

Bill Andrews (Alexander Cross), Department of Commerce Inspector
(Kenneth Harlan), Tom Collins (Ross Alexander), Dave Logan (Pat
O'Brien), and Dad Brunn (Henry B. Walthall) in a publicity still from
China Clipper.

Another wartime buddy, Hap Stuart (Humphrey Bogart), appears in Key
West and joins Dave's organization just as Dave discovers that his wife has
left him and returned to New York City. Sunny Avery (Marie Wilson), Tom's
girlfriend, follows him from Philadelphia to Key West, sporting her new
outfit as part of her trousseau, hinting that he should get around to marrying
her. When he refuses, however, to let her accompany him on his business
trip to New York, she abruptly breaks up with him—a situation that doesn't
appear to alarm Tom.

After a successful flight between Key West and Havana, Dave dominates
the trade loop among the Caribbean Islands before going to Washington to
convince the government to allow him to provide facilities and contractual
agreements with South American countries. When the government
authorities deny Dave's request, he decides to get private sponsorship for the

326

idea and goes back to B.C. Hill to support the development of the Trans-Oceanic Airways System, the new name of the corporation. When a severe hurricane threatens the Caribbean, Dave orders his planes to be at the disposal of local authorities, to be used to bring medical assistance, food, and other supplies necessary to the revitalization of the victims of the storm. For saving twenty-eight thousand people and providing relief to countless others, Trans-Oceanic Airways received a commendation from the United States Red Cross and the Pan-American Union.

As his airway system grows larger, flying from Miami to airports throughout South America, Dave assigns Tom and Hap the responsibilities of establishing a school for pilots and criticizes them snappishly when their progress fails to meet his deadlines. Suddenly, Dave seems obsessive in his managerial style, and nothing and no one seem to be able to achieve his high standard. Hap's attempts to convince Dave to lighten up only serve to get him fired, after which a single punch from Hap knocks Dave to the ground.

Tom Collins (Ross Alexander) and Jean "Skippy" Logan (Beverly Roberts) in *China Clipper*.

In New York, Tom meets Skippy at a bar and tries to convince her to return to Dave (see image above), telling her that Dave has been "daffy," "hard as nails," and "miserable" since she left. Thinking that a reconciliation might be possible, she visits Dave at his New York office. Her visit is interrupted by Tom who reveals that student pilots are walking out because their careers with the airline are too uncertain. Dave suggests that Tom offer them a better deal that can guarantee an actual career with the organization, with a system of promotions, and pensions—a landmark arrangement, offered by no other airline. Tom leaves, excited to deliver the new contract to the students; Skippy remains and asks if Dave would be interested in starting again. Having been wounded by her lack of belief in him previously, Dave tells her that he doesn't trust that she believes in him now, so there is no point in starting over.

Hailing a taxi to take him to Newark Airport, Ross is surprised by Sunny whom he pushes into the waiting taxi and sends her far uptown, as he hails another taxi to his destination (*Silver Screen* for September 1936 revealed that the taxi scene was shot in front of Warner Brothers' studio). At the airline construction site, Dave and Dad are surprised that the government expects the wings of their aircraft to be able to support a weight of seventy-eight tons, well beyond what they understood to be the maximum safe weight. As expected, when the excessive weight is piled upon the wing, it breaks. Dad goes back to the drawing board but, because he needs quick results, Dave approaches several other aircraft engineers, none of whom wants to accept the challenge of designing a passenger plane capable of flying from San Francisco to Macau. Realizing that only Dad has what it takes to see the project through, Dave apologizes for his behavior and asks him to return to work, completely unaware that Dad has a serious cardiac condition and was told by his doctor to stop working. Dad swears his doctor to silence about his disease and continues to struggle with his designs until Dave glibly suggests building a double bottom on the plane, solving the problem of where to keep the fuel.

After Hap gets his job back with Trans-Oceanic Airways, he flies through a hurricane to test the effect of squally weather on the airplane and successfully returns to Miami where he is greeted by Dave who is only concerned about the plane, and Tom who wonders, "What's happened to us? We used to be a couple of sensible pilots. Now we go to school—we go flying through hurricanes—we take a lot of equipment out in the middle of the Pacific Ocean. We've gone completely daffy." When Hap seems lost in thought after Dave exits, Tom inquires what he's thinking about, and Hap replies, "I was just wondering how swell it would have been if he said 'thanks.'" Speaking of "daffy," Tom next appears high on a ladder on Midway Island, inquiring if Gooney Birds have teeth!

Following a montage depicting the construction of the China Clipper, test flights, and the aircraft's arrival in California, Dave assigns Hap to pilot the first flight to China, keeping Tom with him at the command center in Alameda, where Skippy takes a job as Dave's secretary, still hoping for a reconciliation. Once the China Clipper takes to the air, Tom spends all of his time checking weather reports and waiting for the transmissions from the airplane, which must arrive in China by 30 November or the rights to the route will be forfeited. Skippy sends regular reports of the plane's progress to Dad Brunn in the hospital until the China Clipper lands in Manilla, when Mother Brunn (Ruth Robinson) appears to tell Dave that Dad has died. Too busy to grieve, Tom and Dave disagree about how to proceed when storms threaten the lives of the pilots and the safety of the aircraft. When inclement weather downs planes in Manilla, Tom insists that the China Clipper stays on the ground, but Dave, still wanting the plane to fly through the storm, asks Mother Brunn what Dad would have wanted them to do. She says, "Not to fly." Beaten, Dave orders Hap to remain in Manilla until he feels that it is safe to go on.

Hap, however, has a mind of his own and flies the plane into the storm, landing on time in Macau Harbor. Celebrations ensue, with Dave hinting to money-man Hill about following their success with a New York to London route; and Ross telling Sunny that he has to fly to China to do his laundry. Not letting him get away on this occasion, Sunny accompanies him on the trip. Dave and Skippy finally reunite and embrace as they watch the China Clipper fly away.

An experienced pilot, Ross was particularly interested in his role and took every available opportunity to speak to the pilots and ground crews at the Alameda air base of Pan-American Airways where most of the exterior shots for *China Clipper* were filmed. In fact, it was this air base, on the Pacific coast near San Francisco, from which the original China Clipper flew on its journey across the Pacific Ocean. Other exteriors were filmed on Catalina Island, where the foliage resembled that of the various countries serviced by Trans-Oceanic Airways in the film. According to *Photoplay* (August 1936), Ross and Pat O'Brien "waged a battle to see who could keep from blowing up in their lines. They each bet a dollar and before it was over, Ross had lost three and won one. What Warner Brothers, with overhead going full blast, lost on the deal is, of course, something else again" (34). In a syndicated letter directed to Bill Lewis, written during the filming of *China Clipper*, Pat O'Brien noted that "'gagging' lines and situations is a part of every actor's job. If any of us see a place in the script to which we could add a humorous situation or a comedy line we never fail to do so. The director expects it and is the man who passes on it. A lot of them are not accepted. But the ones that are added to the general continuity usually help out a lot. Take our present script. We have been shooting *China Clipper* for about four weeks. During that time eight original gags which were not contained in the script lines have been added by members of the cast, including Ross Alexander, Humphrey Bogart and myself" (*Pittsburgh Sun-Telegraph*, 29 May 1936).

The *Oakland Tribune* (5 July 1936) also provided a behind-the-scenes account of the filming of *China Clipper*:

It is bright, sunny, hot, under the California sky, but stepping into the darkness of a stage on the Warners-First National lot, one hears the unmistakable sound of rain. This is a *China Clipper* set, the interior of a trans-Pacific Airways headquarters on San Francisco Bay. Before the cameras are Pat O'Brien and Ross Alexander in a dramatic scene.

Mingling with the voices of the two actors is the swish of wind-driven rain, beating through the outer darkness of the night upon the office windows. The downpour is ceaseless, punctuated only by flashes of light which tell that the airport beacon is making its measured rounds.

If you move away from the vicinity of the camera, climb over ropes, cables, props, so that you are, in a manner of speaking, out of doors, here is what you can observe: At the top of the exterior of each office window, concealed from view within the scene by partly lowered Venetian blinds are sections of tar paper, held in place by slats. A few inches away short lengths of perforated pipe, two parallel sections to a window. Attached to each a hose, running to a nearby hydrant.

On the floor, sawdust piled against the wall of the set, wooden frames that resemble sleeping cots, with fly-screening instead of springs, placed under the pipes, a low wall of timbers around the entire area. Close to the windows an electric fan on a tall standard, farther back a wind-machine or much larger fan. The scene lighted by carefully arranged cinematographers' lamps, among them an especially powerful arc.

When action begins, water pours down from the pipes, is blown by the fans in uneven gusts against the windows. Drops that escape the fans fall straight down upon the screens, which break them up, prevent their making too much noise for the good of the dialogue. The sawdust keeps the water from invading the office interior, the low wall of timber confines it within proscribed limits. The final illusion, that of the revolving beacon, is obtained by slowly moving the arc lamp beam past the windows, quickly extinguishing it.

On Thursday 21 May, Ross was among the invited guests of society-woman Ysabel (Izzy) Goss at one of her famous "talk-inducer" parties and, a week later, on Wednesday 27 May, he was an impassioned supporter of Benny Barrish in his bout against Ritchie Fontaine at the Los Angeles Auditorium. Even though Barrish lost the fight, the prizefighter hopped over to the Alameda airport where Ross was filming the following day to personally thank him for rooting for him. A mutual liking was immediately established between the actor and the fighter, to the extent that Ross expressed interest in buying in on Barrish's contract, even though sportswriters argued that it was doubtful the fighter's manager, Ben Sharpe, would allow it.

As *China Clipper* moved into June, studio publicists hinted to gossip columnists that Ross and Martha Merrill, another Warner stock player, were an item; that daily marriage proposals come his way; that he was "Hollywood's new Scream find" (images of young women screaming at the sight of Elvis Presley or the Beatles come to mind); that Ross, "who ached so intensely over Anita Louise, has shifted to Olive Jones, the Texas oriole" (*Reading Times*, 16 June 1936); that Ross Alexander, a general study in ebullience, is a back-slapper of the knock-your-lungs-out type and teeters on his heels and slides his thumbs up and down his suspenders, perhaps just the armholes of his vest. Jimmie Fidler in his syndicated column, *In Hollywood* (13 June 1936) also observed that "Ross Alexander dropped in on the *Stage Struck* set, eating an apple. He took a huge bite and kept right on talking. Said [Joan] Blondell: 'You shouldn't talk with your mouth full.' 'It isn't full,' Ross argued, turning his face and pointing: 'Look! One whole side is empty!'" Later, on 29 June, Fidler added that "Whenever I see Ross Alexander, his eyes suggest tragedy; since his wife's suicide they seldom seem to join his lips in smiles."

Following the completion of *China Clipper* on Saturday 20 June, Ross hosted a come-early-and-stay-late bash for his friends, Italian sportsman, Count Mario Gabellini, and his wife, the wealthy and socially prominent actress, Drue Dunne. According to *The Los Angeles Times* (23 June 1936), "Guests gathered early to play badminton or ping pong or just sit to gather strength while chatter was being induced in the usual manner. Lottie Anderson, who has a very special touch on the ivory keyboard, rippled off tunes and more tunes while a group gathered about to sing or dance. The buffet supper included everything from baked beans and potato salad to four kinds of meat and, we're sorry to say, disappeared as though no guest had assuaged the pangs since Saturday morning! Following the vitamins, there was much more piano playing and singing and a large number clustered in the special bar which Ross has outfitted with large brass spittoons, very fine prints [of prizefighters] and a sawdust floor." Ross was keen on the Gabellinis. Two weeks before, he joined them at a roller-skating party sponsored by the Assistance League, one of Drue's charities, at the Culver City Rollerdrome. A week later, Ross hosted them at dinner and took them to see the popular production of W.H. Smith's melodrama, *The Drunkard*, at the Theatre Mart which had opened on 6 July 1933 (and closed twenty-six years later on 17 October 1959). The Count was Ross's age, a heavy drinker, and a big spender. His wife was a high-society beauty who was swept off her feet by the handsome Italian, marrying him after only a ten-day courtship. Mario and Drue viewed one another as trophy spouses, and the couple regarded Ross as a trophy friend. Alexander felt the same way about them. He had an affinity for socially prominent women and well-connected men and needed to feel accepted in their circles. For Ross, the Gabellinis were a match made in heaven.

While *China Clipper* was in production, reviews for *Hot Money* began to materialize with the *Independent Exhibitors Film Bulletin* (27 May 1936) suggesting that "With very little to sell, except Ross Alexander, it will hardly reach average gross generally, but can be expected to build on favorable word-of-mouth. It keeps moving at a lively pace throughout. The dialogue is swift and replete with *nifties*. Alexander gives the difficult role of a typical smart alec a likeable quality which wins the spectator's sympathy. It is a new type of film character for this pleasing young player and his display of versatility will push him further up the ladder to stardom." *The New York Times* (25 July 1936) found *Hot Money* "neither particularly good nor conspicuously poor farce. Thanks to competent editing and direction, it falls quite gracefully into that niche reserved for 'amiable entertainments.' ... Mr. Alexander is especially well-suited to his part." *Variety* (29 July 1936) reported that "Alexander is cast as the super-salesman who manipulates the stock selling. Role enables him to almost shout many of his lines and to gyrate like a college cheerleader. Despite these flaws, he does much better than usual."

William Boehnel writing in the *New York World-Telegram* (27 July 1936), however, complained: "If the piece had been competently written and staged with the sparkle and buoyancy required of farce comedy, the work of Ross Alexander, Joseph Cawthorn and Paul Graetz would have stood out to better advantage and the audience might have been fairly well served. As it stands now *Hot Money* is monotonous farce." The *Motion Picture Herald* (3 October 1936) claimed that "Joe Cawthorn saved this one. The guttural jabbering of the ubiquitous Ross Alexander is horribly monotonous." On 28 November, however, the same publication wrote: "Somewhat screwy story, but Alexander's personality got it across to fair results." Moreover, on 19 December, *Picturegoer Weekly* determined that "Quite an ingenious plot dealing with big business, and well written, snappy dialogue make this quite good entertainment. While humor represents the film's main asset it is not lacking in suspense values and good characterization. Ross Alexander turns in a very good performance as Chick, who floats a company formed to market a chemical which will turn water into petrol. He is very bright in his 'sales' talk, and is admirably backed up by Joseph Cawthorn as Max, his financial backer."

China Clipper was previewed in Los Angeles on 4 August 1936, following which, *Motion Picture Daily* (5 August 1936) reported "Splendid team work by director, cast and producer turns this aviation saga into gripping entertainment that should hold any audience." Noting that *China Clipper* elicited raves from everyone who saw it, Harriet Parsons added that Ross attended the preview with Anne Nagel, a contract player at Warner Bros. who played the minor part of secretary Ruth McElniney in *Hot Money* (*The San Francisco Examiner*, 6 August 1936). Richard Watts, Jr., however, found that "the latest aviation photoplay is a greater tribute to the press agents of the Pan-American Airlines than it is to the men who produced it. There is a line somewhere in the picture wherein one of the players remarks with a touch of bitterness, 'We're all tired and we're getting nowhere.' I suspect that, despite some interesting, if familiar, air scenes and several good performances by the men in the cast, the line can be aptly applied to the film" (*New York Herald-Tribune*, 12 August 1936). Frank Nugent of *The New York Times* (12 August 1936) disagreed: "The Warner Brothers, with the cooperation of Pan American Airways, have added another vivid chapter to the screen's history of aviation in *China Clipper*, which opened last night at the Strand. A fascinating and surprisingly literal dramatization of the China Clipper's trans-Pacific flight of last November, the picture deserves a respectful accolade both for its technical accuracy and for its rather astonishing refusal to describe the flying boat's journey in the stock terms of aerial melodrama. . . . The cast has fulfilled its task with commendable straightforwardness. Mr. O'Brien has contributed a tense portrait of energy incarnate. Humphrey Bogart and Ross Alexander as a pair of pilots, the late Henry B. Wathall as the ship's designer and Addison Richards as the harassed financial backer must be included on the credit side of an entirely creditable film ledger."

Variety (19 August 1936), on the other hand, called *China Clipper*, "an aviation picture without the usual thrills. It fictionalizes recent history and places too much stress on the technical phase of flying, with the result that its value as an educational screen document exceeds its entertainment merits. . . . The romantic part of the story isn't very romantic. O'Brien and the missus (Beverly Roberts) split up over a sappy misunderstanding early in the picture and really don't get together again until the finish. Ross Alexander and Marie Wilson carry on a comedy love affair in which Miss Wilson is 'typed' once more. It would be a good idea to give this promising comedienne a different part now and then. Humphrey Bogart, no gunman this time, does well in a sympathetic role." The *Democrat and Chronicle* (28 August 1936) wished that Bogart had "more of a part," but found that Ross "has some excellent scenes, notably the one in which he refuses Logan's demand that he order the China Clipper on through the storm."

On the same day the above review appeared, Ross, Pat O'Brien, and Beverly Roberts performed scenes from *China Clipper* on the *Hollywood Hotel* program, broadcast on the east coast at 8:00 P.M. on the CBS radio network. Dick Powell continued in his role as master-of-ceremonies of the entertainment that also featured vocalists Frances Langford, Anne Jamison, and Igor Gorin, supported by Raymond Paige's Orchestra. During the first half of the program, entirely devoted to music, Ross sat in the control room of the studio with Mrs. Pat O'Brien. Since seats were scarce, Ross sat on the edge of Mrs. O'Brien's chair and the two gossiped congenially for fifteen minutes, after which Ross left to join his co-stars waiting in the green room. After his exit, an elderly white-haired lady turned to Mrs. O'Brien, not knowing who she was, and said, "I think your boy is wonderful in pictures," evidently referring to Ross, but Mrs. O'Brien understandably thought she meant her husband. The lady continued, "My daughter and I have predicted ever since his first picture that he was going right to the top, and we have followed every one of his pictures with interest. We feel very proud that our prophecy has come true." Mrs. O'Brien beamed with pride and replied, "Thank you. I'll tell him. I know he'll be pleased." After a short pause, the elderly lady remarked in a confidential tone, "I don't like that Pat O'Brien at all. I think he should only play policemen" (*Democrat and Chronicle*, 8 November 1936).

On 7 October 1936, *Modern Screen* claimed that "A giant airliner is the star of *China Clipper*. It is perhaps true that an airplane has no sex appeal, but it usually has something which registers quite definitely at the box office. In this case, the scenes showing the flight of the China Clipper are the most exciting in the film. There's a thrill every moment the camera is focused on the great ship. . . . Pat O'Brien is his usual brusque self as the tough executive. Beverly Roberts seems miscast as the wife. Humphrey Bogart and Ross Alexander are excellent as a pair of aviators, and Marie Wilson contributes comedy as a gal with a yen for Mr. Alexander." Writing in *Picturegoer Weekly* (31 October 1936), however, Lionel Collier felt that *China Clipper* "becomes rather irritating in its insistence on the ruthless driving power of the man who is supposed to start the first Trans-Pacific Airline. . . . Pat O'Brien is quite good but honors go rather to Ross Alexander and Humphrey Bogart as his friends and fellow pilots. Beverly Roberts is fair as the wife. Aerial sequences are very well done and the camera work is excellent but there is a good deal of repetition and the element of thrill is missing."

World Film News and Television Progress (December 1936) published two additional British reviews of *China Clipper* that offered new perspectives on the film. Paul Dehn in *The Sunday Referee* wrote:

The moral of *China Clipper* would appear to be that, so long as the Cause is fundamentally good, one may fight for its attainment by the foulest possible means. Pat O'Brien, for the further advancement of civil aviation in America, built a mammoth airline with the intention of establishing regular flights across the Pacific Ocean. In the pursuit of this end, he alienated his wife's affection, treated her plea for renewed friendship with abominable cruelty, killed a kindly old aeroplane designer through overwork, and drove his exhausted subordinates relentlessly to the point of mutiny. The trans-Pacific flight was a success. Whereat Mr. O'Brien became the hero of the hour, was slapped on the back by an admiring nation, forgiven by his wife, and faded out (by a discreet director) trailing clouds of glory. Let it be. Philosophy or no philosophy, this is a thundering good picture, thronged with every sort of thrill imaginable at high altitudes and a great deal of determined drama at ground level. The film has but one real fault—and that a minor one. It is the Cause, my soul, it is the Cause.

Ignoring a moral or philosophical approach, C.A. Lejeune, in *The Sunday Observer*, was far less impressed with the movie:

The film, I am afraid, is neither as fine nor as exciting as its subject, thanks to a certain stolidity of acting and sentimentality of writing. I am sorry, but Pat O'Brien's playing still seems to me to have just about the subtlety of a trombone, and I have never been able to shout, with the enthusiasm of a Hepburn in *Alice Adams*, "Hurrah, Hurrah for Ross Alexander!" The struggle, however, for wings over the Pacific is still one of the more valid of the season's dramatic subjects.

Boffo reviews or not, *China Clipper* was a happy experience for Ross Alexander who was establishing himself quickly as Pat O'Brien's favorite onscreen wingman. Studio publicity reported that the pair grew short beards during the course of shooting in order to achieve that unkempt and haggard look necessary to depict the long working hours bringing them perilously close to exhaustion. O'Brien quipped that his two-year-old daughter, Mavourneen, ran and hid when he went home at night, unable to understand that the man with the beard was her father. Ross, it seemed, had the opposite experience. He swore that every time he started across the lawn at his farm, his two pet goats, Minnie and Maude, ran after him, aiming for his beard with a fixed purpose in their eyes!

19. *Here Comes Carter* and *Ready, Willing and Able*

Early in June 1936, Ross Alexander was announced as the star of *Loudspeaker Lowdown* (AKA *The Tatler* and *The Voice of Scandal*, but released as *Here Comes Carter*), with singer Jane Froman as the feminine lead, co-staring Glenda Farrell and Craig Reynolds, written by Roy Chanslor from a story by Michael Jacoby, and directed by William Clemens. By the time the production went before the cameras on 22 June, Froman had been assigned to another picture and ingenue Anne Nagle, who had made an appearance in *Hot Money* and *China Clipper*, was cast as her replacement, much to Alexander's delight, since the two would begin a romantic relationship during the production.

Loudspeaker Lowdown opens with Kent Carter (Ross Alexander) walking to his office on the lot of Premium Pictures and listening to his secretary Linda Warren (Anne Nagel) sing "You on My Mind" while she types. They are in love, but she wants to pursue a singing career and Ross wants "a wife, not a long-term contract with options." Since Kent refuses to help her career along, Linda has been keeping company with actor Rex Marchbanks (Craig

339

Reynolds), much to Carter's distress. Marchbanks, in turn, wants Carter's help in disentangling himself from his wife who has sued him for non-support. Arguing that he's "a press agent, not a *sup*press agent," Carter refuses, turns Rex into the police, and is summarily fired from his job, just as Rex had threatened if Kent didn't help him.

Carter finds himself on a park bench looking through the want ads in the newspaper and inadvertently runs into Linda who is also out of work and advises him to "square things" with Premium Pictures. Not convinced, Kent decides to make a living through his inside knowledge of Hollywood and, after a quick stop in a local diner run by Bell (Wayne Morris), where Carter hears a radio announcement that Rex and his wife have reconciled, he goes off to the office of Mel Winter (Hobart Cavanaugh), the dipsomaniacal radio gossip commentator on Station KLA. Met by Winter's wise-cracking secretary Verna Kennedy (Glenda Farrell) who refers to Carter as an "*ex*press agent," he convinces the radio man to hire him at $30.00 a week to feed him the "inside stuff" in Hollywood, not simply the far from juicy material disseminated by the studio press agents. Fortunately for Kent, when Winter is too drunk to deliver his radio broadcast, Carter takes his place, bashes Marchbanks on the air, and becomes an instant success with the radio audience, much to the misery of the actor who forces Premium Pictures to sue the radio station. Undeterred, station boss Daniel Bronson (Joseph Crehan) tells station manager Ben Rogers (John T. Murray) to give Carter a contract and happily agrees to give Linda an audition for the station's musical program, without telling her that Kent arranged it.

The scene changes to Carter's office (formerly Winter's office) at KLA Studios where Verna Kennedy, now his official secretary, asks if it is "prudent to antagonize these birds right at the start." Kent glibly replies, "You ain't seen no antagonism—when I antagonize 'em, they stay antagonized!" Linda appears, thrilled that she has been hired as a vocalist by the radio station. She kisses Carter, much to Miss Kennedy's disappointment and the couple go off to lunch, with Carter quipping as they leave, "If anybody phones, tell 'em to come up and *sue* me sometime." In the meantime, Marchbanks has asked his gangster brother Steve Moran (Norman Willis) to take care of Carter—no rough stuff, just a few scare tactics. Steve assigns Slugs Dana (John Sheehan) to take care of Carter but, since he has tickets to the Diana Davenport film, *Love Larceny*, he only begrudgingly follows orders.

In Carter's office, Slugs complains about Carter's calling him a gangster and a rat on the radio when, in fact, he is a "protection engineer" and messenger from Steve Moran who wants Carter to go easy on Rex Marchbanks. Kent, in turn, promising to apologize on his next broadcast, gives Slugs his Diana Davenport cigarette lighter before the pair go off to watch the preview of her new picture. The scene changes to the radio studio where Linda is performing "You on My Mind" before a live audience, including Carter. He meets her after her performance and the two argue about his "mud-slinging" job, for which he earns $1000.00 weekly. Doggedly, she tells him that she "could never respect a man, spreading brutal, malicious gossip about other people" and Kent realizes that they are philosophically at an impasse.

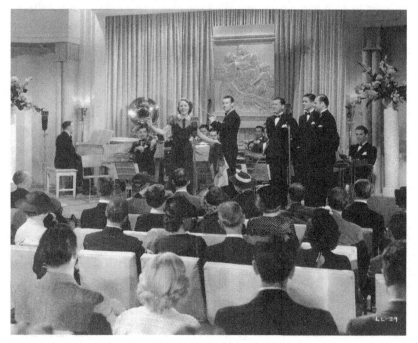

Anne Nagel singing "You on My Mind" in *Here Comes Carter*.

Carter's on-air apology does not placate the gangsters who follow him as he takes Linda home to the Carlton Arms and beat him up. Prior to his beating, however, Kent and Linda had seemingly resolved their differences by his promising to quit his job as soon as his contract was up. Newspaper headlines appear on screen: "Kent Carter Slugged, Beaten: Mystery Surrounds Identity of Attackers." The scene changes to a room in a hospital with Carter, head-bandaged, and lying in bed. He arranges to broadcast from his hospital room just as Linda enters, frightened that thugs will kill him if he continues his on-air diatribes. Against her advice he broadcasts the names of the thugs who beat him up: Louie (Charles Foy) and Boots (George Stone). Bronson appears with Mr. Rogers who want Carter to retract what he said about Rex Marchbanks or face termination of his contract. While they are pleading their case, Kent gets a threatening call from Slugs and pretends that the caller is a Mr. Bancroft of a rival radio station who is offering him $1750 a week. Suddenly, instead of wanting to fire Carter, Bronson matches the bogus offer in order to keep him. Disillusioned by the phony phone call, Linda calls off her engagement, even though Carter tells her that the Bancroft deal was only a ruse.

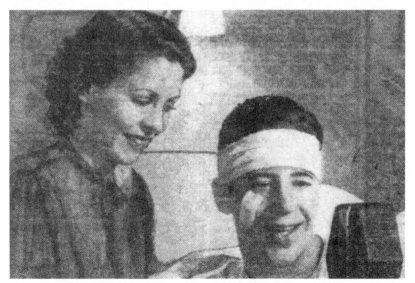

Anne Nagel and Ross Alexander in *Here Comes Carter*.

As she leaves, Slugs enters with a gun on which there are no notches. Carter takes the gun away and talks him out of killing him; in the process, Slugs reveals that Steve Moran killed a bank teller during a recent robbery and that he (Slugs) only served as a lookout man. Carter offers him a lifetime pass to film previews—but makes it known that it is his lifetime, not Slugs's that guarantees the movie passes. Should anything happen to him, the passes are null and void. He also agrees to admit that his identification of the culprits was a mistake. Verna enters to tell Carter that she took down every word of the conversation he has just had with Slugs. Assured that the confession is just for Carter's files, Slugs leaves satisfied but remembers that Carter still has his gun. Carter throws him the gun and subsequently leaves the hospital with Verna.

The hospital sequence took a full week to film, requiring Ross to lay in bed the entire time. "If you think it isn't hard to spend day after day in bed," Ross told reporters, "try it yourself, especially when you feel perfectly well. The fact is, I was so tired out after a day's work in bed that I had to go right home and go to bed" (*The Philadelphia Inquirer*, 13 November 1936).

Newspaper headlines appear on screen: "Kent Carter Disappears. Hollywood Broadcaster Vanishes from Hospital. Foul Play Feared." The scene changes to Carter's office where his fake microphone (which houses his cigarettes) is wired to the broadcast booth to enable him to go on the air from his office. Linda appears and tells Verna that she is worried about Carter. Verna scolds her for her lack of trust in her fiancé, telling her, "When I love a man, I'm there rooting for him, every minute, whatever he does." She reveals that Linda owes her career to Carter, but, gentleman that he is, he wanted her to believe that she did it all on her own. Linda confesses, "Oh, Miss Kennedy, I'm an awful fool." The scene changes again to Steve and Slugs who are listening to the radio. Slugs tells him not to worry, that he has taken care of everything. Nonetheless, Steve gets a phone call telling him that Carter showed up at the police station and fingered Louie and Boots as his assailants. The scene changes again to KLA's studio where Linda is singing "Through the Courtesy of Love" to a studio audience that includes Carter.

343

Ross Alexander and Glenda Farrell in *Here Comes Carter*.

Back in Carter's office, Kent is on the radio with Verna at his side. Carter reveals that the so-called reconciliation between Rex and his wife is bogus, designed only to support Marchbanks's film career. A cut-in interrupts the video of the broadcast depicting the police in one car and gangsters in another, presumably driving to Station KLA. Back to the broadcast, Carter reveals that gangster Steve Moran and Rex Marchbanks are brothers, and apologizes to "the fair men and women of screen" for his peddling dirt during his broadcasts. Steve and Slugs enter, this time Steve has a gun. Not knowing that the microphone is still live and broadcasting, Steve confesses to the murder of a bank teller. He tries to escape but is shot by a policeman. Slugs manages to take advantage of the live microphone, saying "Hello, mom, don't wait up for me," to which Carter responds with his signature, "Oh. Ho!" Following a long embrace with Linda, Carter looks straight at the camera and, in a subdued voice, proclaims "Hey, hey," as the film ends.

A week after production began on *Loudspeaker Lowdown* (hereafter referred to as *Here Comes Carter*) Louella Parsons ran the following article in her syndicated column: "We knew Ross Alexander was an actor of merit when we saw him on the New York stage, and our judgment was confirmed by his picture portrayals. Thus, we acclaim Jack Warner's decision to put Ross in starring spots. The highly-sought and much coveted role of Alabama Pitts in Warden Lawes's story, 'Over the Wall,' will be the first to focus attention on Warners' new white-haired boy. Pitts, you recall, is the former Sing Sing athlete who created such a furor when he quit the big house with a receipt in full for his social debt and began life over as a baseball player" (*The San Francisco Examiner*, 27 June 1936). On 29 June 1936, *The Film Daily* announced that "Ross Alexander will be presented in three Warner-First National pictures scheduled for the immediate future. The first will be *The Go-Getter*, from the story by Peter B. Kyne. Next on the list is *Over the Wall*, based on a story by Warden Lewis E. Lawes of Sing Sing Prison." Later reports in *The Film Daily* advertise that the screenplay for *Over the Wall* will be written by Harry Sauber and Ben Markson, and that Lloyd Bacon will direct. According to *The Brooklyn Daily Eagle* (30 June 1936), the third feature will be *Kid Galahad*, a film version of Francis Wallace's *Saturday Evening Post* story about a clean-cut kid who becomes a boxer and is pushed around by gangsters and racketeers. Film adaptation will be by Seton I. Miller, and Edward G. Robinson is set to co-star.

On 20 July, *Shrinking Violet* (released as *King of Hockey*) began filming, without Ross Alexander or Beverly Roberts. Instead the main roles were portrayed by Dick Purcell and Anne Nagel. Ross, in the midst of filming one picture and already assigned to three more, did not begrudge Purcell the part that Ross had prepared for. Besides, in addition to his duties at the studio, Ross was busy escorting Rosalind Russell, an old friend of Alexander's from his one-a-week stock career, to and from her dinner parties at the Trocadero. At the end of July, Darryl F. Zanuck announced that Twentieth-Century Fox had borrowed Ross for *Pigskin Parade*, a college football musical, staring Judy Garland, Tony Martin, Patsy Kelly, and Betty Grable, but, because production dates of *Pigskin Parade* overlapped those of *Here Comes Carter* and Alexander's other projects at Warner Brothers, the role for which Ross had been cast, "Chip," was consequently performed by Johnny Downs.

On Sunday, 26 July, when Ross welcomed a day off from filming, Drue Gabellini celebrated his twenty-ninth birthday with a pool party that featured an elaborate buffet supper, ping-pong, bridge, and lively conversation in addition to the laughs that arose when party guests, Mrs. Burt Stoddard of Dallas, Texas, and Burt Whitley, teetered on the edge of the pool and fell in with their clothes on! Early in August, Ross and his *Carter* nemesis Craig Reynolds attended the Hollywood preview of *Stage Struck*, starring friends Joan Blondell and Dick Powell. Much to the concern of the featured players at the preview, it was Alexander and Reynolds who were mobbed by autograph seekers and well-wishers. Although Ross was happy to have become the topic of conversation in the film community, he was most gratified to be acknowledged among California's elite social set when on 10 August he was among the A-list guests invited to an afternoon reception for Her Excellency Ruta Bryan Owen, United States Ambassador to Denmark and her husband, Captain Boerge Rohde, guard to His Majesty King Christian X. Among those also invited to the event were Jack Warner, Darryl Zanuck, Hal Wallis, Samuel Goldwyn, Louis B. Mayer, George Cukor, Mary Pickford, Fay Wray, Janet Gaynor, Ginger Rogers, Jeanette MacDonald, Loretta Young, Joan Crawford, Barbara Stanwick, Harold Lloyd, Franchot Tone, Gene Raymond, Pat O'Brien, Nelson Eddy, Cary Grant, Robert Taylor, Jimmy Stewart, and magician-turned-actor Fred Keating. Prior to the reception, Ross and Keating attended the American Legion Parade in Hollywood where they were overwhelmed by youngsters asking for autographs. Not only did they accommodate their requests, Ross and Fred pampered their young devotees with ice cream and sodas at a refreshment wagon!

Here Comes Carter wrapped up filming on 12 August and for the remainder of the month, Ross was free to work at his ranch—planting, building, and tending to his menagerie of animals that included the pigs, Giggi and Rose, two cats, ducks, two pedigreed Toggenburg goats named Minnie and Maude, a coop filled with pigeons adjacent to the chicken coop, a pair of Chinese pheasants, a horse, and a huge, waddling English bulldog named Mr. Watson. Speaking of his cats and Mr. Watson, Ross noted: "I have to have something to talk to. They act hurt if I don't inform them and Mr. Watson how the weather looks for the day and what I'm planning to tell the director the next time he says something I don't like" (*Chicago Tribune*, 26 July 1936).

Ross Alexander chopping wood at his farm.

In the same *Chicago Tribune* article, Ross claimed to have become a teetotaler, saying, "Hollywood's a funny place. If you just like a drink or two and go to a party, someone insists that you take five or six. Then they say, 'Who asked that souse? Throw him out.' The next place you go, when they offer you a drink, you refuse it. They give you the dizzy eye and crack, 'Who asked that holy guy here? What a wet blanket.' It's hard to know exactly what to do, so I'm pleasing myself and drinking nothing right now."

While Ross was busy attending to his livestock, Harriet Parsons announced in her syndicated column (14 August 1936) that Ross and Pat O'Brien would reunite in a prison picture, *San Quentin*, story by John Bright

347

and Robert Tasker, screenplay by Peter Milne and Humphrey Cobb, and directed by Ray Enright, who recently helmed *China Clipper*. Pat would portray the tough captain of the yard who keeps the inmates in line, and Ross would play an obstreperous convict (*The San Francisco Examiner*, 15 August 1936). Not to be outdone, on the same day, *The Los Angeles Times* (15 August 1936) announced that Alexander had been assigned to yet another film, *Ship News*, written by George Bilson, about a waterfront reporter in New York City.

Ross Alexander with a wheelbarrow, watched by Mr. Watson.

Ross Alexander in a contemplative pose with his horse.

Since he met Anne Nagel, there was more to Ross Alexander's life than work on the farm. In the evenings, he was seen on the set of *King of Hockey*, waiting for her to finish work, and escorting her to dinner at Sardi's and dancing at the Palomar Ballroom, a favorite of Alexander's evening spots. All through August and September, gossip columnists pointedly singled them out at cafes and nightclubs, aching to associate Ross with a significant other. Alexander's personal life had become an especially hot topic as his popularity grew among the young female filmgoer. The September 1936 issue of *Photoplay* noted the phenomenon:

A Birdie whispers Dick Powell is a bit worried these days. It seems that

349

feminine visitors on the lot have let their fickle affections drift elsewhere. And Dick has rated top man so long.

A group of girls, high school age, were being shown about the Warner Brothers lot. "Well, did you see Dick Powell?" they were asked by a member of the publicity department.

"Oh yes," was the answer, "but we saw someone much more exciting than Dick. *We saw Ross Alexander.*"

The studio is still wondering about that one. So is Dick.

The girls' reaction and the fact that Ross had become third among Warner's stars getting the most fan mail inspired Hal Wallis to assign him the lead in *Ready, Willing and Able*, the role originally announced for Dick Powell before Daryl Zanuck borrowed him for *On the Avenue*, another backstage musical with songs by Irving Berlin, and co-starring Madeleine Carroll, Alice Faye, and the Ritz Brothers. *Ready, Willing and Able* was based on a *Saturday Evening Post* story by Richard Macauley, with a screenplay by Jerry Wald, Sig Herzig, and Warren Duff, direction by Ray Enright, and costarring Ruby Keeler, Lee Dixon, Allen Jenkins, and Louise Fazenda. Because of his being cast in *Ready, Willing and Able*, Ross was replaced by Humphrey Bogart in *San Quentin*, which began filming location shots at the prison in mid-September.

While he waited for filming to begin, Ross was among Warner's list of contract players designated to appear at London's Teddington film studio as part of the Warner-First National British unit during the 1936–1937 season. In addition to Ross Alexander, the Warner's players assigned to one or more of the twenty pictures planned at the Teddington studio included Zazu Pitts, Glenda Farrell, Hugh Herbert, Joan Blondell, Jean Muir, Anita Louise, and Ian Hunter. In addition, Lloyd Bacon was one of three Hollywood directors assigned to the British unit. *Variety* (30 December 1936) advertised that Ross was particularly wanted to costar with a nineteen-year-old "discovery" named Lesley Brook, who would debut in the Warner's Teddington production of *The Vulture* and go on to a film, stage, and television career.

On 16 September, a day when both Ross and Anne Nagel could free themselves from studio responsibilities, they eloped by plane to Yuma,

Arizona, where they were married by Judge E.A. Freeman, known as the "marrying justice." Born Anna Marie Dolan in Malden, Massachusetts, on 29 September 1915, Anne was given a strict religious education designed to prepare her for a vocation as a nun. After her parents' divorce and her mother's remarriage to Curtis Nagel, a technicolor specialist, the family moved to Hollywood where Anne became less interested in the convent and embraced a career as an actress in film. Taking her step-father's surname, Anne Nagel became a contract player with Fox Film Corporation in the early 1930s, moving over to Warner Brothers in the fall of 1935.

The relationship between Ross Alexander and Anne Nagel began with a faux pas, three months earlier, in the dining rooms at Warner Brothers' studios. Anne had been lunching in the green room, reserved for important film folk, when all of a sudden Ross entered, only to discover that the only empty seat in the room was at Anne's small table. Ross simply sat down opposite Anne, without introducing himself and without waiting for an invitation— something that Anne believed was an impropriety. She responded coldly, "That seat is taken." "Oh, I beg your pardon," Ross said as he got up from the seat and made a quick exit to the common dining room. Enthralled by Anne's sassy attitude and captivated by her lovely face, Ross presently returned to the green room, this time with Errol Flynn, who properly introduced them to one another. Adhering to etiquette, Ross asked, "Now may I sit down?" Anne smiled and said yes.

In a *Movie Mirror* interview with George Madden, published in February 1937, Ross began by saying, "Please don't call our marriage a 'second chance at happiness,' for this is a new adventure Anne and I have just begun—an adventure with a present and a future, but without a past. Our great happiness together is an individual thing that has no relation to anything that has happened to either of us before. We want to keep it that way. We have our eyes and hearts set on the future" (56). Ross continued, "I have few friends out here. I hadn't wanted any, until I met Anne. Can you believe this? I've never been inside the home of anyone on this studio lot and none of them has ever been to mine. I've always lived to myself in Hollywood. And if I was lonely, . . . it was the awful loneliness that comes from wanting just one person, a person to share my life and enjoy the things I enjoyed with me. . . . I found that one person when I met Anne. . . . One Sunday, not so long ago, I picked Anne up early in the morning. We drove out to my ranch and found a marvelous country breakfast waiting for us. We spent part of the day wandering around the ranch—feeding the chickens, picking fruit and talking as we walked. Then, when evening came, we piled a few logs on the fire and set a bridge table in front of the fireplace. We picked up a swell cold supper out of the icebox. After we had finished eating, we just sat there, looking across the table at each other; suddenly I knew that this companionship and Anne were all I wanted out of life! . . . That night I asked Anne if she would marry me" (80–81).

Jimmy Fidler's syndicated column "In Hollywood" provided Anne's memory of her whirlwind elopement:

> Three days before their marriage they told everybody that they were only good friends. Three luncheons later Alexander telephoned, "Pack up! We're going to Yuma to be married." An old-fashioned woman might have answered, "But this is so sudden!" Anne is not old-fashioned; she only said, "But you start a new picture tomorrow!" "That's okay," Ross argued. "We'll be married and back here in time for dinner tonight!" And they were. (*Santa Ana Register*, 30 October 1936)

Immediately after the wedding, Ross and Anne flew back to Los Angeles to begin their honeymoon, scattered between takes of the Warner Brothers' films to which they were assigned. Although Ross denied that having a wife on the ranch would create major lifestyle changes, he did discard his valet, admitting that "Only thing I needed him for was to tie a bow tie for me . . . and Anne can do it better than he" (*The Times*, 29 October 1936).

Anne Nagel, tying a bowtie for Ross Alexander.

Production began for *Ready, Willing and Able* during the week of 21 September 1936, with Bobby Connolly hard at work choreographing a large, pulchritudinous female chorus, and dialogue director Gene Lewis, instructing Ruby Keeler, Winifred Shaw, and Carol Hughes on how to perfect their British accents. While director Ray Enright spent time on establishing shots and camera angles, Ross studied his lines, of which he had a significant amount. Cast as neophyte producer Barry Granville, he strives to take to Broadway a musical comedy he wrote with his song-writing collaborator Pinky Blair (Lee Dixon) called *Fair Lady*. The film begins with Barry on the piano and Pinky singing their latest "hit" called "The World is My Apple," while dressed in coat and tie, but without any trousers (see image below). The pair are impoverished, too poor to come up with $.50 to pay Angelo (Adrian Rosley), the tailor who appears with their pants. They fast-talk him into thinking that they will put his picture on their next song hit, "There's a Little," steal their trousers, and quickly make an exit while the flabbergasted Angelo is enthralled with singing the song.

353

Pinky Blair (Lee Dixon) and Barry Granville (Ross Alexander) in *Ready,*
Willing and Able.

The pair run into J. Van Courtland (Allen Jenkins), an agent and ex-
vaudevillian who once had a successful act with a female partner and trained
seal named Floribell. The three of them go up to the office of Edward
McNeil (Addison Richards) of Amalgamated Pictures; Barry and Pinky go
into McNeill's office, leaving Van Courtland in the outer office with Dot
(Jane Wyman) the secretary, and a violin-scratching Kid (Dickie Jones) who
kicks him in the shins. Meanwhile, in the inner office, McNeil tells Barry and
Pinky that he likes the show, except for the opening, the first act finale, the
holes in the plot, the character of Mendoza, and the fact that "it's been done
before." Nonetheless, he tells them that Amalgamated Pictures will give them
$50,000 to produce the show on two conditions: that the studio gets first
refusal on the movie rights; and that British sensation Jane Clarke (Winifred
Shaw) be hired to star in the show. Barry and Pinky agree without reservation
and, moving to the outer office, Barry cables Miss Clarke, offering her $1500 a

354

week to appear in his show. Now a running gag, Angelo unexpectedly appears with another picture for the song cover as the scene ends.

Jane Clarke (Ruby Keeler), J. Van Courtland (Allen Jenkins), and Angie (Carol Hughes) in *Ready, Willing and Able.*

Following an establishing shot of an ocean liner, Clara Heineman (Louise Fazenda) attempts to talk the ship's Captain (Thomas Pogue) into slowing down the vessel while her wards—the young ladies from college—are performing. When he refuses, she leaves in a huff, and the scene changes to the ladies' dressing room where Jane Clarke (Ruby Keeler) laments having to go back to school and being engaged to Truman Hardy (Hugh O'Connell), who, like her father, disapproves of her wanting to be on stage. Jane and girl's chorus subsequently perform a number called "Handy with Your Feet," which includes various tap dance styles suggesting Flamenco dancing, "Sonja Henie on the ice," and "A drunken husband." As soon as the ship arrives in New York, Van Courtland rushes aboard to place Jane under contract for *Fair Lady.* Knowing that she is not the British star Van Courtland expected, Jane attempts to explain the mix up to him, but he refuses to listen to her.

Encouraged by her friend Angie (Carol Hughes), and always having wanted a career in the theatre, Jane decides to go along with the ruse and sign the contract.

Outside Barry's apartment, two piano movers (Shaw and Lee), who are repossessing Barry's piano, break into a spontaneous dance routine on the sidewalk when Pinky appears and performs on the instrument to convince them not to take it away. Inside, while Barry is trying to persuade his landlady Mrs. Beadle (May Boley) not to evict him, even though he owes her $84.00 in back rent, he learns that Jane Clarke has been signed for his show and his money worries are over—at least temporarily. Barry, Pinky, and Van Courtland meet Jane at her hotel and it is love at first sight between Jane and Barry as he speaks the lyrics to the show's love song, "Too Marvelous for Words."

Barry Granville (Ross Alexander) in *Ready, Willing and Able*.

A reception is held for Jane, during which she speaks to several reporters, providing them with a bogus history of her British ancestry and upbringing. Barry appears in a tuxedo (see image above), for which he had to borrow ten dollars from McNeil to get it out of hock. When the guests clamor for Jane to sing, she claims to be ill and out of voice, so to appease the crowd, Barry sings "Just a Quiet Evening" followed by a tap dance by Jane and Pinky. After the number, Barry sweeps Jane away from the reception and takes her back to the hotel, where he reprises "Just a Quiet Evening" and kisses her goodnight. Back at the reception, Clara tells Van Courtland that she is interested in reigniting her stage career with a role in *Fair Lady*. She provides him with examples of her vocal abilities, sounding more like a foghorn than a singer, though being so self-absorbed, she believes that her artistry, such as it is, is still competitive. In the photo during the reception of her with Pinky Blair at the piano, he looks both surprised and suspicious of the woman whose real-life presence seems like something out of a bad musical comedy.

Clara Heineman (Louise Fazenda) and Pinky Blair (Lee Dixon) in *Ready, Willing and Able.*

357

Fair Lady has been rehearsing for three weeks and Jane has yet to sing a note. Barry, Pinky, choreographer Yip Nolan (Teddy Hart) and the entire cast are concerned, but Van Courtland maintains that "She's so terrific, she could open without a rehearsal." Angelo appears at the theatre with yet another picture for the title page of his song, this one of his entire family—himself, his domineering wife, and his nine children. Barry and Pinky send him away, promising as always to use the photo. In Jane's dressing room, Jane and Angie are listening to a recording of the real Jane Clarke's voice. The sound trickles out to the stage where Barry, Pinky, Yip and all the cast listen rapturously. Barry enters the dressing room to tell Jane that her voice is terrific, and calls for the conductor to play the love song, announcing to the cast that Jane will finally sing. In the meantime, before escorting her on stage, Pinky ecstatically tells Jane that her being cast got them the money for the show, which has been Barry's dream for the past four years. The orchestra plays the introduction to "Too Marvelous for Words" and Barry sings the opening chorus. When it comes time for Jane to sing, however, she freezes and runs back to the dressing room, followed by a very confused Barry, to whom she confesses that she cannot sing, that she is not the real Jane Clarke, just a theatre hopeful who happened to have the same name. Barry feels like the victim of a cruel joke that has cost him $25,000 in costumes, scenery, and salaries. To make matters worse, Truman appears and tells Barry that he is Jane's fiancé, to which Barry replies, "She wasn't even on the level about that." Feeling completely betrayed, he bashes Truman's hat before storming out.

The plot thickens when the real Jane Clarke (Winifred Shaw) threatens to sue Amalgamated Pictures, forcing McNeil to demand the return of their entire $50,000 investment, an impossibility since half the money is already gone. Reminding McNeil of his contract to produce *Fair Lady* on or by 5 September and his intent to honor that contract, Barry angrily exits while McNeil sends a cable to the real Jane Clarke offering her $2000 a week to appear in *Fair Lady* opening in November. Newspaper headlines appear on screen: "*Fair Lady* Folds: Amalgamated Pictures Pulls Out with Backing."

Jane learns that Jane Clarke has sailed from London to New York on the Queen Mary, docking at two o'clock that very day. She, Van Courtland, Angie, and Pinky rush to the dock to speak to Jane before McNeil signs her. To intercept the producer, Pinky picks a fight with him and is instantly knocked to the ground. Police arrive and take both men into custody, ruining McNeil's chances to be first in line to sign Jane Clarke. Barry tries to persuade Jane to appear in the musical but she refuses, saying that she is committed to Amalgamated Pictures. Van Courtland, however, recognizes her as Amy Callahan, his old vaudeville partner, and has a photograph to prove it. Faced with her past being revealed, Jane signs on to do Barry's show. As soon as Amalgamated Pictures realizes that Jane Clarke has signed with Barry, they do everything they can to prevent *Fair Lady* from opening since the studio wants to produce the musical themselves. Telegrams appear on screen from creditors, obviously influenced by Amalgamated Pictures: Atlas Costume Company "will not ship costumes until balance is paid"; Boris Dukes "must have check before delivery of last act scenery"; and Genda Theatrical Equipment Company threatened "if final payment on revolving stage not met by tomorrow noon will get injunction against your opening."

The bogus Jane, who is still in the show because Van Courtland forced Barry to honor her contract, learns from Pinky that unless they come up with $10,000, the show cannot open. Jane finds Truman locked in an embrace with the real Jane Clarke, and persuades him to go to Barry and put up the money, which he does in the long-winded, meandering, idiosyncratic style he exhibits throughout the film. Flash forward to opening night, with the marquee of the Hammond Theatre lit up advertising Barry Granville and Jane Clarke in *Fair Lady*. Clara and Truman arrive and find themselves among hundreds of patrons entering the theatre. Engaging in their usual rambling and self-absorbed conversation, with Clara recalling the dogs in a revival of *Uncle Tom's Cabin*, and a horse that sat on a leading man, the pair manage to find their way up a ramp and into a truck filled with wild animals. Inside the theatre, while the overture is playing, McNeil is chastised by Brockman (Charles Halton), the big wig at Amalgamated Pictures who threatens, "If that curtain goes up, you're fired." The curtain does indeed go up and McNeil responds with, "I quit."

A montage of chorus girls onstage in elegant gowns is overlaid with pages from the theatre program, flipping to indicate a passage of time in the production, and including a brief clip of a Busby Berkeley triple-revolving-stage routine borrowed from *Forty-Second Street*.

Jane Clarke (Winifred Shaw) and Barry Granville (Ross Alexander) in the "Two Marvelous for Words" number in *Ready, Willing and Able*.

The faux Jane meets Barry backstage and asks him how she did in a previous number. His terse reply: "No bargain at $1500 a week." Tired of apologizing and getting the cold shoulder from him, Jane tells Barry that she tore up that contract and that after her next number, she's quitting the show. After she has gone, Angie tells Barry that it was Jane and Van Courtland who forced the real Jane Clarke to appear in Barry's musical, and that it was Jane who persuaded Truman to provide Barry with the money so that he could open the show. Her rebuke of Barry is very reminiscent of the scene in *Here Comes Carter* in which Verna tells Linda that it was Carter who arranged for her to have a singing career. Just as Verna managed to change Linda's attitude toward Carter, Angie's revelation changes Barry's attitude toward Jane as *Fair Lady* moves on to the "Too Marvelous for Words" number, for which Bobby Connolly was nominated for the Academy Award for Best Choreography.

The stage is dominated by a large curved library backdrop, complete with books and ladders and stunning librarians and secretaries, chief of whom is Jane Clarke, secretary to Barry Granville, a man unable to find the right words to put in a letter to his beloved. Jane sings the first chorus of the song, interrupted by Barry's insertion of words and phrases. Barry takes the second chorus, interrupted by librarians on ladders who sing portions of the melody as if suggesting words to Barry, all while the secretaries are typing out the letter, which is sent to the faux Jane who reads it to another chorus of attractive women. Because she does not know what "tintinnabulous" means, Jane telephones Barry to inquire, and a patter section follows in which Barry rattles off a great many words from a great many dictionaries provided by a great many beautiful girls, after which Barry falls to the floor from exhaustion. The celebrated typing dance follows on which Jane and Pinky tap the words on the keys of a gigantic typewriter while chorines dressed in black tights function as the mechanism by which the individual letters are pressed to paper. After Jane and Pinky finish their tap dance, Barry enters on the typewriter, tapping an apology to Jane that signals the end of the number and brings the film to a close. Ross believed that he was, in some small way, the inspiration for the number, for the word around Hollywood was that ever since he arrived, he learned a new word every day from the various dictionaries and encyclopedias that cluttered his home. Even though he didn't graduate from high school Ross had developed a healthy intellectual curiosity, stimulated by his study of elocution with Hugh Towne.

On 29 September, Ross managed to arrange his shooting schedule for *Ready, Willing and Able* so that he could throw his new bride a birthday party at Café LaMaze on Sunset Boulevard. Trailing behind both of them at the party was their pet dachshund who traveled everywhere with them, including Sardi's and nightclubs. According to Hollywood gossip, they even let their dog run freely around the floor (*Hollywood*, February 1937). Ross obviously received special consideration wherever he went.

Three weeks after the party, Ross rushed Anne to Hollywood Hospital after she experienced severe abdominal pains. An emergency appendectomy was performed on Wednesday 14 October by Dr. Franklyn Thorpe, the former husband of film star Mary Astor. Because he was at the studio for most of the day, Ross took the room next to Anne's at the hospital so that he could be by her side during all his free time. Complications must have occurred during the appendectomy because, advised by pathologist Dr. V.L. Andrews, Dr. Thorpe performed a hysterectomy on the actress as well. What is perhaps most peculiar about the second operation is that Anne was not informed about it until eleven years later, when she discovered that she could not bear children. It is difficult to fathom how such an operation could pass unnoticed by hospital staff, billing, and insurance, and kept from Ross who lived in the room next to hers. Was Ross advised about the hysterectomy? Did he agree to it? If so, why would he keep from telling his wife? In 1947, Anne sued Dr. Thorpe for $350,000, charging that he sterilized her without her consent during the appendectomy. Thorpe responded that Anne was well aware of the surgery, its necessity, and its consequences, and gave her full consent. If true, Ross would have known, if only after the fact—there would have been no reason to conceal an operation that had been consented to, especially if it were necessary because of a cancerous growth or other life-threatening disorder. Did Warner Brothers' publicity department keep the hysterectomy out of the news, believing that such an operation would taint the gossip surrounding their latest studio marriage? Was an appendectomy actually performed, or was it only a press-friendly cover-up for the actual operation? The lack of evidence renders a conclusion impossible, and adds yet more substance to the contradictions and mysteries that enveloped the life of Ross Alexander.

No sooner did Ross take Anne home from the hospital than reviews of *Here Comes Carter* began to accrue with Karl Krug announcing "Ross Alexander, who has supplanted Robert Montgomery, as the screen's leading flippant threat, is cast as a dirt-dishing radio commentator in *Here Comes Carter*, another of the efforts to mix gangsters and music, and to give him due credit, it is the best thing I have seen young Mr. Alexander do" (*Pittsburg Sun-Telegraph*, 23 October 1936). *Motion Picture Daily* (24 October 1936) agreed, noting that "Ross Alexander as the racy, fast-talking Hollywood press agent, turned radio commentator specializing in production scandal-mongering, imparts to this otherwise ordinary yarn its active character," and *Photoplay* (November 1936) gushed, "Brimming over with fast action, plenty of laughs and good comedy performances, this little picture, displaying the inside story of the methods used by Hollywood radio gossip columnists, emerges as swell entertainment. Ross Alexander, as the publicity man who takes to the air for revenge, is grand."

Script (31 October 1936) called the film, "An unpretentious program-filler that lampoons radio, gangsters, the motion picture industry and, quite unconsciously, itself. You've undoubtedly heard those gossip spielers over the air—those fast-talking gents who tread with their heels and leave a swath of ruffled reputations in the wake of each broadcast . . . Not a very likeable person, and Ross Alexander accentuates the bombastic character to the point of irritation. Ross purveys a laugh that's an annoyance. . . Glenda Farrell isn't done right by, in assignment or camera work." However, *The New York Times* (14 November 1936) found that "Mr. Alexander seems to be a younger, sprightlier Jack Benny, with a better gag-man than Jack's and at least as glib a delivery—the ease and self-assurance of his performance having never been exceeded by Mr. Benny himself," and the *Daily News* (14 November 1936) stated, "With their usual aplomb, Ross Alexander and Glenda Farrell are tossing off bon mots at the rate of a Florida hurricane at the Palace Theatre in a sharp little piece about a news commentator's lowdown on Hollywood higher-ups. Ross is the garrulous young man who reveals the star's secrets and Glenda is his just-as-garrulous secretary who knows all the answers as well as the questions."

Variety (18 November 1936) determined that *Here Comes Carter* was an "Air-gangster story that does not quite click, not only on account of its implausibility but because it is slowly paced and too dependent upon the effervescent actions of Ross Alexander, who is more and more overworking his expression and his manner. He is growing smart-alecky rather than breezy and if given too much of the footage is apt to tire if the story cannot carry him along. . . . Dialog is frequently too flippant to be acceptable and many scenes require more talking than their value warrants. Direction keeps the story moving along, but mostly in retarded tempo. The story does not entirely bore, but neither does it hold interest." The *Independent Exhibitors Film Bulletin* (18 November 1936) called the film, "An unimportant, mild little yarn about another one of those fast and loud talking radio dirt-dishers . . . a typical Warner quickie containing some well-known faces, but no box-office names. . . . Alexander's performance is principally responsible for holding the spectator's interest. A pleasant fellow, he handles Cagney's old line adequately, if without as much punch. Glenda Farrell hasn't as much to do as usual, but does it well enough. Anne Nagel is an acceptable heroine."

In addition, on 18 November, the *Pittsburgh Post-Gazette* ran Louella Parsons's syndicated column:

THE POSTPONED *Marriage Clause* goes into production at Warner's immediately with Ross Alexander in the Robert Montgomery role opposite Olivia de Havilland. I personally don't feel that Warners have a thing to worry about over the loss of Montgomery, since Ross Alexander is a swell actor and gaining in popularity all the time. Montgomery's failure, however, to show up at the studio is said to have cost Warner Brothers $30,000 in sets, costumes and delays. Since Metro still owes them the loan of a star, another deal will undoubtedly be made.

The film, based on Dana Burnet's *Saturday Evening Post* story, "Technic," about an actress who falls in love with her director, but is unable to marry him because of a "no marriage clause" in her contract, had been made into a silent film in 1926. Ross Alexander may have been chosen as Montgomery's replacement, but the film was never made.

Just as *Ready, Willing and Able* neared completion in mid-December, newspapers and trade papers announced that Ross Alexander would appear with Ruby Keeler in *Variety Show*, another "musical with all the collegiate trimmings," with a screenplay by Fred Pederson, songs by Richard Whiting and Johnny Mercer, the same pair who composed the songs for *Ready, Willing and Able*, direction by William Keighley, and choreography by Busby Berkeley.

Epilogue: 2 January 1937

Wives and female relatives are responsible
for eighty percent of all necktie buying.
And the Lord never saw fit to create a woman
with the ability to select a modest, attractive male necktie.

—Ross Alexander

Ready, Willing and Able finished production by 19 December 1936, just in time for Ross and his new wife to prepare for their first Christmas together, which they hoped would be peaceful even though Ross's parents were driving from Rochester to spend the holidays with the newlyweds. In addition, Anne's grandmother and her aunt (and husband), who had traveled to Los Angeles from Boston to spend Christmas with her mother, promised to drop by. Anne was thrilled to share the holidays with members of her family particularly since her marriage to Ross was a solitary business. According to Gordon Palmer, writing in *Photoplay* (June 1937), marriage to Ross Alexander "was for two people to share, not for many people to mar. He wanted nothing more than Anne's close companionship. Dinner-for-two was his idea of heaven. A game of ping pong, a long talk before the fire, reading a good book aloud and a few other two-way bits of entertainment were not only all he wanted—they were all he would tolerate. Not only did he refuse all invitations but he extended none" (49).

With in-laws on both sides making an appearance, Ross and Anne felt that everything—from the eggnog to the artificial snowflakes and icicles in the windows—had to be worthy of Filene's or Macy's holiday decorations. As a result, the couple spared no expense, which, predictably, became another source of stress since they didn't want their families to accuse them of extravagance. Ross and Vivian Jones his gardener drove out to buy the best tree they could find and returned with a bushy, perfectly-shaped, nine-foot spruce that would assume pride of place in the living room. As Ross and Vivian struggled to get the tree through the back door, Anne and Cornelius Stevenson, butler and chauffeur, rushed out to find lights and ornaments that would be perceived as tasteful rather than ostentatious. By the time Ross and Vivian managed to secure the tree, aptly christened "Bruce (the spruce)," in an upright position, Ross remembered that they needed wrapping paper and bows—lots of bows—to cover the presents going under the tree and into the Christmas stockings—"Did Anne think to buy stockings for our guests?" he wondered. "Better to be prepared, just in case," he decided, "I'll get a dozen They won't go to waste"—and off they went on their quest.

By midnight on 22 December, with help from Cornelius and his wife Elta, the cook, the Alexanders completed the holiday decorations, creating an elegant, festive ambiance throughout the house. The flurry of activity continued the following day with the hanging of stockings, wrapping of presents, preparing the guest room, and cleaning the house of discarded paper, ribbons, and needles that fell from the tree during its trimming—just in time to greet Ross's parents arriving from their four-day journey from Rochester.

Christmas eve was something of a circus with both families coming together for the first time at dinner, a delectable smorgasbord of grilled steak, prepared by Ross since grilling was his specialty, turkey, Alaskan crab, cornbread stuffing, corn on the cob, sautéed green beans with slivered almonds, garden salad, prosciutto-wrapped melon, fresh breads, pecan pie, and butter-pecan ice-cream. When dinner was done, everyone retired to the living room where the guests were given gifts, and everyone nestled by the piano, singing merry holiday songs and popular favorites while Ross played. Anne's family, due to the evident fatigue of her elderly grandmother, was the first to leave, even though Anne's mother and Mrs. Smith, having been engaged in a spirited dialogue throughout the evening, did not appear ready to interrupt their conversation. Anne's aunt complemented her on the Cape Cod ambience of the interior of her house with early American maple furniture, hook rugs, and old prints decorating the walls. Her husband complimented Ross on his choice of cigars, and the size and upkeep of the ranch. Grandmother appreciated the work invested in trimming the tree and decking the halls with holiday wreaths and other festoons and told her granddaughter as much.

Ross's parents took their cue from the departure of Anne's relatives and quickly hastened to bed to allow their son and daughter-in-law time to be alone together on their first Christmas Eve. Ross and Anne appreciated the gesture and heaved a heavy sigh of relief, feeling that one major hurdle of the holiday had been overcome. They sat in the living room gazing at the lighted tree, wondering what joy would be brought to them on Christmases to come. Their reverie was briefly interrupted by Elta and Cornelius, having put away the surplus food and washed and dried the dinner dishes and silverware, before retiring to their quarters behind the house and above the garage. After their departure, Ross turned to his bride and said, sincerely, "I've never brought happiness to anyone, Anne, but I'm going to turn over a new leaf and make you the happiest woman in the world."

Early on Christmas morning, Ross brought in a setting hen, nest and all, and placed it beneath the Christmas tree. A tiny jewel box was hidden in the nest for Anne to find, and when she opened it, she found a wedding ring on which was a cluster of baguette diamonds. When the couple eloped, given their film commitments, there was no time to choose a proper wedding ring so they borrowed Anne's mother's ring at the marriage ceremony—Mrs. Nagel had chaperoned the elopement. As Anne put on her new wedding ring, Ross suggested that, "If you're a good little girl, I'll have the Easter

Bunny bring you a new setting for your engagement ring" (*The Boston Globe*, 7 January 1937).

The remainder of the day was spent opening presents and eating the leftovers from the previous day's dinner. Anne had given Ross a new guitar for Christmas, so he spent much of the time in his cellar "man-cave," where he had set up his trains, practicing the guitar and writing poetry. The almost idyllic nature of the holiday thus far was shattered on Boxing Day when Alexander's over-concerned mother, Maude, began to reprimand him about his extravagances and his drinking. Ross reacted badly to his mother's lectures, arguing that he had been on the wagon for months—he had been injured in an automobile accident and sentenced by the judge to sobriety or the slammer. He chose sobriety, even though his definition of sobriety permitted him to drink, but not get drunk. As the days edged closer to New Year's Eve, Ross's mother redoubled her efforts to reform him, warning that unless he changes his ways, he is in danger of infecting his sweet young bride with his vices, useless extravagance, and alcoholism. She evidently did not recall that Ross had repeatedly helped out his father financially after the leather business was adversely affected by the Depression. That she should attempt to tell him how to spend his money seemed to Ross both ungracious and uncalled for. What made her admonishments even worse was that his father never came to his defense.

By Wednesday 30 December, Ross had had enough of his parents. He packed a bag and moved himself and his wife to a hotel in Hollywood, leaving his family at the house in Encino. From the hotel, Ross telephoned his mother to tell her that as long as she and his father were visiting, he and his wife would remain at the hotel. As a result, Ross's parents left early on New Year's Eve, taking the unfinished sweater Aleta had been knitting for Ross before her suicide, and which Anne had graciously promised to finish for him. Maude told Elta that she found it unfair to Anne to have to deal with such a morbid reminder of Ross's previous wife. Its removal was likely a relief to Anne, but Ross felt the loss very deeply, perhaps as deeply he regretted losing his patience with his mother and forcing his parents to return to Rochester because of one of his dark moods.

New Year's Eve included a trip to Warner Brothers' studios, where Ross happily took pictures of Anne on the empty sets of *Ready, Willing and Able*, and as dusk approached, the couple returned to Encino, where they enjoyed being alone in their home on their first new year together. Whether it was because of an innate sense of inferiority, or jealousy, or possessiveness, or all three, Ross did not enjoy sharing his wife with family or friends. He bristled when they encountered her friends at restaurants, or theatre premieres and, except when she was at the studio, and sometimes even then, Ross kept a close watch on her. Even when she was in the hospital, Ross took the room beside her. His mood improved significantly during New Year's Day as the couple consumed a champagne brunch and drove out to Pasadena to watch third-ranked Pittsburgh beat fifth-ranked Washington, 21–0 at the Rose Bowl. Back at home, Ross retired to his basement retreat where he fiddled with his trains, composed a few lines of poetry, and rehearsed a few popular melodies on the guitar, before eating a late cold supper and going to bed.

On Saturday, 2 January 1937, Ross and Anne spent the morning playing badminton and dismantling Bruce (the spruce), with the help of Vivian Jones who assisted Ross in carrying the tree into the back yard, where it would be chopped into logs and wood chips for use on the farm. During the afternoon, Ross played the guitar and sang for his wife, a totally enraptured and delighted audience. Anne said, "[Ross] was light hearted. We planned a 'honeymoon' trip to New York, and he had already made arrangements with his manager. You know we never had a real honeymoon" (*The San Francisco Examiner*, 4 January 1937). Anne continued, "After passing a quiet day at home last Saturday, we sat in our front room. I was crocheting. Ross was toying with his pistol. Pretty soon we both started playing with the gun, after he removed the cartridges. Finally, Ross told me he was going upstairs to write some poetry. The house was full of the little verses he composed. But after scribbling for a moment, he went out to the barn. He planned to shoot a duck for dinner next day" (*The Los Angeles Times*, 7 January 1937).

371

Gardener Vivian Jones recalled that "Twice Saturday morning while I was taking care of the chickens in the barn Mr. Alexander climbed the ladder to the edge of the loft. Later, I caught a duck for dinner and went looking for the ax. He came out with a gun and said, 'Let me shoot that duck.' I told [him] not to, it would be better to chop its head off. I did and he turned away, saying that he didn't like the sight of blood" (*The Los Angeles Times*, 4 January 1937).

Barn behind Ross's home on 17221 Ventura Boulevard. Arrow points to where Ross was found by Cornelius Stevenson.

At about 7:10 P.M., while Anne was in the front room crocheting, Ross told Cornelius Stevenson that he was going out to the barn to kill a duck. After telling Cornelius to call him from the barn when dinner was ready, he left the house carrying a flashlight and a .22 caliber nine-shot target pistol. Stevenson heard a shot but, thinking it was Ross shooting a duck, he wasn't concerned. "We heard the shot. After 15 minutes I went to the barn and found the body in the hayloft" (*Chicago Tribune*, 3 January 1937). Believing that Ross was asleep, Cornelius called out to him several times before climbing up to the loft, where he discovered blood on the side of Alexander's

372

head. On a pile of grain sacks, and still holding the gun in his left hand, Ross was fatally wounded by a bullet that had pierced his left temple. Cornelius revealed that Ross's suicide, while tragic, was not entirely unexpected since, on more than one occasion, when his master had been drinking and torn to pieces emotionally, he had had to prevent Ross from doing away with himself. Earlier in December, for example, on the anniversary of Aleta's suicide, he had to wrestle a gun away from his master who had been drinking and wanted to kill himself. The June 1937 edition of *Photoplay* added that "When there are dizzy flights to the pinnacle of happiness, there are also the extremes of melancholy and depression undreamed of by normal folk. Ross Alexander suffered from such flights and falls, and when he had been drinking, sank to the depths of despondency. The [restaurants in the] Grove knew this and [were] worried. It is their business to see all, know all, and avoid trouble. One night at Victor Jory's Pasadena home, Ross went into suicide mood and his friends had a wrest a gun from him. Thereafter waiters were never more than a few feet away from Ross's table at the Grove. Eventually the complex brought about his self-inflicted death, a cruelly selfish solution by a man who had everything to live for." Stephenson's wife, Elta, knew how important the unfinished sweater was to Ross and blamed herself for his suicide:

> He used to come in the kitchen often and talk about his other wife, and the things like cream gravy she liked for me to make, . . . but I know he and Miss Anne were very happy and that he loved her. He just didn't know what he was doing sometimes. If he had come out the backdoor Saturday night, instead of slipping out the front door, I would have headed him off and he would have been alive now. I knew he was drinking, although he didn't always show it. When Steve went to call him for dinner and found he was in the barn . . . my heart went into my boots. Steve came running back, his face was green on one side and black on the other. I said, "You don't have to tell me what happened. I know."
> (*The Boston Globe*, 7 January 1937)

Elta immediately called Anne's mother and the police. The Smiths who were on their way back to Rochester, were contacted by Vernon Wood, Ross's business manager, through a friend in Little Rock, Arkansas. As soon as they received the news, Alexander's parents turned around and began the long drive back to Los Angeles. Although Detective Lieutenant Ray Guise determined that Ross had committed suicide, Coroner Frank Nance ordered an inquest into the actor's death at the W.M. Strother Mortuary to which the body had been removed. At the inquest on Wednesday 6 January at 9:30 A.M., no new information was unearthed, so the coroner accepted the police findings with a "death by suicide" verdict.

The Little Church of the Flowers, from a contemporary postcard.

On Friday 8 January, Ross's body was taken in an open coffin to the Little Church of the Flowers within the grounds of Forest Lawn Memorial Park in Glendale, California, where simple funeral services were held. Reverend Glen McWilliams gave a brief eulogy that suggested, "Ross was a credit to his profession—pleasant, straight-forward, always known as a good fellow" (*Democrat and Chronicle*, 9 January 1937). The church was filled with many representatives of the Hollywood film community, including Ross's widow Anne Nagel, Ray Enright, Henry Fonda, Jimmy Stewart, Pat O'Brien, John Eldredge, Dick Powell, John Arledge, Ruby Keeler, Dick Foran, Eddie Acuff, Joan Blondell, Anita Louise, Humphrey Bogart, Rosalind Russell, Zazu Pitts, Glenda Farrell, Errol Flynn, Josephine Hutchinson, Lee Dixon, Louise Fazenda, Winifred Shaw, Teddy Hart, Allen Jenkins, Franchot Tone, Guy Kibbee, Bette Davis, Claudette Colbert, Mickey Rooney, Olivia de Havilland, and Patricia Ellis, who claimed Ross was her favorite leading man. Ross Alexander's burial at Forest Lawn, Sunrise Slope, Lot 292, was delayed until Saturday, 9 January, when his parents arrived.

Not long after Ross was buried, Jack Warner, Hal Wallis, and director Ray Enright met to consider reshooting all of Alexander's scenes with another leading man, so strong was their concern that the public would not accept a film in which the principal character had died. It was noted that Henry B. Walthall had died previous to the release of *China Clipper*, but he was not the principal romantic interest in that film, and his name was dropped from the opening credits. Because of the money that had already been spent on *Ready, Willing and Able*, a decision was made to elevate Lee Dixon as leading man, and reduce Ross to sixth place in the credits. The producers considered the decision a gambol, but one that eventually paid off in the reviews.

On 8 January 1937, Louella Parsons wrote, "Anne Nagel who so suddenly and so cruelly was made a widow by Ross Alexander's tragic death, will immediately be put into the lead in *Steel Highway* by Jack Warner. Unfortunately, young Alexander, who made a large salary, saved nothing and when he died, he left only a meager $200—not enough to bury him—and a much-involved estate with lots of debts. . . . At a meeting attended by Harry Warner and Hal Wallis, it was decided to rush *Steel Highway* in production as a means of helping the unfortunate bride and widow to forget her tragedy" (*Pittsburgh Post-Gazette*, 9 January 1937).

In his syndicated column, Harrison Carroll wrote that "Ross Alexander is now in his grave. Only a few of the late star's intimate friends knew that he had been carrying a heavy financial load—debts contracted during a long period when he was down on his luck and which Ross began paying off as soon as he came into money at Warners. One item was a stay of [several] months in the hospital after an accident in which he lost most of his teeth. Part of his face had to be made over at the time. Ross didn't advertise all this, but the debts were being paid, dollar for dollar" (*The Evening News*, 14 January 1937).

On 16 January, Anne petitioned the court to appoint her mother, Mrs. Veronica Nagel, administratrix of the Alexander estate, worth less than $10,000 ($183,552.86 in 2019 dollars). Near the end of January, Anne discovered a life insurance policy that Ross purchased one year and eleven months previously, about the time he married Aleta Freel. It contained a suicide clause which pledged him not to take his own life within two years of the issuance of the policy. Had Ross postponed his suicide for just another month, he would have left his beneficiaries—Maude and Alexander Smith—$35,000. As a result of his poor timing, Ross's parents received only $3.500.

On 6 March 1937 *Ready, Willing and Able* was released, following a series of preview performances that garnered mixed review, praising the cast but finding the story lacking in originality and interest. The *Hollywood Spectator* (13 February 1937), for example, wrote, "Hollywood has the notion that an elaborate dance number can fit into nothing except a backstage story; and it is also under the impression that Main Street cannot be given too much of Times Square. It is a disease which ultimately will wear off." Regarding the performances, however, it continued, "For Hollywood its gaiety is dampened somewhat by the presence of the late Ross Alexander in the cast, the feeling of regret being accentuated by the fact that his performance is the best he gave on screen. It would have advanced him a long way toward stardom." *The Boston Globe* (26 February 1937) again found the film representative of Warner Brothers' formulaic musical talkies, but noted that "A willingness to overlook the long arm of coincidence and the lack of integrated effort, however, will reward filmgoers with a rare treat in eye-filling tableaux, ear-soothing songs and rib-tickling dialogue that provide more than their own meed of entertainment." Complimenting Bobby Connolly and Ruby Keeler, the reviewer continued, "But the same can be said for all the principals, particularly Ross Alexander, whose promising Hollywood career ended so tragically in death recently. He was never better than in this film."

Harrison's Reports (13 March 1937) found that the film had too much talk and too few songs and dances in a hackneyed plot with no attempt at novelty. Addressing the elephant in the room, it continued, "One of the other things against it is the fact that Ross Alexander, the leading player, is now dead; sensitive people may be disturbed at seeing him. The fact that the heroine at first deceives the hero into believing she is a star when she is just a novice does not put her in a good light, particularly since her doing so almost costs the hero his career. Otherwise, the music and dance routines are good, and the comedy at times enjoyable." Frank Nugent writing in *The New York Times* (15 March 1937) was less kind in his estimation, finding that the clichéd story "was told with magnificent dullness and a colossal lack of humor," and concluding that "The picture has one moment of revelation: Miss Keeler of the wee small voice, listens to a smaller one and admits she can't sing. We've been waiting a long time for that."

Winston Burdett, in *The Brooklyn Daily Eagle* (15 March 1937) wrote that "The late Ross Alexander manages a likeable performance in the dull role of the harassed producer . . . . Since Miss Keeler's forte is dancing, it is too bad that the film doesn't allow her to do more of it. Most of the time she is trying, unsuccessfully, to muster an English accent and simulate an English manner in her impersonation of the London star. How she ever manages to fool anyone is just one of those little mysteries." Similarly, *Variety* (17 March 1937) noted, "Besides being the first starring assignment for Lee Dixon, coupled with Ruby Keeler, this is also a post-mortem release of Ross Alexander. Latter's billing is held down, though his role is the meatiest and his performance the best in the picture. He is the love interest opposite Miss Keeler. Dixon, a promising light comedian, has much less to do as a songwriting-hoofing partner in a stage writing-production setup. Fact that Alexander and Dixon, though unable to pay their rent, are able to promote $50,000 from a picture company to finance a Broadway musical is an absurdity that even the fans can't overlook." Finally, on 28 March 1937, *The Los Angeles Times*, identifying the "Best Performances in Current Films," cited Ross Alexander in *Ready, Willing and Able* and noted "Superior work makes his untimely death all the more regrettable."

Varsity Show, the film for which Ross had been cast prior to his death, was released on 4 September 1937 with Dick Powell in Alexander's role, Charles "Chuck" Daly, a Broadway producer; Fred Waring played Ernie Mason, a student chorale director; Ted Healy acted William Williams, Daly's manager; and Rosemary Lane performed Barbara "Babs" Stewart, Daly's love-interest, and the role previously advertised for Ruby Keeler. Richard Whiting and Johnny Mercer created ten songs for the musical film, Busby Berkeley organized the dances, and William Keighley directed.

Kid Galahad, the other film for which Ross had been advertised in the title role, was filmed in January–February and released on 29 May 1937, with Wayne Morris as Kid Galahad, Edward G. Robinson as boxing manager Nick Donati, Humphrey Bogart as gangster Turkey Morgan, and Bette Davis as Donati's mistress Louise Phillips (AKA "Fluff"). According to publicist Jerry Asher, Ross had been constantly maneuvering to be cast in a film with Bette Davis, so it is difficult to understand why he would kill himself when finally presented with the opportunity. According to Davis's biographer, Lawrence J. Quirk, Asher also revealed that Ross was obsessed with her, writing love notes to her that intimated they were having a physical relationship. Quirk suggests that while Davis was filming *Satan Met a Lady*, she told her husband Ham Nelson to "get him off my fucking back" and Ham responded by giving Ross a black eye during an altercation that took place in a studio men's room (Quirk 1990, 136–137).

What makes this suspect is the timeline it suggests. *Satan Met a Lady* began filming on 1 December 1935 and, following a dispute with Warner Brothers, Bette appeared at work on 3 December, while Ross was busy filming *Brides Are Like That*, so Ross and Bette and Ham would have been at the studio during that time. However, just four days later, on 7 December 1935, Alexander's wife Aleta died of a self-inflicted gunshot wound sustained the previous evening. For the remainder of the month, Ross had to divide his time between inquests, dealing with Aleta's father who had come to Los Angeles to investigate, traveling with her body to New Jersey, attending her funeral, completing his film, and escaping to Rochester to spend the holidays in seclusion with his parents. Anything, of course, is possible, but the probability of his having time and opportunity to appear in the scene described by Quirk is rather low. What also makes Quirk's depiction suspicious is his following paragraph:

> The resulting black eye prevented Ross from beginning the filming of his next picture. He stayed home, brooded, and drank. Ross's wife, Anne Nagel, a pretty young actress who had fallen deeply in love with him, left him several times when she discovered his half-finished notes to Davis under his desk blotter. (Quirk 1990, 137)

Satan Met a Lady completed filming in mid-January 1936, if Davis did so instruct her husband to chastise Ross, it most likely had to have been when Ross returned from Rochester to begin production on *I Married a Doctor* also in mid-January. What is troublesome, however, is the identification of Ross's wife as Anne Nagel, whom he married in September 1936, eight months after the completion of *Satan Met a Lady*. Even if Quirk misspoke and meant Aleta Freel as the wife, most film historians (as well as Ross's best friend, Henry Fonda) suggest that Ross's brooding and alcoholic behavior began after (and was in response to) Aleta's suicide. In any event, what Quirk describes as Ross's conduct most likely would have occurred in January 1936, but Henry Fonda, who had been candid about Ross's alleged infidelities before Aleta's death and his subsequent alcoholism, never mentioned an altercation during January 1936, even though Ross was living with him in Brentwood at the time. If Ross took a publicity agent (Asher) into his confidence, what would have prevented him from unburdening himself to his best friend (Fonda), especially if he was unmarried at the time and under the influence of alcohol.

Quirk provides another interesting detail to Ross Alexander's biography in suggesting that the actor picked up a male hobo, had sex with him, then found himself the victim of blackmail threats. Quirk reports that "Ross appealed to the Warner's lawyers, who managed to hush the mater up. In January 1937 he killed himself. Jack Warner hired people to get all unsent love letters to Davis out of his house before police and reporters found them" (Quirk 1990, 137). It is understandable that Ross believed he could not survive a homosexual scandal, but the fact that he felt a vagrant, whose word could easily be questioned, could ruin his career is quite telling, because it demonstrates his inability to deal with adversity. In her article, "The Real Reason Why Ross Alexander Killed Himself," Caroline Somers Hoyt explained: "All of his life, he had too much—too much charm, two much talent, too much persuasiveness, too much his own way, too much love. Everything came easy. He never had to fight for what he wanted. Even his early failure to get into pictures, those lean months when the breaks were bad, he dramatized until hardship became an adventure which he would rather have had than not. And so he never learned the meaning of something which we all must understand if we are to live happily with others and ourselves. He never learned the meaning of discipline. When things that mattered—really mattered—came into his life, he didn't know how to handle them" (*Movie Mirror* April 1937, 30). That he had a homosexual dalliance is not in question. Many a Hollywood star of the 1930s engaged in such practices, married or not, and their various studios managed the fallout with great aplomb. It is also no surprise that there was a purge by the studio of Ross's notes, letters, and poems immediately following his suicide in an attempt to protect the studio by controlling how Ross's life would be immortalized in the press and police records. That he was still infatuated with Bette Davis by the time he committed suicide is, nevertheless, a bit of a reach.

Hollywood responded to Ross Alexander's death by spinning illusory theories about his continued mourning for Aleta Freel, his feeling responsible for her suicide, his inability to measure up to other leading men, his boredom from playing similar wise-guy characters, but there is no simple, reductive, answer that accounts for his behavior. The *Democrat and Chronicle* (16 April

1937) from Rochester, New York, Alexander's adopted hometown, took particular interest in the demise of one of its favorite sons:

One day this winter a young man who seemed to have everything to live for went to the barn behind his San Fernando Valley ranch house and shot himself. Ross Alexander killed himself on the eve of his greatest success. The best part he ever had in pictures was in *Ready, Willing and Able* which was just ready for release when he suddenly found existence unbearable. Why did he? No one knows exactly. . . . Ross was introspective and a bit too highly geared emotionally. He was unstable so far as women were concerned. Unhappy in her love, his [second] wife committed suicide. Did that prey on his mind? . . . But Ross had married again only a few months before; married in good faith, of course. Think of the desolation of his widow, young Anne Nagel, who was just beginning a screen career and is bravely trying to carry on. It is always sad enough when a bride who loves him loses her husband. How doubly tragic when it is because he chooses to leave her.

Ross claimed to be present-conscious, able to discard memories and relationships, his own mistakes and those of others; if we can take him at his word, then Aleta would have been a past relationship and therefore able to be expunged. If he was unable to erase her, Ross would be out of control of the situation, and that presented a problem since, in his idealism, he must always be in control. Caroline Somers Hoyt knew Ross better than he knew himself when she wrote:

I knew Ross Alexander—knew the brilliance, the ego, the selfishness, the impulsiveness, the charm that made him what he was. And knowing him I am sure of something else. He did not kill himself because he mourned Aleta Freile Alexander and couldn't live without her. True, he had loved her, but he had found solace after her death and a new love with little Anne Nagel. He loved *her* as deeply and sincerely as Ross Alexander could love anybody.

No, Ross Alexander killed himself, not because of Aleta Alexander's suicide, but because he had broken his own heart! . . . Because Ross Alexander had another side. There was in his strange, contradictory being an idealism, fine and strong, which he recognized and respected but which he couldn't always measure up to. He tried, I know. He tried almost as Dr. Jekyll fought against changing into Mr. Hyde. But he often failed, and I am as certain as I am certain of night and day that it was those failures which finally broke his heart and prompted the shot that ended his life. (*Movie Mirror* April 1937, 30, 100)

Later in the same article, Hoyt quotes from a conversation about Anne Nagel in which Ross said somberly, "Anne is a wonderful girl. I love her and I hope I deserve her. I am trying to make her happy." "You can if you want you," Hoyt replied, but Ross shook his head. "I don't know. I haven't made anyone else happy—quite the contrary. I try to tell myself that what is done is done and, honestly, I do love Anne. But I can't forget that if Aleta and I hadn't quarreled that night she—she—All of the quarrels I ever had with anyone were my own fault" (*Movie Mirror* April 1937, 103).

Anne Nagel continued making films until 1951 when she began appearing intermittently in television roles. Her film appearances included *The Green Hornet* (1940), *The Green Hornet Strikes Again* (1940), *Never Give a Sucker an Even Break* (1941), *Stagecoach Buckaroo* (1942), *The Mad Monster* (1942), *Murder at the Music Hall* (1946), *Blondie's Holiday* (1947), *The Spirit of West Point* (1947), *One Touch of Venus* (1948), and *Mighty Joe Young* (1949). In 1951, her second husband, Air Force Lieutenant Colonel James H. Keenan, sued for divorce claiming that she had embarrassed him by drinking to excess after being released from a clinic for the treatment of alcoholism. In 1966, at the age of fifty, Anne died at Sunray North Convalescent Hospital in Hollywood, following surgery for hepatocellular carcinoma (cancer of the liver). She was interred in Holy Cross Cemetery in Culver City, California.

Ross Alexander's suicide has up to now defined his position as a theatre and film artist. "Ross Alexander?" biographers, encyclopedia editors, and critics inquire, "Isn't he the one who committed suicide," as if his life and entire body of work could be reduced to that single act. If nothing else, Ross presents biographers with a complex mass of contradictions, the least of which was his bisexuality, upon which most, if not all of his biographers are in agreement, even if the contention that, during his theatrical career, he was seduced by older actors, two prominent directors, and kept by wealthy men (Quirk 1990, 135) is difficult to verify. Without wishing to appear glib, my own experience in the theatre has witnessed evidence of such behavior toward young male juveniles to this day—the allegations made against Kevin Spacey and others are cases in point—and many a well-known, admittedly heterosexual male actor has been known to have had same-sex experiences for amusement and/ or advancement. Given Ross's good looks, talent, and charismatic personality, it is more probable than not that many a same-sex liaison would have been available to him.

Of greater consideration are contradictions that stem from Alexander's own autobiographical statements. In some interviews he portrays himself as a poor deprived child, growing up without the advantages available to other children, while in others, he is the only child of a prosperous New York family, with the funds to send him to the fashionable Brooklyn Model School. Biographers continue to suggest that Ross grew up in Rochester, New York, even though the United States Census and City Directories prove otherwise. Several publications present Ross saying that after being expelled from Erasmus Hall High School in Brooklyn, he went to New York to study acting, while others, more correctly, indicate that Ross left West High School in Rochester, prior to leaving for the Big Apple. In "Movie Facts and Fancies" published in *The Boston Globe* (4 November 1935), Marjory Adams reported that Ross Alexander "is one of the few actors on the lot who thinks he would starve to death if the studios burned down and the legitimate theatre closed," yet in the October 1936 *Movie Mirror* article, "Ross Alexander the Great," Ross told Katharine Hartley that as a teenager, he was a successful salesperson of men's fashions, a talented window dresser, and an entrepreneur who served as cook, waiter, and cashier of a small Bohemian establishment close to the

Eastman School of Music in Rochester. He told Caroline Somers Hoyt that he fathered a baby girl, but census records do not substantiate his claim, nor have biographers managed to find a birth certificate naming him as father. Co-workers, all of whom are dead and cannot be interviewed, found Ross either a cheery, upbeat, and clever extrovert, or a high-strung, sensitive, and eminently vulnerable introvert—suggesting that Hoyt's assessment of a Jekyll-Hyde personality is well argued. Even Ross's self-deprecation that runs through most of his interviews is challenged in Hoyt's article, "On His Way" in *Modern Screen* (31 March 1936) in which she writes, "He has absolute faith in one person, himself, and upon himself he relies with complete confidence. The ease with which he has taken to a theatrical career shows that."

Perhaps the greatest contradictions exist between Ross's statements about romance and fidelity, and those promulgated by studio press agents, and friends. Ross has often confirmed that "I'm a man who likes a home and a wife. Playing around doesn't interest me" (*Motion Picture*, February 1937) but Henry Fonda, his best friend, asserted that "The nights supposedly spent at Warner Brothers turned out to be nights spent by Ross in the arms of other women" (Fonda 1981, 103), or other men, as others have avowed. Fonda believed that Aleta committed suicide after discovering Ross's womanizing; perhaps, instead, it was the discovery of Ross's same-sex behavior that propelled Aleta to kill herself. Knowing exactly what causes someone to take action, however, is always a matter of conjecture; even when the individual gives reasons for an action, he/she/they may not realize the real cause. Ross's statement above, like many of the so-called "factual" statements made to the press must be taken in an ideal sense, behavior to which he aspires—or believes he should aspire to—rather than a statement of actual conduct. Ross the homosexual aspired to the reputation of being a ladies' man who radiated excessive masculinity and complained about womanish, lisping men, but, in reality, he abandoned his first wife and abused his second, and, knowing his inability to make anyone happy in the past, Ross was afraid that he would strike out with Anne as well. He claimed to be cynical (or realistic) and hardboiled but he was inherently sensitive and vulnerable. He called himself, a "no-account," because of his self-perception of his inability to measure up to his own standards; yet, at the same time, he idealized the concept of "no-accountness" through which he rationalized those same inabilities. Denigrating himself provided an easy escape for any and all transgressions, but since Ross was too intelligent not to know that an easy escape was just an easy excuse, demeaning himself also came with a great deal of guilt.

Ross constantly contradicted himself in interviews and in his own behavior, in an attempt to be perceived in a way that reflected an ideal that he created for himself and only known to him. He understood how to "Hollywood-speak" to columnists and be generous with fans, and, even if his statements might have been at odds with verifiable facts, they were delivered in the sincere attempt to simplify an answer to a question, not consciously to mislead. Ross knew the power of words in print, so he chose his words carefully when dealing with his relationships and matters that were meaningful to him. When dealing with details about his early life, he was less assiduous to detail, suggesting that, perhaps, his early, formative years meant little to him. Even with that consideration, it is quite telling that in every interview about his pre-Boston theatrical experiences, Rose fails to mention Hugh Towne, the actor-teacher-director who mentored him and who was quite probably his romantic partner.

Why, exactly, did Ross Alexander kill himself? I don't pretend to know. Perhaps the more appropriate question is "Why has all of Alexander's life and work been reduced to a single moment in a barn on 2 January 1937?" What I hope is that an audience will continue to be entertained and impressed by his often-exemplary performances throughout a career that was cut too short. Beyond that, I hope that wandering through these pages of data and dates and dialogue, readers might discover something new about the performer that will help them unravel the ambiguity that was Ross Alexander.

I leave you with the image of Mr. Watson, Ross's enormous and faithful bulldog, who, on the day of Alexander's death, longingly sniffed the open closet where Ross had hung his clothes. As if expecting the arrival of his master, he spent a moment in silence, waiting for familiar footsteps that did not come. With an exasperated look on his face, he lay down in front of the closet to sleep—and snored robustly!

Select Bibliography

Scripts

Abbott, George and Ann Preston Bridgers. *Coquette: A Drama in Three Acts.*
In *The Best Plays of 1927–28.* Edited by Burns Mantle. New York: Dodd,
Mead, 1966.

Akins, Zoe. *The Greeks Have a Word for It.* Clear carbon of 1930 play. Comden
and Green Papers. Billy Rose Theatre Collection, the New York Public
Library for the Performing Arts: *T-Mss 1986-004.

Barry, Philip. *Holiday: A Comedy in Three Acts.* New York: Samuel French,
1928.

Bartlett, Sy, Ralph Block, and Dan M. Templin. *Backfire* (AKA *The Cinch*,
released as *Boulder Dam*). Unpublished screenplay, dated 28 March 1935.
Box 40, folder 1. United Artists Corporation: Series 1.2: Warner Brothers
Scripts, 1935.

_____. *Backfire* (AKA *The Cinch*, released as *Boulder Dam*). Changes to
unpublished screenplay, dated 17 October 1935. Box 40, folder 1. United
Artists Corporation: Series 1.2: Warner Brothers Scripts, 1935.

_____. *Backfire* (AKA *The Cinch*, released as *Boulder Dam*). Changes to unpublished screenplay, dated 18 October 1935. Box 40, folder 1. United Artists Corporation: Series 1.2: Warner Brothers Scripts, 1935.

_____. *Backfire* (AKA *The Cinch*, released as *Boulder Dam*). Changes to unpublished screenplay, dated 21 October 1935. Box 40, folder 1. United Artists Corporation: Series 1.2: Warner Brothers Scripts, 1935.

Bein, Albert. *Heavenly Express: A Play in Three Acts*. New York: Samuel French, 1940.

Butler, Rachel Barton. *Mamma's Affair: A Comedy in Three Acts*. New York: Samuel French, 1925.

Chapin, Anne Morrison. *Broken Doll*. Carbon copy. In Billy Rose Theatre Collection, the New York Public Library for the Performing Arts: 1934.

Craven, Frank. *That's Gratitude: A Comedy in Prologue and Three Acts*. New York: Samuel French, 1931.

Crothers, Rachel. *Let Us Be Gay: A Comedy*. New York: Samuel French, 1929.

Daves, Delmar and Lou Edelman. *Flirtation Walk*. Unpublished screenplay. 2nd revised final: 1934.

Davis, J. Frank [and Edward Knoblock]. *The Ladder*. Carbon copy with autograph revisions. Edward Knoblock Papers 1893-1945. Houghton Library, Harvard University: bMS Thr 167 (154).

Dunning, Philip. *Night Hostess: A Dramatic Comedy*. New York: Samuel French, 1928.

Fitch, Clyde. *The Woman in the Case*. In *Plays by Clyde Fitch*. Vol. 4. Boston: Little, Brown: 1919.

Flint, Eva Kay and George Bradshaw. *Under Glass: A Comedy in Three Acts*. Carbon copy. In Billy Rose Theatre Collection, the New York Public Library for the Performing Arts: 1933.

Galsworthy, John. *Loyalties*. In *Contemporary Drama: English and Irish Plays*. Vol. 2. New York: Charles Scribner, 1931.

Herbert, F. Hugh and Brown Holmes. *We're in the Money*. Story by George Bilson. Adaptation by Erwin Gelsey. Unpublished screenplay. Box 429, folder 8. United Artists Corporation: Series 1.2: Warner Brothers Scripts, 1935.

Hoffe, Monckton. *The Faithful Heart: An Original Play*. London: William Heinemann, 1922.

Ibsen, Henrik. *The Wild Duck*. Mineola, NY: Dover, 2000.

Jacobs, William. *Hot Money*. Unpublished screenplay. Box 185, folder 7. United Artists Corporation: Series 1.2: Warner Brothers Scripts, 1936.

Jeffreys, Stephen. *The Libertine*. London: Nick Hern, 1995.

Kaufman, Edward and Sy Bartlett. *Going Highbrow*. Additional dialogue by Ben Markson. Revised final of *Social Pirates*. Unpublished screenplay. Box 155, folder 9. United Artists Corporation: Series 1.2: Warner Brothers Scripts, 1935.

Kaufman, George S. and Edna Ferber. *Minick: A Comedy in Three Acts*. New York: Samuel French, 1922.

Kennedy, Mary and Ruth Hawthorne. *Mrs. Partridge Presents: A Comedy in Three Acts*. New York: Samuel French, 1924.

Kusell, Daniel. *The Party's Over: An American Comedy*. Carbon copy. In Billy Rose Theatre Collection, the New York Public Library for the Performing Arts: 1933.

Loos, Anita and John Emerson. *The Social Register*. Carbon copy. Jones and Green Collection. Billy Rose Theatre Collection, the New York Public Library for the Performing Arts: NCOF + Loos.

McLaurin, Kate L. *Whispering Wires: A Play in Three Acts*. Boston: Walter H. Baker, 1934.

Markson, Ben. *Red Apples*. Unpublished screenplay. Box 41, folder 6. United Artists Corporation: Series 1.2: Warner Brothers Scripts, 1935.

Maugham, W. Somerset. *The Circle*. In *Contemporary Drama: English and Irish Plays*. Vol. 2. New York: Charles Scribner, 1931.

Megrue, Roi Cooper and Walter Hackett. *It Pays to Advertise: A Farcical Fact in Three Acts.* New York: Samuel French, 1917.

Raphaelson, Samson. *The Wooden Slipper: A Romantic Comedy in Three Acts.* New York: Row, Peterson, 1934.

Robinson, Casey. *Captain Blood.* Adapted from the novel by Rafael Sabatini. Unpublished screenplay. Revised final: 1935.

Shakespeare, William. *A Midsummer Night's Dream.* Edited by Barbara A. Mowat and Paul Werstine. Washington, D.C.: Folger Shakespeare Library, n.d.

_____. *Much Ado about Nothing.* Edited by Barbara A. Mowat and Paul Werstine. Washington, D.C.: Folger Shakespeare Library, n.d.

Shaw, George Bernard. *Caesar and Cleopatra.* In *Complete Plays with Prefaces.* Volume 3. New York: Dodd, Mead, 1963.

_____. *Captain Brassbound's Conversion.* In *Complete Plays with Prefaces.* Volume 1. New York: Dodd, Mead, 1963.

Solow, Eugene and Robert L. Johnson. *Just Out of College.* Unpublished screenplay. Box 149, folder 1. United Artists Corporation: Series 1.2: Warner Brothers Scripts, 1934.

Stange, Hugh and John Golden. *After Tomorrow: A Play in Three Acts.* New York: Samuel French, 1931.

Varesi, Gilda and Dolly Byrne. *Enter Madame: A Play in Three Acts.* New York: Longmans, Green, 1926.

Wald, Jerry, Harry Sauber, and Lawrence Hazard. *Maybe It's Love.* Revised final of *Halfway to Heaven.* Unpublished screenplay. Box 254, folder 2. United Artists Corporation: Series 1.2: Warner Brothers Scripts, 1934.

White, Jessie Braham [Winthrop Ames]. *Snow White and the Seven Dwarfs: A Fairy Tale Play Based on the Story of the Brothers Grimm.* With music by Edmond Rickett. New York: Samuel French, 1925.

Films

Captain Blood. Warner Bros., 1935. Supplementary material compiled by Turner Entertainment Company, 2005. Burbank, CA: Warner Home Video, 2005.

China Clipper. Warner Bros., 1936. Packaged by Turner Entertainment Company, 2012. Burbank, CA: Warner Home Video, 2012.

Flirtation Walk. Warner Bros, 1934. Packaged by Turner Entertainment Company, 2009. Burbank, CA: Warner Home Video, 2009.

Here Comes Carter. In *Glenda Farrell Triple Feature.* Warner Bros, 1936. Packaged by Turner Entertainment Company, 2017. Burbank, CA: Warner Home Video, 2017.

I Married a Doctor. Warner Bros., 1936.

A Midsummer Night's Dream. Warner Bros., 1935. Supplementary material compiled by Turner Entertainment Company, 2007. Burbank, CA: Warner Home Video, 2007.

Ready, Willing and Able. Warner Bros., 1937. Supplementary material compiled by Turner Entertainment Company, 2009. Burbank, CA: Warner Home Video, 2009.

Shipmates Forever. Warner Bros., 1935. Packaged by Turner Entertainment Company, 2009. Burbank, CA: Warner Home Video, 2009.

Books and Articles

Allen, John R., Jr. "Ross Alexander." In *Classic Images: People.* www.classicimages.com/people/article_2d4ddd12-a.

Amburn, Ellis. *Olivia de Havilland and the Golden Age of Hollywood.* Guilford, CT: LP, 2018.

Anger, Kenneth. *Hollywood Babylon.* New York: Dell, 1975.

Behlmer, Rudy. *Inside Warner Bros. (1935–1951).* New York: Viking, 1985.

Birnes, William, and Richard Lertzman. *The Life and Times of Mickey Rooney*. New York: Gallery Books, 2015.

Blau, Herbert. *The Audience*. Baltimore: The Johns Hopkins University Press, 1990.

Bordman, Gerald. *American Theatre: A Chronicle of Comedy and Drama 1914–1930*. New York: Oxford University Press, 1995.

_____. *American Theatre: A Chronicle of Comedy and Drama 1930–1969*. New York: Oxford University Press, 1996.

Carroll, Brendan G. *The Last Prodigy: A Biography of Erich Wolfgang Korngold*. Portland, OR: Amadeus Press, 1997.

Chauncey, George. *Gay New York: Gender, Urban Culture, and the Making of the Gay Male World. 1890–1940*. New York: BasicBooks, 1994.

The Chronicles: History of Erasmus Hall High School from 1906 to 1937. Brooklyn: Erasmus Hall, 1937.

Downs, Alan, PhD. *The Velvet Rage: Overcoming the Pain of Growing Up Gay in a Straight Man's World*. Second edition. Boston: Da Capo Press, 2012.

Duchen, Jessica. *Erich Wolfgang Korngold*. 20th-Century Composers series. London: Phaidon, 1996.

Eyman, Scott. *Hank and Jim: The Fifty-Year Friendship of Henry Fonda and James Stewart*. New York: Simon and Schuster, 2017.

Fishgall, Gary. *Pieces of Time: the life of James Stewart*. New York: Scribner, 1997.

Fonda, Henry. *Fonda: My Life*. As told to Howard Teichmann. New York: New American Library, 1981.

Frasier, David K. *Suicide in the Entertainment Industry*. Foreword by Kenneth Anger. Jefferson, North Carolina: McFarland, 2002.

Froh, Riley. *Edgar B. Davis: Wildcatter Extraordinary*. Luling, TX: Luling Foundation, 1984.

Golden, John and Viola Brothers Shore. *Stage-Struck John Golden*. New York: Samuel French, 1930.

Hartley, Katharine. "Ross Alexander the Great." *Movie Mirror* Vol.9 no.5 (October 1936): 62–63; 113–114.

Hart, Moss. *Act One: An Autobiography*. New York: St. Martin's Griffin, 1989.

Houghton, Norris. *But Not Forgotten: The Adventure of the University Players*. New York: William Sloane, 1951.

"How Fate Tricked Ross Alexander!" *Hollywood* (March 1937): 26, 77.

Hoyt, Caroline Somers. "On His Way." *Modern Screen* (31 March 1936): 86–88.

_____. "The Real Reason Why Ross Alexander Killed Himself." *Movie Mirror* Vol.10, no.5 (April 1937): 30–31; 100–103.

Isherwood, Christopher. *Prater Violet*. New York: Bard, 1978.

Kleiser, Grenville. *Talks on Talking*. New York: Funk and Wagnalls, 1917.

Knoblock, Edward. *Round the Room: An Autobiography*. London: Chapman and Hall, 1939.

Kübler-Ross, Elizabeth. *On Death and Dying: What the dying have to teach doctors, nurses, clergy, and their families*. New York: Scribner, 1969.

_____. *Questions and Answers on Death and Dying*. New York: Simon and Schuster/Touchstone, 1972. Reprint. New York: Quality Paperback Book Club, 1992.

Langman, Larry. *Encyclopedia of American Film Comedy*. New York: Garland, 1987.

Les Adieux. Yearbook, West High School Class of January 1924. Rochester, NY: West High, 1924.

Logan, Joshua. *Josh: My Up and Down, In and Out Life*. New York: Delacorte Press, 1976.

Madden, George. "Why Ross Alexander Married Again." *Movie Mirror* Vol.10 no.5 (February 1937): 56; 78–81.

Manbeck, John B., consulting editor. *The Neighborhoods of Brooklyn*. Introduction by Kenneth T. Jackson. New Haven, CT: Yale University Press, 1998.

Mann, William J. *Behind the Screen: How Gays and Lesbians Shaped Hollywood 1910–1969*. New York: Penguin, 2001.

McKegg, William H. "Rejected Guest." *Picture Play* (March 1935), 47, 79.

Meeker, Richard [pseudonym of Forman Brown]. *Better Angel.* Introduction by Hubert Kennedy. Epilogue by Forman Brown. Boston: Alyson, 1990.

Meredith, Burgess. *So Far, So Good: A Memoir.* Boston: Little, Brown, 1994.

Meyers, Jeffrey. *Inherited Risk: Errol and Sean Flynn in Hollywood and Vietnam.* New York: Simon and Schuster, 2002.

Morgan, Michelle. *The Mammoth Book of Hollywood Scandals.* Philadelphia: Running Press, 2013.

O'Brien, Pat. *The Wind at My Back: The Life and Times of Pat O'Brien.* Garden City, NJ: Doubleday, 1964.

Palmer, Gordon. "They Discovered Friendship through Heartbreak." *Photoplay* (June 1937): 48–49, 108–109.

Pemberton, Murdock. "Walking under the Ladder." *Esquire* (February 1939): 82–83; 155–157.

Phillips, Brent. *Charles Walters: The Director Who Made Hollywood Dance.* Lexington, KY: University Press of Kentucky, 2014.

Quirk, Lawrence J. *Fasten Your Seat Belts: The Passionate Life of Bette Davis.* New York: HarperCollins, 1990. Paperback edition. New York: William Morrow, 2018.

Reinhardt, Gottfried. *The Genius: A Memoir of Max Reinhardt.* New York: Alfred A. Knopf, 1979.

Rooney, Mickey. *I.E An Autobiography.* New York: G.P. Putnam's Sons, 1965.
_____. *Life's Too Short.* New York: Villard Books, 1991.

Schatz, Thomas. *The Genius of the System: Hollywood Filmmaking in the Studio Era.* With a new preface by Steven Bach. A Metro paperback. New York: Henry Holt, 1996.

Shoemaker, Rachel Walter Hinkle. *Advanced Elocution.* Philadelphia: Penn, 1910.

Spensley, Dorothy. "I'll Never Have a Star Complex! — Ross Alexander." *Motion Picture* (February 1937): 38, 78–79.

Stricklyn, Ray. *Angels and Demons: One Actor's Hollywood Journey.* Los Angeles: Belle, 1999.

Stuart, Ray. *Immortals of the Screen.* New York: Bonanza, 1965.

Styan, J.L. *Max Reinhardt*. Directors in Perspective series. Cambridge: Cambridge University Press, 1982.

Thomas, Bob. *Clown Prince of Hollywood: The Antic Life and Times of Jack L. Warner*. New York: McGraw-Hill, 1990.

Todd, Matthew. *Straight Jacket: Overcoming Society's Legacy of Gay Shame*. London: Black Swan, 2018.

Wagner, Laura. "Ross Alexander: 'His Eyes Suggest Tragedy.'" *Films of the Golden Age* 87 (Winter 2016/17): 52–53.

Walker, Stanley. "Where Are They Now: Mr. Davis and His Millions." *The New Yorker* (26 November 1949): 35–47.

Wallis, Hal and Charles Higham. *Star Maker: The Autobiography of Hal Wallis*. With a special introduction by Katharine Hepburn. New York: Macmillan, 1980. Paperback edition. New York: Berkley, 1981.

Warner, Jack L. with Dean Jennings. *My First Hundred Years in Hollywood*. New York: Random House, 1965.

Yurka, Blanche. *Bohemian Girl: Blanche Yurka's Theatrical Life*. Athens, OH: Ohio University Prses, 1970.

Zeruk, James Jr. *Peg Entwistle and the Hollywood Sign Suicide: A Biography*. Foreword by Eve Golden. Jefferson, North Carolina: McFarland, 2014.

Index

Abie's Irish Rose, 66

Abbott, George, 123, 180

Accent on Youth, 241

Acuff, Eddie, 254, 255, 256, 260, 262, 282, 375

Adair, Jean, 123

Adams, Leslie, 224

Adler, Stella, 160

Admirable Crichton, The, 151

Advanced Elocution, 40

After Tomorrow, 85, 86, 91, 93–94, 99–107, 171

Akins, Zoe, 126

Alexander, Katherine, 137, 138, 139, 140, 141, 147

Alexander, Ross: Accidents, 76–77, 294, 298, 370; Acting training, 2, 3, 7–8, 11, 111–112; Alcoholism, 171–175, 308, 315–316, 370; Arrests, 315–316; Birth, xvi, 2; Boy scouts, 4, 325; Broadway career, *see individual titles*; Camping, 325; Clothes, 8, 324; Death, xv, 372–375; Early theatrical experiences, 2, 5, 11–40, 42–52; Education, 2, 4–5, 6, 7, 115; Electric trains, 323; Fear of appearing effeminate, 44–45, 88–89, 211, 217, 384; Films, *see individual titles*; Health issues, 76, 77, 79, 286, 293–294, 298; Homosexuality, xii–xiii, 4, 9–10, 84, 150, 152, 308, 315,

380, 383, 384, 385; Interest in aviation, 234, 330, 350, 352; Inquests, 296–297, 374; Jobs, 8–9; Lawsuit, 294; Marriages, 71–72, 90, 109, 179, 202–203, 233–235, 256, 257–258, 294–295, 350–352, 362, 371; Personality, xv–xvi, xvii, 3, 4, 85, 106–107, 111, 112, 114, 116, 118, 129, 155, 162, 176, 181, 182, 234, 257–258, 296, 297, 307, 320–321, 332, 381–382, 383–385; Pets, 90–91, 233, 298, 324–325, 337, 346–347, 385–386; Relationships, xiii–xiv, 2, 9–10, 73–74, 89, 90, 91, 116–117, 119, 129, 148, 150, 152, 176, 190–191, 233–235, 240–241, 278, 299, 303, 308, 314, 315, 332–333, 339, 345, 346, 349, 378–379; Residences, 2, 4, 6, 10–11, 14, 42, 72, 84, 88, 93, 99, 114, 116, 121, 122, 131, 149, 181, 308, 322; School pranks, 7; Shakespearean difficulties, 24–26, 211, 217–219, 231; Sports, xvii, 185, 286, 322, 331–332, 371; Warner Bros. contract, 183–184

Allen, John R., xiv, 111, 112

Alone Together, see *Two Can't Be Happy*

Altman, Ruth, 166

American Hide and Leather Company, 2, 5

American Tragedy, An, 66

Ames, Winthrop, 19

Anchors Aweigh, see *Shipmates Forever*

Anderson, Dallas, 21, 23, 24, 25, 37, 39

Anderson, Lottie, 332

Anderson, Mary, 6

Anderson, Maxwell, 180, 199

Androcles and the Lion, 89

Angels and Demons, xiii

Anger, Kenneth, xv

Anglin, Margaret, 67, 68

Anne of Green Gables, 198

Applesauce (film), see *Brides Are Like That*

Applesauce (play), 289

Arledge, John, 117, 185, 187, 190, 252, 254, 255, 256, 259, 260, 262, 263, 375

Armstrong, Charlotte, 151, 152

Armstrong, Margaret, 110

Arnold, Philip, 208

Arthur, Jean, 122, 123, 129

Asay, R.A., 294

Asher, Jerry, xiii, xiv, 116, 117, 118, 150, 198, 378, 379

Astaire, Fred, 208, 222

Astoria Studio, 110, 112, 114, 116, 160

Astor, Mary, 362

Atkinson, J. Brooks, 55, 105, 136, 139, 154, 170, 174

Atwill, Lionel, 264, 277

Auburn, Dennis D., 263

Aylesworth, Arthur, 192, 193

Backer, George, 137

Backfire, see *Boulder Dam*

Bacon, Lloyd, 345, 350

Bankhead, Tallulah, 149

Barbier, George W., 94, 97

Barlow, Reginald, 264

Baron, Leo, 302

Barrat, Robert, 264, 265, 269, 272, 273, 276, 277, 310, 321

Barrie, James M., 23, 39, 89

Barrier, Frank, 294

Barrish, Benny, 331–332

Barron, Mark, 176

Barrymore, Ethel, 85, 153, 155

Barrymore, John, 208

Barrymore, Lionel, 115–116, 315

Barry, Philip, 110, 127, 129, 137, 180

Barthelmess, Richard, 298

Bartlett, Sy, 235, 279

Baum, Vicki, 165

Beery, Wallace, 208

Behind the Screen, xiii

Behlmer, Rudy, xv

Behrens, Arthur, 15, 17, 18, 37

Bein, Albert, 121

Bellamy, Ralph, 123

Bell, James H., 27

Benchley, Robert, 157, 160

Beranger, George Andre, 316

Berkeley, Busby, 189, 221, 222, 360, 365, 378

Berlin, Irving, 350

Big Broadcast, The, 241

"Big Rock Candy Mountain," 121

Bilson, George, 348

"Black Thursday," 83

Blau, Herbert, xi

Block, Ralph, 279

Blondell, Joan, 117, 231, 242, 243, 245, 247, 249, 251, 332, 346, 350, 375

Blondie's Holiday, 382

Boebnel, William, 228

Bogart, Humphrey, 326, 330, 335, 336, 350, 375, 378

Bohnen, Roman, 151

Bolden, William (butler), 294, 295, 296

Boles, Glen, 185, 187, 190

Boley, May, 356

Borzage, Frank, 185, 190, 252, 262

Borzage, Lew, 256

Boulder Dam, 278, 279–288, 302, 309, 314, 324

Boulton, Milo, 171

Bourne, Charles, 314

Boyd, William, 110, 112, 115, 117, 118

Bradshaw, George, 150

Brady, Alice, 122, 123

Brady, William A., 122

Brae Burn, 88

Braggioni, Francesca, 208, 209

Braggiotti, Mario, 160

Bramley, Jane, 150

Breakston, George, 225, 284

Brecher, Egon, 282, 284, 287

Brent, George, 123

Bricker, George, 322

Brides Are Like That, 287, 289–293, 297, 298, 300–302, 307, 309, 315, 316, 324, 378

Bridgers, Ann Preston, 123

Briggs, Harlan, 247, 248

Bright, John, 347

Broadway, 66

Broken Doll, see *No Questions Asked*

Broken Lullaby, 115

Brook, Lesley, 350

Brooklyn Dramatic Model School, 2, 3, 383

Brooks, Phyllis, 314

Brown, Chamberlain, 180

Brown, Frank Chouteau, 13

Brown, Joe E., 210, 217, 222, 230

Brown, John Mason, 136

Brown, Houston, 130

Brown, Tom, 117

Bruce, Virginia, 123

Bryant, Geoffrey, 141, 147

Bryant, Nana, 134

Buckler, Hugh, 57, 59

Buckley, Harold, 298

Bughouse Square, 84

Bunting, Emma, 151

Bunyea, Ninon, 133

Burdett, Winston, 230, 287, 322, 377

Burnet, Dana, 364

Burroughs, Helen, 71, 109, 116

But Not Forgotten, xiv

Byington, Spring, 172

Caesar and Cleopatra, 29–34

Cagney, James, xvii, 210, 217, 230, 253, 257, 279, 364

Cameron, Kate, 228

Cape Playhouse, 151, 152

Capra, Frank, 315

Captain Blood, 28, 263–278, 279, 314, 315

Captain Blood: His Odyssey, 263

Captain Brassbound's Conversion, 26–28

Captive, The, 66

Carmichael, Hoagy, 308

Carroll, Earl, 10

Carroll Gardens, 1
Carroll, Harrison, 375
Carroll, Madeleine, 350
Carroll, Nancy, 116
Casey, Rosemary, 129
Casey, Stuart, 264
Cavanaugh, Hobart, 211, 243, 265, 340
Cawthorn, Joseph, 199, 203, 289, 293, 301, 316, 319, 333, 334
Chanslor, Roy, 339
Chapin, Anne Morrison, 171, 175
Chaplin, Charlie, 208
Chapman, John, 106
Chief Little Wolf, 244
China Clipper, 325–332, 333, 334–337, 339, 348, 375
Chippendale, Lenore, 15, 18, 19
Chotzinoff, Samuel, 137
Churchill, Marguerite, 75, 77
Circle, The, 35–37
Clark, Myrtle, 94, 97
Classmates, see *Shipmates Forever*
Clemens, William, 298, 339
Cleopatra's Night, 33–34
Clurman, Harold, 160
Cobb, Humphrey, 348
Cody, Joe, 267
Cohan, George M., 176
Cohen, Catherine Woodruff (grandmother), 1
Cohen, Maude Adelle, see Smith, Maude Adelle Cohen (mother),
Cohen, William Henry (grandfather), 1
Cohn, Harry, 148, 157
Colbert, Claudette, 110–115, 117–118, 375
Collins, Charles, 230
Colt, Ethel Barrymore, 153
Columbia Pictures, 148, 157
Conklin, Peggy, 141, 143, 147
Connolly, Bobby, 188, 189, 190, 221, 353, 361, 376

Connolly, Walter, 208

Connor, Barry, 289

Constant, Ann, 50

Cook, Elisha Jr., 148, 323

Cooper, Gary, 208

Coq D'Or, Le, 9

Coquette, 123–126, 129, 130

Cornell, Katharine, 148

Cosbey, Ronnie, 284

Costello, Don, 46

Countess Maritza, 66

Craig, Edward Gordon, 274

Crashing Society, see *Going Highbrow*

Craven, Frank, 94, 96, 98, 99

Crawford, Joan, 117, 208, 226, 346

Creelman, Eileen, 228

Crehan, Joseph, 290, 291, 325, 340

Cromwell, Richard, xiii

Crothers, Rachel, 79, 85, 122

Crouse, Russell, 141

Crown Heights, 2

Crumit, Frank, 261

Cukor, George, 346

Cullen-Harrison Act, 147

Cunningham, Joe, 316

Curtiz, Michael, 263, 267, 269, 273, 274, 275

Darrow, John, xiii, 187

Daves, Delmar, 183, 254

Davidson, John, 28

Davis, Bette, xii, xiii, xiv, 117, 123, 191, 234, 267, 315, 375, 378, 379, 380

Davis, Boyd, 151

Davis, Edgar B., 53, 54, 56, 64, 65, 66, 68, 79

Davis, J. Frank, 41, 42, 53, 54, 55, 65, 67

Davis, Owen, Jr., 148, 323

Dean, Alexander, 151

Dear Brutus, 89

De Cordoba, Pedro, 269

Dee, Frances, 123

Deep River, 66

DeHart, Gail, 75

De Havilland, Olivia, 208, 210, 213, 215, 226, 228, 264, 273, 274, 277, 278, 314, 364, 375

Dehn, Paul, 336

Del Rio, Dolores, 249

DeMille, Cecil B., 315

Depression, The, xi, 83–84, 100, 116, 127, 140, 141, 191, 226, 370

Desert Song, The, 66

De Wit, Jacqueline, 208

Dickstein, Martin, 117

Dieterle, William, 210, 211, 219, 221, 228

Dietrich, Marlene, 117

Dill Pickle Club, 84

Dinehart, Allan, 99

Dinty, 157

Divine Drudge, A, 165

Dixon, Lee, 350, 353, 354, 357, 375, 377

Dixon, Mort, 280

Dolan, Anna Marie, *see* Nagel, Anne

Donat, Robert, 222

Donlevy, Brian, 148, 150, 323

Donnelly, Ruth, 200, 201, 204

"Don't Give Up the Ship," 255

Doré, Adrienne, 117

Douglas, Melvyn, 112, 115, 118, 123

Downs, Alan, xiii

Downs, Johnny, 346

Doyle, John, 151

Doyle, Laird, 279

Doyle, Maxine, 222

Dress Parade, see *Shipmates Forever*

Dreyfus, Max, 73

Dubin, Al, 261

Duckworth, Dortha, 151
Duff, Warren, 350
Dunne, Drue, 332, 333, 346,
Durante, Jimmy, 123
Dvorak, Ann, 123, 192, 193, 279, 322
Dwyer, John T., 128
Earlie Trouble, Ye, 73
Eastern Service Studios, 160
Eddy, Nelson, 346
Edelman, Lou, 183
Einstein, Albert, 226
Eldredge, John, 185, 190, 375
Ellis, Patricia, 279, 281, 282, 284, 286, 287, 314, 375
Emperor Jones, The, 66
Encyclopedia of American Film Comedy, xii
English Speaking Union, 226
Enright, Ray, 242, 325, 348, 350, 353, 375
Enter Madame, xii, 11, 14–19, 20, 41
Entwistle, Peg, 15, 19, 20, 22, 24, 25, 28, 35, 37, 39
Erasmus Hall, xiv, 4, 5, 6, 383
Ervine, St. John, 78
Every Girl for Herself, see *Brides Are Like That*
Fairbanks, Douglas, 257
Fair Lady, 353, 355, 357, 358, 359, 361
Faithful Heart, The, 42–44
Farmer Takes a Wife, The, 233
Farnum, William, 208, 209
Farrell, Charles, 107
Farrell, Glenda, 242, 243, 247, 251, 339, 340, 344, 350, 363, 364, 375
Fasten Your Seat Belts, xii
Faye, Alice, 222, 350
Fazenda, Louise, 313, 321, 322, 350, 355, 357, 375
Ferber, Edna, 34
Ferriday, Carolyn, 15
Fidler, Jimmie (Jimmy), 311, 332, 352
Fields, W.C., 208

Finkel, Abe, 298
First Year, The, 73
Fischer, Bobby, 6
Fischer, Robert, 114, 118
Fishgall, Gary, 148
Flagstad, Kirsten, 226
Fledermaus, Die, 219
Fleming, Victor, 233
Flint, Eva Kay, 150
Flint, Helen, 43, 44, 45, 46
"Flirtation Walk," 188, 190
Flirtation Walk, xii, 183, 185–189, 190, 196–198, 204, 205, 222, 223, 224, 248, 277, 289
Flynn, Errol, 222, 263–275, 277, 278, 314, 351, 375
Fonda, Henry, xiv, 89, 90, 91, 148, 149, 150, 179, 224, 233, 234, 303, 308, 309, 379, 384
Fontaine, Ritchie, 331
Foran, Dick, 148, 192, 193, 197, 252, 254, 259, 260, 262, 375
Ford, Grace, 222
Ford, Wallace, 123
Forty-Second Street, 360
Foster, Norman, 77, 78, 114, 298
Fox Film Corporation, 351
Foy, Charles, 342
Foy, Eddie, Jr., 85
Francis, Kay, 249
Franklin, Dwight, 257
Frasier, David K., xii
Fray, Jacques, 160
Frederick, Pauline, 158, 161
Freedman, Maurice, 75
Freel (Freile), Aleta (wife), xii, 89, 90, 91, 123, 126, 128, 129, 131, 136–137, 149, 179–182, 197, 198, 202, 210, 224, 226, 234, 235, 257–258, 278, 294–297, 300, 307, 308, 370, 373, 376, 378–379, 380, 381–382, 384
Freeman, Judge E.A., 351
Freeman, Susan, 43, 44, 46, 52

Freile, Dr. Eva, 297
Freile, Dr. William (father-in-law), 89, 179, 203, 296
Freile, Williammena (mother-in-law), 178
French, Dixie, 85, 299
Friedlander, William B., 152, 155
Frohman, Daniel, 226
Froman, Jane, 339
Gabellini, Drue, 332–333, 346; *see also* Dunne, Drue
Gabellini, Count Mario, 332–333
Gable, Clark, 117, 208, 315
Galsworthy, John, 28
Game of Thrones, The, x–xi
Garbo, Greta, 111, 208, 308
Gargan, William, 279
Garland, Judy, 345
Garrick, David, x
Garvie, Edward, 158
Gaynor, Janet, 233, 346
Gentlemen Are Born, 189, 190–197, 198, 204, 223, 289, 314
Getting Gertie's Garter, 133
Gilmore, William, 301–302
Goddard, Paulette, 222
Go-Getter, The, 345
Going Highbrow, 235–241, 250–251
Golden, John Lionel, xiv, 71, 72–74, 76, 78, 79, 85, 90–91, 94, 99–100, 105, 106, 114, 121, 151, 163, 165, 171, 176, 299, 300, 307
Goldwyn, Samuel, 346
Gone with the Wind, 233
Goodman, Benny, 148
Goodman, Edward T., 171
Gordon, Ruth, 168
Gorin, Igor, 335
Goss, Ysabel ("Izzy"), 331
Grable, Betty, 345
Graetz, Paul, 316, 333
Graham, George, 141, 147

Grant, Cary, 346

Granville, Charlotte, 80, 85

Greeks Had a Word for It, The, 126–127

Green Hornet, The, 382

Green Hornet Strikes Again, The, 382

Grot, Anton, 210, 220

Guilfoyle, Paul, 167

Guise, Detective Lieutenant Ray, 374

Haendler, A.A., 219

Half Way to Heaven, see *Maybe It's Love*

Hall, Dorothy, 166, 169

Haller, Ernest, 221

Hall, Eva Walsh, 24

Hall, Louis Leon, 31, 37

Hall, Mordaunt, 118

Hall, Porter, 74, 151

Halton, Charles, 359

Hammond, Percy, 139

"Handy with Your Feet," 355

Harbach, Otto, 46, 69

Harlan, Kenneth, 325, 326

Harlan, Otis, 211

Harlow, Jean, 117

Harris, Averell, 75

Hartley, Katharine, xiv, 7, 8, 109, 320, 383

Hartzell, Rachel, 137, 138, 140

Harvey, Forrester, 265, 277

Harvey, Georgette, 145

Hassell, George, 264

Hatton, Fanny, 133, 136

Hatton, Frederic, 133, 136

Haydon, Julie, 208, 209

Hayes, Helen, 123, 148, 176

Hays, Will H., 226

Hazard, Lawrence, 199

Healy, Ted, 378

Heartbreak House, 34

Heavenly Express, 121–122

"Hellcat Crew," 286

Henry Jewett Players, 11, 13–40

Henry, William, 208, 209

Herbert, Hugh F., 210, 217, 242, 243, 257, 350

Here Comes Carter, 141, 339–346, 361, 363–364

Hermann, Ida, 262–263

Her Wild Oat, 157

Herzig, Sig, 350

Heyward, Herbert, 193

Hobson, Valerie, 314

Holiday, 127–129, 137, 180, 181

Holloway, Sterling, 208, 209

Holman, Russell, 116

Holmes, Brown, 242

Honeymoon, 137–141, 150, 183

Hopkins, Charles, 165

Hopkins, Miriam, 176

Horton, Edward Everett, 235, 241, 250, 322

Hot Money, 316–320, 323, 333–334, 339

Houghton, Norris, xiv, 89, 90, 224

Howard, Leslie, 89, 179

Howlin, Olin, 284

Hoyt, Caroline Somers, xiv, xv–xvi, 71, 257–258, 380, 381–382, 384

Hubbard. Penelope, 93, 94

Hubbell, Raymond, 73

Hughes, Carol, 353, 355, 356

Hull, Henry, 150

Hull, Howard, 68

Hull, Josephine, 93

Humbert, George, 192

Hunter, Ian, 211, 215, 228, 314, 350

Hurst, Fannie, 226

Huston, Walter, 208

Hutchinson, Josephine, 196, 309, 310, 311, 313, 321, 375

I Married a Doctor, 309–314, 320–322, 379

Inside Warner Bros, xv

Irwin, Boyd, 153

Irwin, Carlotta, 22

Isherwood, Christopher, 110–111

It Pays to Advertise, 50–52

Jacobs, William, 316

Jacoby, Michael, 339

Jamison, Anne, 335

Jason, Sybil, 322

Jeffreys, Stephen, ix

Jenkins, Allen, 257, 350, 354, 355, 375

Jewell, Isabel, 315

Jewett, Frances, 23

Jewett, Henry, 11–12, 13, 14, 23, 24, 25, 26, 39, 41

Johnson, Malcolm, 228

Johnson, Robert L., 191

Johnson, Samuel, x

Jolson, Al, 198, 222, 322

Jones, Olive, 222, 332

Jones, Robert Edmond, 67

Jones, Vivian, 368, 371, 372

Jory, Victor, 211, 212, 230

Just Out of College, see *Gentlemen Are Born*

Katja, 66

Kaufman, Edward, 235

Kaufman, George S., 34

Keane, Robert Emmett, 291, 319

Keating, Fred, 346

Keeler, Ruby, xii, 183, 185, 187, 188, 190, 198, 204, 223, 252, 254, 255, 261, 322, 350, 353, 355, 365, 375, 376–378

Keenan, Lieutenant Colonel James H., 382

Keighley, William, 365, 378

Keith, Robert, 150

Kelly, Patsy, 345

Kendall, Cy, 316

Kent, Gerald, 96, 97

Kenyon, Charles, 210

Kerry, Anita, 242, 243, 247

Kershaw, William, 15, 24, 25, 27, 35, 37

Kettle House, 149

Kibbee, Guy, 123, 235, 241, 264, 272, 273, 277, 315, 375

Kid Galahad, 345, 378

King, Joseph, 172

King of Hockey, 345, 349

Kingsley, Sidney, 160

Kirkland, Alexander, xiii, 157, 158, 160, 161, 176

Kiss in a Taxi, A, 133

Kleiser, Grenville, 40

Knoblock, Edward, 55, 56, 65

Knowlton, Charles, 39

Korngold, Erich Wolfgang, 210

Kottow, Hans, 133

Krug, Karl, 363

Kübler-Ross, Elizabeth, 307

Kussell, Daniel, 141

Kyne, Peter B., 345

La Rocque, Rod, 129

Laite, Charles, 75

Lanchester, Elsa, 222

Lane, Rosemary, 378

Lang and Smith, 5, 6

Langford, Frances, 335

Langman, Larry, xii

Larrimore, Francine, 80, 83, 84

Laurel, Stan, 315

Lawes, Warden Lewis E., 345

Lawless, Sue, 1

Leatherbee, Charles Grant, 87, 89, 90, 224

Lee, Sam, 356

Lejeune, C.A., 337

Leroy, Mervyn, 315

Let Us Be Gay, 79–86, 91, 109, 122, 123, 129, 176
Levinson, J.B., 208
Levy, Benn W., 126, 180
Lewis, Bill, 330
Lewis, Gene, 353
Lewis, Sinclair, 309
Libertine, The, ix
Life with Father, 141
Lightnin', 73
Light, Robert, 192, 255, 260, 262
Lindbergh, Anne Morrow, 294
Lindbergh, Charles, 325
Lindsay, Howard, 141
Lindsay, Margaret, 192, 193
Little Church of the Flowers, 374
Little Minister, The, 39
Livingston, Margaret, 158, 160, 161
Lockhart, Gene, 289, 293, 301, 315
Lockhart, Kathleen, 289, 293
Lodge, John, 208, 209
Logan, Joshua, 224
Logan, Stanley, 217
Lloyd, Harold, 346
"Long Gone Baby," 280
Lord, Robert, 267–268
Lotus Eater, The, 157
Loudspeaker Lowdown, see *Here Comes Carter*
Louise, Anita, 211, 222, 289, 291, 293, 301, 309, 314, 315, 332, 350, 375
Love Begins at Twenty, 309, 315, 316
Love, Elizabeth, 151
Love Is Not All, see *Two Can't Be Happy*
Love Is Not Important, 129, 130
Love, Montagu, 168
Loyalties, 28–29
Loy, Myrna, 208
Lubitsch, Ernst, 115

Lyons, Ruth, 77
Macauley, Richard, 350
MacDonald, Frank, 279, 280, 287
MacDonald, Jeanette, 119, 346
MacMurray, Fred, 222
Madden, George, xiv, 3, 351
Mad Monster, The, 382
Main Street, 309
Mamma's Affair, 46–49
Mammoth Book of Hollywood Scandals, The, xv
Mamoulian, Rouben, 9
Man Mountain Dean, 242, 244
Mann, Louis, 23
Mann, William J., xiii
Mantle, Burns, 56, 57, 105, 136, 139, 147, 155, 170, 175
March, Frederic, 198
Maricle, Leona, 153
Markson, Ben, 289, 345
Marriage Clause, 364–365
Marsh, Thelma, 94, 97, 98
Martel, June, 235, 239, 240, 241
Martin, Eleanor, 46, 49, 50, 52
Martin, Tony, 345
Marx, Chico, 119
Marx, Groucho, 188
Mason, Louis, xiii
Mason, William, 25, 27
"Maternity Acres," xiv
Maybe It's Love, 199–202, 203–205, 207, 224, 316
Mayer, Louis B., 346
Mayer, Ray, 313, 321
Mayo, Archie, 309, 315, 322
Mayo, William H., 150, 152
McCall, Mary, Jr., 210
McComb, Kate, 171
McCormick, Muriel, 180

McCormick, Myron, 89, 91, 100, 102, 106, 148, 224
McGann, William, 199, 289, 301, 316
McHugh, Frank, 201, 204, 211, 222, 257
McKegg, William H., 234
McWilliams, Reverend Glen, 374
Maugham, W. Somerset, 35
Meek, Donald, 93, 94, 100, 104, 105, 106, 265
Mendelssohn, Felix, 208, 210, 211
Men in White, 60
Mercer, Johnny, 308, 365, 378
Meredith, Burgess, 148, 224
Meredith, Charles, 24, 27
Merkel, Una, 117, 300
Merrill, Martha, 255, 332
"Merry Macs," 308
Metro-Goldwyn-Mayer, 182, 364
Meyers, Jeffrey, 277
Midsummer Night's Dream, A, 104, 207–222, 224, 225–231, 233, 289, 315
Mighty Joe Young, 382
Mikado, The, 5
Miller, Frank, 225
Miller, Seton I., 345
Milne, A.A., 180
Milne, Peter, 348
Miltern, John, 157
Milton, John, 119
Minick, 34–35
Mitchell, Grant, 211
Mitchell, Irving, 44, 45, 46, 48, 49, 50, 52
Mitchell, Thomas, 85, 138, 140
Mohr, Hal, 221
Molly Pitcher Hotel, 122, 131
Monmouth County Players, 122–131, 180
Montgomery, Douglas, xiii, 176
Montgomery, Robert, 181, 363, 364
Moore, Colleen, 157, 158, 159, 160, 161

Moore, Raymond, 165

Morgan, Frank, 198

Morgan, Michelle, xv

Morris, McKay, 122, 124, 126, 127, 129, 130, 131

Morris, Wayne, 340, 378

Motion Picture Production Code, xii, 182

"Mr. and Mrs. Is the Name," 188

Mrs. Partridge Presents, 20–23, 24

Mr. Watson, 233, 298, 347, 348, 385–386

Much Ado about Nothing, 24–26, 219

Muir, Gavin, 129, 131

Muir, Jean, 192, 193, 210, 212, 213, 215, 216, 218, 222, 226, 228, 230, 314, 350

Murder at the Music Hall, 382

Murphy, John Daly, 151

Murray Hill, 89, 179

Murray, John T., 340

Nagel, Anne (wife), 334, 339, 341, 342, 345, 349, 350, 351, 353, 361–362, 364, 367, 368, 369, 370, 371, 372, 373, 375, 376, 379, 381, 382

Nagel, Curtis (father-in-law), 351

Nagel, Mrs. Veronica (mother-in-law), 369, 374, 376

Nance, Coroner Frank, 374

Natwick, Mildred, 89, 149, 224

Naughty Riquette, 66

Nelson, Harmon ("Ham") O., 190–191, 378–379

Nest of Birds, A, 2

Never Give a Sucker an Even Break, 382

Nielan, Marshall ("Mickey"), 157, 160, 161

Nilson, Einar, 210

Night Hostess, 74–78, 106

Nijinska, Bronislava, 210, 220–221

Nixon, Marion, 298

Nobody but You, see *Two Can't Be Happy*,

"No Horse, No Wife, No Mustache," 188, 190

Nolan, Lloyd, 176

No More Blondes, 46, 69

Norris, Ethel, 133, 134

Novarro, Ramon, 117
Nowhere, 298, 308, 309
Nugent, Frank, 334, 377
Oakie, Jack, 315
O'Brien, Eloise (Mrs. Pat), 335–336
O'Brien, Pat, xvii, 185, 189, 190, 204, 222, 223, 309, 311, 315, 320, 325, 330, 335,
   336, 337, 347
O'Connell, Hugh, 355
Ode to Drury Lane, x
Oh, Kay!, 66
Old New York Club, 322–323
On Death and Dying, 307
O'Neil, Barbara, 148
O'Neill, Eugene, 65
O'Neill, Henry, 185, 190, 222, 243, 247, 284
One Touch of Venus, 382
On the Avenue, 350
Orth, Frank, 316
Ostertag, Barna, 151
O'Sullivan, Maureen, 123
Ouse, Hildur, 151
Over the Wall (film), 345
"Over the Wall" (story), 345
Owen, Ruta Bryan, 346
Packard Theatre Institute, 10
Paige, Raymond, 335
Pallette, Eugene, 211
Palmer, Gordon, 367
Paramount Publix Studios (Paramount Pictures), 106, 107, 109, 110, 114, 116, 119,
   122, 141, 226, 241–242,
Parlor, Bedroom and Bath, 133
Parry, Florence Fisher, 288
Parsons, Harriet, 334, 347
Parsons, Louella, 253, 277, 289, 345, 375
Party's Over, The, 141–149
Pauley, William, 281

Peck, Vernon, Jr., 277
Pederson, Fred, 365
Pemberton, Brock, 41, 42, 55, 56, 57, 65, 66, 180
Pemberton, Murdock, 65, 67, 68, 69
Perkins, Osgood, 176
Perry, Antoinette, 41, 57, 59, 180
Perry, Admiral Robert E., 53
Pickford, Mary, 346
Pigskin Parade, 345
"Pink Powder Puffs" 44
Pitts, Zazu, 231, 235, 240, 241, 350, 375
Plewes, Limey, 249–250
Pogue, Thomas, 355
Pollock, Arthur, 105, 134, 136, 140, 147, 155, 170, 175
Pollock, Horace, 15, 23, 27, 28, 35, 37
Pons, Lily, 226
"Poor Butterfly," 73
Powell, Dick, xii, 183, 185, 187, 190, 196, 198, 204, 210, 211, 213, 215, 217, 218–219,
    222, 223, 226, 228, 229, 230, 235, 252, 254, 255, 256, 259, 261, 263, 335, 346,
    349–350, 375, 378
Prater Violet, 110–111
Purcell, Irene, 56, 57, 58, 59, 61, 62, 64
Purcell, Richard ("Dick"), 289, 291, 322, 345
Quartermaine, Charles, 28, 30, 35, 39
Quevli, Truman, 49
Quirk, Lawrence J., xiii–xiv, 73, 378, 379–380, 383
Raft, George, 119, 123
Raine, Norman Reilly, 325
Ramblers, The, 66
Raphaelson, Samson, 115, 165, 170
Rathbone, Basil, 270, 277
Raymond, Gene, 315, 346
Reade, Maida, 97
Ready, Willing and Able, 350, 353–361, 365, 367, 375, 376–378, 381
Red Apples, see *Brides Are Like That*
Reddington, John, 229–230, 250, 263

Reed, Philip, 199

Reed, Tom, 309

Ree, Max, 210

Regan, Phil, 2, 222, 242

Reicher, Hedwiga, 310

Reinhardt, Gottfried, 208

Reinhardt, Max, 207–211, 217–220, 224, 225–226, 228–231

Reinhart, Alice, 166

Reynolds, Craig, 339–340, 346

Richards, Addison, 319, 320, 325, 335, 354

Ritz Brothers, 350

Road to Rome, The, 122

Robbins, Barbara, 100, 101, 102, 104, 105, 171

Roberts, Beverly, 298, 317, 325, 327, 335, 336, 345

Roberts, Ralph, 31

Robinson, Casey, 263, 309

Robinson, Edward G., 226, 279, 345, 378

Robinson, Ruth, 329

Rogers, Ginger, 346

Romero, Cesar, 222, 315

Rooney, Mickey, 208–209, 210, 213–214, 217, 225, 229, 375

Rooney, Pat, 85

Roosevelt, Franklyn Delano, 115, 226, 256, 280

Roosevelt, Mrs. James (Sara Ann Delano), 226

Rose Bowl, 221, 371

Rosley, Adrian, 353

R.U.R., 39

Russell, Rosalind, 126, 127, 129, 130, 131, 222, 345, 375

Sabatini, Rafael, 263

San Quentin, 347, 350

Satan Met a Lady, 378–379

Saturday Night, 147

Saturday's Children, 199; see also *Maybe It's Love*

Sauber, Harry, 199, 345

Savage Rhythm, 114

Scarborough Players, 121, 122

Scott, Agnes, 15, 22, 23, 27, 30

Segovia, Andrés, 315

Selznick, David O., 161

Sennwald, Andre, 228

Serves You Right, see *We're in the Money*

Servoss, Mary, 29, 34

Seventh Heaven, 73

Shaffer, Rosalind, 3

Shannon, Effie, 112, 118, 141, 147

Shannon, Harry, 153

Shaw, Al, 356

Shaw, George Bernard, 26, 29, 34

Shaw, Winifred, 222, 353, 354, 358, 360, 375

Sheehan, John, 341

Sherwood, Robert Emmett, 122

Ship News, 348

Shirley, Anne, 198

Shoemaker, Rachel Walter Hinkle, 40

Shrinking Violet, The, 322, 345; see also *King of Hockey*

Sikov, Ed, 267

Smith, Albertson (grandfather), 1

Smith, Alexander Ross (father), 1, 2, 4, 5, 6, 115, 116, 286, 298, 324, 367, 368, 370, 371, 374, 375, 376, 379

Smith, Alexander Ross, Jr., *see* Alexander, Ross

Smith, Margaret Augusta (grandmother), 1

Smith, Mark, 133

Smith, Maude Adelle Cohen (mother), 1, 2, 4, 5, 115, 116, 286, 298, 299, 324, 367, 368, 369, 370, 371, 374, 375, 376, 379

Smith, Winchell B., 76

Snow White and the Seven Dwarfs, 19

Soanes, Wood, 322

Social Pirates, see *Going Highbrow*

Social Register, 157–163, 165, 183

Solow, Eugene, 191

Spirit of West Point, The, 382

Springtime for Henry, 126, 180

Stage Association, 224–225
Stagecoach Buckaroo, 382
Stage Struck, 332, 346
Stander, Lionel, 242–243
Stange, Hugh, 85, 91, 93, 100
Stanwick, Barbara, 346
State of the Union, 141
Stebbins, Helen, 2
Steele, Vernon, 57, 264
Steel Highway, 375
Stehli, Edgar, 55, 67
Stephens, Harvey, 141, 147, 149
Stephenson, Cornelius, 182, 368, 369, 372, 373
Stephenson, Elta, 182, 368, 369, 370, 373, 374
Stephenson, Henry, 270
Sterling, Rear Admiral Yates, Jr., 261
Stewart, Fred, 134
Stewart, James ("Jimmy"), 148, 224, 308, 323, 346
Stillwell, Charles, 24
Stillwell, George, 27, 30
Stone, Fred, 85,
Stone, George, 342
Stone, Lewis S., 252, 254, 262, 263
Stork Is Dead, The, 133–137, 176, 183
Strange Orchestra, 165
Strasberg, Lee, 160
Stricklyn, Ray, xiii
Stuart, Gloria, 199, 200, 201, 203, 204, 208–209
Sullavan, Margaret, 89, 148, 149–150
Sullivan, Fred, 44, 45, 46, 49, 50
Sunny, 66
Swan, The, 39
Talbot, Lyle, 283, 286, 287, 288
Talks on Talking, 40
Tashman, Lilyan, 110, 112, 118
Tasker, Robert, 348

Tatler, The, see *Here Comes Carter*
Taylor, Deems, 226
Taylor, Robert, 288, 315, 346
Taylor, Ruth, 35, 37
Teasdale, Veree, 211, 215
"Technic," 364–365
Tecumseh, 255
Teddington Studio (London), 350
Templin, Dan M., 279
That's Gratitude, 94–99, 176
Theilade, Nini, 208–209, 211
There's Always Tomorrow, 198
There's Millions in It, see *Hot Money*
Thomas, Frank, 30, 34, 35
Thorn, John, 15, 20, 23, 24, 25, 27
Thorpe, Dr. Franklyn, 362
Three-Cornered Moon, 148
"Through the Courtesy of Love," 343
Tinée, Mae, 288
Tombes, Andrew, 316, 317, 319
Tone, Franchot, 110, 112, 118, 192, 193, 196, 197, 223, 226, 346, 375
"Too Marvelous for Words," 356, 358, 361
Towne, Hugh William, 7–8, 9–10, 39, 40, 73, 114, 361, 385
Travis, June, 322
Treacher, Arthur, 211
Trevor, Claire, 141, 147, 149, 222
Trocadero Café, 315, 345
Trumbo, Dalton, 309
Turk, Mark, 294
Turnbull, Hector, 116
Two Can't Be Happy, 151–152
Two Fellows and a Girl, 44
Under Glass, 150, 151, 152–155, 157, 183
United Actors, Inc., 67, 68
United States Naval Academy, 252, 257
University Players Guild, 87–88, 89–90, 91, 180

Up in Mabel's Room, 133

Vale, Rita, 80

Vale, Vola, 110

Vallée, Rudy, 226

Van Buren, A.H., 134

Variety Show, 365

Velvet Rage, The, xiii

Vernon, Dorothy, 151, 172

Viertel, Berthold, 110–111, 114, 115, 116, 211

Virgin Man, The, 66

Voice of Scandal, The, see *Here Comes Carter*

Volstead Act, 4

Vulture, The, 350

"Wabash Cannonball, The," 121

Wagner, Laura, xiv, 77

Walcott, George, 208–209

Wald, Jerry, 161, 199, 350

Wales, Clarke, xiv, 26

Wallace, Francis, 345

Wallis, Hal B., 248, 267, 274–275, 314, 346, 350, 375

Walthall, Henry B., 325, 326, 375

Waring, Fred, 378

Warner Brothers, xii, xiii, xv, 2, 28, 110, 112, 117, 181, 183, 184, 185, 189, 191, 196, 204, 207, 210, 211, 217, 220, 221, 222, 224, 235, 242, 248, 250, 257, 259, 273, 279, 288, 309, 314, 315, 325, 328, 330, 334, 346, 350, 351, 352, 362, 364, 371, 376, 378, 384,

Warner, Jack L., 198, 207, 210, 222, 242, 257, 267, 279, 289, 346, 375, 380

Warren, Harry, 261

Watts, Richard, Jr., 301, 334

Wead, Frank, 325

Weissberger, Felix, 208

We Live Again, 198

We're in the Money, 2, 117, 242–252, 325

Wesselhoeft, Eleanor, 284, 287

Westcott, Gordon, 239

Westchester Playhouse, 149–150, 180

West High School, xiv, 6–7, 115, 230, 383

Westman, Nydia, 300

West Point, 183, 184–185, 186, 189, 223, 257

"Whispering Wires" (story), 49

Whispering Wires (play), 49–50

Whiteman, Paul, 160

White Parade, The, 198

Whiting, Richard, 365, 378

Wild Duck, The, 11, 14, 24, 37–38, 39

Wild Rose, The, 66

Williams, Quinn, 190

William, Warren, 80, 82, 123, 222

Willis, Norman, 341

Wilmot, John, Second Earl of Rochester, ix, xv

Wilson, Marie, 326, 335, 336

Wiman, Dwight Deere, 165, 171

Windust, Bretaigne, 87, 90, 224

Winninger, Charles, 158, 160, 161, 180

Wiser Sex, The, 110–114, 115–116, 117–119, 183, 211

Wizard of Oz, The, 233

Woman in Room Thirteen, The, 45–46

Wong, Anna May, 117

Wooden Slipper, The, 165–171

Woods, A ("Al"), H., 133, 134, 136

Woods, Donald, 211, 222

Wood, Vernon D., 296, 374

"World Is My Apple, The," 353

Wormser, Richard, 253

Wray, Fay, 346

Wright Players, 42–52

Wrubel, Allie, 280

Wylie, I.A.R., 298

Wyman, Jane, 354

"You Have to Learn Sometime," 253

"You on My Mind," 339, 341

Young, Loretta, 198, 346

Young Nowheres, 298
Young, Roland, 176
Yurka, Blanche, xii, 11, 14, 15, 17, 18, 20, 22, 23, 24, 37, 41
Zanuck, Darryl F., 345, 346, 350
Zukor, Adolph, 116, 226

Made in the USA
Monee, IL
08 July 2020